Your

TEACHER GUIDE

CHOICE

JOHN FOSTER, SIMON FOSTER
& KIM RICHARDSON

William Collins's dream of knowledge for all began with the publication of his first book in 1819.

A self-educated mill worker, he not only enriched millions of lives, but also founded a flourishing publishing house. Today, staying true to this spirit, Collins books are packed with inspiration, innovation and practical expertise. They place you at the centre of a world of possibility and give you exactly what you need to explore it.

Collins. Freedom to teach.

Published by Collins
An imprint of HarperCollins*Publishers*
The News Building
1 London Bridge Street
London SE1 9GF

Browse the complete Collins catalogue at
www.collins.co.uk

British Library Cataloguing-in-Publication Data

A catalogue record for this publication is available from the British Library.

Series editor: John Foster
Authors: John Foster, Simon Foster and Kim Richardson
Commissioning editor: Catherine Martin
Development editor: Jo Kemp
Copyeditor and typesetter: Hugh Hillyard-Parker
Proofreader: Catherine Dakin
Cover designer: The Big Mountain Design, Ltd
Production controller: Katharine Willard

Printed and bound by CPI Group (UK) Ltd, Croydon, CR0 4YY

MIX
Paper from
responsible sources
FSC   www.fsc.org   FSC™ C007454

This book is produced from independently certified FSC™ paper to ensure responsible forest management. For more information visit:
www.harpercollins.co.uk/green

The publishers gratefully acknowledge the permission granted to reproduce the copyright material in this book. Every effort has been made to trace copyright holders and to obtain their permission for the use of copyright material. The publishers will gladly receive any information enabling them to rectify any error or omission at the first opportunity.

An extract on p.36 abridged from 'Sexual attraction and orientation', KidsHealth, https://kidshealth.org/en/teens/sexual-orientation.html. Reproduced by permission; Poems on pp.42, 76, 102 © John Foster. Reproduced with the author's permission; An extract on p.108 from *The Girls' Guide to Growing Up Great* by Sophie Elkan, copyright © Sophie Elkan, 2018. Reproduced by Green Tree, an imprint of Bloomsbury Publishing Plc; An extract on p.126 from 'Tackling inequalities faced by Gypsy, Roma and Traveller communities Seventh Report of Session 2017–19', House of Commons, © Parliamentary Copyright House of Commons 2019. Reproduced under the terms of the Open Parliament Licence; Extracts on pp.132, 238 from 'Clinic opens to help teens hooked on illegal pills bought online' by Dulcie Lee, *The Guardian*, 27/01/2018; and 'Stabbing deaths among young people hit eight-year high' by Alan Travis, *The Guardian*, 08/02/2018, copyright © Guardian News & Media Ltd, 2019; Extracts on pp.221, 222 from *Abortion: decisions and dilemmas: An educational resource for those working with young people aged 13 to 18*, Brook, 2013, https://learn.brook.org.uk/. Reproduced with permission; An extract on p.250 from *Mind Your Head* by Juno Dawson, Hot Key Books, 2016, pp.33-35. Reproduced by permission of Bonnier Zaffre; and the infographic on p.258 'Young People and Gambling 2018', Gambling Commission, 2018, https://www.gamblingcommission.gov.uk. Reproduced with permission.

The links included in the Further information and support boxes are live at the time of going to press. If a deeper link to specific content has expired when you come to use the lesson plan, please try searching on the main website using the search term provided before the link. Teachers should review the recommendations to determine whether they are appropriate to pass on to their students. The publisher cannot take any responsibility for the content in these sites.

Contents

Introduction

The *Your Choice Teacher Guide* provides ready-made, editable teaching resources that will help schools to use the *Your Choice* books to deliver effective RSE and PSHE lessons.

This introduction demonstrates how the three *Your Choice* books meet the requirements of the statutory 'Relationships and sex education' and 'Health education' curriculum, providing a coherent programme of PSHE lessons for Years 7 to 9. It explains how the lesson plans are structured so that they can be adapted to fit a school's own programme for delivering RSE and PHSE.

It also contains advice on developing group discussions and the importance of setting ground rules for RSE and PSHE lessons. There are sections on how assessment can be carried out and how lessons can be differentiated, offering suggestions for helping students with additional needs.

How the *Your Choice* books meet the requirements for RSE and PSHE

Planning your course

The Your Choice books together meet the requirements for RSE and PSHE at Key Stage 3, as shown in the mapping grid on pages ix-xviii. Using the *Your Choice* books as the core of a Key Stage 3 course, therefore, ensures that a school is covering the statutory curriculum for relationships and sex education and health education, as well as the framework guidelines for PSHE.

The books set out what might be suitable for Years 7, 8 and 9, but schools themselves should decide which topics are taught in each year and in which order, according to the particular needs of their context and cohort, and following the RSE policy agreed with parents. Whatever approach a school adopts, there is enough material to provide a full three-year course in RSE and PSHE.

The units in the *Your Choice* books are divided into four strands:

* Personal wellbeing and mental health
* Relationships and sex education
* Physical health and wellbeing
* Social education.

It is therefore possible to plan to deliver the course strand by strand. This arrangement may suit schools in which the course is being delivered by different teams of teachers. It would be possible, for example, for a team of form tutors to deliver the PSHE units, while a team of senior teachers delivered the RSE units. Alternatively, the RSE strands could be delivered with the help of outside bodies, since the units are freestanding. Schools can plan to use the units in whatever sequence they choose or to use them in the order which they appear in the books.

In planning the course for their school, senior managers or the PSHE coordinator can follow the ten steps set out in the 'Roadmap to statutory RSE' prepared by the Sex Education Forum and the PSHE Association.

To help guide their planning, it can be useful for the PSHE coordinator to talk to local organisations or public service providers such as the police and sexual health clinics, to gather information on the particular issues that may affect young people in the area and in the school.

Planning a unit

Each unit in *Your Choice Books One, Two* and *Three* covers a specific area of the RSE or PSHE curriculum, divided into topics that comprise a lesson each (one double-page in the student books). The lessons are planned so that there is a clear progression in the building of the student's knowledge and understanding of the subject of the unit. Thus, in *Your Choice Book One,* the unit on 'You and the internet' begins with a lesson on personal safety online. This is followed by lessons on cyberbullying and how students can protect their identity on the internet. Similarly, in *Your Choice Book Two* the unit on 'Sexual relationships – your responsibilities' starts with a lesson on giving consent, followed by a lesson on encouraging students to consider whether they are ready to have sex and how to avoid feeling pressurised into having sex before they are ready, followed by a lesson exploring how people's first experiences of sex can be very different.

The RSE units are self-contained and can be adapted for use according to the school's policy.

Each lesson plan is presented on a single sheet, so that it can be duplicated and given to all the teachers in the team responsible for delivering RSE and PSHE. The lesson plans clearly indicate which strand of the RSE curriculum and/or the PSHE programme is covered and what the objective of the lesson is.

Coordinators can use the lesson plans in two ways. They can circulate them at a planning meeting with the appropriate team members present and, after discussion, adapt them to the needs of particular classes. Alternatively, they can distribute them to individual teachers.

Setting guidelines

The course is designed to provide students with opportunities to explore the topics, providing them with essential information to enable them to have informed and frank discussions and to share their views. Students are encouraged to use exploratory talk to help them to formulate their own opinions. Thus, they will be empowered to make their own choices when faced with real-life situations.

Because many of the topics are sensitive, it is essential that discussion of these areas be controlled to safeguard students who might otherwise find them upsetting. It must be made clear that students have the right not to reveal anything that they do not want to reveal and not to be pressurised to talk about things they do not want to talk about. When group or pair discussions are being set up, teachers need to think carefully about which students will be working together, in which lessons they will allow students to choose their own groups and in which lessons they will decide the groups. Mixed-ability pairings can work well.

Since so many of the activities involve discussions, it is vital to make students aware of how they are expected to behave in group discussions. **Worksheet 1.1a** 'Our rules for class discussions' can be used at the beginning of Year 7 to establish rules for students to follow. It can be referred to as is necessary in Years 8 and 9.

In Year 8, students start to hold more formal debates in addition to discussions and guidance on these is provided in **Worksheets 5.1b** and **15.3**.

The group discussions in many cases do not ask for the group to reach agreement. For a variety of reasons, such as an individual's religious beliefs, members of the group may hold very different views on a particular topic. Such differing opinions must be tolerated and no one should feel it necessary to withhold an opinion because it is controversial or because it goes against the view of the rest of the group. Students are expected to learn to agree to disagree. Teachers and TAs should carefully monitor paired work, group discussions and role plays to ensure these guidelines are being followed.

Using the lesson plans and worksheets

Each lesson plan follows the same structure.

* The **strand** of the RSE curriculum and/or the PSHE programme and the **learning objective** are stated clearly at the top of the lesson plan, with details of any **resources** that are required for the activities. (Please note that most lessons include research tasks that require internet access.)

* A short **starter** activity is suggested as a way in to the topic. It is designed to occupy no more than five minutes of the lesson.

* The main part of the lesson plan offers **suggested activities**, including those set out in the student book, and guidance on when and how to use the related worksheet(s). Many of the activities require students to read an article, a scenario or some information prior to discussing the issues raised in pairs or groups. Others provide a series of statements expressing different opinions on a controversial issue. Students are asked to consider the statements on their own before debating them with the rest of the class. **Scenarios** give students a safe space to explore issues without needing to share their own personal experiences.

* There are suggestions for **writing tasks** ranging from paragraphs of three or four sentences to reports of two or three paragraphs and replies to problems sent in advice columns.

* There are enough activities to fill a typical RSE/PSHE session of between 30 and 45 minutes. However, the length of the session may determine which activities the teacher uses. The more activities are completed, the more comprehensively a topic will be covered. But often it is not necessary for all the activities to be included for the objective of the lesson to be achieved.

* The **plenary** is designed to round off the lesson by focusing on what has been learned. This is often an oral activity that summarises the main points of the lesson.

- In addition, the **extension activity** enables students to explore the topic in greater depth or is designed to stretch students who require more challenge.
- Finally, a **Further information and support** box provides details of useful links to organisations, websites and articles, and sometimes to short videos, for both teachers and students. (Please note, these links are live at the time of going to press. If a deeper link to specific content has expired when you come to use the lesson plan, please try searching on the main website using the search term provided before the link. Teachers should review the recommendations to determine whether they are appropriate to pass on to their students.)

There is a supporting worksheet for most lessons, included immediately after the lesson plan to which it relates. The overall aim of the worksheets is to increase students' understanding of a topic. Worksheets are also included to provide scaffolding for students' writing.

Assessment and reviewing

Each of the units contains at least one writing activity that can be used to assess and record evidence of students' learning.

At the end of this introduction, on pages xix-xxi, are worksheets that invite students to review their learning. If the course is delivered in separate strands, the worksheets can be adapted and introduced when all the lessons in a particular strand have been completed. Alternatively, they can be used at the end of the year.

Differentiation

Differentiation means having a variety of tasks at different levels, to suit the way and the pace at which different students learn. As noted above, extra challenge and support have been built into the lesson plans and worksheets to help you support the full range of learners.

Students respond best when they are presented with information in a variety of different ways, and are engaged in a variety of different activities, so this has been incorporated into the design of each unit. In many units, there will be paired work and work in groups of different sizes, including as a whole class, all in one lesson. This will encourage a range of different skills.

Receiving information

Listening

Learning to listen is a key skill that should be developed while teaching PSHE, and as such has its own lesson in *Your Choice Book One*, 18.2. It is important that teachers recognise the level of different students and set them tasks that are appropriate. So, a student who has difficulty listening should not be thrown into a class debate listening to others for 20 minutes. Instead, they should be given tasks that recognise their level and then gradually build up their listening skills – from listening to a partner for one minute in paired work, to two minutes, then to listening in a group for up to five minutes and eventually to listening in a longer class debate.

Remember that there are conditions and situations that can affect a student's listening ability and concentration. These include ADHD and other medical conditions, the time of day, the day of the week, or what term the lesson is occurring in, and what a student has had to eat before a lesson. Play to the students' strengths and learn how to get the best out of them. They will need to develop their state management skills, which is covered in *Your Choice Book One*, lesson 10.1.

Reading

There will be plenty of literacy resources in your school, particularly in the English department – make sure you use resources and teachers who specialise in this area. Remember, there are several different reading skills, such as skimming for the gist (what the article is generally about) and scanning for specific information (looking for a specific word or phrase). In most cases in these books, reading for gist is the main skill being developed. Again, the important thing is to set a task that is at a student's ability level. This can be done by providing simpler or shorter text material for some readers, and paired work where a more confident student can guide one needing more support. Extra support should be given to students with dyslexia (see 'Students with additional needs' below).

Producing information

Speaking

Students will have different levels of confidence when it comes to speaking. Speaking in front of a group can be daunting for some students. Therefore, be careful to gauge ability and confidence, getting students to speak either in pairs or groups before speaking to the class, where appropriate. Also, remember that students will themselves differentiate between formal and informal speaking. For example, a student who needs more support may not want to get up in front of the class, but may respond to a question in the class, if they are sitting down, in an informal setting. Again, use your judgement here, based on the needs of each individual student.

Writing

Both the complexity and speed of writing tasks should be varied. The worksheets provided will scaffold students' writing for longer tasks. For students who struggle, pairing them together may also help when doing writing tasks. The length of time should also be varied for writing tasks. This should be done positively rather than negatively. So, if you have some students who write slowly, allow the entire class the time the slower students require. Fast finishers can then be given extra tasks. Again, extra steps should be taken for those with dyslexia (see 'Students with additional needs' below).

Students with additional needs

There is a wide variety of students with additional needs in both mainstream and SEND school settings. This section aims to give some general advice and approaches for supporting students to access learning regardless of their challenges. Inclusion and equality are vital for ensuring that everyone can achieve. It is important to be aware that learning differences can include those that are physical, cognitive, sensory, behavioural and related to mental health. It is therefore the role of the practitioner to be creative in their approach to supporting students as best as possible.

Dyslexia

Dyslexia is very common, but it may present differently in each individual student. Many students will have difficulty reading, with words appearing to 'dance' around the page. Talk to the student first to see if they have their own coping strategies. Often, a student can read much more easily if there is a colour background to the writing, rather than the bright glare of a white page. Therefore, photocopying materials onto a background colour, or providing the student with a plastic filter of that colour, may make a real difference. Computer presentations can also be filtered by changing the background colour. Some students may be given a computer to work on. This could be used as a resource and, by getting students to research extra information in class, using a laptop can be turned into a positive.

Extra time for reading and writing may also be appropriate for dyslexic students. Remember students should be encouraged to see themselves positively. It is important to monitor students and assess them, to be aware of students whose cognitive ability is way above their reading and writing ability.

ASD: Autism Spectrum Disorder

There are a wide range of traits that can present on the autistic spectrum, including students with Asperger's Syndrome. It is important for you to get to know where a student lies on the spectrum, and what particular needs they have. Talking to the student, their learning assistant, the SEN coordinator, and reviewing their Educational Statement and Learning Plan if they have one, will all help.

For some activities, you may need to give a student an explanation of the topic in more simplistic terms, and check their understanding of more complex issues. This also applies to students with learning differences (see below).

One particular strategy that helps is that of adopting a regular routine. This provides a pattern which autistic students respond to well. For example:

- Starter – Every student comes in and writes one point on the board from the previous lesson. This cannot be a point that anyone else has written. The first activity is then for all students to stand up and explain their point.

Students are encouraged to arrive early or on time so that they get the easiest points. Everyone participates at the beginning of the class, so the activity is inclusive. It also a provides a routine – every student knows what is going to happen at the beginning of the class.

- Finisher – Before they leave, every student has to tell the teacher one thing they have learned in that class. No student can repeat a point that has already been made. Again, this encourages active listening, and provides a routine. It also gives the teacher feedback on what a student has learned in the lesson.

Learning differences

If a person has learning differences then the processing speed of their brain may work differently from a more neuro-typical brain. Cognition and memory can be affected, which in turn can hinder a learner from internalising information and making progress. This may affect the speed at which they can learn, and also the complexity of the ideas they can comprehend.

You may find that a student has a learning support assistant with them in class, in which case, work closely with the assistant by providing them with a lesson plan in advance, leaving space for clarification during the lesson, and speaking to the assistant and possibly the student after each lesson. The aim of full inclusion is to adapt teaching styles to engage every individual. It can take time to get to know a student with learning differences, so observation can be very important in developing teaching strategies.

Tasks can be simplified and extra time can be designed into the lesson to accommodate any additional needs.

Physical needs

Some students may have physical needs. These include anything from visual or hearing impairment to mobility issues. Strategies for assisting visually impaired students include using large text, enlarged photocopied resources, specific easier-to-read typefaces, or braille if the need is severe. Strategies for assisting students with hearing impairments can include using audio material, or using voice software on computers. In some cases, hearing loops, subtitles or visual material may be required as a substitute. A student may have mobility needs and require support in the form of voice dictation and scribing.

The *Your Choice* course is designed to prepare students for life in contemporary society, presenting them with information on key issues that will enable them to develop not only their understanding of the topics but also the skills necessary to make informed choices and thus to lead safe and healthy lifestyles. We hope that the wide variety of materials and activities that the course provides will lead to lessons involving a lively exchange of views that both teachers and students will enjoy and find rewarding.

John Foster, series editor

Coverage of the curriculum

PHYSICAL HEALTH AND MENTAL WELLBEING

Curriculum objective	Where it is covered in the Your Choice series
Mental wellbeing	
Pupils should know • how to talk about their emotions accurately and sensitively, using appropriate vocabulary.	**Book One** 3.1 Feeling worried or anxious 10.1 State management 15.1 Managing your emotions 15.2 Managing grief 15.3 Dealing with divorce or parents splitting up **Book Two** 11.1 Dealing with anger 11.2 Jealousy 11.3 Dealing with fear 12.1 Signs of stress 12.3 Coping with stress **Book Three** 1.1 Building your confidence 1.2 Self-esteem 1.3 Coping with challenges and change 1.4 Problem-solving
• that happiness is linked to being connected to others.	**Book One** 5.1 You and your family 15.1 Managing your emotions 17.1 How you spend your time 19.1 Being a good neighbour **Book Three** 8.1 Different types of partnership 8.2 What makes relationships work? 13.1 Attending to your wellbeing 13.4 Getting help and giving help
• how to recognise the early signs of mental wellbeing concerns.	**Book One** 3.1 Feeling worried or anxious **Book Two** 12.1 Signs of stress 12.2 What stresses you? 12.3 Coping with stress **Book Three** 10.1 Eating disorders 13.1 Attending to your wellbeing 13.2 Mindfulness 13.3 Mental illness 13.4 Getting help and giving help
• common types of mental ill health (e.g. anxiety and depression).	**Book Two** 12.1 Signs of stress 12.2 What stresses you? 12.3 Coping with stress **Book Three** 10.1 Eating disorders 13.3 Mental illness 13.5 Managing anxiety 13.6 Managing depression

Curriculum objective	Where it is covered in the Your Choice series
• how to critically evaluate when something they do or are involved in has a positive or negative effect on their own or others' mental health.	**Book One** 4.3 Regrets and saying sorry 5.1 You and your family 5.2 What makes a good friend? 5.3 Rivalries 8.1 What is bullying? 8.2 Dealing with bullies 9.2 Cyberbullying **Book Two** 1.1 Becoming an adult 1.2 Problems with parents 1.3 Being responsible 2.1 Close relationships 2.2 What makes a healthy relationship? 2.3 Unhealthy relationships and feelings of rejection **Book Three** 1.1 Building your confidence 1.2 Self-esteem 1.3 Coping with challenges and change 1.4 Problem-solving 13.4 Getting help and giving help
• the benefits and importance of physical exercise, time outdoors, community participation and voluntary and service-based activities on mental wellbeing and happiness.	**Book One** 14.1 Exercise 14.2 Exercise, sleep and your mental health 15.1 Managing your emotions 17.1 How you spend your time 19.1 Being a good neighbour **Book Two** 12.3 Coping with stress **Book Three** 13.1 Attending to your wellbeing
Internet safety and harms	
Pupils should know • the similarities and differences between the online world and the physical world, including: the impact of unhealthy or obsessive comparison with others online (including through setting unrealistic expectations for body image), how people may curate a specific image of their life online, over-reliance on online relationships including social media, the risks related to online gambling including the accumulation of debt, how advertising and information is targeted at them and how to be a discerning consumer of information online.	**Book One** 3.2 The laws of attraction 4.2 Who do you admire? 9.1 Personal safety online 17.2 Internet gaming addiction **Book Two** 7.4 Are you addicted to your mobile phone? **Book Three** 5.2 Your online reputation 9.1 Social media and body image 12.3 Online literacy and responsibility 14.1 What is gambling? 14.2 Problem gambling 14.3 How to manage gambling
• how to identify harmful behaviours online (including bullying, abuse or harassment) and how to report, or find support, if they have been affected by those behaviours.	**Book One** 9.1 Personal safety online 9.2 Cyberbullying 9.3 Protecting your identity online **Book Two** 5.1 Child abuse 5.2 Grooming 5.3 Sexting – it's no laughing matter **Book Three** 5.2 Your online reputation 12.1 Fake news 12.2 Radicalisation 12.3 Online literacy and responsibility

Curriculum objective	Where it is covered in the Your Choice series
Physical health and fitness	
Pupils should know • the positive associations between physical activity and promotion of mental wellbeing, including as an approach to combat stress.	**Book One** 14.1 Exercise 14.2 Exercise, sleep and your mental health 17.1 How you spend your time **Book Two** 12.1 Signs of stress 12.2 What stresses you? 12.3 Coping with stress **Book Three** 13.1 Attending to your wellbeing 13.2 Mindfulness 13.4 Getting help and giving help
• the characteristics and evidence of what constitutes a healthy lifestyle, maintaining a healthy weight, including the links between an inactive lifestyle and ill health, including cancer and cardio-vascular ill-health.	**Book One** 13.1 Healthy eating 13.2 You and your weight 14.1 Exercise 14.2 Exercise, sleep and your mental health **Book Three** 10.1 Eating disorders
• about the science relating to blood, organ and stem cell donation.	**Book Two** 15.4 Blood, organ and stem cell donation
Healthy eating	
Pupils should know • how to maintain healthy eating and the links between a poor diet and health risks, including tooth decay and cancer.	**Book One** 13.1 Healthy eating 13.2 You and your weight **Book Two** 10.2 Caring for your teeth, ears and eyes **Book Three** 10.1 Eating disorders
Drugs, alcohol and tobacco	
Pupils should know • the facts about legal and illegal drugs and their associated risks, including the link between drug use, and the associated risks, including the link to serious mental health conditions.	**Book One** 12.1 What are drugs? 12.2 What effects do drugs have? **Book Two** 7.1 Recreational drugs 7.2 New psychoactive substances 7.3 How can I tell if a drug is safe? **Book Three** 6.1 Heroin and cocaine 6.2 The impact of drugs
• the law relating to the supply and possession of illegal substances.	**Book One** 12.1 What are drugs? 12.2 What effects do drugs have? **Book Two** 7.2 New psychoactive substances **Book Three** 6.1 Heroin and cocaine 6.2 The impact of drugs
• the physical and psychological risks associated with alcohol consumption and what constitutes low risk alcohol consumption in adulthood.	**Book Two** 8.1 Alcohol: the facts 8.2 Alcohol: the risks 8.3 Alcoholism **Book Three** 5.1 Safety at parties
• the physical and psychological consequences of addiction, including alcohol dependency.	**Book Two** 8.2 Alcohol: the risks 8.3 Alcoholism
• awareness of the dangers of drugs which are prescribed but still present serious health risks.	**Book Two** 7.3 How can I tell if a drug is safe?
• the facts about the harms from smoking tobacco (particularly the link to lung cancer), the benefits of quitting and how to access support to do so.	**Book One** 11.1 Smoking facts 11.2 Smoking versus vaping

Curriculum objective	Where it is covered in the Your Choice series
Health and prevention	
Pupils should know • about personal hygiene, germs including bacteria, viruses, how they are spread, treatment and prevention of infection, and about antibiotics.	**Book Two** 9.1 Immunisations and health checks 10.1 Looking after your skin
• about dental health and the benefits of good oral hygiene and dental flossing, including healthy eating and regular check-ups at the dentist.	**Book Two** 10.2 Caring for your teeth, ears and eyes
• (late secondary) the benefits of regular self-examination and screening.	**Book Two** 4.1 STIs 4.2 Symptoms of STIs 4.3 Sexual health clinics 9.1 Immunisations and health checks
• the facts and science relating to immunisation and vaccination.	**Book Two** 9.1 Immunisations and health checks **Book Three** 12.1 Fake news
• the importance of sufficient good quality sleep for good health and how a lack of sleep can affect weight, mood and ability to learn.	**Book One** 14.2 Exercise, sleep and your mental health **Book Two** 12.1 Signs of stress 12.3 Coping with stress **Book Three** 13.1 Attending to your wellbeing
Basic first aid	
Pupils should know • basic treatment for common injuries.	**Book One** 20.1 First aid: what to do in an emergency
• life-saving skills, including how to administer CPR.	We think these skills are better taught by an expert in person than through a textbook. In the *Teacher Guide* we have provided links to training providers and online guidance.
• the purpose of defibrillators and when one might be needed.	
Changing adolescent body	
Pupils should know • key facts about puberty, the changing adolescent body and menstrual wellbeing.	**Book One** 2.1 Puberty 2.2 Periods: the facts **Book Three** 2.3 Understanding gender identity
• the main changes which take place in males and females, and the implications for emotional and physical health.	**Book One** 2.1 Puberty 2.2 Periods: the facts 7.1 Exploring your sexuality **Book Two** 1.1 Becoming an adult 1.2 Problems with parents 1.3 Being responsible **Book Three** 2.3 Understanding gender identity
Additional This should enable pupils to understand how their bodies are changing, how they are feeling and why, to further develop the language that they use to talk about their bodies, health and emotions	**Book One** 2.1 Puberty **Book Two** 1.1 Becoming an adult

RELATIONSHIPS AND SEX EDUCATION

Curriculum objective	Where it is covered in the Your Choice series
Families	
Pupils should know • that there are different types of committed, stable relationships.	**Book One** 5.1 You and your family **Book Three** 8.1 Different types of partnership 8.2 What makes relationships work?
• how these relationships might contribute to human happiness and their importance for bringing up children.	**Book Three** 7.4 Good parenting 8.2 What makes relationships work?
• what marriage is, including their legal status, e.g. that marriage carries legal rights and protections not available to couples who are cohabiting or who have married, for example, in an unregistered religious ceremony.	**Book Three** 8.1 Different types of partnership
• why marriage is an important relationship choice for many couples and why it must be freely entered into.	**Book Three** 3.3 Forced marriage, honour-based violence and FGM 8.1 Different types of partnership 8.2 What makes relationships work?
• the characteristics and legal status of other types of long-term relationships.	**Book Three** 8.1 Different types of partnership
• the roles and responsibilities of parents with respect to raising of children, including the characteristics of successful parenting.	**Book Three** 7.3 Teenage parents 7.4 Good parenting
• how to: determine whether other children, adults or sources of information are trustworthy: judge when a family, friend, intimate or other relationship is unsafe (and to recognise this in others' relationships); and, how to seek help or advice, including reporting concerns about others, if needed.	**Book One** 4.2 Who do you admire? 5.1 You and your family 5.2 What makes a good friend? 8.1 What is bullying? 8.2 Dealing with bullies 9.1 Personal safety online 9.2 Cyberbullying **Book Two** 2.1 Close relationships 2.2 What makes a healthy relationship? 2.3 Unhealthy relationships and feelings of rejection 5.1 Child abuse 5.2 Grooming 5.3 Sexting – it's no laughing matter **Book Three** 3.2 Violence against women 3.3 Forced marriage, honour-based violence and FGM 12.2 Radicalisation
Respectful relationships, including friendships	
Pupils should know • the characteristics of positive and healthy friendships (in all contexts, including online) including: trust, respect, honesty, kindness, generosity, boundaries, privacy, consent and the management of conflict, reconciliation and ending relationships. This includes different (non-sexual) types of relationship.	**Book One** 1.2 Your personality 4.1 Right and wrong 4.2 Who do you admire? 4.3 Regrets and saying sorry 5.2 What makes a good friend? 7.1 Exploring your sexuality 7.2 Sex: your rights and responsibilities 7.3 Attitudes to sex 10.2 What influences your decisions **Book Two** 2.1 Close relationships 2.2 What makes a healthy relationship? 2.3 Unhealthy relationships and feelings of rejection 3.1 Giving your consent 5.1 Child abuse 5.2 Grooming 5.3 Sexting – it's no laughing matter **Book Three** 8.1 Different types of partnership 8.2 What makes relationships work?

Curriculum objective	Where it is covered in the Your Choice series
• practical steps they can take in a range of different contexts to improve or support respectful relationships.	**Book One** 4.3 Regrets and saying sorry 5.2 What makes a good friend? **Book Two** 2.1 Close relationships 2.2 What makes a healthy relationship? 2.3 Unhealthy relationships and feelings of rejection 3.1 Giving your consent **Book Three** 8.2 What makes relationships work?
• how stereotypes, in particular stereotypes based on sex, gender, race, religion, sexual orientation or disability, can cause damage (e.g. how they might normalise non-consensual behaviour or encourage prejudice).	**Book One** 1.4 Gender and your identity **Book Two** 6.1 What is stereotyping? 6.2 What is prejudice? 16.1 Disabilities and learning differences 16.2 Dealing with ageism **Book Three** 3.1 Women's rights 3.2 Violence against women 3.4 LGBT+ rights 4.1 Racism in education and at work 4.2 Racism and society 12.2 Radicalisation
• that in school and in wider society they can expect to be treated with respect by others, and that in turn they should show due respect to others, including people in positions of authority and due tolerance of other people's beliefs.	**Book One** 1.1 Your identity 1.3 Who am I? 1.4 Gender and your identity 4.3 Regrets and saying sorry 7.1 Exploring your sexuality 8.1 What is bullying? 8.2 Dealing with bullies **Book Two** 6.1 What is stereotyping? 6.2 What is prejudice? 14.1 Laws and the rights of children 14.2 You and the police 15.2 You and human rights 16.1 Disabilities and learning differences 16.2 Dealing with ageism **Book Three** 2.1 Your developing sexuality 2.2 What influences your attitudes to sexuality and gender? 3.1 Women's rights 3.2 Violence against women 3.4 LGBT+ rights 4.1 Racism in education and at work 4.2 Racism and society
• about different types of bullying (including cyberbullying), the impact of bullying, responsibilities of bystanders to report bullying and how and where to get help.	**Book One** 7.1 Exploring your sexuality 8.1 What is bullying? 8.2 Dealing with bullies 9.2 Cyberbullying **Book Three** 3.4 LGBT+ rights
• that some types of behaviour within relationships are criminal, including violent behaviour and coercive control.	**Book One** 6.2 Sex and the law 7.2 Sex: your rights and responsibilities **Book Two** 2.3 Unhealthy relationships and feelings of rejection 3.1 Giving your consent 5.1 Child abuse 5.2 Grooming 5.3 Sexting - it's no laughing matter **Book Three** 3.2 Violence against women 3.3 Forced marriage, honour-based violence and FGM

Curriculum objective	Where it is covered in the Your Choice series
• what constitutes sexual harassment and sexual violence and why these are always unacceptable.	**Book One** 6.2 Sex and the law 7.2 Sex: your rights and responsibilities **Book Two** 3.1 Giving your consent 5.1 Child abuse **Book Three** 3.1 Women's rights 3.2 Violence against women 3.3 Forced marriage, honour-based violence and FGM 3.4 LGBT+ rights
• the legal rights and responsibilities regarding equality (particularly with reference to the protected characteristics as defined in the Equality Act 2010) and that everyone is unique and equal.	**Book One** 7.1 Exploring your sexuality 7.2 Sex: your rights and responsibilities **Book Two** 6.2 What is prejudice? 16.1 Disabilities and learning difficulties **Book Three** 3.1 Women's rights 3.2 Violence against women 3.4 LGBT+ rights 4.1 Racism in education and at work 4.2 Racism in society

Online and media

Pupils should know • their rights, responsibilities and opportunities online, including that the same expectations of behaviour apply in all contexts, including online.	**Book One** 6.2 Sex and the law 9.1 Personal safety online 9.2 Cyberbullying **Book Two** 5.2 Grooming 5.3 Sexting – it's no laughing matter **Book Three** 5.2 Your online reputation 12.3 Online literacy and responsibility
• about online risks, including that any material someone provides to another has the potential to be shared online and the difficulty of removing potentially compromising material placed online.	**Book One** 6.2 Sex and the law 9.3 Protecting your identity online **Book Two** 5.2 Grooming 5.3 Sexting – it's no laughing matter **Book Three** 5.2 Your online reputation 12.3 Online literacy and responsibility
• not to provide material to others that they would not want shared further and not to share personal material which is sent to them.	**Book One** 6.2 Sex and the law **Book Two** 5.3 Sexting – it's no laughing matter **Book Three** 5.2 Your online reputation 12.2 Radicalisation 12.3 Online literacy and responsibility
• what to do and where to get support to report material or manage issues online.	**Book One** 9.1 Personal safety online 9.3 Protecting your identity online **Book Two** 5.2 Grooming 5.3 Sexting – it's no laughing matter **Book Three** 5.2 Your online reputation 12.2 Radicalisation
• the impact of viewing harmful content.	**Book One** 9.1 Personal safety online **Book Three** 2.2 What influences your attitudes to sexuality and gender? 12.2 Radicalisation

Curriculum objective	Where it is covered in the Your Choice series
• that specifically sexually explicit material e.g. pornography presents a distorted picture of sexual behaviours, can damage the way people see themselves in relation to others and negatively affect how they behave towards sexual partners.	**Book One** 9.1 Personal safety online **Book Three** 2.2 What influences your attitudes to sexuality and gender? 9.1 Social media and body image
• that sharing and viewing indecent images of children (including those created by children) is a criminal offence which carries severe penalties including jail.	**Book One** 6.2 Sex and the law **Book Two** 5.2 Grooming 5.3 Sexting – it's no laughing matter **Book Three** 2.2 What influences your attitudes to sexuality and gender?
• how information and data is generated, collected, shared and used online.	**Book One** 9.3 Protecting your identity online **Book Three** 12.3 Online literacy and responsibility

Being safe

Pupils should know • the concepts of, and laws relating to, sexual consent, sexual exploitation, abuse, grooming, coercion, harassment, rape, domestic abuse, forced marriage, honour-based violence and FGM, and how these can affect current and future relationships.	**Book One** 6.2 Sex and the law **Book Two** 3.1 Giving your consent 5.1 Child abuse 5.2 Grooming **Book Three** 3.2 Violence against women 3.3 Forced marriage, honour-based violence and FGM
• how people can actively communicate and recognise consent from others, including sexual consent, and how and when consent can be withdrawn (in all contexts, including online).	**Book One** 6.2 Sex and the law 7.2 Sex: your rights and responsibilities **Book Two** 3.1 Giving your consent

Intimate and sexual relationships, including sexual health

Pupils should know • how to recognise the characteristics and positive aspects of healthy one-to-one intimate relationships, which include mutual respect, consent, loyalty, trust, shared interests and outlook, sex and friendship.	**Book One** 3.2 The laws of attraction 5.2 What makes a good friend? **Book Two** 2.1 Close relationships 2.2 What makes a healthy relationship? 2.3 Unhealthy relationships and feelings of rejection **Book Three** 8.1 Different types of partnership 8.2 What makes relationships work?
• that all aspects of health can be affected by choices they make in sex and relationships, positively or negatively, e.g. physical, emotional, mental, sexual and reproductive health and wellbeing.	**Book One** 3.2 The laws of attraction 6.3 Safer sex: contraception 7.1 Exploring your sexuality 7.2 Sex: your rights and responsibilities **Book Two** 4.1 STIs 4.2 Symptoms of STIs 4.3 Sexual health clinics **Book Three** 7.1 Pregnancy
• the facts about reproductive health, including fertility and the potential impact of lifestyle on fertility for men and women, and menopause.	**Book One** 2.2 Periods: the facts **Book Two** 4.1 STIs 4.2 Symptoms of STIs **Book Three** 7.1 Pregnancy
• that there are a range of strategies for identifying and managing sexual pressure, including understanding peer pressure, resisting pressure and not pressurising others.	**Book Two** 3.1 Giving your consent 3.2 Am I ready to have sex? 3.3 Having sex – teenagers' experiences

Curriculum objective	Where it is covered in the Your Choice series
• that they have a choice to delay sex or to enjoy intimacy without sex.	**Book Two** 3.1 Giving your consent 3.2 Am I ready to have sex? 3.3 Having sex – teenagers' experiences
• the facts about the full range of contraceptive choices, efficacy and options available.	**Book One** 6.1 Sex: facts and myths 6.3 Safer sex: contraception **Book Two** 4.3 Sexual health clinics **Book Three** 7.1 Pregnancy
• the facts around pregnancy including miscarriage.	**Book Three** 7.1 Pregnancy
• that there are choices in relation to pregnancy (with medically and legally accurate, impartial information on all options, including keeping the baby, adoption, abortion and where to get further help).	**Book Three** 7.1 Pregnancy 7.2 What to do if you are pregnant 7.3 Teenage parents 7.4 Good parenting
• how the different sexually transmitted infections (STIs), including HIV/AIDs, are transmitted, how risk can be reduced through safer sex (including through condom use) and the importance of and facts about testing.	**Book One** 6.3 Safer sex: contraception **Book Two** 4.1 STIs 4.2 Symptoms of STIs 4.3 Sexual health clinics
• about the prevalence of some STIs, the impact they can have on those who contract them and key facts about treatment.	**Book Two** 4.1 STIs 4.2 Symptoms of STIs 4.3 Sexual health clinics
• how the use of alcohol and drugs can lead to risky sexual behaviour.	**Book One** 6.2 Sex and the law 7.2 Sex: your rights and responsibilities **Book Two** 3.1 Giving your consent 8.2 Alcohol: the risks **Book Three** 5.1 Safety at parties
• how to get further advice, including how and where to access confidential sexual and reproductive health advice and treatment.	**Book Two** 4.3 Sexual health clinics 7.1 Pregnancy 7.2 What to do if you are pregnant

Additional

| The Law in relation to
• marriage
• consent, including the age of consent
• violence against women and girls
• online behaviours including image and information sharing (including 'sexting', youth-produced sexual imagery, nudes, etc.)
• pornography
• abortion
• sexuality
• gender identity
• substance misuse
• violence and exploitation by gangs
• extremism/radicalisation
• criminal exploitation (for example, through gang involvement or 'county lines' drugs operations)
• hate crime
• female genital mutilation (FGM) | **Book One**
6.2 Sex and the law
12.1 What are drugs?
12.2 What effects do drugs have?
Book Two
3.1 Giving your consent
5.2 Grooming
5.3 Sexting – it's no laughing matter
6.1 What is stereotyping?
6.2 What is prejudice?
7.1 Recreational drugs
7.2 New psychoactive substances
7.3 How can I tell if a drug is safe?
Book Three
2.3 Understanding gender identiy
3.2 Violence against women
3.3 Forced marriage, honour-based violence and FGM
3.4 LGBT+ rights
4.2 Racism and society
6.1 Heroin and cocaine
6.2 The impact of drugs
7.2 What to do if you are pregnant
11.2 Gangs and knife crimes
12.2 Radicalisation |

Curriculum objective	Where it is covered in the Your Choice series
• Schools should address the physical and emotional damage caused by female genital mutilation (FGM). They should also be taught where to find support and that it is a criminal offence to perform or assist in the performance of FGM or fail to protect a person for whom you are responsible from FGM. As well as addressing this in the context of the law, pupils may also need support to recognise when relationships (including family relationships) are unhealthy or abusive (including the unacceptability of neglect, emotional, sexual and physical abuse and violence, including honour-based violence and forced marriage)	**Book Two** 2.3 Unhealthy relationships and feelings of rejection 5.1 Child abuse 5.2 Grooming **Book Three** 3.2 Violence against women 3.3 Forced marriage, honour-based violence and FGM
• Internet safety should also be addressed. Pupils should be taught the rules and principles for keeping safe online. This will include how to recognise risks, harmful content and contact, and how and to whom to report issues. Pupils should have a strong understanding of how data is generated, collected, shared and used online, for example, how personal data is captured on social media or understanding the way that businesses may exploit the data available to them.	**Book One** 9.1 Personal safety online 9.2 Cyberbullying 9.3 Protecting your identity online **Book Three** 12.3 Online literacy and responsibility

- Think about what you have learned in each strand of the course.
- Use the questions on each strand to draft a statement about the knowledge and skills you have developed from studying those units.
- In your statement, include any important views, expressing the attitudes and values that you have formed as a result of discussing the issues raised in those units.

Personal wellbeing and mental health

What have you learned about the following?

- Yourself – your identity, personality and gender
- Dealing with anxieties and worries
- How to manage your emotions, especially when dealing with grief or divorce
- Your values – knowing right from wrong, qualities you admire and dealing with regrets
- Managing your money – pocket money and budgeting
- How you spend your leisure time
- Internet gaming addiction
- How you make decisions

Relationships and sex education

What have you learned about the following?

- The changes that occur during puberty
- Relationships with families and friends
- Dealing with rivalries
- Facts and myths about sex
- Sex and the law
- Contraception
- Your developing sexuality
- Attitudes to sex
- Bullying and dealing with bullies
- The internet and personal safety online, including protecting your identity online
- Cyberbullying

Physical health and wellbeing

What have you learned about the following?

- Smoking and vaping
- Drugs and drug taking
- Healthy eating
- The importance of exercise and getting enough sleep

Social education

What have you learned about the following?

- How to express your opinions
- How to be a good listener and give feedback
- Being a good neighbour

- Think about what you have learned in each strand of the course.
- Use the questions on each strand to draft a statement about the knowledge and skills you have developed from studying those units.
- In your statement, include any important views, expressing the attitudes and values that you have formed as a result of discussing the issues raised in those units.

Personal wellbeing and mental health

What have you learned about the following?

- Becoming an adult – your rights and responsibilities
- Dealing with problems with parents
- Managing your emotions – dealing with anger, jealousy and fear
- Managing stress
- Managing your money – managing bank accounts, saving and borrowing

Relationships and sex education

What have you learned about the following?

- Close relationships and what makes relationships work
- The signs of unhealthy relationships
- How to cope with rejection
- The importance of consent
- Teenagers' experiences of having sex
- Safer sex, STIs and sexual health clinics
- Child abuse, grooming and sexting

Physical health and wellbeing

What have you learned about the following?

- Cannabis, MDMA, LSD, new psychoactive drugs and prescription drugs
- The dangers of drug taking and what to do in an emergency caused by drug taking
- Becoming addicted to your mobile phone
- Alcohol and alcoholism
- Immunisations and health checks
- Allergies
- Looking after your skin
- Caring for your teeth, eyes and ears
- Caring for your feet and back
- Getting tattoos and piercings

Social education

What have you learned about the following?

- Stereotyping and prejudice
- Laws and the rights of children
- The role of the police and attitudes towards the police
- Democracy and voting
- Human rights and pressure groups
- Blood, organ and stem cell donations
- Treating people with disabilities and learning differences with respect
- Dealing with ageism

- Think about what you have learned in each strand of the course.
- Use the questions on each strand to draft a statement about the knowledge and skills you have developed from studying those units.
- In your statement, include any important views, expressing the attitudes and values that you have formed as a result of discussing the issues raised in those units.

Personal wellbeing and mental health
What have you learned about the following?
- Developing confidence and self-esteem
- How to cope with challenges and change
- Problem-solving
- Looking after your mental health
- Mental illness
- Managing anxiety and depression
- Mindfulness
- How to manage gambling
- Your rights as a consumer
- Financial choices

Relationships and sex education
What have you learned about the following?
- Your developing sexuality
- Gender identity
- Women's rights and violence against women
- Forced marriages, honour-based violence and FGM
- LGBT+ rights
- Safety at parties
- Your online reputation
- Pregnancy and parenthood
- Partnerships and marriage

Physical health and wellbeing
What have you learned about the following?
- The impact of drug taking
- The dangers of hard drugs – heroin and cocaine
- Social media and body image
- Eating disorders

Social education
What have you learned about the following?
- Racism, prejudice and discrimination
- Young people and crime
- Gangs and knife crime
- Fake news and radicalisation
- Online literacy and responsibility
- Climate change and how to combat it
- Poverty
- Genetic engineering

1.1 Your identity

Strand:
- Personal wellbeing and mental health

Resources:
- Book One: pp. 6–7
- Worksheets 1.1a and 1.1b

Learning objective:
- To understand the factors that shape a person's identity

Key words:
identity, influences, religion, traditions, environment

STARTER

- Since many of the activities in this course involve discussions, it is vital to make students aware of how they are expected to behave in group discussions.

- Give students copies of **Worksheet 1.1a** to establish the ground rules you expect everyone to follow. Invite them to discuss the reasons for each of the rules, and whether there are any other rules they would add. Alternatively, encourage groups of students to draw up their own sets of rules first and share them in a class discussion before comparing these with those on **Worksheet 1.1a**. Students can then discuss any they would like to add to the worksheet.

- With students, study the identity chart on page 6 of *Your Choice Book One* and discuss the various facts that Vikram has included in his chart. Ask: What different factors are important to his identity? (e.g. *religion, immediate family, extended family, nationality, hobbies and career aspirations*)

ACTIVITIES

- Hand out copies of **Worksheet 1.1b** and ask students to draw their own identity charts. Encourage them to share their chart with a partner and suggest any facts they could add. For example, 'Who is in your immediate family? Who is in your extended family? What is your nationality/religion/ethnic background?' Share students' charts in a class discussion, considering whether different students have focused on different aspects of their identity.

- As a class, read the survey results on page 6. Organise students into groups to discuss the main findings of the survey; then discuss them as a class and list them on the board. Discuss whether students think their view of themselves will remain the same throughout their lives. If they think it will change, why do they think that?

- With students, read the list of factors that influence a person's identity on page 7. Ask them to study it and rank the factors in order of importance. Then encourage individuals to share their views in a class discussion.

PLENARY

- Ask students to write a paragraph stating which three factors from those listed on page 7 they think have the most influence on a person's identity.

RESEARCH

- Ask students to research three traditions or religious festivals that have been brought to the UK by immigrants from different cultures, such as celebrating Diwali or Chinese New Year.

EXTENSION

- Show students the BBC Bitesize videos listed in the links below and ask them to take notes and then draw an identity chart for one of the children. Then ask them to work in pairs to compare how their own identity is different from the person's in the video.

Further information and support for students:
BBC Bitesize, Understanding identity (3 videos): www.bbc.com/bitesize/topics/z66hvcw/resources/1

Further information and support for teachers:
Identity charts: www.facinghistory.org/resource-library/teaching-strategies/identity-charts

1. I will respect the comments made by other members of the class.

2. I expect other members of the class to respect my contributions to the discussion.

3. Personal remarks about others in the class will not be tolerated.

4. I do not have to reveal anything I do not want to about myself, my thoughts or my feelings.

5. I do not have the right to pressurise anyone to join in.

6. I must wait my turn to speak and not interrupt.

7. If I feel someone is behaving inappropriately, I have the right to say so.

8. If I am asked a question by anyone other than the teacher, I do not have to answer it but should still reply politely.

9. I should not try to force other people to agree with me.

10. I have the right to keep facts about my relationships and experiences private.

Anyone who does not keep these rules will be asked to leave the room.

Suggestions for additional rules:

....

....

....

....

....

....

....

....

Create your own identity chart, similar to Vikram's on page 6 of *Your Choice Book One*, using the spider diagram frame below. You can add more legs if necessary.

Some factors you might want to include are listed below. You don't have to include all of these, and you can include others if you'd like to – whatever you feel is most important to your identity.

- Family
- Gender
- Age
- Appearance

- Nationality
- Where you live
- Culture
- Religion

- Language
- Hobbies and interests
- Friends
- The media

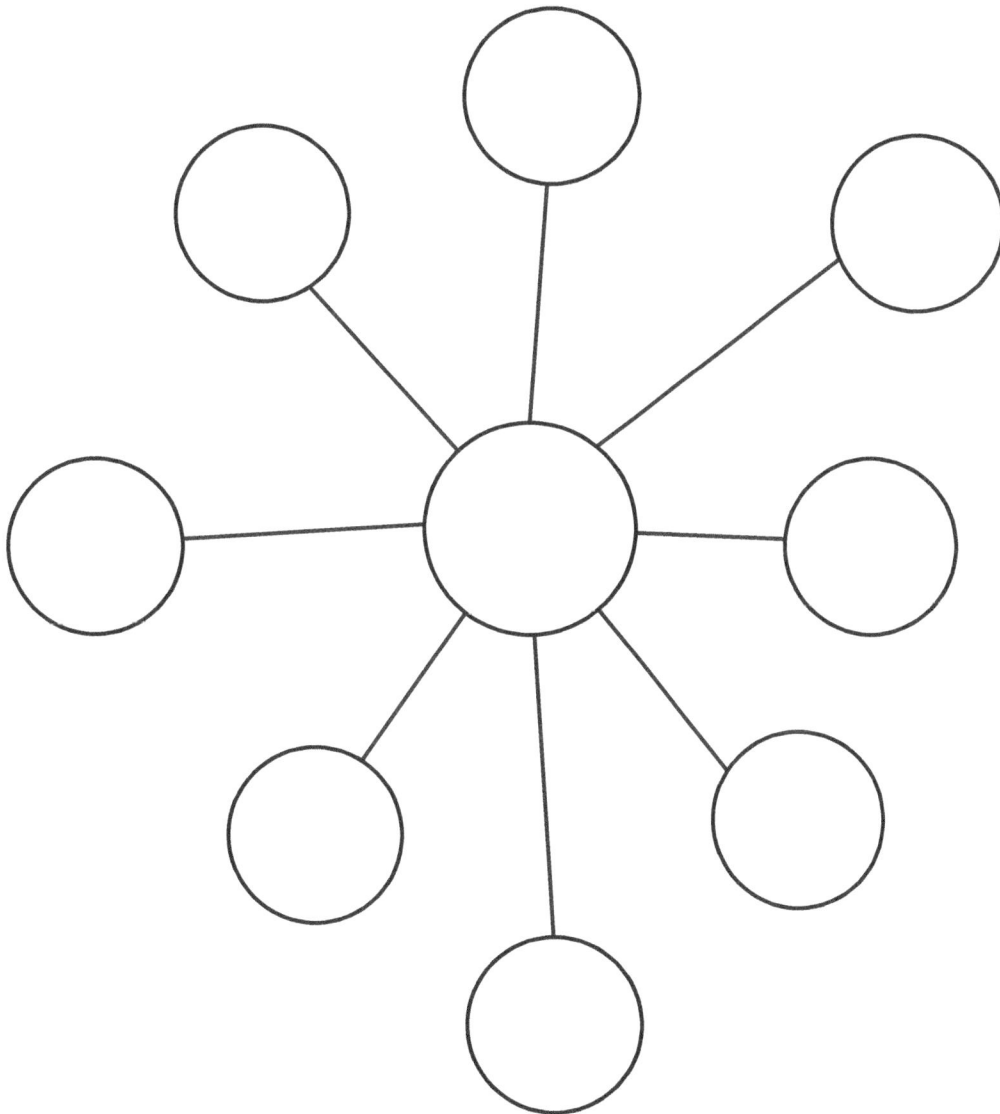

Strand:	**Resources:**
• Personal wellbeing and mental health	• Book One: pp. 8–9 • Worksheet 1.2

Learning objective:	**Key words:**
• To understand how your personality is formed, how it affects your behaviour and the differences between extroverts and introverts	personality, nature, nurture, environment, introvert, extrovert

STARTER

• Write the word 'personality' on the board and ask students what it means. Collect their responses on the board and then write up this definition: 'the combination of characteristics and qualities that make up an individual's character'.

• With students, read the introductory section and 'Nature or nurture?' on page 8 of *Your Choice Book One*, and discuss how a person's personality is formed by a combination of their genes and upbringing. Explain that experts disagree as to which is the more important.

ACTIVITIES

• Encourage students to think about the qualities they have by doing the discussion activity 'What sort of person are you?'. Then read with them the paragraph beneath the activity about other factors.

• Ask students to read the five situations described on page 8 and think about how they would react in each. Then ask them, in pairs, to say what this tells them about their personalities. Example responses: *Situation 1 – I am frightened, so I tell my friend I don't want to go on with them. This shows I am confident enough to tell other people how I feel and to only do what is comfortable for me.*

• Give out copies of **Worksheet 1.2** for students to complete. Then ask them to share what they found out with a partner.

• Invite students to read the information on 'Are you an introvert or an extrovert?' on page 9. As a class, discuss the characteristics of introverts and extroverts and ask: 'What are the advantages and disadvantages of being an extrovert or an introvert?' Be sure to point out the advantages of both: for example, while extroverts may take the lead and provide energy, introverts may come to a more thoughtful and considered form of action by thinking things over.

PLENARY

• Ask students to write one or two paragraphs stating what they have learned about their identity and personality from this lesson and the previous lesson.

RESEARCH

• Ask students to think about the strengths and weaknesses in their own personality and to research what strategies they could use to help them overcome or cope with any negative aspects.

EXTENSION

• Ask students, on their own, to think about what sort of person they would like to be when they are an adult and to write down three things. Then invite them to discuss these in pairs, thinking about how their personality might develop as they get older.

Further information and support for teachers:

Information on the Myers-Briggs personality types as it applies for teenagers, which can be adapted for use in class:
www.psychologyjunkie.com/2017/09/23/teenage-struggles-every-myers-briggs-personality-type/

The enneagram for teenagers – written by one 17-year-old with cartoons to help:
https://allymarthontheenneagram.wordpress.com/2015/01/16/the-enneagram-for-teens-follow-up/

Worksheet 1.2 Your personality

Consider these statements. Put a tick beside the ones that apply to you. When you have finished, share your answers with a partner and say what the answers tell you about your personality.

✓

1. I like to be surrounded by people. ☐

   I prefer to be on my own or with a close friend. ☐

2. I am excited by new challenges. ☐

   I am very nervous when I have to do something new. ☐

3. I am willing to take risks. ☐

   I am very cautious. ☐

4. I am easily embarrassed. ☐

   It takes a lot to embarrass me. ☐

5. I will always join in discussions and express my opinion. ☐

   I won't offer an opinion unless I'm asked to do so. ☐

6. I am quick-tempered. ☐

   I remain calm even when I'm provoked. ☐

7. I work best on my own. ☐

   I work well in a group. ☐

8. I always look on the bright side. ☐

   I always think about what could go wrong. ☐

9. I'll always volunteer if volunteers are wanted. ☐

   I'll never volunteer for anything. ☐

10. I'm bossy and willing to take the lead. ☐

    I'll do what others suggest. I'll follow others rather than lead them. ☐

11. I'm patient and take my time working things out. ☐

    I'm impulsive and always in a rush to do things. ☐

12. I'm ambitious and want to do the best I can. ☐

    I'm easy-going and not very ambitious. ☐

13. I care about what people think of me. ☐

    I don't care what other people think of me. ☐

14. I have a high opinion of myself. ☐

    I don't think I'm very good at anything. ☐

15. I get upset when people make insulting remarks about me. ☐

    I take no notice if people say nasty things about me. ☐

Unit 1.3   Who am I?

Strand:
- Personal wellbeing and mental health

Resources:
- Book One, pp. 10–11
- Worksheet: 1.3

Learning objective:
- To understand that you are a citizen of the country in which you are born and entitled to a passport of that country, and how others may be entitled by residency or by parentage

Key words:
ethnicity, identity, nationality, refugee, immigration, deportation, amnesty, residency, ethnic group, descent, double descent

STARTER

- Read the introduction on page 10 of *Your Choice Book One* and the section starting 'You are a citizen...' on page 11. Discuss how a person is a citizen of the country in which they are born and is entitled to a passport issued by that country. Explain that you can also qualify for citizenship by living in a country – this is known as 'residency'.

ACTIVITIES

- Ask students, in twos or threes, to study Marlon's family tree on page 10 and discuss his ethnic background. Point out that, depending on who their parents and grandparents are, one person may come from a number of different backgrounds. Ask them to discuss how easy it was to classify Marlon.

- Hand out **Worksheet 1.3** and, with the class, read the information about descent and double descent. Check that they understand what these terms mean. Then ask them to do the discussion task on page 10 in the same pairs or threes. Bring the class back together to share students' findings.

- Support students to complete the research task on the Windrush generation. *Answers:* **1.** *The* Empire Windrush *was a ship that brought people to the UK from the Caribbean from 1948 until the early 1970s.* **2.** *The immigrants were invited to come because of labour shortages after the Second World War.* **3.** *Because they were considered British subjects, most lived and worked in the UK without additional paperwork – their landing cards served as proof of their arrival in the UK. In 1971, the Immigration Act granted indefinite leave to remain to all Commonwealth citizens already living in the UK. However, it did not provide any paperwork to confirm this. During a recent government crackdown on illegal immigration, many in the Windrush generation have had difficulty proving their legal right to remain in the UK. This was especially true after records of their landing cards were destroyed by the Home Office in 2010. This caused a political controversy in 2018 when it came to light.*

- Ask students to read the left-hand column of page 11 and then to work in groups on the writing task.

- Now, with students, read the poem 'Immigration Trap' and invite groups to discuss the issues it raises about immigration. Ask students if they empathise with Farida's situation. If it were their mother being deported, how would they feel?

- Draw students' attention back to **Worksheet 1.3** and invite them, in pairs, to produce a 'True or false' quiz, and then to give it to another pair to do.

PLENARY

- Ask students, in pairs, to discuss what they have learned about people's heritage/background and about immigration, and how the two are linked. Bring the class together to share their ideas.

EXTENSION

- In groups, and then as a class, encourage students to discuss what backgrounds people have in the class, in the school and in the local area, and what positive things each brings.

Further information and support:

BBC Bitesize, series of videos on 'Diversity in the UK': www.bbc.com/bitesize/topics/z8dj6sg/resources/1

Celebrating diversity, Black history month: www.blackhistorymonth.org.uk/

Worksheet 1.3 The right to a British passport

Your right to a British passport depends on a number of factors.

Birth

If you are the son or daughter of a British citizen and were born in the UK, you have British nationality and are entitled to a British passport.

You may be entitled to a British passport if you were born in the UK and your parents are not British citizens. It will depend on how and why they came to Britain.

Descent

You are entitled to a British passport if one of your parents is a British citizen.

Double descent

You are entitled to apply for a British passport if one of your grandparents was/is a British citizen.

Residency

You may apply for British citizenship, which will entitle you to a British passport if you have been resident in the UK for 5 years, speak English and have passed the 'Life in the UK' test.

You may apply for British citizenship if you are stateless: for example, if you fled from war in your country and came to the UK as a refugee.

Marriage

You can become a British citizen by marriage to a British citizen after you have been married for two years.

Your application for citizenship may be rejected if:

- you entered the country illegally
- you applied for asylum as a refugee, but are not considered to have justification for leaving your native land
- you have **been** convicted of a criminal offence.

In pairs, use the information on this page to make up a 'True or false' quiz about who has the right to a British passport. Include some statements that are true and some that are false. Then give it to another pair to do. An example has been included in the table below to help get you started.

Statement:	True or false?
1. To be a British citizen, both of your parents must be British.	
2.	
3.	
4.	
5.	

Strand:	**Resources:**
• Personal wellbeing and mental health	• Book One, pp. 12–13 • Worksheet 1.4

Learning objective:	**Key words:**
• To understand how far gender shapes your identity, what gender stereotypes are, and how to challenge them	gender, sex, stereotypes

STARTER

• Ask students as a class if there are any common views of what girls and boys can and can't do at school. For example, are there certain sports, such as netball or rugby, that only girls or boys can play? Note two or three examples on the board, avoiding any that are listed on **Worksheet 1.4** (see below).

ACTIVITIES

• With the class, read the introduction on page 12 of *Your Choice Book One*. Make sure that students understand the difference between sex and gender.

• Ask students to work in pairs to read 'Gender development' and then discuss the questions in the 'Discuss' box. Bring the class together to share their answers and discuss any differences in opinion.

• Hand out **Worksheet 1.4** and ask students, in their pairs, to read 'Stereotypes' on page 12 and then do task **1** of the worksheet. Bring the class together to discuss their responses to the task. Do they generally agree on the sorts of stereotyping that they are aware of at school? Do they think people realise that they are stereotyping?

• Organise students into groups to read 'Changing times' on page 13 and encourage them to do the research task individually outside class time. At the start of the next lesson, you could ask them what they found out, and which approach they prefer and why.

• Ask groups to read 'Challenging stereotypes' and 'When your gender doesn't feel right' before doing the discussion task on page 13.

PLENARY

• In a class discussion, invite students to discuss their responses to the discussion task. Bring their attention to task **2** on **Worksheet 1.4** and use the prompts to discuss the best ways to combat stereotyping.

EXTENSION

• Encourage students to work in pairs to do the second research task on page 13.

Further information and support for teachers:

Ten ways to challenge stereotypes in the classroom:
http://lettoysbetoys.org.uk/ten-ways-to-challenge-gender-stereotypes-in-the-classroom/

The Telegraph – article on what happened when a primary school went gender-neutral:
www.telegraph.co.uk/women/life/happened-primary-school-went-gender-neutral/

You could search on YouTube for the full documentary, *No More Boys and Girls*. There are a few short clips on the BBC site: www.bbc.co.uk/programmes/b09202jz/clips

Gender stereotype resources from the NSPCC and the PSHE Association:
https://learning.nspcc.org.uk/research-resources/schools/making-sense-relationships/

Worksheet 1.4 Gender stereotypes

1. Which types of gender stereotyping are you aware of at your school?
   Tick any that you are aware of in the second column.

   Now decide whether you think each stereotype is fair or unfair, or you're not sure.
   Say which in the third column.

   There are some empty rows for you to fill in with any other stereotypes you think are occurring at your school.

Stereotype	Believed by some at your school?	Is this fair? Yes/no/ not sure
1. Girls are more emotional than boys.		
2. Boys are better at science and computing; girls are better at arts subjects.		
3. Only boys should be allowed to play football.		
4. Boys should never cry in public, but it's OK for girls to.		
5. Boys should never wear pink.		
6. Girls are more mature than boys.		
7. Boys find it hard to sit still.		
8.		
9.		
10.		

2. Which of the following do you think is the best way to combat stereotyping?
   Give reasons for your views.

   - Having a positive role model
   - Education
   - Taking stereotypes to their extreme to show how ridiculous they are
   - Using humour and laughing at stereotypes
   - Challenging stereotypes wherever you find them

....

....

....

....

....

2.1 Puberty

<table>
<tr><td>

Strand:
- Relationships and sex education

</td><td>

Resources:
- Book One, pp. 14–15
- Worksheet 1.1a

</td></tr>
<tr><td>

Learning objective:
- To explain the changes that take place during puberty

</td><td>

Key words:

puberty, period, hormone, ovary, penis, testicle, pubic, masturbation, erection, ejaculate, semen

</td></tr>
</table>

STARTER

- As this is the first lesson in which you are going to be dealing with facts and issues concerning puberty and sex, you need to ensure that students are aware of the ground rules that you expect them to follow. Remind them of the rules for class discussion from Unit 1 and, if necessary, go through **Worksheet 1.1a** with them again.

ACTIVITIES

- Divide the class into small groups to read 'Growing and changing' on page 14 of *Your Choice Book One* and then to do the discussion activity that follows the comments. Encourage groups to notice the main changes that boys and girls are undergoing. If you feel it is appropriate, you could introduce the idea that some students may feel that they do not fit this binary.

- Bring the class back together to read 'Puberty: your questions answered'. Invite questions about physical changes during puberty. Then ask students, in pairs, to read Christian's and Eveline's letters to Erica on page 15 and draft replies to them.

- Read 'Thoughts and feelings' with the class and discuss how these change as people become young adults. Then ask pairs to read 'Ask Erica' and do the first part of the writing activity. Stronger students can do this activity on their own.

- Introduce the idea of a question box that allows students to ask questions anonymously. Place the box on your desk. Give out slips of paper and ask everyone to do part **2** of the writing activity. Explain that you will answer some of the questions in the next lesson – you can decide which are appropriate for this.

PLENARY

- Remind the class that people develop and change at different times: one person may enter puberty aged 10, another at 13, while some people's bodies don't change until later.

RESEARCH

- Ask students to look at the diagrams on page 15 in pairs. They should use a dictionary to look up any terms they are not familiar with.

EXTENSION

- Ask students, in groups, to list the differences between boys and girls during puberty, and then discuss what they could do to help each other (e.g. respecting a girl when she has her period, not teasing boys if they don't start shaving until much later or when their voices break).

Further information and support:

NHS, 'Stages of puberty':
www.nhs.uk/live-well/sexual-health/stages-of-puberty-what-happens-to-boys-and-girls/

BBC Bitesize, 'Puberty': www.bbc.com/bitesize/guides/z9fgr82/revision/6

2.2 Periods: the facts

Strand:
- Relationships and sex education

Resources:
- Book One, pp. 16–17
- Worksheet 2.2

Learning objective:
- To understand the basic facts about periods

Key words:
ovulation, menstruation, menstrual cycle, ovary, menopause, vagina, cervix, fallopian tube, uterus, sanitary towel, tampon

STARTER
- Explain that the focus of the lesson will be periods and that the term 'period' is that commonly used to describe the process of menstruation.
- With the class, read the introduction on page 16 of *Your Choice Book One* and 'What happens during a period?'. Check understanding of the terms 'ovaries', 'uterus' and 'fallopian tube' and explain as necessary using the diagrams on page 16.

ACTIVITIES
- Now ask pairs to read through 'Periods: your questions answered' together.
- Ask students to do the test-yourself quiz on page 17 on their own, before comparing their answers in a class discussion. *(Answers: 1. Fact; 2. Myth; 3. Myth; 4. Myth (periods end with the menopause); 5. Fact; 6. Myth; 7. Myth (it varies from individual to individual); 8. Myth; 9. Myth; 10 Myth.)*
- Organise students into mixed-gender groups to read **Worksheet 2.2** and then discuss what they think the most important information and best pieces of advice are on the worksheet. *(Answers to worksheet: 1. Exercise, meditation, fruit and vegetables, sleep; 2. Salty food, snacks, caffeine, stress.)*
- In the discussion, make the point that once periods are established, very heavy bleeding, excessive pain that disrupts everyday life and bleeding between cycles are not normal. Anyone who experiences these things should see their doctor, as they could be a sign of an underlying condition, such as endometriosis, fibroids, pelvic inflammatory disease or polycystic ovary syndrome. The NHS website gives further information on heavy and painful periods (see below).
- Read 'Tampon tax' with the class, then ask students for their views. Encourage students to do the research task to find out how the campaign to make tampons free of VAT is going and to find out whether their local MP supports it. They can contact their MP via the link below.

PLENARY
- Invite students to read 'Ask Erica' and draft their replies to Tess. Share them in a class discussion.

EXTENSION
- Encourage students to use the tampon tax calculator in the weblinks below to work out how much tampons cost a woman each year, and how much she could save over a year it there was no VAT.

Further information and support for teachers:

Samples can be obtained from Tampax and Always, who can also provide speakers:
www.always.co.uk/en-gb/puberty-education-programme-always-tampax

BBC PSHE, Lara's first period (video):
www.bbc.com/teach/class-clips-video/pshe-ks2--ks3-laras-first-period/zjxn382

Free sanitary products for schools: www.bbc.co.uk/news/uk-47553449

Menstrual health: www.bbc.co.uk/news/newsbeat-47350835

For students:

BBC Tampon tax calculator: www.bbc.co.uk/news/health-42013239

NHS, Starting your periods, period problems, heavy periods:
www.nhs.uk/conditions/periods/starting-periods and www.nhs.uk/conditions/heavy-periods

Contacting your local MP: www.theyworkforyou.com

Worksheet 2.2 What is premenstrual syndrome?

What is premenstrual syndrome?

Premenstrual syndrome (PMS) is the term used to describe the symptoms a woman may have in the weeks before her period. Most women will experience some of the symptoms at some time in their lives. But the symptoms vary from person to person and can vary from month to month.

What are the symptoms of PMS?

The most common symptoms are:

Emotional symptoms

- Mood swings
- Feeling depressed or anxious
- Feeling irritable
- Feeling upset

Physical symptoms

- Headaches
- Bloating or abdominal pain
- Tiredness and trouble sleeping
- Breast tenderness
- Spotty skin and/or greasy hair
- Weight gain due to fluid retention
- Changes in appetite/food cravings

The symptoms usually disappear within four days after the period starts. But while they persist, they can be severe enough to affect a person's daily life.

Can I do anything about PMS?

Many women find that they can manage their symptoms themselves. Things you can do include:

- Taking some form of exercise regularly.
- Altering your diet so that you eat healthily.
    - Cut down on salty food and snacks to reduce bloating and fluid retention.
    - Eat plenty of fruit and vegetables.
    - Eat smaller meals to feel less bloated and full.
    - Avoid caffeine.
- Trying to reduce your stress levels, for example by meditating.
- Taking painkillers such as paracetamol or ibuprofen.
- Making sure you get plenty of sleep.

If your PMS is severe, you can see your doctor, who will advise you about treatments that are available.

For a few women, the symptoms occur regularly each month and are so debilitating they affect their whole lives. This form of PMS is called premenstrual dysphoric disorder. Other conditions that can cause particularly heavy or painful periods include endometriosis, fibroids, pelvic inflammatory disease and polycystic ovary syndrome.

Check your understanding:

1. What should you *increase* if you are suffering from PMS? ....

....

....

2. What should you *decrease* if you are suffering from PMS?...

....

....

3.1   Feeling worried or anxious

Strand:
- Personal wellbeing and mental health

Resources:
- Book One: pp. 18–19
- Worksheet 3.1

Learning objective:
- To discuss common worries and anxieties and how to deal with them

Key words:

anxiety, phobia

STARTER

- With the class, read the introduction and 'What worries you?' on page 18 of *Your Choice Book One*. Explain that it is natural to feel worried and anxious at times, but that some worries and feelings of anxiety are more serious than others. It depends what you are anxious about.

- Invite students to read the 12 statements in 'What makes you feel anxious?' and rank them according to their level of seriousness, then to compare their views with a partner's.

ACTIVITIES

- Ask students to think about the advice Erica might give to the people who made the statements and, in pairs, to draft replies to two of them. A sample reply to situation 10 might read: '*You need to talk to your friends and find out what is really going on. Many worries are about things that turn out not to be true or simply never happen. Your friends may have forgotten to invite you. You need to find out what is going on, rather than worrying about it.*'

- Read the rest of page 18 with the class. Then ask students to read 'Ask Erica' on page 19 and, in groups, to discuss her replies to the five people who wrote to her, considering the questions in the discussion task.

- Encourage students to think of a time when they have felt embarrassed or self-conscious and then to do the writing activity. Invite those who are willing to do so to share what they have written.

- Ask students to read the research task and then hand out copies of **Worksheet 3.1**. Read this with the class and then support students to use the internet to complete the task. If any of them have anxieties about something specific that might be considered a phobia, they could research that using the NHS web page below.

PLENARY

- Remind students that a worry shared is a worry halved. Then get them to look again at each of the 12 statements on page 18 and to suggest who might be the best person to share their anxiety with (e.g. a friend, family member, a counsellor or a trusted adult).

EXTENSION

- Ask students to write a short report of two to three paragraphs on their findings in the research task they did earlier. Invite individuals to present their findings to the rest of the class.

Further information and support for teachers:

Anxiety UK, resources for parents and schools:
www.anxietyuk.org.uk/get-help/anxiety-information/young-people-and-anxiety/resources/

NHS, 'Anxiety in children': www.nhs.uk/conditions/stress-anxiety-depression/anxiety-in-children/

Further information and support for students:

Nine tips for public speaking for teenagers:
www.teenvogue.com/story/public-speaking-tips-class-presentations

NHS, 'Phobias': www.nhs.uk/conditions/phobias

Worksheet 3.1 Phobias

What is a phobia?

A phobia is a type of anxiety that causes a person to try to avoid contact with an object or animal, a place or a situation.

Examples of simple phobias are fear of dogs, spiders or snakes, fear of going to the dentist, fear of flying and fear of enclosed spaces such as lifts and caves.

Who is affected?

It is estimated that about 10 million people are affected in the UK. Phobias can affect people of any age.

Simple phobias, such as going to the dentist, often start in early childhood and disappear as you get older.

More complex phobias, such as social phobia (a fear of social situations, such as weddings or performing in social situations, such as speaking in public) often begin during puberty.

Can phobias be cured?

Almost all phobias can be successfully treated and cured. Simple phobias can be treated by gradually exposing the person to the object, animal, place or situation that causes the anxiety. But many people with a simple phobia do not need treatment and find that avoiding the object of their fear is enough to control the problem.

Treating more complex phobias takes longer and often involves counselling and psychotherapy.

Write down which phobias you have researched and what you have found out.

1. ....

....

....

....

2. ....

....

....

....

3. ....

....

....

....

3.2 The laws of attraction

Strand:
- Personal wellbeing and mental health

Resources:
- Book One: pp. 20–21
- Worksheet 3.2

Learning objective:
- To understand anxieties about being attractive and what are attractive qualities

Key words:
attraction, dependability, optimistic, moral integrity

STARTER
- Ask students on their own to write down up to five things they think make a person attractive.
- Share their views in a class discussion and list on the board the qualities or personality characteristics that they suggest. Once you've made this list, ask students whether the characteristics are more to do with personality or the way people look, and which they think are more important.

ACTIVITIES
- With the class, read the introduction and the 'Fact check' on page 20 of *Your Choice Book One*. Then move on to the article by Trinia Newsome. Discuss her view that what makes people attractive is their personality rather than their appearance.
- Ask students, on their own, to pick out the three qualities she lists that they think are the most influential in making a person attractive. Encourage them to compare their choices with a partner and discuss any differences.
- Ask students to read Sonia's story on page 21 on their own. Then, as a class, discuss the reasons why she finds Darren attractive. Ask: 'From what she says, do you think Darren is attractive? What else would you need to know about him in order to decide whether or not he is an attractive person?'
- Next, ask students to read Thomas's story and then discuss the questions in the discussion activity. Ask: 'Do you agree that a person's character is more important than their appearance in making them attractive?'
- Ask students to do the writing task and then encourage a few to share their answers. Points may include that being good looking or clever doesn't necessarily make someone a good friend but being kind and considerate does. People can, of course, be all of these things!
- Give out copies of **Worksheet 3.2** and ask students to do task **1**, deciding which are unattractive and which are attractive ways of behaving. Discuss their responses as a class.

PLENARY
- Ask students to write a paragraph summing up their views on what qualities are most significant in determining whether or not a person is attractive. Compare their responses with the list you wrote on the board at the start of the lesson. Has anything changed in students' views?

EXTENSION
- Ask students to do task **2** on **Worksheet 3.2**. Some sentence starters are provided to help get students going.

Further information and support for teachers:

Psychology Today, 'The four types of attraction':
www.psychologytoday.com/us/blog/valley-girl-brain/201504/the-four-types-attraction

Further information and support for students:

Girls Out Loud (a charity helping teenage girls), the pressures on girls today, including to be attractive:
http://girlsoutloud.org.uk/

Worksheet 3.2 What makes people attractive?

1. Study these statements and put a tick beside those you agree with and a cross beside those you disagree with. Then compare your answers in a group discussion.

a)	I think people who are good at sports are attractive, because they look after their bodies.	
b)	It doesn't matter if someone is useless at sport. It's what sort of person they are that matters.	
c)	You can tell what a person is like by the way they treat animals. People who are cruel to animals are unattractive.	
d)	People who swear a lot are unattractive.	
e)	People who wear glasses are less attractive than people who don't wear them.	
f)	People with tattoos all over them are unattractive.	
g)	A person who smiles a lot is attractive.	
h)	A person who thinks a lot of themselves isn't very attractive.	
i)	People who behave politely and show consideration are more attractive than people who are inconsiderate.	
j)	A person who is daring and adventurous is attractive.	
k)	Clever people are more attractive than other people.	
l)	A rich person is more likely to be attractive because they can afford to look after their appearance.	
m)	It doesn't matter to me what a person looks like or how rich they are; it's their sense of humour that counts – I like someone who can make me laugh.	

2. Write two or three paragraphs for an article entitled 'Why some people are more attractive than others', explaining what you think makes someone attractive and what makes some people unattractive.

Here are some sample sentences openers to help you get started:

'In my opinion, being attractive is about both what's inside and outside…'

'I have a friend who I think is really attractive, for the following reasons…'

'Being attractive is about positive parts of a person's personality. The top thing I find attractive in a person is…'

4.1   Right and wrong

Strand:	Resources:
• Personal wellbeing and mental health	• Book One: pp. 22–23 • Worksheet 4.1

Learning objective:	Key words:
• To consider what is right and wrong behaviour and how attitudes and values change from generation to generation	attitudes, values

STARTER

• Read the introduction and 'What are values?' on page 22 of *Your Choice Book One*. Ask students to think about what they believe is the right way to behave. Elicit answers such as '*treating other people with kindness and consideration*'. Encourage them to draw up their 'Top Ten Rules' on how to behave.

ACTIVITIES

• Ask students to read Jodie's list of rules and compare it with their own, deciding which of her rules they agree with and why. Now ask students to read 'Sticking to the positive'; encourage them to look at Jodie's list and their own lists and to alter them as necessary into positive statements.

• Ask groups of students to discuss any other rules they would include. Then come together as a class to draw up an agreed list of 'Our ten rules for today', consisting of positive statements.

• Talk about how attitudes and values change. With the class, read 'It's all changed since great grandad's day...'. Ask students to discuss what they think the most important difference is between the 1960s and life today: what has had the biggest impact on everyday life?

• Ask students in groups to discuss what they would do in the three situations described in the second part of the discussion task on page 23. Then encourage them to develop role plays in which they show people with different views discussing what they should do.

• Ask students to do the writing activity on page 23 on their own, but pair up students needing more support to do the second part of the activity. Then ask students to compare their answers in groups, giving reasons for their views.

• Give out copies of **Worksheet 4.1** for individuals to complete. Then invite them to share their views in a class or group discussion. *(Suggested responses include: cheating creates an unfair playing field and ruins the point of any test or exam; relationships should be based on honesty and clear understanding of what is acceptable and unacceptable to both parties.)*

PLENARY

• Ask pairs to complete the 'Your choice' ranking activity on page 23 and compare their views, first with another pair's and then in a class discussion. Draw out whether they think that things that hurt other people are the worst points on this list.

• Ask students to complete the research activity at the top of page 23 as homework, talking to parents, carers or older relatives about how values and attitudes changed during the 1960s.

EXTENSION

• Using the link to BBC Newsround below, distribute Jake's story and ask students to complete the questions on the website.

Further information and support for teachers:

Young Citizens, Go-Givers, resources to teach empathy and compassion:
https://www.youngcitizens.org/go-givers

BBC Newsround, 'My life behind bars':
http://news.bbc.co.uk/cbbcnews/hi/newsid_4570000/newsid_4576100/4576161.stm

Worksheet 4.1 Cheating

1. Cheating can mean different things to different people.

   Look at the following list. Decide which involve cheating. Then rate the situation according to how serious you think it is, on a scale of 1 to 5, where 1 is not serious and 5 is the most serious. Give reasons for your views.

Situation	Cheating (yes/no)	Seriousness (from 1 to 5)	Reason
1. Getting a private tutor to help you the night before an exam.			
2. Buying the exam questions the night before an exam from a teacher on eBay who is selling them.			
3. Kissing another person on the cheek without telling your boyfriend or girlfriend.			
4. Answering a piece of homework by looking at several different articles, and then summarising an argument from each of them in your own words.			
5. Kissing another person on the lips without telling your boyfriend or girlfriend.			
6. Copying another person's answers in a multiple-choice exam without their knowledge.			
7. Doing a piece of homework by simply cutting and pasting an article from the internet and passing it off as your own.			
8. Answering a homework question as a group, but not telling the teacher you've collaborated with your friends.			

2. What other instances of cheating can you think of? Which are the most serious? Give reasons for your views.

Situation	Seriousness (from 1 to 5)	Reason

4.2 — Who do you admire?

Strand:	Resources:
• Personal wellbeing and mental health	• Book One: pp. 24–25 • Worksheet 4.2

Learning objective:	Key words:
• To identify qualities that we admire and to consider whether there are unique British values	admiration, attraction, assertive

STARTER

• With the class, read the introduction and 'What is admiration?'. Talk about what admiration is and why we admire certain people. Is it because of their achievements? Because they are celebrities? Because they have particular qualities that we value? Ask: 'If you had to choose one person in the world to meet because you admire them, who would it be?' Encourage some students to give reasons for their choice.

ACTIVITIES

• Ask students to look at the list of people in the discussion activity and say whether they admire them. Get them, individually, to place the people on a scale of 1 to 10, where 1 = not at all worthy and 10 = extremely worthy and explain their reasons for the ranking.

• Read the case studies together. Ask students, in groups, to do the first part of the discussion activity on page 25. Hand out of copies of **Worksheet 4.2**. Ask students to look at Tariq and Stacey's word cloud and then to create one of their own. Then, in pairs, ask them to do the second part of the discussion activity, using the worksheet to help them. Elicit the fact that our opinions can change. Now ask them to do the second part of the worksheet in light of what they've discussed, and then to do the 'Write' activity.

• With the class, read 'How the media influence us' and discuss how some people get more media exposure than others. Ask if they had heard of Bethany Firth. Do they think the media are making an effort to give more exposure to people with disabilities, for example, by covering the Invictus Games? Encourage suggestions for how the media could do more.

• Elicit from students a list of their unsung heroes and note them on the board. Encourage them to consider people like carers. Use the links to 'Jemma's special journey' and 'My hero' in the box below for other examples for students to discuss.

• Ask pairs to read 'British values' and then to do the first part of the discussion task below it. Ask: 'Do you think there are unique British values, or are there universal values that apply in all cultures?' Organise students into groups to do the second part of the discussion activity. Values from other parts of the world could include: respect for nature (Maoris, New Zealand) or respect for your elders (China).

PLENARY

• With students, look at 'The Ministry of Stories' website (see below) and discuss the idea of a paean. Encourage students to work in pairs to write a paean for one of their heroes.

EXTENSION

• Organise a balloon debate. Put the class in groups of about five. Ask each group to choose a person they admire. Imagine these people are in a hot-air balloon that is losing height above a volcano. One of them must be sacrificed to save the others by reducing the weight of the balloon so it can avoid landing in the volcano. Each group must prepare a speech saying why their person's admirable qualities mean they should not be thrown out of the balloon. Listen to all the speeches and then hold a vote to decide who to throw out of the balloon based on which group gave the least convincing speech.

Further information and support for teachers:

BBC, 'Jemma's special journey', video showing a SEN role model: www.bbc.co.uk/worldclass/17211188

British Council, 'My hero', audio (6 mins):
http://learnenglishteens.britishcouncil.org/skills/listening/upper-intermediate-b2-listening/my-hero

The Ministry of Stories, admiration poetry (paeans), includes examples for writing paeans with the class.
www.ministryofstories.org/teacher-resource/paean-admiration-poetry/

1. Tariq and Stacey have made a word cloud of the qualities they most admire in people.

    Make a word cloud of your own in the box below of the qualities you most admire in other people.

Being trustworthy   Being handsome or beautiful

Honesty   Strength

Being pushy

Fitness   Qualities I admire   Being driven

Power   Style

Being successful   Being forthright

Being rich   Assertiveness

2. Compare your word cloud with Tariq and Stacey's. Do you want to add any of the qualities they included but you didn't?

....

....

....

Regrets and saying sorry

Strand: • Personal wellbeing and mental health	**Resources:** • Book One: pp. 26–27 • Worksheet 4.3
Learning objective: • To focus on how people make mistakes that they regret and on how to apologise	**Key words:** regret, apology

STARTER

* With the class, read 'Regrets' on page 26 of *Your Choice Book One*. Ask individuals to think about a mistake they have made and why they made it. Did they act impulsively, without thinking of the consequences? Explain that they do not need to share what they did if they do not wish to, but encourage those who are willing to say what they did and why they regret it. Ask: 'Looking back, how do you wish you had behaved differently?'

ACTIVITIES

* Ask students to work in groups to read the scenarios on page 26 and then do the discussion task based on these. Remind them that they do not have to agree and that members of the group may explain that they would have acted differently from others in their group. Encourage students to think about the consequences for other people, whether they know them or not.

* Then ask groups to move on to think about the question in 'Your choice' on page 27. Encourage them to think about which scenarios might be bullying (e.g. teasing the person in a wheelchair), and how some situations can cause greater emotional harm than others (e.g. if the bench being defaced had a plaque on it dedicated to someone who had died). Ask them to write their views about **a)** and **b)**. Then bring the class back together to discuss different groups' responses. Make it clear to students that, for their own safety, they should not intervene themselves.

* Encourage students, working in groups, to do the second discussion activity. Again, bring the class back together and invite groups to share and compare their answers. Do responses to this and the 'Your choice' activity vary greatly between groups? Are there some areas of agreement?

* Give out copies of **Worksheet 4.3**. Working in pairs, ask students to discuss the situations in task **1** and decide which ones they think the friend should apologise for and how, giving their reasons.

* As a class, read 'Saying sorry and making amends'. Encourage students, in pairs, to choose the two most useful rules for making apologies and then to work together to complete the writing task.

PLENARY

* Ask individuals to complete task **2** on **Worksheet 4.3**.

EXTENSION

* Ask students to create a poster raising awareness of the importance of regrets and saying sorry, to be displayed in school. Suggest that they use an eye-catching headline and image and then bullet points for the best advice they have learned from the lesson, referring to the text on page 27.

Further information and support for teachers:

Teaching Apologies, 'The Anatomy of a Good Apology' – six easy steps you can teach students (from an ESL perspective, but applicable in general):
https://busyteacher.org/14345-how-to-teach-apologies-esl-activities.html

Further information and support for students:

TeensHealth, 'Apologizing': https://kidshealth.org/en/teens/apologies.html

Worksheet 4.3 Apologising

1. Your friend tells you they have been involved in one of the following situations. They're not sure whether or not they should apologise. Do you think they ought to apologise, and if so, how?

Situation	Apologise (yes/no)	How?
1. Your friend has met somebody on the internet who fancies them and has been swapping messages with them behind their partner's back. The messages look innocent.		
2. Your friend has copied from somebody else in the latest English test. They've got higher marks than usual as a result and will be awarded a prize in class tomorrow.		
3. Your friend scratched the next-door neighbour's expensive car by accident and hasn't said anything because they don't want to get in trouble.		
4. Your friend keeps buying clothes from a top sports shop, wearing them on the weekend and then taking them back on the Monday claiming they haven't worn them.		
5. Your friend knows somebody has a crush on them and is leading them on, even though they don't really fancy the other person.		
6. Your friend keeps teasing a boy in the next class who thinks he might be gay.		

2. **a)** Think of a time when you apologised.

   How did this make you feel in your head? ....

   What about in your heart or in your gut? ....

   How did you feel after you had apologised? ....

   b) Now think of a time when you *didn't* apologise.

   How did this make you feel in your head? ....

   What about in your heart or in your gut? ....

   c) Now write two sentences, one describing your feelings after apologising, the other describing how you felt after not apologising.

   ....

   ....

   ....

   ....

5.1   You and your family

Strand:	Resources:
• Relationships and sex education	• Book One: pp. 28–29 • Worksheet 5.1

Learning objective:	Key words:
• To understand that there are different types of family and the importance of communication in your relationships with other family members	blended family, extended family, guardian, sibling

STARTER

* Explain that, in the past, the term 'family' was used to describe a group consisting of a father, a mother and their children, known as a 'nuclear family'. Now the word 'family' is used to describe many different groupings – there is no one type of family. With the class, read the introductory paragraphs on page 28 of *Your Choice Book One* and make sure that students understand the term 'blended families'.

ACTIVITIES

* Ask students, in pairs, to study and discuss the statements in the discussion task and then consider the two questions. In a class discussion, invite students to share their answers to the questions. Elicit that we often have a different relationship with our mum from the one we have with our dad, and that there are many different families (single-parent families, children with two dads, etc.).

* Get students to read 'Communicating with your family members' and Faisal's story, and then to do the discussion activity in groups. Invite some students to share their conclusions with the class.

* Encourage students to reflect on an argument they have had with a parent or carer by writing about it and, if they feel comfortable, sharing it with a partner (see the first 'Write' and two 'Discuss' activities on page 29).

* Explain to students the importance of being positive in their communication with their parents or carers. Ask them to read 'Being positive' and 'Hugs'. For homework, ask students to carry out the final writing task on page 29, keeping a record of the positive and negative comments they receive over a period of a week and considering the results. You could also ask them to think about how often they give or receive a hug over the week and whether this affects how they feel.

* Give out copies of **Worksheet 5.1**. Talk about how Jason lives in a blended family. Then ask students to complete the worksheet in pairs, deciding which roles each member of Jason's family might fulfil. Bring students together in groups, or as a class, to discuss their answers. Draw out the idea that many of the roles will depend on the individual family set-up and the personalities involved, and that some roles will be done by more than one person. Gently challenge any gender stereotyping in the way roles have been allocated, where appropriate. Discuss how it may be more appropriate for the biological parent to take a child to the doctor or to take the lead in telling a young person off, depending on the circumstances.

PLENARY

* Ask students, in pairs, to make lists of who in their family fulfils the roles described on the worksheet. Ask: 'Is the distribution of roles fair, or is there someone in your family who does more than their fair share?'

EXTENSION

* Ask students to make a podcast for other students their age or simply to record a segment of speech on their mobile phone, describing the different types of family that can exist. Examples should include single-parent families, same-sex couples, blended families, adoptive and foster families.

Further information and support for teachers:

Family lives, 'What your teenager needs':
www.familylives.org.uk/advice/teenagers/you-and-your-teen/what-your-teenager-needs/

The Guardian, 'Love it, hate it, can't do without it – teenagers reveal all on family life': www.theguardian.com/lifeandstyle/2015/dec/12/teenagers-siblings-parents-family-life-growing-up-young-adults-children

Worksheet 5.1 Roles within families

Jason's family

Jason lives in a blended family. He has a sister, Chantelle. Their mother, Irene, is divorced from their father, Lonnie. She has remarried Vince, and they live in a blended family with Vince's son, Alfie, from his first marriage to Sylvia. Irene's mother, Daisy, who is 80, also lives with them.

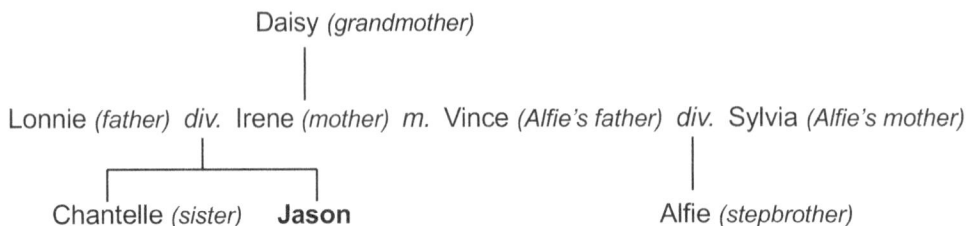

Daisy *(grandmother)*

Lonnie *(father)* div. Irene *(mother)* m. Vince *(Alfie's father)* div. Sylvia *(Alfie's mother)*

Chantelle *(sister)* **Jason**   Alfie *(stepbrother)*

m. = married
div. = divorced

Imagine you are Jason. Look at the list of roles below and decide which person or people in the family might perform that role. Use the lines to write your answers to the questions.

Roles within the family

1. Who goes out to work in the family?
    Do they work full time or part time?

    ....

    ....

    ....

    ....

2. Who tells you off when you have done something bad?

    ....

3. Who helps you with your homework?

    ....

4. Who praises you when you have done something good?

    ....

5. Who would take you to the doctor?

    ....

6. Who do you have the most fun with?

    ....

7. Who do you talk to the most?

    ....

8. Who does the cooking and cleaning in your house?

    ....

9. Who does the DIY or looks after a car?

    ....

10. Who does the washing and ironing?

    ....

11. Who takes the rubbish out?

    ....

12. Who does the gardening?

    ....

Strand:	Resources:
• Relationships and sex education	• Book One: pp. 30–31 • Worksheet 5.2

Learning objective:	Key words:
• To explore levels of friendships and how friends should behave	associates, tolerance, expectations

STARTER

● With the class, read the introductory text on page 30 of *Your Choice Book One* and explain the different levels of friendship. Ensure that students understand the difference between close and distant friends.

ACTIVITIES

● Ask students to write down what they expect from their friends by completing the statements 'A good friend is…' and 'A best friend is…'. Encourage them to share what they have written in pairs before completing the 'Your choice' activity. Invite pairs to share their choices with the rest of class and discuss any differences.

● With the class, read 'The changing nature of friendships' and ask: 'What do Carla's friendship maps show about how friendships may change?'

● Talk about meeting new people and how some people are more confident than others. Give out copies of **Worksheet 5.2**. Ask students to read and complete the worksheet individually, before coming back together as a class to discuss their responses.

● Ask students to read 'How should friends behave?' on page 31, explaining that different groups of friends will have different expectations. Then ask them, in groups, to study and discuss Mika's list of rules. Encourage them to suggest other forms of behaviour they would expect from friends. Bring the class back together to share suggestions.

● As a class, read the paragraph on 'Tolerance' and the questions and list of behaviours in the discussion activity that follows it. Invite students to share their responses to the questions in a class discussion. Points **a)**, **c)**, **e)**, **f)**, **h)** and **j)** are worth challenging outright. Point **b)** can be avoided. Point **d)** is worth broaching with your friend if it keeps on happening, as is point **g)** and point **i)**.

PLENARY

● Ask students individually to do the 'Write' activity, compiling: 'My ten rules for friendship'.

EXTENSION

● Ask students to work in groups to draw up a poster to put up in school showing how we should treat others as we would like to be treated.

Further information and support for teachers:

'Why teenage friendships are important', an Australian site listing factors that apply equally in the UK: https://raisingchildren.net.au/pre-teens/behaviour/peers-friends-trends/teen-friendships#why-teenage-friendships-are-important-nav-title

TES, 'Becoming a teen: friendship' further teaching resources: www.tes.com/teaching-resource/becoming-a-teen-friendship-6182747

NSPCC resources, 'Making sense of relationships': https://learning.nspcc.org.uk/research-resources/schools/making-sense-relationships/

Further information and support for students:

Childline, 'Top tips for making friends': www.childline.org.uk/info-advice/friends-relationships-sex/friends/top-tips-making-friends/

Worksheet 5.2 Meeting new people

Some people may make it look easy to make friends or talk to new people. However, they may be just as nervous as you inside. It's important to remember that everyone can feel nervous from time to time. So, if you're in a new situation, such as a new school, a new class, a new sporting activity or a social event where you don't know anybody, here's a list to help you:

Top tips on how to make meeting new people easier

1. Use balanced breathing (see **Worksheet 10.1**) to help you feel positive about meeting new people.

2. Scan the room to see who you might like to talk to.

3. Notice how other people are in the room. There may be people standing alone who have nobody to talk to and would welcome you talking to them.

4. Listen to what groups of people are talking about and join in the conversation if the topic is interesting.

5. Trust your gut feelings. You'll probably know within the first minute whether you want to talk more with somebody, or if you need to politely move on and talk to somebody else.

6. Approach somebody and either ask their name or start a conversation about what other people are talking about.

7. Remember to make eye contact and smile when you introduce yourself to another person.

8. Listen to what the other person is saying.

9. People like shared experiences where they connect with other people. So if a person plays the same video game, likes the same music, supports the same sports team or lives in the same area as you, comment on this and make that connection.

10. Be fine with rejection. If you talk to five people and you don't have anything in common with four of them, or they don't want to talk to you, that is fine, because the fifth person may turn out to be a really good friend – and that's all that matters.

Study the advice given in the article above. List the three pieces of advice that you think are most useful and say why. Then share them in a group discussion.

Advice:	Why is it useful?

5.3 Rivalries

Strand:	**Resources:**
• Relationships and sex education	• Book One: pp. 32–33
	• Worksheet 5.3

Learning objective:	**Key words:**
• To explore rivalries and how to deal with them	rivalry, superiority, competition, competitiveness

STARTER

* Write the word 'rivalry' on the board. Ask students what they think it means. Then write the following definition on the board: 'competition between people who have the same objective, who want the same things or want to be superior in some way'. Explain that rivalries occur in all walks of life – businesses, sports, politics. They can be between individuals, teams or organisations; they can be personal and can be friendly or unfriendly. Read the introductory paragraphs on page 32 of *Your Choice Book One* with the class.

ACTIVITIES

* Ask students to work in groups to read Susie's and Mike's stories and then do the discussion task. Question 3 is optional and they should only do this if they feel comfortable sharing their experiences.

* With the class, read 'Identity issues' on page 34. Discuss the points made about how rivalries can affect and undermine a person's identity. Ask: 'Why is it important to remember that there is usually someone who is better at something than you? How does the writer suggest you can put it in perspective?'

* Explain that if you are involved in a rivalry, you need to recognise the feelings it may cause. With the class, read 'Sorting out your emotions' – then invite anyone who is willing to do so to talk about their own experiences of how a rivalry made them feel. Ask students to work in groups on the discussion task that follows.

* Give out copies of **Worksheet 5.3** and encourage students to discuss each scenario in groups, saying what causes the rivalries and how best to deal with them.

PLENARY

* Ask students to study the two statements in the discussion task below 'Identity issues'. Then lead a class discussion to find out why they agree or disagree with them.

RESEARCH

* Ask students, in pairs, to use the internet to research a local sporting rivalry or a rivalry between two celebrities. Ask: 'Is the rivalry healthy? Do you think anything can be done to resolve the rivalry?'

EXTENSION

* Encourage students to work in pairs to produce a PowerPoint presentation from the research task to share with the class, explaining the rivalry and how healthy they think it is.

Further information and support for teachers:

Mail Online, 'Sibling rivalry': www.dailymail.co.uk/news/article-2252041/Sibling-rivalry-causes-long-term-psychological-harm-parents-leave-squabbling-teens-to-avoid-damage.html

Worksheet 5.3 Rivalries

1. Martin is good at chess. He can beat everyone in his class until, midway through the year, Zita joins the class. She is a refugee. Her English is not very good, but she can play chess. She learned to play while she was in a refugee camp in Turkey. One of the volunteers at the camp taught her. She challenges Martin and although she loses the first game, she soon works out his strategies and is able to beat him. Jed, who has regularly been beaten by Martin, finds this funny and starts to tease Martin, who gets upset and angry because Zita beats him.

   a) Who are rivals in this situation?

   ....

   b) Is it a friendly rivalry?

   ....

   c) What is the best way to resolve the rivalry?

   ....

   ....

2. Douglas really enjoys football and scores a goal most games. Justin notices this and starts to try and score a goal in every game as well. They play on different teams but are good friends.

   a) Who are rivals in this situation?

   ....

   b) Is it a friendly rivalry?

   ....

   c) What is the best way to resolve the rivalry?

   ....

   ....

3. Tina's best friend is Zoe. Tina is ill and off school for two weeks. When Tina returns, she finds that Zoe is spending all her time with Magda, another girl in the class. Although Zoe is friendly, she spends more time now with Magda than she does with Zoe.

   a) Who are rivals in this situation?

   ....

   b) Is it a friendly rivalry?

   ....

   c) What is the best way to resolve the rivalry?

   ....

Strand:	Resources:
• Relationships and sex education	• Book One: pp. 34–35 • Worksheet 6.1

Learning objective:	Key words:
• To explain myths about pregnancy and about STIs, and to learn what safer sex is	pregnant, safe sex, STI

STARTER

* Explain that although the next few lessons focus on improving students' understanding about sex, the age of consent in the UK is 16. In other words, it is illegal to have sex with someone under the age of 16.

* Ask students what they know about pregnancy and how to prevent it. Note their suggestions on the board, including any myths. (You will point out which ones are facts and which are myths as you continue the lesson.)

ACTIVITIES

* With the class, read the introductory paragraphs on page 34 of *Your Choice Book One*. Then, together, read the myths in 'How much do you know about how people become pregnant?' and the final paragraph on page 34. Point out any myths that were noted on the board in the starter and cross these out.

* Explain that pregnancy is not the only risk in having sex. As a class, read 'What is safer sex?' on page 35 and talk about why people use the term 'safer sex' rather than 'safe sex'. Ask the class to look at the poster on page 34. Ask: 'Why do you think there's a sad emoji over the person's face?' *Answers might include: to show that having an STI can be an isolating, embarrassing or unpleasant experience; you can't tell whether someone has an STI by looking at them.* Do they think the poster is effective in encouraging people to use a condom to protect themselves from catching an STI?

* Ask pairs or groups to discuss Gina's problem on page 35. What should she do? What do they think of her boyfriend's attitude? Ask them to discuss the questions in the discussion task.

* Encourage students to read 'How much do you know about STIs?' and 'Getting treated' and then invite them to ask questions. You may choose to discuss these immediately or prepare an answer to their questions for the next lesson.

* Ask students to do one of the tasks in the writing activity, either making up their own true or false quiz or designing a poster.

PLENARY

* Encourage students, working individually, to write down the three most important things they have learned from the lesson. Invite students to share their views in a class discussion, giving reasons for their choices.

EXTENSION

* Hand out copies of **Worksheet 6.1** for students to complete individually, before comparing and checking their answers in pairs: *Answers: 1. False: it may be harder to know when you are ovulating and you can still get pregnant if you have sex during your period if you have a shorter cycle. 2. True. 3. False: condoms will stretch to fit every size of penis. 4. False: creams that claim to do this rarely do so. 5. True. 6. False: there is no connection between the two sizes. 7. False: you can also catch STI from oral and anal sex. 8. False. 9. False: shaving is less hygienic as the hair protects the sensitive skin around the genitals, acting as a barrier to bacteria and viruses. 10. False.*

Further information and support for teachers:

UK Family Planning Association – factsheet on sexual behaviour of young adults:
www.fpa.org.uk/factsheets/teenagers-sexual-health-behaviour

Further information and support for students:

'Sexual health for teens': www.healthforteens.co.uk/sexual-health/

NHS, '15 things young people should know about sex':
www.nhs.uk/live-well/sexual-health/15-things-young-people-should-know-about-sex/

- Study these statements and decide which are true and which are false, writing T or F next to each one. If you think a statement is false, write a comment in the final column explaining why.
- Then compare your answers with a partner.
- If you are unsure about the answer, use the internet to check.

Statement	True or false?	Comment
1. You cannot get pregnant if your period is irregular.		
2. Sperm can live for up to seven days inside the body.		
3. Condoms don't fit everyone.		
4. During puberty a girl can increase her breast size by using special creams.		
5. A man who has had a vasectomy cannot make a woman pregnant.		
6. People with big feet have larger penises.		
7. You can only catch an STI when having vaginal sex.		
8. You can always tell if you have caught an STI.		
9. Shaving your pubic hair is more hygienic than leaving it as it is.		
10. You can stop yourself getting pregnant if you douche yourself with coke immediately after having sex.		

6.2 Sex and the law

Strand:
- Relationships and sex education

Resources:
- Book One: pp. 36–37
- Worksheet 6.2

Learning objective:
- To understand the laws in the UK about sex

Key words:
consent, indecent assault, exploitation, obscene, predator, upskirting

STARTER
- Ask: 'What do you know about the laws about sexual activities in the UK?' Answers should include the fact that all sexual activities (such as vaginal, oral or anal sex and mutual masturbation) with anyone under 16 are against the law. Ask why students think they are illegal. Bring out the point that the law is there to prevent young people from being abused or exploited. Then, together, read the 'Fact check' on page 36 of *Your Choice Book One*. You could refer to the FPA factsheet (see the link below) to help clear up any confusion about the distinction made between under 16 and under 13.

ACTIVITIES
- Invite students to read 'The age of consent' and 'What does consent mean?'. Ask them to discuss as a class what is meant by 'consent' (giving your permission for something). Ensure that they understand that consent must be given freely and that a person can change their mind and withdraw consent.

- Discuss how different countries have different ages of consent. Hand out **Worksheet 6.2** for students to discuss and complete in groups. Ask students to share their views about the reasons why 16 may have been chosen as the age of consent. Elicit ideas such as: *most young people have gone through puberty by that point; you can marry at 16; the law protects young people who might not be able to read a situation with an adult or older teen as exploitative or who might not feel able to say 'no' to them.*

- With the students, read the sections on 'Rape and sexual assault', 'Indecent exposure' and 'Indecent images'. Explain the difference between rape, sexual assault and assault by penetration, using the definitions in the FPA factsheet (see the link below).

- As a class, discuss Craig's and Molly's questions to Erica and her replies to them.

- Ask students to read the newspaper article on upskirting. As a class, discuss what students think of people who take such pictures. Then ask pairs of students to work together on the role-play activity. This activity will need to be managed carefully to make sure that students take it seriously. Invite pairs to share their role play with the rest of the class and mediate feedback from the rest of the class.

PLENARY
- Give students time to work in groups on the discussion activity about sentencing. Then bring the class back together to compare and discuss the groups' decisions. *Suggested sentences could be as follows: **a)** Community service and a criminal record. **b)** Formal caution. **c)** Formal caution. **d)** Prosecution for statutory rape (trial and sentencing would usually happen in a Crown Court).*

EXTENSION
- Ask students to watch the video '6 simple ways to understand content' (see the link below) and to discuss in groups whether they think it's a good way to help people understand consent. Then ask them to write a bullet list of key points they have learned from the video.

Further information and support for teachers:

FPA factsheet, 'The law on sex': www.fpa.org.uk/factsheets/law-on-sex

BBC News, 'Upskirting – how one victim is fighting back': www.bbc.co.uk/news/magazine-40861875

Further information and support for students:

Brook, 'How to get and give consent': www.brook.org.uk/your-life/consent

PSHE Association resources on consent: www.pshe-association.org.uk/curriculum-and-resources/resources/disrespect-nobody-teaching-resources-preventing

Video: '6 simple ways to understand consent' (2 minutes): www.healthforteens.co.uk/sexual-health/consent-and-the-law/video-6-simple-ways-to-understand-consent/

Worksheet 6.2 The age of consent

The age of consent varies from country to country. It is 14 in some countries, including Germany, 15 in France, 16 in the UK, and 17 in Ireland and some states in the USA.

Why do you think the age of consent in the UK is set at 16?

In groups, list below the arguments for and against 16 as the age of consent.

1. ....

....

2. ....

....

3. ....

....

4. ....

....

5. ....

....

6.3	Safer sex: contraception

Strand:	Resources:
• Relationships and sex education	• Book One: pp. 38–39 • Worksheet 6.3 • a condom

Learning objective:	Key words:
• To learn about different methods of contraception	contraceptive, condom, rhythm method

STARTER

• Introduce the lesson by recapping the facts about how intercourse can lead to a sperm fertilising an egg and the woman becoming pregnant. Talk about how there weren't reliable methods of preventing pregnancies in the past. Women became pregnant much more frequently and as a result had much larger families than is common today.

ACTIVITIES

• Explain that the focus of the lesson is on different methods of contraception available today. With the students, read the three introductory paragraphs on page 38 of *Your Choice Book One*.

• With the class, read the information about in 'Condom facts' and 'Where can you get condoms?' and show students a condom. Invite questions and discussion before supporting students to do the research activity on condoms on page 39. *Answers:* **1.** *False.* **2.** *False: condoms are 98% effective if used properly.* **3.** *True: check the expiry date.* **4.** *False: condoms should only be used once.* **5.** *False: don't use oil-based lubricants such as Vaseline, which can damage a condom; use lubricants without oil, such as KY Jelly.* **6.** *True.* **7.** *True: condoms sometimes split, but only if they catch on something sharp like a fingernail or piece of jewellery, or if air is caught in the tip.* **8.** *True: wrap them in tissue and put them in the waste bin.* **9.** *False: they are tough and don't break easily.* **10.** *You don't need to use a condom to protect you from pregnancy if your partner is on the pill. However, a condom gives extra protection against pregnancy as well as protecting you against STIs.*

• With the class, read 'The contraceptive pill' and 'Is the pill fool-proof?'. Stress how the pill is only effective if taken regularly.

• Then read the information about 'The morning after pill'. Invite any questions from students.

• Ask students to read Alicia's and Vikram's letters to Erica and then to compose Erica's replies. When they have done this, encourage them to share what they have written in a class discussion.

PLENARY

• Hand out **Worksheet 6.3** and ask students, in pairs, to note down the five key facts they have learned during the lesson and then to share these in a class discussion. Are there aspects of contraception they would like to find out more about? They can make a note of these on the worksheet.

EXTENSION

• Support students to research other methods of contraception, such as injections, implants and patches. Invite students to work in pairs or groups of three, and then to report their findings to the rest of the class orally.

Further information and support:

Brook, 'Sexual health and wellbeing for under 25s': https://www.brook.org.uk and (for teachers) https://learn.brook.org.uk

NHS, 'Getting contraception': www.nhs.uk/live-well/sexual-health/getting-contraception/

Childline, 'Contraception and safe sex': www.childline.org.uk/info-advice/friends-relationships-sex/sex-relationships/contraception-safe-sex/

Worksheet 6.3 Contraception

What five key facts have you learned during this lesson?

1. ....

   ....

2. ....

   ....

3. ....

   ....

4. ....

   ....

5. ....

   ....

What would you like to find out more about?

....

....

....

....

Strand:	Resources:
• Relationships and sex education	• Book One: pp. 40–41 • Worksheets 1.1a, 7.1

Learning objective:	Key words:
• To explore sexual attraction and orientation and to reassure students who may be unsure and confused by their feelings	sexuality, sexual orientation, heterosexual, homosexual, gay, lesbian, bisexual, transgender

• This is an extremely sensitive topic as there are likely to be some students who are confused and uncertain about their sexual feelings. Remind students of the ground rules for discussions set out in **Worksheet 1.1a**.

STARTER

• Introduce the topic by writing the words 'sexuality' and 'sexual orientation' on the board. Ask: 'What do they mean?' Guide the discussion so that students understand that sexuality means the romantic and sexual feelings people have towards others. Make it clear that there are different types of sexuality and that for some people, it can be confusing as they try to work out what their sexuality is. Explain that a person's sexual orientation, which is part of their sexuality, describes who they are attracted to – members of a different sex, members of the same sex, both or neither.

ACTIVITIES

• With the class, read and discuss 'What's right for you is right for you'. Ask: 'Is it easier for people who only have strong feelings towards the opposite sex than for those with strong feelings towards people of the same sex, or towards both sexes?' Then ask students to do the discussion activity in groups.

• Focus on 'Exploring your feelings'. Ask: 'Is it a good idea to discuss with adults about how you feel? How easy is it to discuss your feelings with your parents? If you feel you can't discuss them with your parents, who else could you discuss them with?' Then ask students to do the discussion activity in groups.

• Encourage students to study the 'Fact check' explaining some of the terms used to describe a person's sexuality and then to read the text at the top of page 41.

• With the class, read the three letters to Erica and then ask students to complete the writing activity individually. Then, in groups, they can do the discussion activity about Erica's responses.

• Encourage students to share their own replies in a group discussion. Ask the groups to draft a reply that includes the best points made in their group; then to choose someone to read it to the rest of the class.

PLENARY

• Give out copies of **Worksheet 7.1**. Read and discuss the article, and then ask students to do the research task on page 41 using the weblinks to Stonewall and The Proud Trust below. Encourage them to write down the three most important things they have learned from this lesson.

RESEARCH

• Research what is meant by each of the letters in longer versions of the acronym LGBT, e.g. LGTBIQ+. Produce a list explaining each of the letters or characters and why it is important to include them all.

Further information and support for teachers:

PSHE Association resources:
www.pshe-association.org.uk/content/government-equalities-office-anti-homophobic

Reachout, Sexuality and teenagers, including 'Parents: understanding sexuality' video (4 mins):
https://parents.au.reachout.com/skills-to-build/wellbeing/sexuality-and-teenagers

Further information and support for students:

Stonewall Youth, 'Coming out as LGBT': www.youngstonewall.org.uk/get-support/coming-out-lgbt

Childline, 'Sexuality': www.childline.org.uk/info-advice/your-feelings/sexual-identity/sexual-orientation/

Worksheet 7.1 Sexual attraction and orientation

Adolescence is a time of change

During the teen years, the hormonal and physical changes of puberty usually mean people start noticing an increase in sexual feelings. It's common to wonder and sometimes worry about new sexual feelings.

It takes time for people to understand who they are and who they are becoming. Part of that involves better understanding of their own sexual feelings and who they are attracted to. […]

What is sexual orientation?

Sexual orientation is the emotional, romantic or sexual attraction that a person feels towards another person. There are several types of sexual orientation […].

During the teen years, people often find themselves having sexual thoughts and attractions. For some, these feelings and thoughts can be intense and seem confusing. This can be especially true for people who have romantic or sexual thoughts about someone who is the same sex as they are. […]

Being interested in someone of the same sex does not necessarily mean that a person is gay – just as being interested in someone of a different sex doesn't mean that a person is straight. It's common for teens to be attracted to or have sexual thoughts about people of the same sex *and* people of the opposite sex. It's one way of sorting through emerging sexual feelings.

Some people might go beyond just thinking about it and experiment with sexual experiences with people of their own sex or the opposite sex. These experiences, by themselves, do not necessarily mean that a person is gay or straight.

Do people choose their sexual orientation?

Why are some people straight and some gay? There is no simple answer. […] Most medical experts believe that in general sexual orientation is not something that a person voluntarily chooses. Instead, sexual orientation is just a natural part of who a person is.

Source: https://kidshealth.org/en/teens/
sexual-orientation.html

What are the three most important things you have learned from this lesson?

1. ....

2. ....

3. ....

Sex: your rights and responsibilities

Strand:	Resources:
• Relationships and sex education	• Book One: pp. 42–43 • Worksheet 7.2

Learning objective:	Key words:
• To explore rights and responsibilities with regard to sex	harassment, confidentiality

STARTER

• Explain that the purpose of the lesson is to make students aware of their rights and responsibilities with regard to sexual activities. Read the first paragraph on page 42 of *Your Choice Book One* with students and tell them that the five rights you will be focusing on are consent, protection, privacy, communication and the right to choose.

ACTIVITIES

• Focus on each of the five rights in turn. First, read with students what the right is and then, before reading what responsibilities they have as a result, ask pairs to write down what they think the responsibilities are. Then tell them to read the information about the responsibilities in the book and compare it with what they have written.

• When focusing on consent, stress that consent can be given but then withdrawn at any time during sex. Emphasise the importance of picking up clues from a person's body language to suggest that they are uncomfortable about continuing. Ask the students to do the discussion activity in groups and then come together as a class to share and compare their thoughts.

• When dealing with the right to choose, stress that people in same-sex relationships have the same rights and responsibilities as everyone else.

• Invite students to discuss the rights and responsibilities of the people in the six situations described on page 43. The following points should be made: *1. Liam must stop kissing Scarlett. If he continues, he could be guilty of harassment. 2. Theo must stop touching Becca. If he continues, he could be guilty of harassment. 3. Jasmine is guilty of breaking a confidence. Ask students how they would feel if they were Rachel. 4. Jenny needs to take the photos down. She is breaking the law as Jed hasn't given his permission. 5. Jacob needs to go and be tested and tell the girls that they should get tested too. 6. Sinead's friends should stop teasing her. They should accept her sexuality and not bully her.*

• Hand out copies of **Worksheet 7.2** and ask students to discuss the scenarios in pairs. You could ask all of them to discuss all the scenarios, or you could ask different pairs to discuss different scenarios and then invite them to share their conclusions with the rest of the class.

PLENARY

• Ask students to do the writing activity on page 43, writing their statement on **Worksheet 7.2**, and then invite some of them to share what they have written.

EXTENSION

• Ask students to work in groups to write a questionnaire on 'Sex: rights and responsibilities'. It should include 8–10 questions aimed at other Year 7 students. They could then use the questionnaire to survey other students in the year to find out what they know. Invite them to share their results in a class discussion. Questions might include: 'Is it against the law for under-18s to take and share nude photos of someone?' *(yes)*; 'What is the legal age of consent in the UK?' *(16)*; 'If a person tells you to stop kissing or touching them, must you stop?' *(yes)*

Further information and support for teachers:

Brook, 'Sex, relationships and your rights': www.brook.org.uk/your-life/sex-relationships-and-your-rights

The law on sex, factsheets: http://www.fpa.org.uk/factsheets/law-on-sex

Human relations media, 'Before you hook up', video (4 mins):
www.hrmvideo.com/catalog/before-you-hook-up

Lesson plans for Key Stage 3 on inappropriate sexualised behaviour, from the NPSCC, *Making Sense of Relationships*, 'Inappropriate sexualised behaviour':
https://learning.nspcc.org.uk/media/1405/ks3-lesson-plan-4-sexualised-behaviour.pdf

Worksheet 7.2 Sex: rights and responsibilities

1. Read each scenario below and then discuss it.

Scenario 1

Beth and Hannah are babysitting Beth's little brother while her mum is out. They are sitting on the sofa watching TV when Beth puts an arm round Hannah. Hannah feels comfortable with Beth's arm round her. She snuggles up to Beth, who bends down and starts kissing her. Hannah responds but when Beth puts her hand under Hannah's sweater, she stiffens. Beth persists and starts to undo Hannah's bra. Hannah tries to pull away. She is confused and uncertain what to do.

- Discuss what rights and responsibilities Beth and Hannah have in this situation.

Scenario 2

Jake and Ayla have been seeing each other for several weeks. Ayla wants to make their relationship official. However, Jake doesn't want his brother Callum to know, because he's afraid he will tease him. Ayla keeps pressurising him because she wants to tell all her friends. Jake gets angry and threatens to break up with Ayla if she keeps on about the issue.

- Discuss what rights and responsibilities Jake and Ayla have in this situation.

Scenario 3

Fiona and Tom are both 15 and recently had sex. Fiona tells Tom that he is now her boyfriend. Tom says it was only a one-night thing and that he doesn't want a relationship. Fiona says that he has to be her boyfriend now, otherwise she will tell the police that they have had sex.

- Discuss what rights and responsibilities Fiona and Tom have in this situation.

Scenario 4

Kim is gay, and has kissed another guy, Louis. Louis says that he is going to tell other people that Kim is gay. Kim wants to keep this private, as he hasn't come out to anyone yet, including his parents.

- Discuss what rights and responsibilities Kim and Louis have in this situation.

Scenario 5

Jodie and Brian were going out, until Jodie abruptly ended the relationship. When Brian asks to talk about what has happened, Jodie refuses.

- Discuss what rights and responsibilities Jodie and Brian have in this situation.

2. Complete the following statement:

The most important points I have learned in this lesson are:

....

....

....

....

....

7.3 Attitudes to sex

Strand:	**Resources:**
• Relationships and sex education	• Book One: pp. 44–45

Learning objective:	**Key words:**
• To understand that attitudes to sex vary according to age, religion and culture	premarital, taboo, generation, exploit, promiscuous

STARTER

• Explain that different people have different attitudes to sex and that it is up to individuals to decide what their attitude is, for example, whether sex before marriage is acceptable. Get students to write on a slip of paper, without showing anyone else, either 'Yes' to indicate that they think it acceptable and 'No' if they don't. Collect the slips, count them and discuss the result.

ACTIVITIES

• Talk about how people of different generations and different religions may have particular views: for example, a family with strong religious beliefs may encourage their children not to have sex before marriage.

• With the class, read 'How you feel about sex' on page 44 of *Your Choice Book One*. Talk about how people have different feelings and attitudes and that there is not one right way to feel or behave. Discuss what casual sex is and why it can involve risks.

• Ask students to study Sam's letter to Erica and then do the writing activity.

• Focus students' attention on the statements in the discussion activity and invite them, in groups, to say whether or not they agree with them and why.

• With the students, look at the information in the 'Fact check' on page 44. Ask them to discuss, in pairs or groups, whether they are surprised by any of the survey results. Come back together as a class to share responses.

• Ask students to read Carrie's and Carl's letters to Erica and then do the writing activity in pairs. Invite some pairs to share their replies with the class.

• With the class, read the 'Fact check' on page 45 and then the article by Nicola Wordsmith. Talk about how attitudes can differ from generation to generation.

PLENARY

• Ask students to consider the question in the discussion activity and invite responses. Guide them in a class discussion.

EXTENSION

• Using the BBC link below, ask students to discuss what they think of the recent trends in teenage sexual activity.

Further information and support for teachers:

BBC, 'Are teenagers having less sex?' – useful for a discussion on recent trends for teenagers and sexual activity: www.bbc.co.uk/news/uk-44902411

8.1 What is bullying?

Strand:
- Relationships and sex education

Resources:
- Book One: pp. 46–47
- Worksheets 1.1a, 8.1
- Your school's bullying and child protection policies

Learning objective:
- To identify different types of bullying and to explore what it feels like to be bullied

Key words:
bullying, provoke, scornful

STARTER

- Remind students of the rules for class discussion on **Worksheet 1.1a**.

- Then ask: 'What is bullying?' Encourage students to work in pairs to list all the types of behaviour they think constitute bullying and to distinguish between banter (having a joke) and teasing (making fun of somebody at their expense). Explain how teasing, if it persists, can develop into bullying. Ask pairs to share their ideas and note them on the board.

ACTIVITIES

- With the class, read the introductory text on page 46 of *Your Choice Book One* about different types of bullying and then do task **1** of the discussion activity.

- Ask: 'Are some people more likely to get bullied than others?' Clarify that it is never acceptable to bully somebody. Develop the idea of how an imbalance of power can sometimes lead to bullying (e.g. an established friendship group over a child who has just joined the school). Then ask students to read 'Who gets bullied?'.

- In a class discussion, encourage students to say how they think it feels to be bullied. Then ask them to work in groups on task **2** of the discussion task. Invite groups to share what they have learned from Kyle and Martin about bullying.

- Hand out **Worksheet 8.1** and read 'I feel bad about Sharon'. Discuss with the class how people often witness bullying but don't intervene. Why do students think this happens?

- Ask students, in groups, to read 'How does it feel to be bullied?' on page 47 and do the discussion task that follows it. Then encourage them to read the poem 'And how was school today?' on page 47 and consider the statements in the discussion activity above it.

- Invite students to read and discuss the rest of the poems on the worksheet. Focus on each poem in turn. Start with 'Why won't they talk to me?' and discuss how the person in the poem feels. Then discuss what happens in 'If he hits you'. Ask: 'Is it best not to fight back? Is there anything to be gained by standing your ground?' Next, focus on 'If you tell'. Do students think the person in the poem should put up with the bullying? Is reporting bullying 'telling tales'? Has someone who is being bullied got the right to tell an adult?

- Draw students' attention to your school's bullying and child protection policies, making sure they know who they can talk to and how bullying will be dealt with.

- Then focus on 'Walk tall' and 'I was bullied once'. Discuss how difficult it can be to walk tall when bullies are threatening you. Ask if they think it is likely that people who were bullied become bullies (it is).

PLENARY

- Encourage students to write poems of their own about bullying and invite those who feel comfortable with it to share their poems with the class.

EXTENSION

- Ask students to work in groups of four to make an anti-bullying poster, to be displayed in the classroom or across the school. It should include what bullying is, why it is harmful and who the safeguarding contacts are at the school.

Further information and support for teachers:

Bullying UK, Anti-bullying week resources:
www.bullying.co.uk/anti-bullying-week/anti-bullying-week-resources/

TES PHSE resources, bullying: www.tes.com/articles/teachers-tv-secondary-pshe-resources-bullying

Preventing and tackling bullying, DfE guidance:
https://assets.publishing.service.gov.uk/government/uploads/system/uploads/attachment_data/file/62389
5/Preventing_and_tackling_bullying_advice.pdf

Further information and support for students:

Bullying statistics in 2017: www.ukwristbands.com/bullying-statistics

BBC, 'Being bullied – Jake's story', video (5 mins):
www.bbc.com/teach/class-clips-video/pshe-ks2-being-bullied/zdds382

1. Read these poems about bullies and bullying by John Foster. What do you learn from them about:

    a) bullies and why they bully

    b) what it feels like to be bullied

    c) how someone may feel if they see someone being bullied and do nothing

    d) what can happen if you get involved in a fight?

2. Discuss which poem you think is the most powerful.

3. Write your own poem about bullying.

I feel bad about Sharon

I feel bad about Sharon.
I feel bad about what I did.
But when I saw them coming,
I ran away and hid.
I watched as they laughed and spat.
I watched as they made her cry.
I didn't stand up for her.
I didn't even try.
I feel bad about Sharon.
I feel bad about what I did.
But when I saw them coming,
I just ran away and hid.

If he hits you

'If he hits you, hit him back.'
That's what my father said.
So I hit him and now I am
In trouble with the Head.
He hit me first. He started it.
I didn't want a fight.
Now I'm in trouble with the Head
and I don't think that's right.

Why won't they talk to me?

Why won't they talk to me?
Each day it's just the same.
No one will talk to me.
To them it's like a game.
When I walk into the room,
They turn their heads away.
No one will sit by me.
No one asks me to play.
What have I done to them?
Why do they pick on me?
What am I doing wrong?
Please someone, talk to me.

Walk tall

'Walk tall,' Dad said. 'Hold up your head.
Don't ever let them see
you're scared.'
But there are four of them
and only one of me.
As I walk past, they turn and stare,
but I don't let them see
I'm scared.
'Cause there are four of them
and only one of me.

If you tell

'If you tell we'll get you.'
That's what they always say.
So I give them what they want.
It's easier that way.
They take my things.
They break my things.
They know I'll never tell.
For telling tales is never done.
But not telling tales is hell.

I was bullied once

I was bullied once.
Now I'm a bully too.
They took it out on me.
So I'll take it out on you.

8.2 Dealing with bullies

Strand:	**Resources:**
• Relationships and sex education	• Book One: pp. 48–49
	• Worksheet 8.2

Learning objective:	**Key words:**
• To explore why some people become bullies and how to deal with bullying	insecure, inadequacy, intimidation

STARTER

• Introduce the theme of the lesson by asking students individually to write one or two sentences saying what they think is the best way of dealing with bullies. Invite some of them to share their ideas.

ACTIVITIES

• Ask students to read the statements in 'Your choice' on page 48 and discuss what they think is the best advice.

• With the class, read 'Why do some people become bullies?'. Encourage class discussion of the reasons given. Ask: 'Which do you think are the main reasons? Can you suggest any others?'

• Ask students to do the writing activity on page 49 independently. Then encourage pairs to do the role-play activity. Pair up students who are used to working with one another so they feel more comfortable doing this task. Ask them to do it twice, taking it in turns to be the bully. Monitor the role plays, giving feedback by stopping the students and asking them how they feel at the most appropriate points in the activity. Then, in a debriefing discussion, ask what they felt when they acted as the bully.

• Invite someone to read the poem 'If you want to join the gang' and then, as a class, do the discussion activity above it. Talk about people who see an act of bullying. Ask: 'Is the person in the poem as guilty of bullying as those who bullied Tony Chang?'

• With the class, read 'How to beat the bullies'. Ask students, on their own, to choose the two pieces of advice they think are most helpful, and then to share their ideas in a class discussion.

• Encourage students to do the role-play activity of the TV discussion on page 49. Choose the participants carefully, so that anyone who might be being bullied does not have to play the part of the person being bullied and that a potential bully is not cast in the role of a bully. If the opportunity occurs, halt the discussion at an appropriate moment and ask the participants to say how they are thinking and feeling at that point.

PLENARY

• Ask students, on their own, to read 'Ask Erica' and do the writing task. Then invite some of them to share what they have written.

RESEARCH

• Ask students, in pairs or on their own for stronger students, to research whether their local council, football team or place of worship has an anti-bullying policy. Then ask them to compare these in groups alongside the school's anti-bullying policy (lesson 8.1) and to decide which they think is best, and why.

EXTENSION

• Give out copies of **Worksheet 8.2** and invite students, in groups, to suggest what the policy should say. Then agree on a policy as a class. Make a copy for everyone and put one on display in the classroom.

Further information and support for teachers:

Kidscape, anti-bullying resources: www.kidscape.org.uk/resources-and-publications/

The literacy shed, anti-bullying week resources: www.literacyshed.com/anti-bullying-shed.html

CBBC, 'What counts as bullying?':
http://news.bbc.co.uk/cbbcnews/hi/newsid_4440000/newsid_4440000/4440024.stm

Worksheet 8.2 A class bullying policy

List all the types of behaviour that you consider to be bullying and unacceptable.
Then state the procedure to be followed by anyone who is subjected to an act of bullying.

We the members of Class .... regard the following behaviours to be unacceptable and acts of bullying:

....

....

....

....

....

....

....

....

Anyone who is being subjected to an act of bullying should follow this procedure:

....

....

....

....

....

....

....

....

Strand:	**Resources:**
• Relationships and sex education	• Book One: pp. 50–51
	• Worksheet 9.1

Learning objective:	**Key words:**
• To evaluate the advantages and disadvantages of the internet	internet, pornography
• To highlight the problems of pornography and the dangers that surround teenage modelling	

STARTER

• Ask the students what they think are the best and worst things about using the internet. Note their answers on the board. Highlight the very best and very worst in each case.

ACTIVITIES

• Divide the class into groups of three or four to read 'Is the internet good or bad?' on page 50 of *Your Choice Book One* and then to do the discussion task that follows.

• Invite groups to share their responses to the discussion activity with the rest of the class. Compare these with the views listed on the board during the starter activity and see if there is anything they would like to add or take away in light of their discussions.

• Organise students into pairs to read 'Pornography' on page 51 and then do the discussion task that follows it. Closely monitor the pairs while they are doing this, closing down any inappropriate conversations and directing them back to the task. Then bring the class back together and ask pairs to share their responses and explain their views.

• Now organise students into groups to read 'Darcia's story', and then do the discussion task that follows. *Responses to question 2 might include: finding out more about the opportunity in advance, including whether she needed to pay for the portfolio, whether it was for a professional and reputable modelling agency, asking to see examples of their work in the past and taking an adult along to the shoot.*

• Ask students to work in pairs to do the 'Your choice' activity. Then ask them to compare their responses with those of another pair.

PLENARY

• Bring the class back together and discuss which pairs had the same opinions as each other about the 'Your choice' activity and which differed. Is it possible to come to a consensus, or do the students think that some of them will have to agree to disagree?

EXTENSION

• Ask students to complete the matching task on **Worksheet 9.1**.
  Answers: 1 – B; 2 – E; 3 – A; 4 – C; 5 – G; 6 – D; 7 – F.

Further information and support for teachers:

UK Safer Internet Centre, resources for 11–19s:
www.saferinternet.org.uk/advice-centre/young-people/resources-11-19s

Gov.uk, 'Education for a Connected World':
https://assets.publishing.service.gov.uk/government/uploads/system/uploads/attachment_data/file/683895/Education_for_a_connected_world_PDF.PDF

Children's Commissioner 2018 report on social media use among 8–12 year olds:
www.childrenscommissioner.gov.uk/wp-content/uploads/2018/01/Childrens-Commissioner-for-England-Life-in-Likes.pdf

Further information and support for students:

Think u know for 11–13 year olds: www.thinkuknow.co.uk/11_13/

Safety net kids, 'Online Safety': www.safetynetkids.org.uk/personal-safety/online-safety/

Improve your understanding of ways you can stay safe online by completing this matching task.
Draw a line to match each term to its correct definition.

| 1. Block | | A. Email that you do not wish to receive and that has no value. |

| 2. Catfished | | B. What you can do on Facebook and other apps, so you have no contact with somebody online. |

| 3. Spam | | C. The part of the internet that is used for trading illegal goods, but which most people can't access. |

| 4. Dark Web | | D. Allows you to only see only some information online, whilst harmful information is automatically excluded. |

| 5. Parental controls | | E. When you are tricked by somebody pretending to be someone else who is more attractive so that they can become romantically involved with you. |

| 6. Filter | | F. The company responsible for providing the means for you to view the world-wide web via a computer, tablet, phone or other device. |

| 7. Internet service provider | | G. Allows adults to prevent their children from viewing harmful content. |

Strand:	Resources:
• Relationships and sex education	• Book One: pp. 52–53 • Worksheet 9.2

Learning objective:	Key words:
• To investigate cyberbullying and how to deal with it	trolls, cyberbullying

STARTER

• Ask: 'What is cyberbullying?' Encourage students to suggest what forms cyberbullying takes and list examples on the board. Then read with them the introductory text on page 52 of *Your Choice Book One*.

ACTIVITIES

• Read with the class the section about trolls and the information in the 'Fact check' box. Then ask them to read the 'Top tips to deal with trolls' in groups. Staying in their groups, ask them to do the discussion activity on page 53.

• Bring the class back together and discuss their responses to the discussion activity. These may include views on freedom of speech on the internet, but point out that people also have the freedom to live their lives free from cyber-bullying, discrimination and harassment.

• Ask students to focus on the advice given in 'Be streetwise'. Encourage students to discuss what they should do in the following situation: Someone comes up to them in the street and says they're working for a magazine called *Town and Out*. They would like to take a photo of them as they want a photo of a teenager to go alongside an article on young people in their town. You could refer back to Darcia's story in 9.1 for the types of response to expect, and also elicit suggestions about seeing the person's ID, signing consent forms and getting parental permission.

• Instruct students to read 'Ask Erica' and then do the writing task that follows. *Suggested answers could include: finding out who is spreading the rumours and asking them to stop (or reporting them to a parent/teacher if you know them from school); using the report buttons on social media to report either the post or the person posting the material (for some sites this may involve filling out an online form); blocking the person circulating these rumours on all social media platforms. They should also save the evidence by taking a screen shot.*

PLENARY

• Give out copies of **Worksheet 9.2**. Encourage students to read and discuss the article in groups. Ask them to decide which piece of advice they think is the most useful and to suggest other strategies that people can use to counter cyberbullying.

EXTENSION

• Ask students to work in pairs to compile two lists of key points, one for how to avoid cyberbullying and one for how to deal with it. Ask them to draw up a written code of conduct of what is and is not acceptable behaviour on the internet.

Further information and support for teachers:

Internetmatters.org, Cyberbullying facts and advice to support children: www.internetmatters.org/issues/cyberbullying

The Telegraph, 'Cyberbullying makes young people twice as likely to self harm or attempt suicide': www.telegraph.co.uk/science/2018/04/22/cyberbullying-makes-young-people-twice-likely-self-harm-attempt/

Further information and support for students:

BullyingUK, 'Cyberbullying': www.bullying.co.uk/cyberbullying/

If you have been bullied online, it may have affected your self-confidence. Here are some ways that you can set about rebuilding your confidence.

1. **Share how you feel** with someone you can trust to listen to you – an adult such as a teacher, parent, sibling, grandparent or friend.

2. **Remember it isn't your fault.** You may have begun to feel that you must have done something wrong and that you deserve to be bullied. But if hurtful messages about you are being posted online, you aren't to blame. It's the bully who is responsible.

3. **Don't respond.** The bullies want to get a reaction from you. It makes them feel powerful and gives them a chance to continue attacking you. Instead of responding, which will only make it worse, switch off your phone or tablet and do something active.

4. **Take a cyber break.** The easiest way to avoid being affected by what is being said on social media about you is to take a break from using social media and the internet for a while. What you don't see or hear being said about you cannot affect you. The more you can push the bullying to the back of your mind, the less it will affect you.

5. **Try something new.** If you find it difficult to stop checking what the bullies are saying about you, try doing something different to take your mind off the bullying. You could join a group playing a new game or be the first person to reply to a message. You could use the internet to research a topic that interests you.

6. **Take action against the bullies.** Don't allow the bullies to make you feel worthless. Use the anger you feel to take action against them. Collect evidence by taking a screenshot of what they are doing. Then block them and report them.

7. **Put it in writing.** Either keep a diary in which you write about your feelings or write yourself notes in which you remind yourself that it's not your fault that you are being bullied, that you are not going to respond to what they post and express how you intend to use your anger positively against them. You can put what you write in a box so that you can read the notes at times when the bullying leaves you feeling low.

In groups, discuss the advice that is given in the article. Which piece of advice do you think is the most useful?

....

Suggest other things that would help someone who is being bullied online to regain their confidence.

....

....

....

....

....

Strand:	Resources:
• Relationships and sex education	• Book One: pp. 54–55 • Worksheet 9.3

Learning objective:	Key words:
• To explain the need to protect yourself online and to give advice on how to do so	virus, malware, phishers

STARTER

• Introduce the topic by asking students to explain the measures they take to protect themselves when they go online. Write their answers on the board. Ask: 'What dangers do we face if we don't take such measures?' Again, note their suggestions on the board.

ACTIVITIES

• Read the extract from Sophie Elkan's book on page 54 of *Your Choice Book One*. Discuss with students what she says about giving out too much personal information and why it is wise not to do so. Ask: 'What does she say about posting pictures of yourself?' Then ask students to work in groups to do the discussion activity.

• Ask students to study 'Unwanted emails' on page 55 in pairs and discuss why they should not open or respond to them.

• Still in their pairs, ask students to read 'Ask Erica' and then do the writing task that follows. *Suggested responses could be that Alfie should contact the safeguarding officer at school and the police, that Leila should ignore the email as it's a scam, and that Heidi must tell someone about the photo straight away – such as her parents or the safeguarding officer at school.*

• Organise students into different pairs. Introduce **Worksheet 9.3** and go through the advice Abigail Green offers. Then ask students to complete the second writing task on page 55 (THINK BEFORE U CLICK) by writing their top tips on how to protect themselves when using the internet. You could direct them to the appropriate page of Thinkuknow website, listed below, to give them more ideas.

• Support students, working in groups, to do the research task to find out more about staying safe online. You could suggest that they look at the websites listed below.

PLENARY

• With the class, refer back to the list of measures students suggested at the start of the lesson to protect themselves when online. Ask them if they'd like to add any more now that they have had a chance to discuss it in class.

RESEARCH

• Encourage students to check the privacy settings on all of their social media and to look back at the sorts of things they have been sharing and posting. Ask them to decide if, now they know more about online safety, there are any steps they need to take to protect their identity and safety online.

Further information and support for students:

Staying safe online: www.safetynetkids.org.uk/personal-safety/staying-safe-online/

Thinkuknow, advice about online safety: www.thinkuknow.co.uk/11_13/

BBC Webwise, ten online safety tips: www.bbc.co.uk/webwise/0/21259413

Childnet International: www.childnet.com/

Abigail Green offers advice about how to avoid the dangers of the internet.

The internet is great for communicating swiftly and for finding information at the tap of a keyboard. But for all its pluses, there are lots of minuses ready to snare the unwary.

When you are surfing the net, you need to be aware of the dangers. There are predators waiting to catch and groom young people and to exploit them sexually. There are bullies ready to hurt you. There are fraudsters out to steal your personal information. There are pornographers offering a distorted view of sex, and hackers ready to attack your computer or break into your online accounts.

So what can you do to stay safe?

- When you chat, guard your personal information. Never let people know your location, your name, your address or where you go to school.
- Don't chat with strangers or accept e-mails from strangers or open attachments from strangers. Don't respond to unusual requests and never agree to meet an online friend alone.
- Don't let anyone know your password. Think up a complex password and change it every now and again. Don't use the same password for everything.
- Be selective who you share with, especially if you are sharing pictures or videos. Before you click, ask yourself: Would I be happy if my parents or any teacher saw this? Could someone who wanted to get at me use it against me? What if someone were to share the pictures with somebody untrustworthy or dishonest? What about the issue of sharing photos without the consent of the person who is in them?
- When you are surfing the net, use a filter. Don't click on a site that looks suspicious or does not have a safety security certificate (a warning will appear on your computer if this is missing). If you feel at all unsure about a site, trust your instinct and don't go on it.

Take my advice. Use the internet wisely. A few sensible precautions will help you to avoid the pitfalls. Don't click silly. Click savvy!

Now summarise what you think are the top tips for keeping yourself safe online.

My top tips on how to protect yourself online.

....

....

....

....

....

....

....

....

Strand:	Resources:
• Personal wellbeing and mental health	• Book One: pp. 56–57 • Worksheet 10.1

Learning objective:	Key words:
• To complete a balanced breathing exercise • To become aware of how their head, heart and gut are involved in different types of decision making • To develop strategies to improve decision making	balanced breathing, head brain, heart brain, gut brain

STARTER

• Ask students to think of a really good decision they made. How did they make it? Elicit the best strategies for making decisions and write them on the board. As a class, read the introductory paragraphs on page 56 of *Your Choice Book One*.

ACTIVITIES

• As a class, talk about the fact that as students enter puberty, they may feel emotions more intensely on the one hand, but on the other hand, will be expected to act more maturely and take more responsibility for their decisions.

• Take students through the balanced breathing exercise on **Worksheet 10.1**. Explain that this can be a helpful way of calming and controlling their state of mind, in preparation for making decisions.

• Invite students to read 'Focusing on your head' on page 56 and then to work in groups on the first discussion task. Examples of what helps them might include having plenty of energy, feeling relaxed, having time to think, writing things down to see them visually. Examples of what hinders them might include feeling tired, being rushed, being influenced by others.

• Next, ask them to read 'Focusing on your gut', and then, again in their groups, to do the second discussion activity. Get students to focus on the language they use to describe their feelings, such as 'I knew in my gut'; 'It was a gut feeling'; 'I had butterflies in my stomach'.

• If any groups finish quickly, ask them to discuss how making decisions with their gut differs from making decisions with their head.

• Instruct all students to move on to reading 'Focusing on your heart' and then, this time in pairs, to discuss the first two questions in the next discussion activity.

• Organise students into new pairs and ask them to discuss task **3** in the activity.

• Ask students to read 'Making good decisions' and then, in pairs, to do tasks **1–4** of the final discussion activity as a template for making a decision.

PLENARY

• In pairs or groups of three, ask students to draw a flowchart of how they make good decisions. Support them by asking them to think of the steps they used to make a good decision in the past (refer back to the starter on the board if necessary), e.g. *I was asked to go out on Thursday night. I really wanted to (in my heart). I always have fun with this friend, but they live a long way away so I'd get back late and be tired the next day. My head reasoned that I shouldn't do this on a school night. My gut feeling now is not to do this. I decided to say no, but suggested we meet up at the weekend.*

EXTENSION

• Ask students to write a report of two or three paragraphs on what they have learned about making good decisions, and how they will put this into practice in the future.

Further information and support for teachers:

TES, Psychology for teenagers on making the most of themselves:
www.tes.com/teaching-resource/psychology-for-teenagers-making-the-most-6061534

The Independent, 'Why are teenagers so moody?':
www.independent.co.uk/news/science/why-are-teenagers-so-moody-a6874856.html

The Guardian, 'Emotional intelligence: why it matters and how to teach it': www.theguardian.com/teacher-network/2017/nov/03/emotional-intelligence-why-it-matters-and-how-to-teach-it

Worksheet 10.1 Making a good decision: balanced breathing

- Find a nice, calm, quiet place to relax where you won't be disturbed.

- Sit on a chair, comfortably, with your back supported and without slouching. Keep your legs uncrossed and your feet flat on the floor.

- Take a moment to notice how you are feeling at the beginning of this exercise, so you can refer back to this later.

- Become aware of your breathing.

- You can keep your eyes open or, if you prefer, close your eyes.

- Begin to breathe in through your nose and out through your mouth equally on a count of 6 or 8 – that is, breathe in for 6 to 8 seconds and then out for 6 to 8 seconds. The important thing is that in-breaths and out-breaths are equal.

- Continue this balanced breathing for at least 2 minutes.

- If thoughts or distractions appear in your head, ignore them. Concentrate just on your breathing and on being mindful.

- Notice how you are feeling more relaxed as your balanced breathing continues.

When you wish to finish:

- Open your eyes (if you closed them earlier).

- Make sure that you are fully aware of your surroundings and are fully back into the room.

- Take a moment now to notice how you are feeling. In particular, notice whether the pace you are thinking and moving has changed to a better speed.

- Later in the day, notice what sort of difference this has made. The effects of balanced breathing should last at least four hours, and in some people can last over eight hours.

Strand:	Resources:
• Personal wellbeing and mental health	• Book One: pp. 58–59 • Worksheet 10.2

Learning objective:	Key words:
• To consider what the good and bad influences are for a student, and what they can change in the future	influence, social media influencer

STARTER

- Ask the class who influences them. Make a list of the most popular suggestions on the board.

ACTIVITIES

- Ask students to read the introduction and then, in pairs, to do the 'Your choice' ranking task on page 58 of *Your Choice Book One*. Invite pairs to compare their list with another pair and discuss any differences.

- Still in their pairs, ask students to read 'John's story' and then do the discussion activity on page 58. They might suggest that John should have ignored his friend's suggestion and realised that the suggested course of action would have serious consequences.

- Ask students, in pairs, to read 'Media influencers' and then, in groups, to do the first of the discussion activities on page 59.

- Hand out copies of **Worksheet 10.2** for students to complete. Encourage them to reflect on this independently outside of the class.

- As a class, read 'Opportunity cost'. Make sure that everyone understands what this means. Then organise students into pairs to do the second discussion task on page 59.

- Encourage students, individually, to keep a diary of what they do for a week, and to make a note of the opportunity costs involved. This can be done as a simple table – what decision they made, what the alternative decision/activity might have been, and whether or not they have made a good decision and why after reflecting back at the end of the week.

PLENARY

- In a class discussion, invite students say what they think are the positives and negatives of social media influencers, based on what they discussed in pairs earlier. Note the main ideas for and against social media influencers on the board. In the discussion, bring out the point that these people are usually paid for what they are doing and ask students to consider how that might affect both their messages and the way their messages are received. You could hold a class vote at the end of the discussion to decide on the main pros and cons.

RESEARCH

- Ask students, in pairs, or on their own for stronger students, to use the internet to research the latest laws and rulings on social media influencers advertising products on the internet. Ask students to find out what steps they now have to take after they have been paid to advertise a product, using the link below.

Further information and support for teachers

The Observer: 'What would you do if your teenager became an overnight Instagram sensation?': www.theguardian.com/technology/2018/jul/22/what-would-you-do-if-your-teenager-became-an-overnight-instagram-sensation-

Top 25 influencers in the UK: https://influencermarketinghub.com/top-25-influencers-in-the-uk-influencers-making-a-name-for-themselves-in-britain/

1. Who influences me in my family:

   a) ....

   b) ....

   c) ....

   d) ....

2. Who influences me at school:

   a) ....

   b) ....

   c) ....

   d) ....

3. What influences me in the media:

   a) ....

   b) ....

   c) ....

   d) ....

4. What is a good influence on my behaviour?

   ....

   ....

5. What is a bad influence on my behaviour?

   ....

   ....

6. What am I going to change in the future?

   ....

   ....

Strand:	**Resources:**
• Physical health and wellbeing	• Book One: pp. 60–61 • Worksheet 11.1

Learning objective:	**Key words:**
• To present facts about the effects of smoking and to explore why people start smoking	chronic, bronchitis, emphysema, passive smoking

STARTER

* Introduce the topic by asking students to write two sentences, one giving their opinion on smoking beginning 'I think smoking…' and the other beginning 'The most important fact I know about smoking is…'. Share some of their statements.

ACTIVITIES

* With the class, read and then discuss the information in the 'Fact check' on page 60 of *Your Choice Book One*. Ask: 'What is the most surprising thing you have learned about smoking? What are the financial implications of being a smoker? Is it fair to call smoking a "dirty habit"?'

* Together, read the other sections of text on page 60 and the article 'Why do people start smoking?'. Do the discussion activity as a class. Ask the class what they think of the warnings on the image of the cigarette packet: how effective do they think such images are? Does removing the branding work?

* Organise students into pairs to do the first role play on page 61. Monitor them and list the most effective arguments on the board (e.g. threat to health, cost, yellow teeth, bad breath). Then split the class into groups to do the second role play. Again, note the most persuasive reasons for smoking on the board (e.g. peer pressure, wanting to look cool, appear older, try something new). Invite pairs and groups to share their role plays with the rest of the class. Discuss whether it was easy to convince the first person to stop smoking and how easy or difficult it was for the second person to resist the pressure to smoke.

* Ask students to read 'Smoking myths' and 'Passive smoking', as well as the five statements in the discussion activity. Lead a class discussion and invite students to share their opinions.

* With the class, read 'Smoking during pregnancy' and then talk through the role play. Ask pairs to act out the discussion and invite one or two to share their role plays with the class.

* Give out copies of **Worksheet 11.1** and ask students to complete the table. In a class discussion, encourage students to express their views on the ten statements. Then ask them to do part **3** of the worksheet on their own.

* Support students in using the internet to research what support is available to those who wish to quit smoking (see the link to the NHS website below). Encourage them to find out what your local council, doctors and hospitals are doing locally to reduce and prevent smoking.

PLENARY

* Invite students, either individually or in pairs, to write 'Ten things you should know before you start smoking' to go on a poster in a youth club.

EXTENSION

* Ask students to write an email or letter to a parent or grandparent explaining why they think they ought to give up and explaining that even if they have been smoking for a long time, it can make a difference.

Further information and support for teachers:
NHS Digital, Statistics on smoking: https://digital.nhs.uk/data-and-information/publications/statistical/statistics-on-smoking/statistics-on-smoking-england-2018/content

Further information and support for students:
Asthma UK, 'Cigarette smoke':
www.asthma.org.uk/advice/triggers/smoking/?gclid=CjwKCAiAv9riBRANEiwA9Dqv1c708PDN6D5qDMahNSASZcnxESCPS-BEMX0_uVkbVl9Yib8f7sXxQhoCqn8QAvD_BwE
NHS, 'Quit smoking': www.nhs.uk/live-well/quit-smoking/

1. Study these statements and decide which you agree with and which you disagree with.

Statement	Agree/disagree
1. Smoking and vaping should be banned in all public places.	
2. Too much fuss is made about smoking.	
3. I've never been tempted to start smoking.	
4. Smokers should have to pay for hospital treatment for smoking-related illnesses.	
5. There should be heavy fines for people who sell cigarettes to children under 16.	
6. Vaping is as anti-social as smoking.	
7. People who smoke are unjustly victimised.	
8. Kissing someone who smokes is like kissing an ashtray.	
9. People should have the right to smoke wherever and whenever they want.	
10. People who drop cigarette stubs on the ground should be fined on the spot.	

2. Now share your views in a class discussion.

3. Use the space below to write two or three sentences giving your views on smoking.

....

....

....

....

....

....

....

....

....

....

Strand:	Resources:
• Physical health and wellbeing	• Book One: pp. 62–63 • Worksheet 11.2

Learning objective:	Key words:
• To explore facts and opinions about vaping, about trying to give up smoking and the laws about smoking and selling tobacco	carcinogenic, precursor, juul

STARTER

• Write the words 'vaping' and 'e-cigarette' on the board and ask: 'What do you know about e-cigarettes and vaping?' Draw a spider diagram of what students know. End this part of the lesson by asking them to put up their hands if they think vaping is safe. Count how many think it is and keep a note of the number.

ACTIVITIES

• With the class, read the information 'What are e-cigarettes?' and 'What are juuls?' on page 62 of *Your Choice Book One*. Talk about how e-cigarettes work and how they are different from cigarettes. Ask students to decide what they think are the two most important facts they have learned about juuls.

• Ask students, in groups, to do the discussion task on page 62. Then ask them, still in their groups, to do the first part of the first discussion task on page 63. In a class discussion, ask groups to share their opinions. Then organise students into pairs to do the second part of the discussion activity. Now ask for a show of hands about whether vaping is safe. Are the numbers the same as when you asked earlier? If anyone has changed their mind, invite them to explain why.

• Read 'Kicking the habit' (page 62) with students. Ask: 'Do any of the figures surprise you?' Then read the 'Fact check' with them and look again at the photograph of the packet of cigarettes on page 60.

• Ask students to read **Worksheet 11.2** in groups, and then do the discussion task on the worksheet. Ask groups to share their opinions and to give reasons for their answers. Stress that the overall benefits of giving up smoking far outweigh the negatives in the long run.

• Ask students to read 'ASH (Action on Smoking and Health)' on page 63 and then, in a class discussion, ask them if they think the suggestions for new laws are a good idea, and why.

• Ask students to do the final discussion activity in pairs. Then come together again to share their conclusions in a class discussion.

PLENARY

• Encourage students to look again at the spider diagram you drew at the beginning of the lesson and to suggest any further facts they have learned about vaping and its safety.

EXTENSION

• Support students in researching the latest evidence on whether vaping is safe (see the links below and look at the NHS website). Then ask students to work in groups to produce a photocopiable sheet on 'Is vaping safe?', to be distributed across your school.

Further information and support for teachers:

The Guardian, 'Teenagers who use e-cigarettes more likely to start smoking':
www.theguardian.com/society/2018/oct/02/e-cigarettes-vaping-study-teenagers-smoking-cigarettes

NHS Smokefree: www.nhs.uk/smokefree

Further information and support for students:

WalesOnline, 'The shocking effects of smoking compared with vaping revealed':
www.walesonline.co.uk/news/health/shocking-effects-smoking-compared-vaping-15603411

British Heart Foundation, 'Is vaping safe?':
www.bhf.org.uk/informationsupport/heart-matters-magazine/news/e-cigarettes

Quitting smoking

Giving up smoking can be hard, because your body has become used to the nicotine in cigarettes. The longer you go on smoking, the harder it is likely to be to quit. So, the sooner you try to give up, the more likely you are to succeed.

There are many good reasons to quit. The most obvious are the benefits to your health.

- The craving for nicotine will gradually reduce and within a month the nicotine receptors in your brain will return to normal.
- The circulation of blood round your body will improve and you will feel more energetic.
- You will be physically fitter because you will find breathing easier.
- Your immune system will work more efficiently and you will be more able to fight off illnesses such as colds.
- Your mouth will be cleaner and your breath won't smell of smoke.
- Similarly, your teeth won't get stained and your clothes won't smell of cigarette smoke.
- Your senses of smell and taste, which have been dulled by smoking, will return to normal.
- The likelihood of developing lung diseases, such as cancer and emphysema, will be dramatically reduced.
- So will the chances of your having a heart attack.
- Overall you are more likely to live longer than if you continue to smoke.

There are financial benefits too. All the money you have been spending on cigarettes, you can now spend on other things.

There are side effects of quitting. You are likely to suffer withdrawal symptoms, as your body craves the nicotine it is no longer getting from cigarettes. When you feel the craving, try to make a conscious effort to do something that will distract you from wanting a cigarette.

The withdrawal symptoms may make you irritable and bad-tempered. You may find that your concentration is poor and you are restless, and your sleep may be disturbed. However, all these effects will disappear with time.

The more determined you are to quit, the more likely you are to succeed, but it is a good idea to get support. The NHS runs a 'Smokefree' support service which you can contact online. A number of websites (including NHS Smokefree) have a timeline that shows how quickly you can expect to benefit from stopping smoking.

Discuss what you think the best benefits are of quitting smoking, and which are the worst problems. Be prepared to give reasons for your views. Write the three best reasons for stopping:

1. ....

2. ....

3. ....

Strand:	Resources:
• Physical health and wellbeing	• Book One: pp. 64–65 • Worksheet 12.1

Learning objective:	Key words:
• To understand the difference between medicinal, social and illegal drugs and to explore why some young people take drugs	stimulant, addictive, excess

STARTER

- Explain that drugs can be divided into three types: medicinal, social and illegal. Ask students, in pairs, to make a lists of drugs for each category. Share their lists in a class discussion. Mention that people sometimes talk about 'recreational drugs'. Ask: 'Which drugs are recreational drugs?' Encourage them to add to their lists any drugs that other people have included, but that were not on their own lists.

ACTIVITIES

- With the class, read about the different types of drugs on page 64 of *Your Choice Book One* and then ask the students, again working in pairs, to do part **1** of the discussion task. Bring the class back together to compare pairs' answers to the questions.

- Organise students into groups to do part **2** of the discussion task. Again, bring the class back together to discuss the groups' views on the statement. Are there differing opinions? Ask the students to support their opinions with reasoned arguments.

- Encourage students to read the magazine article by Luke Haines on page 65 and then, in pairs, to do the discussion task that follows it. Invite pairs to share their answers and lead a class discussion about the differences and similarities in responses.

- With the class, read Sally's story and then read the two discussion questions that follow. Invite students to give their views on what she should do.

- Organise students into groups of three to do the role-play activity in which Sally's parents talk to her brother.

- Organise students into groups to do the research task. Encourage them to focus on a particular type of drug, e.g. painkillers, antibiotics, drugs used for particular illnesses such as heart failure or Parkinson's disease. If appropriate, ask groups to collate their findings into a PowerPoint presentation to show to the rest of the class.

PLENARY

- Recap the reasons that people gave for starting to take illegal drugs. Ask: 'What are the risks involved?' Discuss the view that taking illegal drugs means gambling with your health. Points to raise include addiction, not knowing what is actually in the drug, drug driving (as dangerous as drink driving), sickness, coma (MDMA dehydration), unsafe or nonconsensual sex when on drugs, overdosing and death.

EXTENSION

- Invite students to do the quiz on **Worksheet 12.1**. *(Answers: 1. False – evidence suggests long-term use can damage people's health. 2. False – you can't tell what you are buying. 3. False – it is a depressant. 4. False – the damage remains. 5. False. 6. True. 7. False. 8. False. 9. True. 10. True.)*

Further information and support for teachers:

Brook, 'Drugs': www.brook.org.uk/your-life/drugs

Further information and support for students:

Childline, 'Drugs, alcohol and smoking': www.childline.org.uk/info-advice/you-your-body/drugs-alcohol-smoking/

NHS, 'The effects of drugs': www.nhs.uk/live-well/healthy-body/the-effects-of-drugs/

Decide whether each of these statements is true (T) or false (F).

Statement	True or false?
1. Smoking cannabis is not dangerous.	
2. You can buy drugs safely over the internet.	
3. Alcohol is a drug that speeds up your reactions.	
4. When the good feeling you get from taking drugs wears off, so does any damage to your body.	
5. You always know what you are buying when you purchase drugs like MDMA.	
6. You can become addicted to prescription medicines.	
7. It is easy to stop using drugs like heroin and cocaine.	
8. Taking steroids won't produce any side-effects. The only risk an athlete takes is being caught and labelled a cheat.	
9. Injecting drugs is more dangerous than swallowing them.	
10. You can never tell exactly how a drug is going to affect somebody.	

Strand:	Resources:
• Physical health and wellbeing	• Book One: pp. 66–67 • Worksheet 12.2

Learning objective:	Key words:
• To be aware of the effects illegal drugs have	tolerance, addictive, stimulant, hallucinogen, depressant, perception

STARTER

• Begin the lesson by asking students individually to write down all the effects that taking illegal drugs might have on someone's life. Invite students to share their notes and list all their suggestions on the board in the form of a spider diagram.

ACTIVITIES

• Reinforce the starter in the whole class by reading the introduction on page 66 of *Your Choice Book One* and then reading about and discussing the effects drugs have on health, relationships, work and crime.

• Invite students to study the table on page 66 and then, in groups, to do the discussion activity at the top of page 67. Invite groups to share their opinions with the class.

• Hand out copies of **Worksheet 12.2** and ask students to fill in the 'Effects' column in the table. Answers are in the table on page 66.

• As a whole class, read 'How drugs affect individuals differently' and discuss the factors that influence the effects – the drug, the individual and the environment in which the drug is taken. Next, ask pairs to do the discussion activity that follows. Then invite students to share their suggestions with the class.

• Ask students to study the statements in 'To use or not to use – it's your choice' and discuss the reasons the teenagers give. Organise students into groups to do the 'Your choice' activity. Then ask groups to share their views and see if there is any consensus.

• Taking the role of compere, encourage students to do the role play. Do several role plays, inviting different students to take part. Alternatively, you could appoint a 'Question Time' panel to give their views on drugs and drug taking: someone with a hard-line attitude, someone with a liberal attitude, a police officer, a former addict and a person who works in a drop-in facility for drug taking.

PLENARY

• Ask students to make a list of all the things that can go wrong if you take illegal drugs, and then to share their views in a class discussion.

EXTENSION

• Ask students to fill in the 'Dangers' column on **Worksheet 12.2**. They could use the NHS website link below.

• Ask students, in pairs, to do the 'Research' task about anabolic steroids. (Stronger students could do this task on their own.) Invite individuals to share their presentations with the class. They could use the NHS website listed below to find out information.

Further information and support for teachers:

NHS, 'The effects of drugs': www.nhs.uk/live-well/healthy-body/the-effects-of-drugs/

BBC News, 'Talk to Frank: Do anti-drugs adverts work?': www.bbc.co.uk/news/magazine-21242664

NHS, 'Anabolic steroid misuse': www.nhs.uk/conditions/anabolic-steroid-misuse/

Complete this table, matching the drugs to their effects and then listing the dangers of each.

Drug	Effects	Dangers
Alcohol		
Amphetamines		
Anabolic steroids		
Caffeine		
Cannabis		
Cocaine		
Ecstasy (MDMA)		
Heroin		
Ketamine		
LSD		
Magic mushrooms		
Solvents		

Effects:

- Stimulant – speeds things up
- Hallucinogen – heightens your senses
- Painkiller – blocks nerve impulses
- Depressant – slows down messages to the brain
- Performance enhancer – improves muscle development

Remember: some drugs have more than one effect!

Dangers: addiction, death, dehydration, inability to concentrate and/or sit still, pounding heart, stomach cramps, shaky hands, unconsciousness, vomiting.

Strand:	**Resources:**
• Physical health and wellbeing	• Book One: pp. 68–69 • Worksheet 13.1 • The lunch menu for your school canteen

Learning objective:	**Key words:**
• To understand what a healthy diet is and why it is important	calorie, nutrient, saturated fat, cholesterol

STARTER

• Ask: 'What is a healthy diet?' Use the diagram on page 68 of *Your Choice Book One* to illustrate what constitutes a healthy diet and then read 'What is a healthy diet?'.

ACTIVITIES

• Ask students to study the statements in the 'Fact check' box. Ask: 'Do any of the statements surprise you? In your experience, do the findings of the survey reflect the eating habits of children of your age?'

• With the class, read 'What are junk foods?' and then ask students to do the writing task. Encourage them to create either a cartoon with three or four pictures (perhaps one on each meal of the day and one on snacks) or a script two or three paragraphs long.

• Together, read the 'Top tips for healthy eating' on page 69 and then ask the students to do the discussion task in pairs. Invite pairs to share thoughts with the rest of the class.

• Encourage students to do the writing task to produce a storyboard for a TV advert encouraging teenagers to eat healthily. You could supply them with a storyboard template from the link below.

• Ask students to read 'What's in your lunch box?' and then to do the discussion task in groups. Invite groups to share their conclusions with the rest of the class. *(Tula's is the best/most balanced, followed by Sasha's (although both could reduce the sugar content further), followed by Max's and then Martin's.)* Did all the groups give the same scores to each lunch box? Where they were different, did students give good reasons for their scores? Discuss the suggestions for healthier options.

• Support students to do the research task. Ask them to make notes of what they find out and then invite individuals to share their findings in a class discussion. If you have students from different religious or cultural backgrounds, you could ask them to share their food customs and experiences.

PLENARY

• Provide students with the lunch menu for your school canteen and ask them to decide, in groups, what are the most healthy and the least healthy options. Share ideas in a class discussion.

EXTENSION

• Hand out **Worksheet 13.1**. Ask students to keep a food diary for a week and then think about how they could improve their own diet based on what they have learned in this lesson.

Further information and support for teachers:

British Nutrition Foundation, 'Teenagers': www.nutrition.org.uk/healthyliving/lifestages/teenagers.html

Food Standards Agency, 'The Eatwell Guide': www.food.gov.uk/business-guidance/the-eatwell-guide

Storyboard template: https://creately.com/blog/examples/storyboard-templates-creately/#Storyboard%20download

Further information and support for students:

NHS, 'Eat well': www.nhs.uk/live-well/eat-well/

NHS, 'Vegetarian and vegan diets Q&A': www.nhs.uk/live-well/eat-well/vegetarian-and-vegan-diets-q-and-a/

Keep a food diary for a week and then think about how you could improve your diet from what you have learned in class.

Meal	Protein	Fruit and veg	Carbohydrates	Dairy products	Fats
Breakfast					
Lunch					
Dinner					
Snacks					
Totals					

I need to eat more ....

....

I need to eat less ....

....

When I treat myself, I can have ....

....

<table>
<tr><td>

Strand:
- Physical health and wellbeing

</td><td>

Resources:
- Book One: pp. 70–71
- Worksheet 13.2

</td></tr>
<tr><td>

Learning objective:
- To understand why it is important to be a healthy weight and to avoid fad diets, and to discuss government measures to reduce obesity

</td><td>

Key words:
obese, metabolic rate, nausea, dehydration

</td></tr>
</table>

STARTER

- Explain that what you weigh is an important indicator of how fit and healthy you are. Your weight depends on several factors: the type of foods you eat, the amount you eat, the amount of exercise you do and the rate at which you use up energy (calories). Explain that this final factor is called your metabolic rate, and this varies from person to person. End by reading the first paragraph on page 70 of *Your Choice Book One*.

ACTIVITIES

- With the class, read the British Nutrition Foundation article on page 70. Organise students into groups to do the discussion activity. Bring the class back together and invite groups to share their views on what the three most important points were. Agree a final class list of the top three and write them on the board.

- Read the writing task with the students and make sure they understand what a crash diet is. Then encourage them to complete the task independently.

- Ask students to read 'Should junk food advertising be banned?'. Ask: 'Do you think such measures are likely to have a big effect?' Encourage students to share their views in a class discussion.

- Read 'The sugar tax – will it work?' with the class, then ask them to read through the first three questions in the discussion task before you discuss them as a class. Invite students to give their opinions on how far the government should intervene and try to change people's eating habits.

- Divide the class into three groups and allocate each one a statement from question **4** to discuss. Then ask groups to share their opinions in a class discussion.

- Give out copies of **Worksheet 13.2** for students to complete in pairs. When they have finished, invite pairs to share their views in a class discussion and agree the best additional tip to add to the list.

- Organise students into groups to do the 'Research' task and then invite them to share their findings in a class discussion.

PLENARY

- Hold a class discussion on the following view: 'Diet alone won't solve a person's weight problem – to maintain a healthy weight, people have to look at their whole lifestyle and make changes.'

EXTENSION

- Invite pairs of students to role play a scene between a nutritionist and a journalist in which the journalist asks the nutritionist what advice they would give to teenagers about how to eat healthily and maintain a healthy weight. Give them time to prepare.

Further information and support for teachers:

British Nutrition Foundation, 'Life stages': www.nutrition.org.uk/healthyliving/lifestages.html

Safe Food, 'Fuel your body':
www.safefood.eu/Healthy-Eating/Food-Diet/Life-Stages/Teens/Fuelling-your-sport.aspx

BBC News, 'Children's online junk food ads banned by industry': www.bbc.co.uk/news/health-38239259

'TfL junk food ban will tackle child obesity': www.london.gov.uk/what-we-do/business-and-economy/food/tfl-junk-food-ads-ban-will-tackle-child-obesity

Further information and support for students:

NHS, 'Healthy weight': www.nhs.uk/live-well/healthy-weight/

Brook, 'Healthy weight': www.brook.org.uk/your-life/healthy-weight

Worksheet 13.2 Top tips on how to lose weight

In pairs, read through and discuss the tips below on how to maintain a healthy weight.

Tips for losing weight

1. Cut down on sugary soft drinks. There is a direct link between having lots of sweetened soft drinks and putting on weight. Switch to water.

2. Eat a healthy breakfast – for example, cereal with skimmed/semi-skimmed milk, which contains less fat than full-fat milk. Research shows that if you skip breakfast, you are likely to snack on high-fat foods containing lots of calories in order to alleviate your hunger.

3. Start taking regular exercise. Set yourself a target of at least half an hour a day of moderate exercise outside school – for example, walking to school, taking the dog for a walk, or helping with the housework by hoovering or in the garden by sweeping the path.

4. At least three times a week, take some vigorous exercise, such as bike-riding, swimming, skateboarding or playing football.

5. Limit the amount of time you watch TV and only eat healthy snacks while you are watching – for example, a piece of fruit rather than a packet of crisps.

6. Limit the amount of time you spend playing computer games. Set an alarm to go off after an hour and take a break to do some stretching exercises. The more you sit around, the more likely you are to put on weight because you are storing the calories you get from the foods you eat rather than using them up.

7. Cut down on sweets and chocolate.

8. If you are feeling full, don't worry about leaving some uneaten food on your plate. It's healthier to stop eating than to overeat.

Which three pieces of advice do you think are most useful?

1. ....

2. ....

3. ....

What further tip would you add to the list?

....

....

....

....

....

....

14.1   Exercise

Strand:	**Resources:**
• Physical health and wellbeing	• Book One: pp. 72–73 • Worksheet 14.1

Learning objective:	**Key words:**
• To understand the benefits of exercise	• exercise, physical health, mental health

STARTER

* Begin the lesson by asking students to write down three reasons why it is good to take exercise. Then, during a class discussion, invite students to share the benefits they listed. Record them on the board.

ACTIVITIES

* With the whole class, read Stuart Lewis's article on page 72 of *Your Choice Book One*. See if any of the benefits he includes are on the class list suggested during the starter. Ask: 'What other benefits does he mention?' Add them to the list on the board.

* Focus on the three statements in 'Role play' from people who don't want to exercise. Ask groups to discuss what they would say to these people. Then encourage pairs to do the role play.

* With the students, read and discuss 'The three elements of fitness' and 'Exercise: your questions answered' (page 73). Talk about the risks involved in taking anabolic steroids and support students to do the research task.

* Give out copies of **Worksheet 14.1**. Ask students to read the ten suggestions and to choose two that they would find fun and enjoy. Organise students into groups to discuss their choices and then to rank the list on the worksheet from 1 to 10, where 1 is the most fun and 10 the is the least fun.

* Ask: 'Is it possible to take too much exercise?' Read the article 'Addicted to exercise?' together and then ask pairs of students to do part **1** of the discussion activity that follows it.

PLENARY

* Read 'An exercise challenge' on page 73 with the class. Ask if they think it's a good idea and encourage them to think of an exercise challenge they could work towards over the next month. Then organise them into groups to do the discussion activity at the top of page 73. You will find guidelines on healthy amounts of exercise on the NHS website listed below. Elicit benefits such as feeling good, being able to concentrate and sleep better, and being healthier. Refer back to the list of benefits you compiled in the starter activity.

* Refer back to 'Addicted to exercise?' to consider some of the risks when exercising becomes an unhealthy obsession, and share ideas as a class to complete part two of the final discussion task on page 73.

RESEARCH

* Ask students to look at the 'This Girl Can', and 'Girls Active' websites (see the links below) and discuss how effective they think they might be in getting more girls involved in sport.

EXTENSION

* If practicable, work with the PE department and the students to organise 'The Big Challenge' described in part **2** of the worksheet. This could be done either in PE lessons or outside the normal timetable.

Further information and support for teachers:

NHS, 'Anabolic steroid misuse': www.nhs.uk/conditions/anabolic-steroid-misuse/

BBC Ethics guide on drugs, including steroids: www.bbc.co.uk/ethics/sport/debate/types_1.shtml

Further information and support for students:

KidsHealth, 'Why exercise is wise': https://kidshealth.org/en/teens/exercise-wise.html

NHS, 'Physical activity guidelines for children and young people':
www.nhs.uk/live-well/exercise/physical-activity-guidelines-children-and-young-people/

'This Girl Can', on getting girls involved in sport: https://sportengland.org/our-work/women/this-girl-can

Youth Sport Trust, 'Girls Active': www.youthsporttrust.org/girls-active

---

Worksheet 14.1 Have fun, get fit

1. Read the suggestions below for how to get fit and have fun. Rank them from 1 to 10, with 1 being the one you think will be most fun and 10 the one you think will be least fun.

How to get fit and have fun	Ranking
a) Exercise with a friend. Set yourselves fitness targets. Write down what you aim to have achieved in a month's time, in three months, in six months, in a year. Give it to your fitness buddy to look after.	
b) Be competitive. Set yourselves challenges. Who can ride their bike fastest round the park? Who can walk to school quickest? (No running allowed!) Who can score the most baskets in ten throws?	
c) Join a local sports club or a fitness class. Stay behind after school once a week to participate in whatever is available at your school, e.g. badminton, table tennis or judo.	
d) Dance your way to fitness. Put in your earphones, play your favourite songs and sing along as you dance alone in your bedroom.	
e) Use commercial breaks. Don't sit there bored by the adverts; use the time to see how many press ups or sit-ups you can do. Can you do more than your brother or sister?	
f) Make your exercise pay. Help with the housework and earn some extra cash at the same time. An hour's housework will burn off 190 calories.	
g) Alternatively, wash the car, mow the lawn or tidy out the shed.	
h) Play games on Nintendo Wii Sports.	
i) Make an obstacle course in your local park. See who can complete it the fastest.	
j) Strut your stuff. Imagine you are in the backing group for your favourite star. Rock around the bedroom playing air guitar.	

2. **The Big Challenge**

With the rest of the class, organise a heptathlon, a competition consisting of seven events. Either think up seven events yourselves or use these ideas:

- A penalty shoot-out – Who can score the most goals from ten penalties?

- An obstacle course – Who can do it the fastest?

- A throwing contest – Who can throw a tennis ball furthest?

- A hitting contest – Who can hit a golf ball or a tennis ball furthest?

- A dribbling challenge – Who can dribble a ball round a set of cones fastest?

- A hopping race – Who can hop the fastest for 100 metres?

- A press-ups/sit-ups/step-ups challenge – Who can do ten of each the fastest?

Strand:	Resources:
• Physical health and wellbeing	• Book One: pp. 74–75 • Worksheet 14.2

Learning objective:	Key words:
• To understand the benefits of exercise for your mental health and the importance of getting enough sleep	dopamine, serotonin, endorphins, melatonin

STARTER

• Ask: 'How many of you did some exercise yesterday? What did you do? How did you feel afterwards?'

• Then ask: 'How much exercise did you do during the last seven days? How much do doctors and health advisers recommend you should do?' *(At least 30 minutes, five days a week)* 'How many of you did that amount of exercise?'

• Explain that the reason teachers and adults emphasise the importance of exercise is that, as well as the physical effects, it also affects your mood. It can help you to feel less anxious and less stressed.

ACTIVITIES

• Encourage students to read the article about exercise on page 74 of *Your Choice Book One* and then to do the discussion task in groups. Follow up with a class discussion, encouraging students to give their opinions on the following questions: 'Why does exercise make you feel better? Why do health experts recommend that you exercise regularly?'

• Ask students to study the information given in the 'Fact check' box. Ask: 'What does it tell you about how much sleep teenagers need? What are the effects on teenagers of not getting enough sleep?'

• Ask students to read 'Teenagers' sleep patterns' and 'Top tips to help you get enough sleep' on page 75, and then to do the discussion activity in groups. Follow up with a class discussion, encouraging students to share their opinions on the following questions: 'How do teenagers' body clocks differ from those of adults? What is melatonin and what effect does it have? Why is it not a good idea to use your phone or tablet just before you go to sleep?'

• Invite students to research the amount of sleep they are getting by keeping a sleep diary for a week using **Worksheet 14.2**. Ask them to discuss in pairs what their diaries tell them about their sleeping habits.

PLENARY

• Revisit the 'Top tips to help you get enough sleep'. Discuss each tip with the class and ask students which they think is the most useful piece of advice. Is there a consensus or are there different opinions?

EXTENSION

• Ask the students to keep an exercise diary. In pairs, students should discuss whether they are getting enough exercise (half an hour or more every day).

Further information and support for teachers:

How to look after your mental health using exercise:
www.mentalhealth.org.uk/publications/how-to-using-exercise

Further information and support for students:

NHS, Get active for mental wellbeing:
www.nhs.uk/conditions/stress-anxiety-depression/mental-benefits-of-exercise/

BBC Bitesize, Health and wellbeing: www.bbc.com/bitesize/guides/z3shycw/revision/1

Young Minds, Sleep problems:
https://youngminds.org.uk/find-help/feelings-and-symptoms/sleep-problems/

1. Research the amount of sleep you are getting by keeping a sleep diary for a week using the table below.

	Monday	Tuesday	Wednesday	Thursday	Friday	Saturday	Sunday
What exercise did you do in the day?							
What did you do before you went to bed?							
What time did you go to bed?							
How long did it take you to fall asleep? Did you fall asleep at once? Fairly quickly? After a long time?							
Did you wake in the night? If yes, how many times? How long were you awake?							
What time did you wake up the next morning?							
How many hours of sleep did you have?							
How do you feel the next morning on a scale of 1–5? (1 = bad, 5 = great)							
Describe how you felt: were you refreshed, a bit tired, or irritable and moody?							

2. What does your diary tell you about your sleeping habits?

....

....

....

....

Strand:	Resources:
• Personal wellbeing and mental health	• Book One: pp. 76–77 • Worksheet 15.1

Learning objective:	Key words:
• To learn how to manage your emotions	state management

STARTER

* Ask students if they have ever felt out of control of their emotions. What have they done to get back in control of their emotions? Invite suggestions and write them on the board.

ACTIVITIES

* Ask students to read the introduction on page 76 of *Your Choice Book One* and then, in pairs, to do the discussion activity. Then ask students to compare their lists with another pair or in a class discussion.

* With the class, read 'Heart to heart' and then organise students into groups to do the discussion task that follows. In a class discussion, ask groups to share their answers and list the three most popular suggestions on the board.

* Encourage students to read 'Being in the right mood' and then, in pairs, to do the discussion activity. Then ask students to compare their answers in groups or to share them in a class discussion.

* Ask students to read 'When positive emotions are too much' and 'Breaking the pattern' on page 77, and then to do the discussion task in groups. Invite groups to share their answers in a class discussion, encouraging them to give reasons for their views.

* Organise students into pairs to study the statements in 'What works for you?' and then to do the first part of the discussion task that follows it. Invite some pairs to share their rankings with the class and give their reasons.

* Ask students, in pairs, to do the second part of the discussion activity.

PLENARY

* Ask students to do the writing task, reflecting on what they discussed with their partner in the previous activity.

EXTENSION

* Hand out **Worksheet 15.1**. Ask students on their own (or in pairs for students needing more support) to rank the emotions in the list in task **1**. Invite them to compare their answers in pairs or groups. Then, working in pairs, ask students to do part **2** of the worksheet. Responses might include: *curiosity and determination in a lesson, competitiveness in a sports lesson and determination and calm in an exam.*

* Finally, ask students to keep a mood diary for a week (task **3** on the worksheet). This will help them to find out when they feel best – in the morning, afternoon or evening. Once they have done this, ask them how they can use this new knowledge to their advantage (e.g. doing homework in the mornings at the weekend if they work best in the mornings, or at night during the week if they work best in the evenings).

Further information and support for teachers:

'How to help teens manage their emotions and accept their feelings': www.goodtherapy.org/blog/how-to-help-teens-manage-their-emotions-and-accept-their-feelings-0705175

Further information and support for students:

Moodcafe, 'Managing your emotions': www.moodcafe.co.uk/managing-your-emotions.aspx

PsychCentral, 'Techniques for teens: how to cope with your emotions': https://psychcentral.com/blog/techniques-for-teens-how-to-cope-with-your-emotions/

Childline, 'Feelings and emotions': www.childline.org.uk/info-advice/your-feelings/feelings-emotions/

Worksheet 15.1 Managing your emotions

1. Look at the following list of emotions. Which do you find the easiest and hardest to deal with? Rank them in order from the one you find easiest to manage (1) to the one you find hardest to manage (12). Then compare your answers in a group. Give reasons for your views.

☐ Happiness	☐ Anger
☐ Enthusiasm	☐ Rage
☐ Jealousy	☐ Excitement
☐ Grief	☐ Boredom
☐ Tiredness	☐ Sadness
☐ Confusion	☐ Exhaustion

2. Now, in pairs, consider the following three situations and decide which states of mind you think would be most useful in each. Why? Give reasons for your views.

Determination   Calm   Focus   Creativity   Competitiveness   Curiosity

- in a lesson ....
  ....

- in a sports lesson ....
  ....

- in an exam ....
  ....

3. On your own, keep a mood diary for a week.
   - Which emotions or states of mind do you experience and when?
   - Do you have more positive emotions or states of mind in the morning, the afternoon or the evening?

   Keep a note so you can plan when to do your best work.

Strand:	Resources:
• Personal wellbeing and mental health	• Book One: pp. 78–79 • Worksheet 15.2

Learning objective:	Key words:
• To understand the grief cycle and how to manage grief	denial, anger, bargaining, depression, acceptance, guilt, resentment

• Note: There may be students in the class who have recently suffered a bereavement and who are going through a grieving process. They may find this lesson distressing or they may find it helpful. Be aware of their different needs and leave it up to them to decide whether or not to contribute. The plenary in particular must be approached with great sensitivity. Warn students in the previous lesson that you will be dealing with grief and bereavement so they have the opportunity to raise any concerns with you in advance.

STARTER

• Begin by giving a definition of grief – an intense feeling of sadness and loss. Ask students to suggest the circumstances in which people experience grief, such as the death of a family member or a close friend, the break-up of a long-term relationship, the death of a pet or the end of a friendship. There is also the public grief people feel when there is a tragic accident even if they don't know the people involved, such as the Grenfell Tower fire in 2017. Make the distinction between public grief and private grief. Now ask students to read the introductory paragraphs on page 78 of *Your Choice Book One*.

ACTIVITIES

• Organise students into groups to read and discuss the statements in the discussion task on page 78. Ask them which two statements they think are the best. Then ask the students, individually, to write a statement of their own. Encourage any who are willing to share their statement in a class discussion.

• With the class, read the paragraph below 'Discuss' and then go through the five stages of the grief cycle. Focus on each stage in turn and what it involves. Then organise students into groups to do the discussion task on page 79, before inviting them to share their views in a class discussion.

• Ask students to read 'Showing emotions' and then, in pairs to do the 'Your choice' matching exercise.

PLENARY

• Invite students to write two or three sentences on the best way to help a friend deal with the death of someone they are close to. If appropriate, invite some of them to share what they have written.

RESEARCH

• Ask students, in pairs, to read about different funeral customs on **Worksheet 15.2**, and then to work together to research the funeral customs of another religion or culture.

EXTENSION

• Ask pairs to compile a factsheet about the funeral customs of the religion or culture they researched for the worksheet. Invite pairs to share their factsheet with the rest of the class.

Further information and support

NHS, 'Bereavement and young people':
www.nhs.uk/conditions/stress-anxiety-depression/bereavement-and-young-people/

Child Bereavement UK: https://childbereavementuk.org/young-people/

Teenagers' understanding of death:
www.cruse.org.uk/get-help/for-parents/teenagers-understanding-of-death

---

Rituals for mourning in different religions and cultures

Different religions and cultures have different customs for mourning someone's death. Funerals, whatever form they take, are important because they are a public recognition of a person's life. Friends and family gather together to remember them.

Here are some of the funeral practices of four of the world's major religions:

- Christian burials – many Christians are buried at their church or cemetery after a funeral service. Some people choose to be cremated instead and have their ashes scattered in a particular place important to them, or at sea.

- Islamic burial – according to Muslim tradition, a person must be buried as soon as possible after they die.

- A Hindu practice is that of the last sacrifice, in which the person who has died is cremated on a funeral pyre. Different things will be cremated with them, according to who they were.

- In Judaism, when a person dies, those mourning the death recite the prayer *dayan ha-emet*, recognising God's power as the 'true judge'. Jewish law requires that the body be buried within a day or as soon as practical from the time of death.

Now do some more research on the funeral traditions of one of the religions above or of a different culture or religion, for example hanging coffins in China and the Philippines, what people do in South Korea or Madagascar.

Write notes below.

The name of the religion or culture: ....

The culture's or religion's most important beliefs or traditions related to funerals:

1. ....

   ....

2. ....

   ....

3. ....

   ....

In what way do the funeral practices of this culture or religion help people express their grief or come to terms with their loss?

....

Dealing with divorce or parents splitting up

Strand:	Resources:
• Personal wellbeing and mental health	• Book One: pp. 80–81 • Worksheet 15.3

Learning objective:	Key words:
• To understand how divorce may affect children and to suggest some ways of dealing with divorce	divorce, separation, access, reconciliation, counsellor

• Note: This is another topic that needs to be approached sensitively as there will probably be students in your class whose parents have split up or who are in the process of doing so. They may find this lesson distressing or, conversely, they may find it helpful. As with the lesson on grief, be aware of their different needs and leave it up to them to decide whether or not to contribute.

STARTER

• Recap what grief is (see lesson 15.2) and remind students that the break-up of a relationship can precipitate grief. Read the introduction on page 80 of *Your Choice Book One* with the class and then the poem on **Worksheet 15.3**. Discuss how children can mistakenly blame themselves for their parents separating.

ACTIVITIES

• With the students, read the article 'How to tell kids about divorce: an age-by-age guide' on page 80 of *Your Choice Book One*. Then organise students into pairs to do the role play. Monitor students to check that they are all OK with this activity, paying particular attention to those who have experienced or are experiencing a break-up in their household. If there is an odd number of students, the third student can observe and then feed back what they have learned from watching the role play. They can also say whether they would have said anything different.

• Ask pairs of students to read the statements in the 'Discuss' box and rank them with the most helpful at the top. Then invite them to compare their list with that of another pair, giving reasons for their views.

• Ask students to read 'Dealing with the loss'. Then encourage them, in pairs, to discuss who they would go and speak to in each of the scenarios in the second 'Discuss' box, giving reasons for their views.

• Organise students into groups to read 'Ask Erica' and then write Erica's reply to Rashida.

• With the students read 'Counsellors' and then tell them about any counselling services available in your school.

PLENARY

• Revisit **Worksheet 15.3** from the starter and ask students, working in pairs, to discuss the questions about the poem. Encourage them to extend their emotional vocabulary by using some of the words and phrases suggested on the worksheet.

EXTENSION

• Ask students to work in groups to produce an information leaflet (A4 folded to A5) for students their age about how to cope when parents are separating or divorcing. They should include what they have learned this lesson and can also use the links below to find out more.

Further information and support for teachers:

'Dealing with your parents' divorce as a teenager':
www.ourfamilywizard.co.uk/blog/dealing-your-parents-divorce-teenager

Further information and support for students:

KidsHealth, 'Dealing with divorce': https://kidshealth.org/en/teens/divorce.html

There are four chairs round the table

There are four chairs round the table,
Where we sit down for our tea.
But now we only set places
For Mum, for Terry and me.
We don't chatter any more
About what we did in the day.
Terry and I eat quickly,
Then we both go out to play.
Mum doesn't smile like she used to.
Often, she just sits and sighs.
Sometimes, I know from the smudges,
That while we are out she cries.
Why did he have to leave us?
Why did he have to go?
Was it something that I did?
I suppose I'll never know.

John Foster

Discuss the following questions in pairs.

1. How does the speaker of the poem feel?

2. How do the speaker's brother Terry and his mum feel?

Use any of the words and phrases below in your answers and explain what in the poem tells you this.

sad   regretful   upset   lonely   confused   nostalgic

empty   sympathetic   blaming yourself   avoiding   lost

16.1   Pocket money

Strand:	**Resources:**
• Personal wellbeing and mental health	• Book One: pp. 82–83 • Worksheet 16.1

Learning objective:	**Key words:**
• To explore issues involving pocket money	income, expenses, interest

STARTER

• Introduce the topic by reading the introductory paragraphs on page 82 of *Your Choice Book One*. Ensure that students understand that there is no law saying that parents should give children pocket money; nor is there a rule about how much they should be given – for many parents, pocket money may be unaffordable. Use your knowledge of the students' backgrounds to assess whether pocket money is something many in the class will receive and tailor your questions accordingly. Ask: 'Should pocket money be earned rather than just given?' Invite students to share their opinions.

ACTIVITIES

• Organise students into groups to do the first 'Discuss' activity on page 82, then invite them to share their suggestions with the class. Elicit that the quotation means that money doesn't just appear; it has to be worked for.

• Ask students to read 'Should you have to earn your pocket money?'. Invite students with different views to give their reasons. Hand out **Worksheet 16.1** for students to complete the table on their own following the instructions in part **1**. Then organise them into groups to do parts **1** and **2** of the second 'Discuss' task. Invite groups to share their responses with the class.

• Look at part **3** of the discussion activity with the students to make sure they understand what they need to do. Then ask groups to draw up their contracts, referring to task **2** on **Worksheet 16.1**. Again, invite groups to share their contracts with the rest of the class. Ask if any of them would change their contract having have heard what others have included.

• With the class, look at the findings of the survey in the 'Fact check' box on page 83 and the activity in the 'Discuss' box next to it. Encourage students to decide, on their own, how they would spend or save their £10, before bringing the class together to discuss their choices.

• Talk about borrowing money. Ask: 'Who is it best to approach if you want to borrow money – a parent, your brother/sister, a friend?' Explain what interest is (a charge you pay for borrowing money). Then ask pairs to read 'Ask Erica' and write her reply to Sean. Talk about lending money. Explain that there is a saying: 'Only lend money that you can afford to lose.' Ask students whether they agree or disagree with that statement. Then ask them to write Erica's reply to Sam.

• Encourage groups to discuss Izzy's problem. Read 'Money management tips' with the students. Ask which of the tips they think would help Izzy most. Then ask groups to write a reply to Izzy and invite them to share all three of their replies in a class discussion.

PLENARY

• As a class, ask students to discuss their replies to the 'Ask Erica' activity. Do they think differently about pocket money now? For example, is it a right? Is it precious and something that should be saved or spent carefully? Did writing a pocket money contract make them think differently about it?

Further information and support for teachers:

Young Enterprise, Young Money: www.young-enterprise.org.uk/

The Money Advice Service, 'The power of pocket money' (including 2-minute video):
www.moneyadviceservice.org.uk/blog/power-of-pocket-money

The Money Advice Service, 'How to help teenagers manage their money':
www.moneyadviceservice.org.uk/en/articles/how-to-help-teenagers-manage-their-money

1. Complete the table. Which of the chores listed in the first column do you currently get paid for? Are there chores you do that are not listed? If so, add them in to the table under 'Other'.

   How much do you get paid? Make a note of this in the second column.

   Do you think this is a fair amount or do you think you should be paid a different amount? Make notes in the third column. Finally, make notes on how difficult you think the chore is in the final column.

Name of chore	What you currently get paid	How much you would do this for	How difficult is the chore?
Helping with the washing up			
Tidying your room			
Putting out the rubbish			
Helping with the garden			
Helping hang out the washing			
Helping wash the car			
Other:			
Other:			
Other:			

2. Discuss the idea of having a pocket money contract where you and your parents or carers:

   a) specify what your pocket money is to be used for

   b) agree what you are going to do in return for getting pocket money

   c) specify whether there are any circumstances in which your pocket money will be stopped.

Strand:	Resources:
• Personal wellbeing and mental health	• Book One: pp. 84–85 • Worksheet 16.2

Learning objective:	Key words:
• To distinguish between needs and wants • To distinguish between short-run and long-run costs • To encourage students to budget and save money	needs, wants, necessities, luxuries, short-run and long-run costs, opportunity costs, income, expenditure

STARTER

• Ask students if there is anything they would like to save up for in the future. Note the best ideas on the board. Ask how they are going to save the money and write some of their suggestions on the board.

ACTIVITIES

• Ask students to read the introduction and 'Needs and wants' on page 84 of *Your Choice Book One*. Then ask them to do the writing activity, using Sam's list as a template.

• Now ask students to work in pairs on 'Your choice'. When they have done this, invite them to share their answers and discuss any differences in opinion with the class.

• Back in their pairs, ask students to study Sam's monthly budget in the discussion activity and to answer the questions. Invite pairs to compare their answers in groups, giving reasons for their views.

• Get students to read 'Necessities and luxuries' on page 85 and then, in groups, to do question **1** of the discussion activity that follows it. Invite groups to compare their answers in a class discussion.

• Now ask groups to do part **2** of the discussion activity and then to read the paragraph below it. Hand out **Worksheet 16.2** and ask students to complete it on their own. They should then compare their answers in pairs. There is space for students to add their own suggestions. Then bring the class together to discuss their suggestions for where Sam can save money (for example, does she really need a fizzy drink every day, or could she just drink water?). Remind them that Sam's income for the month is £50 and ask how much she could save if she followed their suggestions.

• As a stretch activity, fast finishers can do the next discussion activity and then share their answers with the rest of the class (for example, Sam may not be able to rely on money from Grandma, but may get some extra money for Christmas).

• Ask the students to read 'Opportunity costs' and 'Short- and long-run costs'. Check that they understand these concepts. Then ask them, either on their own or in pairs (for students needing more support) to do the writing activity. Invite students to compare their lists in groups and check that they have got them right.

• Ask students to read 'The bank of Mum and Dad' and then do the research task that follows, listing the things their parents or carers have to budget for each month. Students can share this information but be sensitive to the individual needs within your class for students from different income backgrounds.

PLENARY

• Lead a class discussion on which items students think are necessities and luxuries to them, which are short- and long-run costs, and where they think they can all save money.

Further information and support for teachers:

'Making money make sense', KS3 resources:
www.moneymakesense.co.uk/section.php?xSec=14&xPage=1

The Money Advice Service, 'How to help teenagers manage their money':
www.moneyadviceservice.org.uk/en/articles/how-to-help-teenagers-manage-their-money

Young Enterprise, Young Money: www.young-enterprise.org.uk/

Worksheet 16.2 Budgeting

Use the table below to create a monthly budget for yourself.

1. Under 'Income' write down all the money you will receive during the next month. Include your weekly pocket money, money for extra chores, money for your birthday or a special occasion such as Chinese New Year.

2. Under 'Expenses', write down all the things you want your money to buy in the next month. Include anything that you are saving for, such as presents for family birthdays and any costly items that you are saving up to buy in the future.

Income	Amount	Expenses	Amount
Pocket money		Food	
Chores		Drinks	
Money from grandparents		Phone contract	
Birthday/Christmas/gift money		Extra data for phone	
Savings from last month		Cinema tickets	
Work		Concerts	
		Clothes and shoes	
Other (specify)		Other (specify)	
Total		**Total**	

3. If your income is greater than your expenditure, how much money are you planning to save each month?

....

....

....

4. If your expenditure is greater than your income, where are you going to spend less in order to balance your budget?

....

....

....

How you spend your time

Strand:	**Resources:**
• Personal wellbeing and mental health	• Book One: pp. 86–87 • Worksheet 17.1

Learning objective:	**Key words:**
• To think about how you spend your leisure time and ways of using it better	relaxation, leisure, free time

STARTER

• Introduce the topic by asking students to think about how much leisure time they have on schooldays. Ask: 'How do you spend that leisure time? How many hours do you spend on average each weekday watching TV? Playing computer games? Messaging friends? Are you making the best use of your leisure time?' Then ask similar questions about how they spend their leisure time at the weekend.

ACTIVITIES

• Ask students, working on their own, to complete the quiz on page 86 of *Your Choice Book One*. Ask them to reflect on what their answers tell them about the use they make of their leisure time. Encourage them to discuss with a partner what they could do to make better use of it.

• Give out **Worksheet 17.1** and ask students to complete the chart and then to discuss with a partner what they learn from it. Then, still in their pairs, ask them to read 'What your answers say about your leisure time' on page 87 and see if this matches what they had suggested in their discussions of the questionnaire and the worksheet chart. Ask them to do the final discussion activity, reflecting back on everything they have learned.

• With the students, go through the 'Ten ways to make better use of your leisure time'. Ask: 'Which do you think is the most useful suggestion from your point of view? Why?'

• Ask students to do the writing activity on their own. The article should be three or four paragraphs long and you could provide them with title prompts such as 'The best way to spend your weekend' or 'How to make the best use of your spare time after school'.

PLENARY

• Encourage students, working in small groups, to share their articles and choose one piece of advice to share with the class.

RESEARCH

• Ask students to research what the latest advice is to parents about how much time children their age should spend on their phones, the internet and watching TV. Direct them to some of the links below.

EXTENSION

• Ask students to share and compare their findings from the research activity in a class discussion. Were they surprised by what they found out, or does the advice match what they already do?

Further information and support for teachers:

'Teenagers and free time':
https://raisingchildren.net.au/pre-teens/entertainment-technology/free-time-activities/free-time

Belfast Telegraph, 'Boys spend 15 minutes more a day than girls on sports activities'
www.belfasttelegraph.co.uk/news/uk/boys-spend-15-minutes-a-day-more-than-girls-on-sports-activities-official-figures-show-36547040.html

BBC News, Teen 24: 'Living in a remote village': http://news.bbc.co.uk/1/hi/uk/7098798.stm

Children's Commissioner 2018 report on social media use among 8-12 year olds: www.childrens commissioner.gov.uk/wp-content/uploads/2018/01/Childrens-Commissioner-for-England-Life-in-Likes.pdf

Further information and support for students:

NHS, 'Teen screen time linked to less sleep':
www.nhs.uk/news/pregnancy-and-child/teen-screen-time-linked-to-less-sleep/

Worksheet 17.1 How do you use your time?

Complete the following chart, noting down in each section how many hours you spend at each time of day doing the following activities.

E = Eating

M = Mental exercises to relax

R = Reading for relaxation

TRV = Travel

V = Playing video games or surfing the internet

F = Spending time with family or friends

P = Physical activity, including sport

S = Schoolwork or study

TV = Watching TV

Day	AM	PM	Evening	Notes
Monday				
Tuesday				
Wednesday				
Thursday				
Friday				
Saturday				
Sunday				

Strand:	Resources:
• Personal wellbeing and mental health	• Book One: pp. 88–89 • Worksheet 17.2

Learning objective:	Key words:
• To understand internet gaming addiction	addictive, adrenaline, immune

STARTER

• Ask students who play computer games what their current favourite games are and how many hours per week they spend playing them.

ACTIVITIES

• With the students, read the information about gaming and gaming addiction on page 88 of *Your Choice Book One*. Divide the class into three groups and instruct each group to discuss one of the questions in the first discussion activity. Then bring the class back together and invite groups to share their responses in a class discussion, giving reasons for their views.

• Ask students to read 'Addicted to gaming' on page 89. Check comprehension by asking the following questions in a class discussion: 'Why do you think gaming made him lose confidence to leave the house?' *(lack of direct contact with other people)*; 'What do you think is meant by "unable to function properly"?' *(Suggestions might include having problems with communicating with people, having no interest in anything but gaming, etc.)*

• Now ask students to read 'Why are games so addictive?' and then, in groups, to do the discussion task that follows it. Bring the class back together and ask groups to share their opinions and give reasons for them.

• Ask students, in pairs, to read 'Ask Erica' and then do the discussion task that follows. Next, they should do the writing task on their own, using what they discussed with their partner to inform their reply.

• Hand out copies of **Worksheet 17.2** for students to read and complete on their own.

PLENARY

• When they have finished the worksheet, invite students to share their rankings in a class discussion, giving reasons for their views.

EXTENSION

• Ask students to use the internet to research what the government is doing to combat internet gaming addiction. Answers can include: *offering support for gaming addiction through the NHS, the classification of games to make them age appropriate, and an investigation by the Gambling Commission into whether some online games now involve gambling.*

Further information and support for teachers:

UK addiction treatment centres, 'The phenomenon of gaming addiction':
www.ukat.co.uk/gaming-addiction/

Family lives, 'Gaming': www.familylives.org.uk/advice/teenagers/online/gaming/

Express, 'Two thirds of teenagers prefer to spend time in their bedrooms glued to their screens':
www.express.co.uk/news/uk/758758/Survey-shows-teenagers-prefer-socialising-online-and-in-their-bedrooms

Why are certain games so addictive? *Asks Daniella Lewknór*

Games like Fortnite are addictive for a number of reasons. In these games, the player takes on an identity which he assumes whenever he plays the game. He meets other players and they interact with each other.

How internet gaming addiction affects people's lives

Internet gaming addiction can affect a person's life in a number of ways:

- Mental health – Emotionally the person can become withdrawn and depressed through lack of direct contact with other people.
- Physical health – The person may be constantly tired through lack of sleep because they are playing throughout the night. They may not eat properly – snacking rather than eating proper meals. They may ignore personal hygiene.
- School life – Their addiction is likely to affect their schoolwork. They may forget or neglect to do homework and perform poorly in school because they are overtired. Their grades suffer as a result.
- Social life – Instead of going out with friends, the person may become isolated, relating only to people online rather than in person.
- Family life – Gaming addiction can cause family problems as parents or carers try to limit the amount of time a boy or girl spends gaming.
- Financial problems – There may be financial repercussions with the addict spending more than they can afford on games and their online characters.

Treating gaming addiction

It can be hard at first to change an addict's behaviour. The first step is to get them to acknowledge that they have a problem. Once this is done, then the next step is to reduce the amount of time they spend gaming.

Treatment usually involves seeing a counsellor who will focus on getting the person to realise the harm that the addiction is causing. The family has a part to play in helping and supporting the person and providing alternative activities for the person to do when previously they would have been gaming.

Rank the six effects of video gaming, with the most negative at the top.

Be prepared to give reasons for your views in a class discussion.

1. ....

2. ....

3. ....

4. ....

5. ....

6. ....

Strand:	Resources:
• Social education	• Book One: pp. 90–91 • Worksheet 18.1

Learning objective:	Key words:
• To understand the difference between assertive, aggressive and manipulative speaking and how to participate in group discussions	assertive, aggressive, manipulative, formal, informal

STARTER

* Introduce the topic by writing the terms 'assertive', 'aggressive' and 'manipulative' on the board. Ask students what they mean. Give them definitions: *assertive means being confident and not being frightened to say what you want or believe; aggressive means behaving in an angry or violent manner; manipulative means behaving so as to get what you want by controlling and influencing a person.*

ACTIVITIES

* With the students, read the text on page 90 of *Your Choice Book One* that explains the difference between speaking assertively, aggressively and manipulatively. Can they think of examples of where someone has been manipulative towards them (not talking about anyone in the room)? Is there anyone they admire for speaking assertively without being aggressive? Ask students if they have any questions and discuss these as a class. Ask students what their parents or carers have said to them when they haven't done their chores or their homework. Have they shouted at them? Calmly discussed it with them? Bribed them with pocket money or another incentive? How did this make them feel? Would another approach have been better?

* Invite pairs of students to role play a scene in which someone is upset about something, such as being told by the person on the door at a concert that their ticket is forged. Ask them to do the scene twice, once with the person speaking aggressively to the door person and once with them behaving assertively.

* Ask students, in pairs, to study statements **a)** to **h)** in 'Your choice' and then do task **1**. Next, for task **2**, invite pairs to compare their answers and discuss their reasoning if they have different opinions. They can then move on to do task **3** in their groups.

* Ask students to read 'Speaking in groups' on page 91. Invite them to share what they have learned about what makes a good group discussion.

* Give out copies of **Worksheet 18.1** and ask students to do task **1** individually. Then ask them to do task **2**, outlining which discussion skills they have and which ones they need to improve.

* Encourage students to recall the best group discussions they have had – if they can't think of any, you could suggest a class discussion that you think went particularly well. Then ask them to do the discussion activity in groups and then compare their lists from part **2** with another group.

PLENARY

* Organise the students into pairs to perform the role play suggested on page 91. Encourage students to use anything they have learned from the lesson to make the role-play discussion as successful as possible. In a class discussion, ask what things they learned in the lesson helped and in what way.

EXTENSION

* Ask students what they think the role of a chairperson is in a debate or discussion and clarify any misunderstandings. Then organise them into groups to discuss how and why having a chairperson in certain types of group discussion might be helpful. Bring the class back together to share ideas.

Further information and support for the teacher

Relate, 'Teen aggression and violence': www.relate.org.uk/relationship-help/help-family-life-and-parenting/parenting-teenagers/behaviour/teen-aggression-and-violence

Health direct, 'Teen aggression and arguments': www.healthdirect.gov.au/teenage-aggression-and-arguments

1. Circle the option that applies to you for each statement below.

   a) I listen attentively.   a) usually   b) sometimes

   b) I interrupt others.   a) occasionally   b) frequently

   c) I wait till it is my turn to speak.   a) always   b) sometimes

   d) I join in the discussion.   a) usually   b) only if I'm asked directly

   e) I stick to the point of the discussion.   a) usually   b) only if it interests me

   f) I introduce new and relevant points.   a) frequently   b) not very often

   g) I give reasons for my point of view.   a) usually   b) not very often

   h) I help to refocus the discussion if the group wanders off task.   a) sometimes   b) never

   i) I ask someone to elaborate if they make a good point.   a) sometimes   b) not very often

   j) I am prepared to change my opinion if I find someone else's argument convincing.   a) usually   b) not often

   k) I am prepared to agree to disagree with other people's opinions.   a) sometimes   b) not usually

   l) I am willing to negotiate and compromise if the group is asked to make a decision.   a) usually   b) only rarely

   m) I respect others' points of view.   a) always   b) only if they are sensible.

   n) I dominate discussions by talking loudly and aggressively.   a) not very often   b) frequently

2. Now write one or two paragraphs about which discussion skills you think you have and which you could improve, based on your answers above.

....

....

....

....

....

....

....

....

....

Listening and giving feedback

Strand:	Resources:
• Social education	• Book One: pp. 92–93
	• Worksheet 18.2

Learning objective:	Key words:
• To understand what makes a good listener and how to give feedback	feedback

STARTER

• Draw two columns on the board, one labelled 'Good listener', the other 'Poor listener'. Ask: 'What do you think are the skills of being a good listener? What makes someone a poor listener? How does a person's body language tell you whether or not they are listening?' Collect students' ideas on the board. Explain that the focus of the lesson is listening effectively and giving feedback.

ACTIVITIES

• With the students, read 'Listening to others' on page 92 of *Your Choice Book One*. Organise them into groups to do the discussion activity. Invite groups to compare their answers with those of other groups.

• Encourage students to assess their own listening skills by doing part **1** of **Worksheet 18.2**. Then ask them to answer the question in part **2**.

• Get students to read questions **1** and **2** of the writing activity on page 92 and then answer question **3** on the worksheet. Encourage them to write their action plan on the worksheet.

• Talk about giving and receiving feedback after making or listening to a speech. Elicit ideas such as limiting feedback to two or three main points and giving positive feedback before offering suggestions for improvements. With the class, read 'Giving and receiving feedback' on page 93. In a class discussion, ask students what they have learned and whether they agree with the list of rules. Do they think they're helpful?

• Organise students into groups to talk about the situations in the discussion activity at the top of page 93. Explain the need to be firm but tactful when giving feedback in difficult situations.

• Encourage students to work on the role play in pairs, bearing in mind the rules for giving feedback. If they can't think of an example they've already experienced, ask them to think of a potential future scenario, such as giving a summary of a homework tasks in class. Then ask them to do the writing task. Encourage them to include what went well, what didn't work and what they would do differently next time.

PLENARY

• Organise students into pairs or groups to do the final discussion task and then get them to share their views in a class discussion.

RESEARCH

• Support students to research information available on the websites below that would be useful for teenagers to help with public speaking. Then ask them to record a short podcast (2–3 minutes) on their phones, summarising this advice for others.

EXTENSION

• In groups, ask students to write two or three paragraphs summarising what they have learned from their research and in class. The summary should include advice to students their age for improving their public speaking.

Further information and support for the teacher

BBC Skillswise, 'Speaking and listening': www.bbc.co.uk/skillswise/topic-group/speaking-and-listening

Samaritans, 'Developing listening skills': www.samaritans.org/education/deal/connecting-with-others/developing-listening-skills

British Heart Foundation, '10 tips for active listening': www.bhf.org.uk/informationsupport/heart-matters-magazine/wellbeing/how-to-talk-about-health-problems/active-listening

---

Worksheet 18.2 Assessing your listening skills

How good are you at listening in group discussions?

1. Give yourself a score from 1 to 5 for each question below, where 1 = sometimes and 5 = always.

Question		Score
a)	Do you give the person who is speaking your full attention?	
b)	Do you think about what you hear?	
c)	Do you allow the speaker to talk without interrupting them, even if you disagree with what they are saying?	
d)	Do you make an effort to listen without being distracted by other people, noise or the surroundings?	
e)	Do you wait for people to finish or for the chairperson to invite you to speak?	
f)	Do you keep focused on the topic being discussed?	
g)	Can you challenge an argument by quoting someone's reasons and saying why you disagree with them?	
h)	Can you identify the main points that are made and summarise them?	
i)	Are you prepared to listen to others' arguments and to change your mind if you find them convincing?	
j)	Can you think of and ask appropriate questions?	
k)	Can you recall later what you heard?	

2. What makes a good listener?

    ....

    ....

    ....

3. How good a listener are you and what could you do to improve?

    ....

    ....

    ....

4. Make an action plan of what you are going to do to listen carefully in the future:

    ....

    ....

    ....

    ....

Strand:	Resources:
• Social education	• Book One: pp. 94–95
	• Worksheet 19.1

Learning objective:	Key words:
• To think about what makes a good neighbour and how to deal with any problems in your neighbourhood	neighbourhood, graffiti, fly tipping

STARTER

* Introduce the topic with the whole class by reading the introduction and 'What is a neighbour?' on page 94 of *Your Choice Book One*. Ask students individually to list two or three things they think make a person a good neighbour. Then invite some of them to share their ideas. Note these on the board, building up a spider diagram.

ACTIVITIES

* Encourage students, in groups, to read the statements in the first discussion activity on page 94 and to talk about which ones they agree with and why.

* Ask students to think about the questions in the second discussion activity. Then ask them to discuss, in pairs, how they think a perfect neighbour would behave and how *they* would behave and treat people in order to be a perfect neighbour.

* With the class, read the information about 'Neighbourhood Watch'. Ask students what they think of the scheme. Is it a good idea? What makes it effective? Are there any drawbacks to the scheme?

* Ask students to read 'Improving your neighbourhood' on page 95 and then go through the first 'Your choice' activity with them before asking them to do it in pairs. When they have finished, encourage them to compare their answers with those of another pair, then share the correct answers with the class:
  1. Local council 2. You 3. Neighbourhood Watch 4. You and your neighbour 5. You 6. Local council 7. Local council 8. You and your neighbour.

* Read 'Street scene champions' with the class and then ask students to work in pairs to do the second 'Your choice' activity. Encourage pairs to share their rankings with those of another pair and then, in groups, to do the discussion task. Ask: 'Would you ever consider being a street scene champion? Give your reasons.'

PLENARY

* In a class discussion, ask students: 'What do you think could be done to improve your neighbourhood? What do you think are the most important priorities? Who should you contact in order to take action? Is there anything you could do yourself to help deal with the problems?'

RESEARCH

* Give out copies of **Worksheet 19.1**. Ask students to complete the questionnaire individually, and then compare their answers with a partner. Bring the class back together and discuss the results as a class.

EXTENSION

* Divide the students into small groups and give each student ten copies of **Worksheet 19.1**. Tell them to ask ten people they know who live in the local area to complete the questionnaire (not classmates). Then ask them to work in their groups to collate the results, before bringing the whole class together to collate all the results, using this as an opportunity to embed numeracy skillls (collation).

Further information and support for teachers:

Good Neighbours Network: www.goodneighbours.org.uk/

TES, 'Being a good neighbour', free resources:
www.tes.com/teaching-resource/being-a-good-neighbour-unit-3-6078281

BBC news, 'Noisy neighbours "top nuisance list"': www.bbc.co.uk/news/29211402

Worksheet 19.1 Checking out your neighbourhood

Your name: ....

Date: .... Location: ....

Survey questions (fill in the answers provided by the person you are speaking to):

Question	Yes	No	Don't know
1. Do you think there is a good range of shops in your neighbourhood?			
2. Is there a post office in your neighbourhood?			
3. Is there a park or playground in your neighbourhood?			
4. Is there a library in your neighbourhood?			
5. Is there a swimming pool or sports centre in your neighbourhood?			
6. Is there a community centre in your neighbourhood?			
7. Is there a youth centre in your neighbourhood?			
8. Do you feel safe in your neighbourhood?			
9. Do you think your local roads are safe?			
10. Is there enough parking in your local area?			
11. Are there a lot of potholes in your local area?			
12. Do you think you have enough street lighting in your local area?			
13. Is there a lot of litter in your local area?			
14. Are there good recycling facilities and recycling collections from your house in your area?			
15. Is graffiti a problem in your local area?			
16. Is any of the water in local ponds, rivers, lakes or canals in your area polluted?			
17. Is the air quality good or bad in your local area?			
18. Are there flowerbeds and trees provided by the council that are in good condition?			
19. Is there anything else you would like to add that is particularly good or bad about your local neighbourhood?			

Strand:	Resources:
• Physical health and wellbeing	• Book One: pp. 96–97 • Worksheet 20.1

Learning objective:	Key words:
• To understand what first aid to give for common injuries	first aid, recovery position, shock

- Please note that these books do not cover all the first aid objectives from the Health Education curriculum guidance, e.g. defibrillators. You might also want to get an expert trainer to help to deliver first aid lessons.

STARTER

- Introduce the topic by asking: 'Where do you think most accidents occur?' Explain that there are more accidents in the home than anywhere else. What do they think is the commonest type of accident? Explain that it is a fall.

- Ask how many children under 15 they think go to A&E departments each year in the UK. The answer is two million. Emphasise that because accidents are so common, it is important for everyone to have some knowledge of first aid.

ACTIVITIES

- Focus on first aid for each type of accident or emergency on page 96 of *Your Choice Book One* in turn, reading each section with the class. Ask a few questions to check comprehension, e.g. 'Should you move a person after a fall?' *(no)*; 'How long should you cool a burn under cold running water?' *(at least ten minutes)*; 'What should you do with a cut or wound, if possible?' *(raise the injured area above the person's chest to slow down the blood flow)*

- Ask if any of student has ever made an emergency telephone call and discuss what the procedure is. Hand out **Worksheet 20.1** and read it through with the class, recapping the procedure and making sure they all understand what they should do.

- Write the following details on the board. Then organise students into pairs to act out making the emergency call, one of them taking the part of the ambulance service operator, the other the part of Sam Turner, Mr Turner's grandchild: *The call is from 15 Bury Street, Newtown NT1 1NT from phone number 01234 556677 asking for an ambulance for Alfred Turner, aged 74, who has fallen from a chair while standing on it trying to change a lightbulb. He was knocked out but is now conscious.* Invite a pair to perform the role play for the class. Then discuss it and invite questions.

- Still in their pairs, encourage students to discuss the six questions in the 'Discuss' box and then to write their answers individually. Then ask them to read 'Ask Erica' on their own and to write Erica's reply to Jo.

PLENARY

- Ask students to use the second part of **Worksheet 20.1** to prepare the role play on page 97. The sketch should last two to three minutes and give at least three key pieces of first aid advice. Monitor the students closely, so you know which sketches you can use for the extension activity (see below).

RESEARCH

- Instruct students, in pairs, to visit the St John's Ambulance website (see below) to learn more about the recovery position.

EXTENSION

- Invite appropriate pairs to act out the sketches they wrote for the role-play activity in the plenary above.

Further information and support for teachers

British Red Cross, 'First aid learning for young people':
www.redcross.org.uk/get-involved/teaching-resources/first-aid-learning-for-young-people

First aid for life, 'First aid for teenagers': https://firstaidforlife.org.uk/first-aid-courses/first-aid-teenagers/

St John's Ambulance, teaching resources: www.sja.org.uk/sja/teaching-resources.aspx

In an emergency, you should call the emergency services.

- Dial 999.

- You will be asked which service you need.

- Ask for the ambulance service.

- An operator will ask you what phone number you are calling from, what the address is (including the postcode if you know it) and what has happened.

- An ambulance will then be sent.

- Meanwhile, you will be asked some more questions, such as the patient's name, sex and age, whether they are conscious and breathing, exactly what the injury is and how it happened.

Role play: First aid advice from Felicity the First Aider to Donald Doitright

Plan your sketch by answering the questions below and making notes.

1. Where does your sketch take place?

....

2. What is Donald's role in the sketch?

....

3. What is Felicity's role in the sketch?

....

4. What is the first piece of first aid information you wish to get across in the sketch?

....

5. How will you get this across to your audience?

....

6. What is the second piece of first aid information you wish to get across?

....

7. How will you get this across to your audience?

....

8. What is the third piece of information you wish to get across?

....

9. How will you get this across to your audience?

....

10. Is there any humour you could introduce into the sketch? If so, how?

....

Strand:	**Resources:**
• Relationships and sex education	• Book Two: pp. 6–7 • Worksheet 1.1

Learning objective:	**Key words:**
• To understand what teenagers' rights are and what rights their parents and carers have	right, privilege, privacy, sexuality, teenager

STARTER

* Ask the students if they know the difference between rights and privileges. A right is something that may be legally defined in law, e.g. the right to freedom of movement, the right to legal advice in custody, or something that you are morally entitled to, e.g. the right to choose your friends. A privilege is something that you do not have automatically and can be taken away from you, e.g. your parents may let you stay up late as a treat, but this is privilege, not a right.

ACTIVITIES

* Draw a line down the middle of the board and label one side 'Teenagers' rights' and the other 'Parents'/carers' rights'. Divide the class into groups and ask half of them to decide what rights teenagers have and the other half what rights parents/carers have. List their suggestions on the board and draw attention to any rights that are conflicting.

* Invite students to read the introduction and 'Teenagers' rights' on page 6 of *Your Choice Book One*. Ask: 'Are any of the rights listed actually privileges rather than rights?' Hand out **Worksheet 1.1** to help them to decide which are rights and which are privileges. Ask them to work in pairs to do 'Your choice' on page 6 and then to complete part **2** of the worksheet.

* Next, ask them to do the writing task, based on what they have discussed in 'Your choice' and their responses on the worksheet.

* In the same pairs, get students to read 'Parents' rights' and then to do the first 'Discuss' task on page 7. When they have finished compiling their lists, ask pairs to share and compare their lists (parents'/carers' rights and teenagers' rights) in a class discussion.

* With students, look at the 'Fact check'. Ask: 'Do you think it is right that teenagers can go to these appointments without their parents or carers knowing?'

* Encourage students to read 'Pria's problem' and then do part **1** of the discussion task in small groups. Bring the class back together and compare students' responses to the questions. Ask: 'Is being asked to wear a Gator an infringement of Pria's rights and an offence to her dignity, as well as an invasion of her privacy? Are there any circumstances in which you would agree to wear one?'

PLENARY

* As a class, discuss the two statements in part **2** of the discussion activity. Dangers teenagers may not be aware of include internet safety, exposure to violent behaviour and stereotypes on TV, the addictiveness of drink and drunk, spiking of drinks and date rape.

EXTENSION

* Make copies of the lists of teenagers' rights and parents'/carers' rights that the class identified and encourage students who wish to do so to take the lists home to discuss them with their parents/carers.

Further information and support for teachers:

BBC Future, 'How our teenage years shape our personalities':
www.bbc.com/future/story/20180608-how-our-teenage-years-shape-our-personalities

The Heroic Journey of Teenagers (contains information on suicide – use discretion with this material):
http://teenheroicjourney.org/challenge-1-forming-identity/

Further information and support for students:

Better Health, 'Teenagers and communication':
www.betterhealth.vic.gov.au/health/healthyliving/teenagers-and-communication

1. As a person and a member of a family, you have certain rights to be treated in particular ways. Read what this group of teenagers have to say about their rights.

    Nat: You're entitled to have a place to live, to have a home.

    Gemma: Yes, and to have enough food to eat.

    Trudie: And clothes to keep you warm.

    Nat: You're entitled to feel safe at home.

    Trudie: Yeah. You've got a right not to be bullied or threatened.

    Gemma: What about being smacked?

    Trudie: Some parents hit their children. I think you're entitled to live without the fear of being treated violently.

    Theo: What about the rules families have? Like what time you have to be in by. Haven't I the right to set a time myself?

    Nat: That's not a right though, is it?

    Trudie: What about our privacy? Do our parents or carers have the right to know where we are and who we're with all the time?

    Theo: And what about giving us pocket money?

    Gemma: Is that a right? Some parents can't afford to give pocket money.

    Theo: If I do something wrong, my parents stop my pocket money. Is it fair to use stopping our pocket money as a punishment?

2. With a partner, write down what you think your top three rights are and what the top three privileges are that your parents give you.

My top three rights	My top three privileges

Why are these your top three rights and privileges? Give reasons for your views.

....

....

....

....

....

....

Strand:
- Relationships and sex education

Resources:
- Book Two: pp. 8–9
- Worksheet 1.2

Learning objective:
- To discuss ways of dealing with problems with parents and to consider the value of contracts

Key words:
contract, negotiate, compromise, independence

STARTER

- Begin the lesson by writing some sentence starters on the board, such as: 'When I try to talk to my parents….'; 'The problem with parents is…'; 'My parents won't…'; 'Talking doesn't get you anywhere because…'; 'Parents always think…'. Ask students to complete one or two of the statements individually, and then to share what they have written in a class discussion. What does this activity reveal about the problems they encounter when talking with their parents?

ACTIVITIES

- Introduce the idea of teenagers drawing up a contract with their parents or carers, reading the introduction on page 8 of *Your Choice Book Two* with the class. Discuss what Marcia and her parents included in their contract. Ask: 'What else might they have included?' Ask pairs to do the writing task. Then give out copies of **Worksheet 1.2** and suggest that the students use it for reference to draw up a contract that they would be prepared to sign. Invite some pairs to share their responses and their contracts, and discuss differences and similarities.

- Ask students to read the 'Top tips on talking with parents' on page 8 and then to work in small groups on the discussion activity. Invite groups to share their top three tips and see if the class can agree a final list.

- Encourage students to read 'Who's responsible?' and then to do the 'Your choice' task individually, before discussing their answers in groups. Bring the class back together and ask: 'Do you think you take as much responsibility for these tasks as you could/should?'

- With students, read what Eileen Pickersgill says about accepting responsibility and do part **1** of the 'Discuss' task. Invite students to share examples of times when they have had to take responsibility for their actions now that they are teenagers.

- Then ask the students to read 'Zara's problem' and to do part **2** of the discussion task, again in small groups. Invite groups to share their responses with the class and discuss any differences.

PLENARY

- End the lesson by asking students to write a paragraph saying what they have learned from the lesson about how to deal with problems they have with parents. Invite some of them to read out what they have written.

EXTENSION

- Encourage students to show the contracts they have drawn up to their parents/carers and, if their parents/carers agree, to make any changes they accept and to sign a contract.

Further information and support:

Teens with Problems, 'How to write a home rules contract':
www.teenswithproblems.com/home_contract.html

'Teenagers and rules – a win/win for all':
https://yourteenmag.com/family-life/discipline/teenagers-negotiate-rules

'How to negotiate with your parents' video (5 mins) from Date Right can be found by searching on YouTube

I agree to talk to my parents/carers when they request a meeting to discuss a problem and to listen to what they have to say.

In return, my parents/carers agree to listen to what I have to say.

I agree to speak calmly and to control my temper and not to shout and swear.

My parents/carers agree to remain calm and to control their tempers.

I agree to do my share of the chores.

I agree to be in by a certain time.

My parents/carers agree to negotiate the time depending on where I am going and when.

I expect my parents/carers to respect my opinions and to allow me to make my own decisions.

My parents/carers agree to let me make my own decisions provided that my decisions are not going to be harmful to me or to anyone else.

I have the right to choose my own friends and to go out when and where I want, provided I tell my parents.

My parents/carers do not have the right to criticise my friends.

If I am punished at school, I do not expect to be punished at home as well.

I have the right to privacy in my own room.

I have the right to see a doctor without telling my parents/carers.

My parents/carers agree to respect my privacy.

Strand:	**Resources:**
• Relationships and sex education	• Book Two, pp. 10–11 • Worksheet 1.3

Learning objective:	**Key words:**
• To think about how to be a responsible teenager	responsibility, freedom, independence

STARTER

• Ask students to give examples of the things they have to do now, and the things they think they will have to do at 18. Note some of their suggestions on the board. Then ask them how they think they will take control of their lives. Allow them five minutes to discuss this in pairs and then note their suggestions on the board.

ACTIVITIES

• Ask students to read the introduction on page 10 of *Your Choice Book Two*, as well as 'Take control of your life' and 'Take control of your money'. Ask: 'How does the list in the book compare with the lists on the board?' Discuss this as a class.

• Working individually, ask students to read 'My health checklist' and then support them to do the first part of the 'Research' task. When they have finished, work through the checklist with them and make sure they know how to find any information they don't already know. Explain that they could ask their parents and carers for some of the information; they could look online to find the nearest pharmacy and A&E and the contact details of the GP practice where they are registered. Then hand out **Worksheet 1.3** for students to do the second part of the 'Research' task, creating their factsheet.

• Organise students into small groups to read 'What I regret most' on page 10 and then to do the discussion task that follows. Ask them to list what they can learn from the experiences described. Then invite representatives from the groups to share their lists and compare them in a class discussion.

• Ask students to read 'Think about the future' and to list three things they are going to do as a result of reading this and 'Take control of your money' from earlier in the lesson. Then encourage them to compare their lists in groups.

PLENARY

• Organise the class into seven groups or pairs. Allocate each group or pair two jobs from the list in the final 'Discuss' task and then instruct them to carry out the task. Bring the class back together to compare and discuss their answers.

EXTENSION

• Ask students to discuss which skills from the plenary are transferable between jobs and are therefore the most important. They should give reasons for their views.

• Ask students to write an article for an advice column in a teenage magazine entitled 'Don't do anything you might later regret!'. Suggest that they include anecdotes from teenagers about the kind of things they have regretted doing and why.

Further information and support:

Young Minds, Supporting adolescence and mental health: https://youngminds.org.uk/

WikiHow, 'How to be a responsible teen': www.wikihow.com/Be-a-Responsible-Teen

ActiveNationUK, 'Responsibility', video (2 mins) from ActiveNationUK can be found by searching on YouTube

Worksheet 1.3 Health check

Use this sheet to create a factsheet containing the information listed.

My health checklist

My GP's name, address and telephone number, and how to make an appointment either by phone or online:

....

....

....

Name and address of the nearest pharmacy where I can get prescriptions:

....

....

Details of the nearest hospital with an Accident and Emergency department:

....

....

My national health number and where my national health card is kept:

....

....

Immunisations I have had and any I am due to have in the future (see Unit 9.1):

....

....

Any allergies I have (e.g. nut allergy, see Unit 9.2):

....

....

Any medical conditions I have (e.g. asthma) and medicines I take for them:

....

....

Any childhood illnesses I have had (e.g. chicken pox):

....

....

....

Strand:	**Resources:**
• Relationships and sex education	• Book Two, pp. 12–13 • Worksheet 2.1

Learning objective:	**Key words:**
• To distinguish between friendship, infatuation and being in love, and to understand that there are different types of love	infatuation, friend, love, being in love

STARTER

• Read the introduction with students and then invite them to suggest what they think are the qualities of a close friendship. Note suggestions on the board. Elicit ideas such as wanting to spend lots of time together, sharing their thoughts and feelings, having shared interests or a similar sense of humour.

ACTIVITIES

• Ask students to read 'What does being in love mean?' on page 12 of *Your Choice Book Two* either on their own or in pairs (for students needing more support), and then to do the discussion activity in pairs. After the discussion, ask them to write two or three sentences on their own about what they think being in love means (question **1** of 'Write' on page 13). Encourage them to share and compare their answers in small groups.

• Then ask them, again on their own or in pairs, to read 'How do you that know that you're in love?' and then to do the second discussion activity in pairs. When they have done this, ask them to do question **2** of the 'Write' activity (page 13) on their own. Encourage them to share their answers in small groups.

• Ask students to read 'Sharing your thoughts and feelings' and 'Ask Erica' on page 13. Then ask them to write Erica's reply, either on their own or in pairs if they need more support. Invite students to share their responses with the class and discuss any differences in the advice they've given.

• Organise students into groups of three to read 'Jay and Tanya's dilemma' and then to do the role-play activity about it. Instruct students to take it in turns to be either Jay, Tanya or an observer, with the observer making notes of anything they think is important in the conversations. When they have all taken their turns, ask them to compare their notes and discuss what they have learned from the activity.

PLENARY

• Hand out **Worksheet 2.1** for students to complete on their own and then discuss their responses as a class. See if the class agree which of statements describe features of both close friendships and romantic relationships: trusting someone completely, thinking about them every day, missing them when they are not with them, being able to tell someone a secret or being able to talk to them when they are upset. Perhaps ask them which type of relationship they think is more important at their age.

RESEARCH

• Ask students to work in pairs to research how teenagers define 'mates', 'friends' and 'being in love' by devising a short survey to circulate among their form group. Ask them to then write two or three paragraphs to summarise their findings.

EXTENSION

• Ask students to make a poster of what it is like to have a friend, what they expect of a friend and what a friend can expect of them in return.

Further information and support for teachers:

Love Island – what it teaches us about how not to treat people in relationships:
www.ljmu.ac.uk/about-us/news/blog/2018/6/26/love-island-not-treat-romantic-partners

Further information and support for students:

Teenagers' thoughts on falling in love: https://kidshealth.org/en/teens/love-thoughts.html

Love and romance: https://kidshealth.org/en/teens/love.html

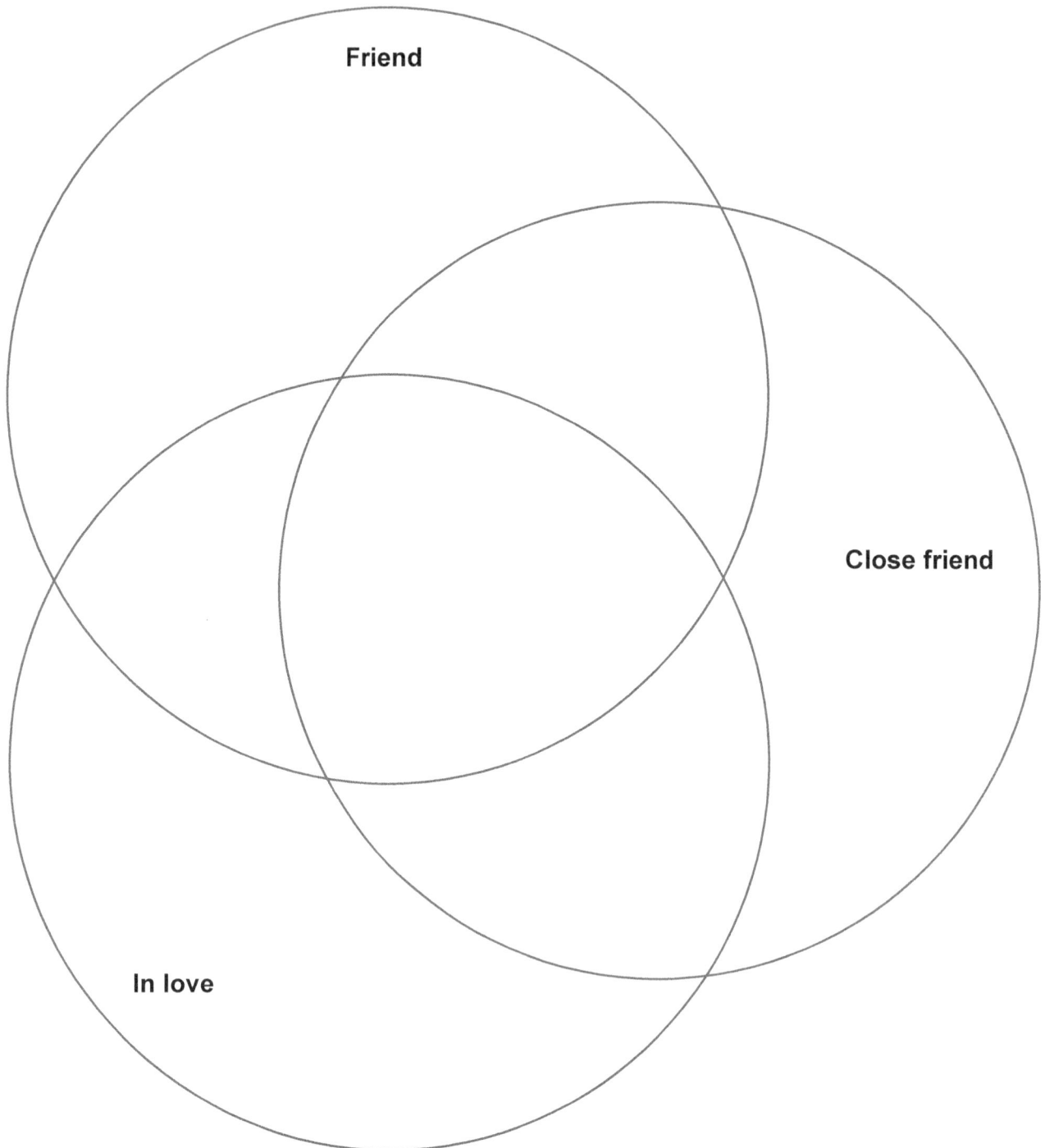

Write the following phrases in the section of the Venn diagram where you think they fit:

Trust completely   Like to spend time with them

Like to be around   Take an interest in their life

Think about them every day   Like to do the same things

Miss them when not with them   Like to play games / have fun with them

Can tell them a secret   Can talk to them when upset

Friend

Close friend

In love

Strand:	Resources:
• Relationships and sex education	• Book Two, pp. 14–15 • Worksheet 2.2

Learning objective:	Key words:
• To explore what makes a good relationship	trust, compromise, respect, communication

STARTER

* Ask students what they think makes a healthy relationship. Note their ideas on the board. Elicit and highlight trust, communication, compromise and respect.

ACTIVITIES

* Ask students to read 'Keys to a healthy relationship' on page 14 of *Your Choice Book Two* and then, in pairs, to rank the features listed from most to least important in contributing to a healthy relationship. Invite pairs to share and compare their lists in a class discussion, giving reasons for their views.

* Ask students to work in pairs to read 'Adam's story' on page 15 and then to do the role play that follows it. Encourage pairs to share their role play with another pair. Then invite some pairs to come up and perform their role play for the rest of the class. As a class, discuss any differences in approach.

* Get students to read the 'Top tips for good relationships' on their own and then, in pairs, to do the first part of the 'Your choice' activity. Combine pairs into groups to compare and discuss their answers, and agree a top three for the group. Invite groups to share their final top three with the rest of the class and discuss any differences.

* Hand out **Worksheet 2.2** and ask students to read the poem and work on parts **1** and **2** in pairs, before tackling part **3** on their own. Invite students to share their responses in a class discussion.

PLENARY

* Lead a class discussion about what students think are the most rewarding things about having friends. Answers could be: *having someone to support you, companionship, shared interests.* Also discuss what are the most challenging things about friendships. Answers could include: *compromise, flexibility, dedicating time to them.*

EXTENSION

* Give students the following challenge: 'Imagine you are giving support to someone who finds it difficult to make new friends. What advice would you give them? Why?' Answers could include meeting people who have shared interests through a sports club or hobby, and talking to people with shared interests first. Use the information from the 'Friendless teens' link below to support students.

Further information and support for teachers:

NSPCC, 'It's Not OK: teaching resources about positive relationships': https://learning.nspcc.org.uk/research-resources/schools/its-not-ok/

'Friendless teens': www.maggiedent.com/blog/friendless-teens/

The importance of strong, close friendships: https://qz.com/1059666/having-a-stronger-closer-friendship-as-a-teenager-predicts-less-depression-as-a-young-adult/

Disrespect NoBody teaching resources: www.pshe-association.org.uk/curriculum-and-resources/resources/disrespect-nobody-teaching-resources-preventing

Further information and support for students:

'Friends, frenemies and fakers': www.thinkuknow.co.uk/11_13/Need-advice/friends-frenemies-and-fakers

Childline, 'Friends': www.childline.org.uk/info-advice/friends-relationships-sex/friends/

A Friend Is...

A friend is someone you can rely on
A shoulder to cry on.
A friend is someone who cares.
A friend is someone who shares.
A friend is someone who won't let you down
Someone who sticks by your side.
A friend is someone who listens to you
And in whom you can confide.
A friend is someone who won't force you
To do things you don't want to do.
A friend is someone who will always
Keep their promises to you.
A friend is someone you can trust.
A friend is loyal and true
Someone you can depend on
Who is always there for you.

John Foster

1. List the qualities the poem says a friend has.

....

....

....

2. Are there any other personal qualities that you look for in a friend?

....

....

Here is what some teenagers said when they were asked what quality they valued most in a friend.

A good sense of humour

Honesty

Someone who respects you

Someone who is sympathetic

Confidence

Sincerity

Someone who is caring

Reliability

Intelligence

Someone who respects you

3. Write a paragraph stating which qualities you most value in a friend.

....

....

....

....

....

Strand:	**Resources:**
• Relationships and sex education	• Book Two, pp. 16–17 • Worksheet 2.3

Learning objective:	**Key words:**
• To distinguish between a healthy and unhealthy relationship • To develop strategies to deal with rejection	healthy relationship, unhealthy relationship, rejection

STARTER

• Ask students what they think might be some of the characteristics of a healthy and an unhealthy relationship and note their suggestions on the board. During this lesson, be sensitive to the needs of students who might be in an unhealthy relationship or have family members in unhealthy relationships.

ACTIVITIES

• Ask students to read the introduction and 'What are the signs of an unhealthy relationship' on page 16 of *Your Choice Book Two*. Then ask them to do the 'Your choice' activity in pairs. Encourage pairs to compare their responses with another pair and then invite groups to share their answers with the rest of the class, giving reasons for their views. During the discussion, look back at the characteristics of an unhealthy relationship listed during the starter and ask if students would like to add anything to it or remove anything.

• Either on their own, or in pairs for students needing more support, ask students to do the 'Write' task on page 16, based on what they have learned so far in the lesson.

• Ask students, in pairs, to read the first 'Ask Erica' on page 17 and then do the discussion task that follows it. Invite pairs to share their responses in a class discussion. Then, either in their pairs or on their own (depending on how much support they need), ask the students to read the second 'Ask Erica' and write a reply. Again, invite students to share their responses in a class discussion.

• Get students to read 'Feeling rejected' and then to work in pairs on part **1** of 'Your choice' on page 17. Combine pairs into small groups to do part **2** of 'Your choice', comparing their answers.

PLENARY

• Still in their groups, ask students do to do part **3** of 'Your choice', discussing what other advice they would give someone. Then bring the class back together to discuss groups' responses. See if you can agree a final ranking for the advice suggested and can agree on the best piece of additional advice.

RESEARCH

• Direct students to the websites listed below and ask them, in pairs, to find out more about rejection and how to deal with it. Ask them to make a short podcast (writing a script and, if possible, recording it) giving advice to people their age, based on what they've learned.

EXTENSION

• Hand out copies of **Worksheet 2.3** for students to complete in pairs, before comparing their answers in groups. As a further stretch activity, students can think up other problems (there is space for this on the worksheet) and how they would deal with them.

Further information and support for teachers:

Rescue Youth, '12 tips for teaching your teenagers to deal with rejection': www.rescueyouth.com/12-tips-for-teaching-your-teenagers-to-deal-with-rejection/

Further information and support for students:

'Rejection and how to handle it': https://kidshealth.org/en/teens/rejection.html

'Dealing with rejection': http://teenhealthsource.com/relationships-selfesteem/dealing-with-rejection/

'Being loved, or being used?': www.thinkuknow.co.uk/11_13/Need-advice/Relationship-abuse-and-exploitation/

Worksheet 2.3 Solving relationship problems

In pairs, complete the table, suggesting a solution for each of the problems.

Problem	Solution:
A friend is lying to you about little things, but you have caught them out.	
A friend keeps letting you down at the last minute after you have arranged to see them.	
A friend keeps gossiping about everyone, and it's beginning to annoy you.	
A friend often interrupts you and speaks over you when you are talking.	
You told a friend a secret and then found out from another friend that they told them about it.	
A friend keeps being negative about another friend, whom you actually like.	
A friend has suddenly stopped talking to you, and you don't know why.	
A friend has started hanging out with a different group of friends, and you miss spending time with them.	
A friend keeps pestering you and doesn't understand that you are sometimes busy with other things such as homework.	
A friend has told you a third friend no longer wants to be friends with you. You have no idea whether this is true.	

3.1 Giving your consent

Strand:	Resources:
• Relationships and sex education	• Book Two: pp. 18–19 • Worksheet 3.1

Learning objective:	Key words:
• To understand that consent must be given for any sexual activity	consent, permission

• Note that this is potentially a sensitive/embarrassing topic, so think about the students you'll be teaching and consider speaking to some of them one to one before the lesson about what is and is not appropriate to say in class (particularly any students who have been inappropriate in previous lessons).

STARTER

• Ask: 'What does consent mean when we're talking about sex?' Write students' suggestions on the board. Then read the introductory paragraphs on page 18 of *Your Choice Book Two*. Explain that consent must be given to take part in any sexual activity; without consent, sexual activity is a criminal offence. (Remind them that the legal age of consent is 16, and why that is the case, particularly to protect young people from harmful relationships with adults.) With the class, reach the 'Fact check' and make sure everyone understands the information.

ACTIVITIES

• Ask students to read 'Five things you should know about consent'. Then, to consolidate their understanding, get students, in pairs, to close their books and to take it in turns to tell each other one of the five key things they need to know about consent.

• With the class, read 'Asking for consent', referring back to the introduction to remind them of the kinds of thing they need to get consent for, including oral sex, genital touching, vaginal or anal penetration. If students need guidance on what these terms mean, you could refer to **Worksheet 3.3**.

• Explain that it is also important to know how to say 'No'. With the class, read 'Saying "No"' on page 19 and then lead a class discussion about what students have learned so far in the lesson.

• Next, encourage students to read the four scenarios in small groups and then to do the discussion task. Invite groups to share their responses in a class discussion, giving reasons for their views.

• Organise students into pairs or groups to do the writing task, creating a podcast for teenagers about what consent means, why it is important and how to ask for it.

PLENARY

• Hand out **Worksheet 3.1** and ask students to work through it in pairs to recap the importance of obtaining consent before and during sexual activities, of not putting pressure on a partner to do something, of stopping when a partner says no, and of being aware of non-verbal cues.

EXTENSION

• Encourage and support students to research what a person who is the victim of a sexual assault should do, using some of the links below. Share students' advice in a class discussion.

Further information and support for teachers:

PSHE Association guidance on teaching about consent: www.pshe-association.org.uk/curriculum-and-resources/resources/guidance-teaching-about-consent-pshe-education-key

NHS, 'Help after rape and sexual assault':
www.nhs.uk/live-well/sexual-health/help-after-rape-and-sexual-assault/

Video, 'All about consent – what does consent look like' (4 mins – NB this is quite a mature video):
www.plannedparenthood.org/learn/teens/sex/all-about-consent

Further information and support for students:

Rape Crisis national freephone helpline: 0808 802 9999. Open all year 12–2.30 p.m. and 7–9.30 p.m.

Video, '6 simple ways to understand consent' (2 mins): www.healthforteens.co.uk/sexual-health/consent-and-the-law/video-6-simple-ways-to-understand-consent/

C is for **Checking**

Check that your partner is comfortable with what you are doing together. Consent needs to be ongoing. So you need to keep checking that they are enjoying themselves and want to continue. Remember that they have the right to change their mind and to withdraw consent at any point if they don't like what you are doing.

O is for **Objecting**

If you want to stop what you are doing, make your objection clearly and firmly, so that there can be no doubt that you are objecting to it.

N is for **No**

No means no. If you continue after your partner has said no, you are committing an offence. You could end up in serious trouble.

S is for **Stop**

If your partner objects and says no, then it is up to you to stop. Otherwise you will be taking advantage of your partner and abusing them.

E is for **Ensuring**

Whatever sexual activity you are participating in, it is up to you to ensure that your partner is a willing participant. If you get the impression through your partner's body language that they have ceased to enjoy themselves, you need to find out whether they want to continue.

N is for **No**

A reminder that no always means no.

T is for **Talking**

A lot of problems can be avoided if you talk to your partner before you have sex and while you are having sex. Tell each other what you would like to do and what you don't want to do. Communicating your thoughts and feelings about what is acceptable and unacceptable will help to prevent misunderstandings and help you to have enjoyable experiences, rather than ones that you may later regret.

Strand:	**Resources:**
• Relationships and sex education	• Book Two: pp. 20–21 • Worksheet 3.2

Learning objective:	**Key words:**
• To identify strategies to deal with being pressured to have sex	sex, virginity, pressurisation, consent

• As with the previous lesson, think about the students you'll be teaching and consider speaking to some of them one to one before the lesson or changing some parts of your lesson plan if necessary. For example, are there students who have misbehaved in class before and may be likely to make inappropriate comments? Or students with safeguarding issues who may have experienced or witnessed inappropriate sexual activity or comments? Think carefully about where extra care needs to be taken.

STARTER

• Ask students if there is too much discussion and focus on sex for teenagers, and where this pressure might be coming from. Ask them to read the introduction and 'Fact check' on page 20 of *Your Choice Book Two*, reminding them of the legal age of consent.

ACTIVITIES

• Ask students to read 'Deciding whether you are ready to take things further' before working in small groups to do questions **1** and **2** of 'Your choice'. Invite groups to share their responses in a class discussion, giving reasons for their views.

• Next, ask students to read 'Sex and peer pressure' and 'How to deal with sexual pressure', before doing the 'Discuss' task in small groups. Again, invite groups to share their responses in a class discussion, giving reasons for their views. Encourage them to try to come to a consensus on how best to deal with sexual pressure.

PLENARY

• Hand out **Worksheet 3.2** and ask students, in pairs, to read the extract from *The Girls' Guide to Growing Up Great* and answer the questions that follow it. Invite pairs to share their responses in a class discussion. *Answers: **1.** Someone who has never had sex; **2.** No; **3.** Yours – no one should force you; **4.** 16; **5.** Yes – it is an offence that could ruin your career; **6.** Some cultures and religions say you shouldn't have sex before marriage.*

RESEARCH

• Direct students to some of the links below and ask them to do more research. Ask them to write a list of anything new they have learned from these websites not already covered in the lesson. Invite students to share their lists with the rest of the class, so that everyone can benefit from the findings.

EXTENSION

• Ask students to fold a sheet of A4 paper in half and to make an A5 leaflet on the ways of dealing with sexual pressure, how to manage peer pressure and how to make good decisions about sex.

Further information and support:

Childline advice on sex and relationships: www.childline.org.uk/info-advice/friends-relationships-sex/sex-relationships

Brook provides free and confidential sexual health and wellbeing advice and support: www.brook.org.uk

NSPCC, '40% of teenage girls pressured into having sex':
www.nspcc.org.uk/what-we-do/news-opinion/40-percent-teenage-girls-pressured-into-sex

Losing your virginity

You may have heard people talking about losing your virginity and wondered what that means. Or perhaps your mates have been discussing who is and who is not a virgin. A virgin is someone who hasn't had sex, so losing your virginity is a way of describing the first time you've had sex. That's it. There is no hidden meaning there. Sometimes people will call someone a virgin in a nasty way, as if to say there is something wrong with them. That's just not true. There is nothing wrong in not having sex with someone; even once you are over 16, having sex with someone should be your choice and your choice only. Your body, your choice and your business.

The age of consent

The more you hear about sex, the more you talk about it with friends, or see stuff on telly, music videos, or movies, the more interested you'll get. Of course, at some stage you'll want to experiment. It's really natural to want more but – and this is the most important thing I can say – do remember that the law of this country is that girls and boys must not have sex until they are 16. This is known as the age of consent. The idea is that the average boy or girl who is under 16 will not be ready for the emotional consequences of sex. Letting someone get that close to you is a massively big deal. Don't ever think about doing it to make someone like you, don't even think about doing it to look good in front of your mates and don't even think about doing it until you are good and ready and know you can really trust the person you are with. Seriously. And when I say it is against the law, I mean that you or the person you are with (especially if they are over 16) can get into trouble with life-long consequences. Plenty of people don't have sex until they are much older than 16 – late teens/early 20s (and some maybe older still). In some cultures or religions and/or according to some people's personal belief systems, couples should not have sex until they are married.

From Sophie Elkan, *The Girls' Guide to Growing Up Great*

1. What is a virgin?

   ....

2. Is there anything wrong with being a virgin?

   ....

3. Whose choice is it to have sex?

   ....

4. What is the age of consent?

   ....

5. Can you get in trouble with the law for having sex under 16?

   ....

6. Where else do restrictions on having sex come from?

   ....

   ....

Strand:	**Resources:**
• Relationships and sex education	• Book Two: pp. 22–23 • Worksheet 3.3

Learning objective:	**Key words:**
• To explore issues around when is the right time to start having sex and examine the dangers of having sex too early	contraception

• See the advice given at the start of 3.1 and 3.2. For this lesson, think in particular about shy students who might be embarrassed to get things wrong, particularly when it comes to sex myths at the beginning. **Worksheet 3.3** has been included to help you answer any questions students might have. This could be shared at any point in the teaching sequence for Unit 3.

STARTER

• Introduce some myths about sex, such as you can't get pregnant if you have sex standing up, it always hurts when you have sex, and having sex makes a guy grow taller. Ask students to discuss any myths they have heard about sex. Encourage students to laugh about the ones that clearly aren't true.

ACTIVITIES

• Ask students to read 'The first time' on page 22 of *Your Choice Book Two*, and then go on to read 'Teenagers talk about their first experiences of sex'. Organise students into small groups to do the first discussion task, before bringing the class back together to compare groups' responses and discuss the issues raised in the text. Ask if they were surprised to read what percentage of young people felt they had not been ready when they lost their virginity. Explore the reasons for not feeling ready, e.g. not being open and honest with the person it happened with. Remind them of their discussions about peer pressure in the previous lesson.

• On their own, or in pairs if students need more support, ask students to read 'Ask Erica' and then to do the writing task that follows. Invite students to share their replies with the class and discuss the different advice they gave.

• Get students to read Kristen's story, and then, in groups, to do the discussion activity that follows it. Bring the class back together to share groups' responses and discuss their opinions. Do they have different views on how Kristen, her friends and Carl should have behaved?

PLENARY

• Organise students into groups of four and ask them to write a script of what Kristen's parents might have said to her if she had told them. Tell them that they are going to act out the scene, with one person playing Kristen, two playing her parents and the fourth person observing.

• Observe groups' role plays and then invite one or two groups to perform theirs in front of the class. You could choose one role play where the parents are understanding and one where they are not. Then lead a class discussion on what they have learned from the lesson as a whole.

EXTENSION

• Ask students to write an article two to three paragraphs long, to go on a teen website, about the importance of not having sex until you are ready, using what they have learned in the lesson as well as additional online research.

Further information and support for students:

NHS, 'When sex goes wrong': www.nhs.uk/live-well/sexual-health/when-sex-goes-wrong/

'What happens the first time you have sex?': www.plannedparenthood.org/learn/teens/sex/virginity/what-happens-first-time-you-have-sex

Q. Does having sex for the first time hurt?

A. The first time can be really enjoyable for both of you, if you feel ready and are considerate to each other. If sex feels uncomfortable, stop what you're doing, talk to your partner, and try something different if you choose to start again.

Q. Is it normal if I bleed after having sex for the first time?

A. Some girls may bleed the first time they have sex. Sometimes the hymen – the ring of tissue that covers the opening to the vagina – may tear if it stretches too quickly. For others, the hymen may already have been broken by sports or inserting tampons.

Q. What is anal sex?

A. Anal sex is when a boy puts his penis into the anus of his partner. It is important to use a condom when having anal sex to protect against STIs. It is also helpful to use a water-based lubricant during anal sex. (Remember, oil-based lubricants such as Vaseline® can stop a condom working.)

Q. What is oral sex?

A. Oral sex is when someone uses their mouth and tongue to stimulate their partner's genitals. A boy's partner will put his penis in their mouth in order to stimulate him. A girl's partner will use their mouth to stimulate her genital area, including her clitoris. It is wise to use a condom or a dental dam during oral sex to protect against STIs.

Q. What if I don't have an orgasm during sex?

A. Everybody is different and over time you will work out what feels good for you. Talk to your partner about how you feel. If sex is painful, stop and try again another time. If you feel your body is not ready before you begin, spend longer on kissing and foreplay until you do feel ready.

Q. I'm worried that my penis is too small.

A. Penises come in many shapes and sizes, though they are more similar in size when they are erect. You and your partner should be able to enjoy sex whatever size your penis is.

Q. What is masturbation and does everyone do it?

Masturbation is when someone strokes or rubs their own genitals in order to get sexual pleasure. Some people masturbate regularly. Others do not masturbate at all. Masturbation should always be done in private.

4.1 STIs

Strand:	Resources:
• Relationships and sex education	• Book Two: pp. 24–25 • Worksheet 4.1 • Bananas and condoms

Learning objective:	Key words:
• To examine what STIs are and how to protect yourself against them	chlamydia, protected sex, unprotected sex, STI

• This is another lesson dealing with a sensitive topic. Think about how you are going to teach this lesson beforehand (particularly the worksheet) with strategies that allow a sensible level of humour without it turning into one big joke. This can involve talking to individual students (the 'class clowns') beforehand, and owning and directing the humour yourself.

STARTER

• Ask students what they think 'unprotected sex' means. Elicit from them what they think the dangers of unprotected sex are, and why. Dispel any myths and clarify any areas of confusion.

ACTIVITIES

• Read 'STIs: your questions answered' and 'Protecting yourself against STIs' on page 24 of *Your Choice Book Two* with the class. Lead a discussion of the issues raised and make sure all students understand the answers to the questions. Ask what they think is the most important information they have learned from these two sections, giving reasons for their views.

• If you feel it's appropriate, you could use **Worksheet 4.1** to demonstrate putting a condom on a banana, and/or getting students to do it. Be prepared for lots of laughing, but make sure they understand that there is a serious side to the activity.

• Ask students, on their own or in pairs, to read 'Ask Erica' and then write Erica's reply to Penny. Encourage students to share their replies in groups and invite some to share them in a class discussion.

• Organise students into pairs or groups to read 'Chlamydia: a "silent" STI' and 'Jayden's story', and then to do the research task. They could visit some of the websites listed below. They should then design a poster warning about what chlamydia is and its dangers.

PLENARY

• Hold a class discussion where students talk about what more can be done to help young people protect themselves from STIs, and what will work best in persuading young people to take this seriously, based on what they have learned in the lesson.

RESEARCH

• Support students to use the links below to find out more about the other STIs mentioned, such as herpes and genital warts – how they are transmitted and how best to protect themselves against them.

EXTENSION

• Ask students to create a podcast for teenagers, warning about the top five dangers of unprotected sex. These could include: pregnancy, serious STIs (HIV, syphilis), problematic STIs (herpes, genital warts), anxiety (from not knowing whether you're infected or a symptomless carrier) and regret.

Further information and support:

NHS, 'STIs': www.nhs.uk/conditions/sexually-transmitted-infections-stis/

NHS, 'Sexual health': www.nhs.uk/live-well/sexual-health/

Teens Health, 'Chlamydia': https://kidshealth.org/en/teens/std-chlamydia.html

Brook, 'STIs': www.brook.org.uk/your-life/category/stis

Sexwise, 'STIs': www.sexwise.fpa.org.uk/stis

Here is some information on how to use a condom. You can practise putting on a condom using a banana and following the first five steps below.

1. Carefully open the foil packaging which the condom is wrapped in, taking care not to tear the condom.

2. Hold the tip of the condom between your forefinger and thumb to make sure it's put on the right way round and no air is trapped inside (the condom may split if air is trapped inside).

3. Place the condom over the tip of the penis.

4. While squeezing the tip of the condom, roll it down over the length of the erect penis.

5. If the condom will not unroll, it's probably on inside out – start again with a new condom as there may be sperm on it.

6. Make sure that the condom stays in place while you're having sex. If it comes off, stop and put on a new one.

7. After ejaculation (when the boy or man has come) and while the penis is still hard, hold the condom in place and carefully withdraw the penis from your partner's body.

8. You should only take the condom off the penis when there's no further contact with your partner's body.

9. Wrap the used condom in a tissue and put it in the bin. You should never flush condoms down the toilet as they may block the toilet and can cause environmental damage.

Source: www.nhs.uk/conditions/contraception/how-do-i-use-condom/

Symptoms of STIs

Strand:	Resources:
• Relationships and sex education	• Book Two: pp. 26–27 • Worksheet 4.2

Learning objective:	Key words:
• To identify the symptoms of several major STIs, and how to protect yourself against these	STI, gonorrhoea, syphilis, genital warts, pubic lice

STARTER

* Before the lesson, check the current rates of infection for different STIs within the UK on the Gov.UK site, looking particularly at rates of infection for young people. Draw on this knowledge during the lesson.

* Ask students what STIs they know of and if they know what the symptoms are. Emphasise that it is possible to have an STI without having any obvious symptoms.

ACTIVITIES

* Explain that you are going to do something different this lesson, called 'Jigsaw reading'. Organise students into groups of five, with each student reading about a different STI as described on pages 26 and 27 of *Your Choice Book Two*. One student reads about gonorrhoea, one about syphilis, one about HIV, one about genital warts, and the fifth about genital herpes and pubic lice. They then describe the STI to the rest of the group. Once everyone in the group knows about all of the STIs, they work together to rank the diseases in order of seriousness. Invite groups to share their rankings with the rest of the class and discuss any differences. There is no correct order, but students should explain their rankings.

* Ask students to work in their groups again to do the first discussion task on page 27, before bringing the class back together to share their responses and give their reasons.

* On their own, or in pairs for students needing more support, ask students to read 'Ask Erica' and then write a reply. Encourage students to compare their replies in groups.

* Ask students to complete the crossword on **Worksheet 4.2**. Again, students requiring more support can do this in pairs. *Answers: 1. herpes; 2. test; 3. syphilis; 4. symptoms; 5. pregnancy; 6. condom; 7. virgin; 8. unsafe; 9. wart; 10. chlamydia.*

* With the students, read the final writing task and discuss what information they think the video should contain.

PLENARY

* Ask students to create a storyboard giving details of what each part of the video would contain. Then bring the class back together to discuss their stories.

EXTENSION

* Ask students to choose one of the STIs from the first activity and research recent infection rates for that STI in the UK. Encourage them to summarise their findings in a report of two or three paragraphs.

Further information and support for students:

NHS, 'STIs': www.nhs.uk/conditions/sexually-transmitted-infections-stis/

Brook, 'STIs': www.brook.org.uk/your-life/category/stis

NHS, 'Sexual health': www.nhs.uk/live-well/sexual-health/

Sexwise: www.sexwise.fpa.org.uk/

Annual rates of STI infection: https://www.gov.uk/government/statistics/sexually-transmitted-infections-stis-annual-data-tables

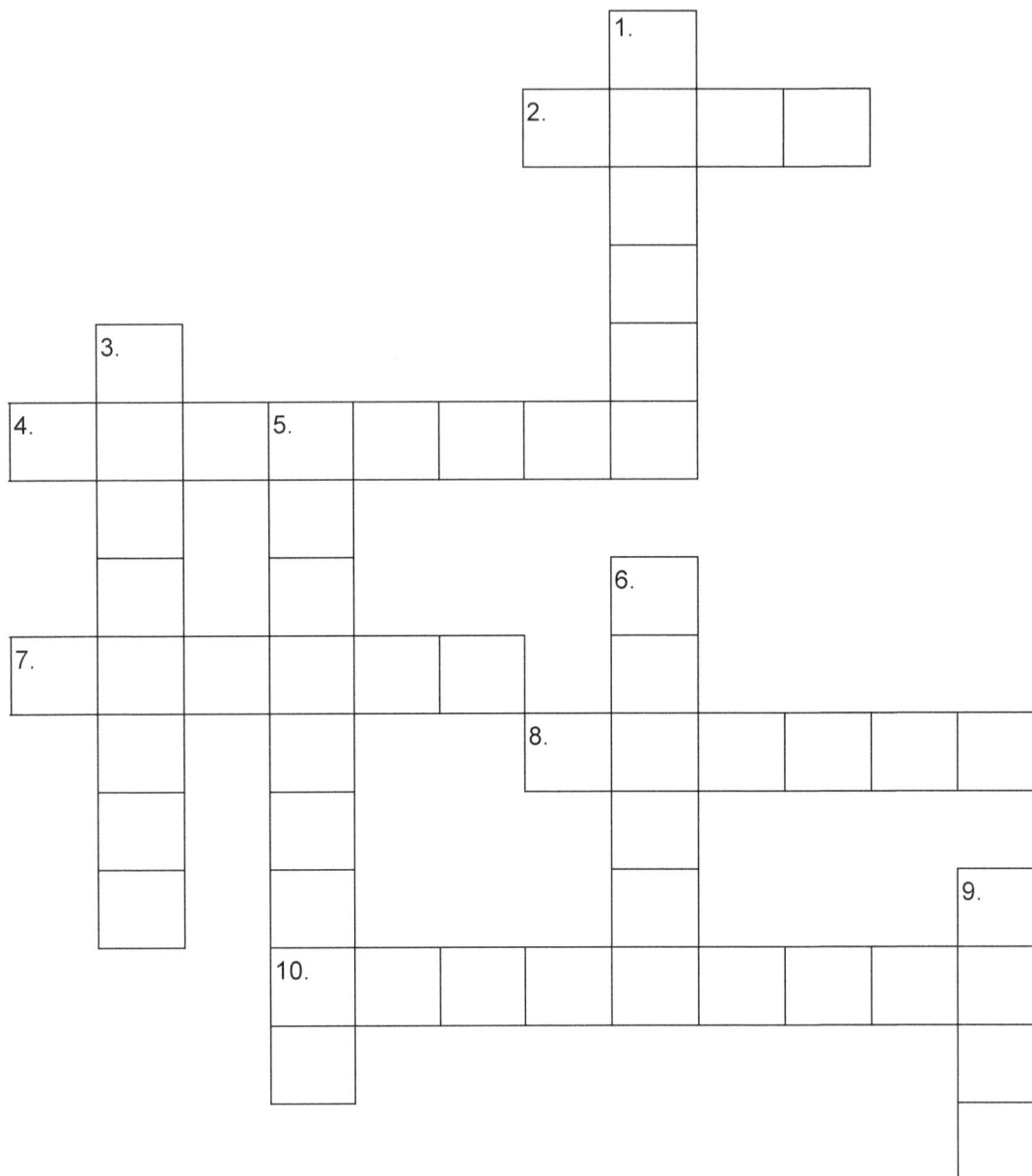

Across

2. At a sexual health clinic samples of your blood and urine are taken to ____ whether you have an STI. (4)
4. Many people do not know they have an STI because they have none of these. (8)
7. Someone who has never had sex, and therefore cannot have caught an STI. (6)
8. Another word for 'unprotected' in terms of sex. (6)
10. Type of STI that is very common among young people and can lead to infertility. (9)

Down

1. A virus that can appear around the mouth as sores, but also has a genital version which is an STI. (6)
3. A serious STI which can lead to insanity and death. (8)
5. Possibly the biggest consequence of unprotected vaginal sex. (9)
6. A good form of protection against STIs. (6)
9. One of these on a man's genitals is an indication he has an STI. (4)

Strand:	Resources:
• Relationships and sex education	• Book Two: pp. 28–29 • Worksheet 4.3

Learning objective	Key words:
• To understand what a sexual health clinic does and how to deal with an STI	STI, screening, C-Card

STARTER

• Elicit from students what they already know about sexual health clinics, noting their answers on the board. Keep any myths up there, and rub these out as the lesson continues, replacing them with the correct information.

ACTIVITIES

• Ask students to read 'Sexual health clinics: your questions answered', 'How to deal with an STI' and 'Screening for STIs' and then to do the first discussion task in small groups. Get them to list what they think are the five most useful pieces of advice and to rank them in order from the most useful. Encourage groups to share their lists in a class discussion, comparing them and discussing which pieces of advice surprised them most, giving reasons for their views.

• Ask if they have any other questions and if there is anything they would now like to add or remove from the list on the board.

• Organise students into pairs or groups to read the newspaper article on page 29, and then discuss the questions that follow it. Again, invite students to share their responses in a class discussion.

• Ask students to read the information about the C-Card scheme on page 29 and then to do the discussion activity that follows it as a class.

PLENARY

• Ask students to complete the true/false activity on **Worksheet 4.3** to consolidate what they have learned in this lesson. *All the statements are true, apart from the following, which are false: **2**, **6** (the true figure is half) and **7**.*

EXTENSION

• Students should use the internet to research where there is a sexual health clinic in their local area, or how to sign up to the C-Card scheme.

Further information and support

NHS, 'Guide to sexual health services': www.nhs.uk/using-the-nhs/nhs-services/sexual-health-services/guide-to-sexual-health-services/

Brook Young People, 'STIs': www.brook.org.uk/your-life/category/stis

Free chlamydia testing kit: www.freetest.me/

Study these statements and decide which are true and which are false, writing T or F next to each one. Then compare your answers with a partner.

Statement	True or false?
1. Self-testing kits are free to order on the internet.	
2. The majority of young people have a sexually transmitted disease.	
3. If you see a doctor and they find out you have an STI, they will keep your information confidential.	
4. You should have an STI check when you change partners.	
5. If you think you have an STI, you should stop having sex.	
6. One third of young people do not use condoms for sex with a new partner.	
7. You always have to make an appointment for an STI clinic.	
8. Condoms significantly reduce the chance of catching many STIs.	

Strand:	Resources:
• Relationships and sex education	• Book Two: pp. 30–31 • Worksheets 5.1a and 5.1b

Learning objective:	Key words:
• To distinguish between different types of abuse	physical abuse, emotional abuse, sexual abuse, verbal abuse, neglect

• Please note that both lessons 5.1 and 5.2 contain sensitive topics, with the potential to trigger traumatic memories for those who have suffered abuse. You might like to consider speaking to some students one to one before these lessons and adapting the lessons to fit the students' needs through differentiation, paying attention to the emotional reaction of students as the lesson is being taught, and intervening or changing what is being taught as appropriate.

STARTER

• Write the definition of abuse from page 30 on the board. Ask students whether abuse is occurring in these situations: a student is shouted at by a parent every day, regardless of their behaviour; a student is being slapped at least once a week by a parent. Both are clear examples of abuse – verbal and physical.

ACTIVITIES

• Ask students to read 'Types of child abuse' and 'Physical abuse' and then work in small groups to do the discussion task that follows. Then hand out **Worksheet 5.1a**, for students to complete in pairs. *Answers: 1. Physical abuse; 2. Verbal abuse; 3. Sexual abuse; 4. Neglect (or poverty); 5. Emotional abuse; 6. Physical abuse; 7. Sexual abuse; 8. Emotional abuse; 9. Sexual abuse; 10. Verbal abuse. Note that this is a good opportunity to review the lesson, and stop it and teach alternative material if any student is clearly showing signs of reacting negatively and emotionally to the material.*

• Ask students to read 'Facts about abuse' and then to do the discussion task in pairs. Pair students who require more challenge with those who need more support. Some of the facts may surprise them – in particular, **b)** and **e)**. Other points worth discussing further are: **a)**, **d)**, **g)** and **j)**.

• Divide the class into groups to read 'Sexual abuse – it's important to tell someone' on page 31 and then do the discussion task that follows. *Answers: 1. In order to stop the abuse; 2. It can make it difficult to trust people, to form relationships and to concentrate on school work; it can cause low self-esteem and depression or serious mental illness in the long term.*

• Organise students into pairs to read 'Help and support' and do the research task that follows it.

PLENARY

• Hand out **Worksheet 5.1b** and go through it with the students, making sure that everyone is clear about how a formal debate works. Then allocate roles (you might like to be the Chair) and divide the class into for and against, explaining that you are going to hold a debate on the motion 'It is a child's right not to be physically punished in any way'. Point out that smacking somebody is a form of physical abuse, and that the laws against smacking have been tightened up in recent years (e.g. banned in Scotland).

EXTENSION

• Based on their research and what they've learned in the lesson, ask students to create a poster for children their age giving information about types of abuse and details of who to contact for help.

Further information and support for teachers:

NHS, 'Spotting child abuse': www.nhs.uk/live-well/healthy-body/spotting-signs-of-child-sexual-abuse/

Guardian, 'How to get your whole class debating':
www.theguardian.com/higher-education-network/teacher-blog/2012/jun/18/pupil-class-debate

Further information and support for students:

NSPCC, 'Types of abuse': http://www.nspcc.org.uk/preventing-abuse/child-abuse-and-neglect/

Childline, 'Abuse and safety': www.childline.org.uk/info-advice/bullying-abuse-safety/abuse-safety/

Thinkuknow, 'What is sexual abuse?': www.thinkuknow.co.uk/11_13/Need-advice/Sexual-abuse/

Young Minds, 'Abuse': https://youngminds.org.uk/find-help/feelings-and-symptoms/abuse/

Worksheet 5.1a Types of abuse

Each incident described below is an example of abuse. Decide what kind of abuse it is and note that down in the right-hand column.

Incident	Type of abuse
1. A parent kicks a child regularly as a punishment.	
2. One teenager is constantly bullying another at school by making nasty comments about their clothes, appearance and family.	
3. A person on the internet is grooming a child, with the aim of getting naked photos of them.	
4. A child doesn't have enough to eat each week.	
5. A teenage girl is never allowed to go out with her female friends, because her boyfriend controls her social life and forbids it.	
6. Hard smacking is used as a punishment on a child, and it leaves a mark.	
7. A group of boys is always shouting sexual remarks at a group of girls in the school corridor.	
8. A parent is very strict with their child and never lets them go out to play with others.	
9. A much older man in a chatroom wants to talk with a young person over the phone because he finds it sexy.	
10. A young person can't go on Facebook because a group of girls is always posting nasty, negative things about them.	

Worksheet 5.1b Holding a formal debate

A formal debate is different from a group discussion. For a debate, the class will be divided into sides of an argument, one in favour, the proposition, and one against, the opposition. The sides take it in turns to present their arguments and respond to the other side, trying to persuade the rest of the class one way or the other.

The 'audience' (the rest of the class) has the opportunity to question the speakers and to give their own opinions.

A chairperson and a timekeeper, who keep events moving, oversee the whole thing.

Chair:	This is the person who decides who will speak in the debate, and ensures that a range of different opinions are heard.
Vice-Chair (or Timekeeper):	This is the person who keeps track of the order in which people will speak, and assists the Chair.
Motion:	This is what is going to be discussed. For example: 'This house believes that Brexit is a bad idea.'
Amendments:	These change the motion that is being discussed. For example: 'This house believes that a hard Brexit is a bad idea, but a soft Brexit is a good one.'
Proposer:	This is the person who argues first in favour of the motion. They speak first in the debate, usually for 3–5 minutes.
Opposer:	This is the person who argues first against the motion. They speak second in the debate, usually for 3–5 minutes.
Seconders:	There is one seconder in favour of the motion, and one against. They speak third and fourth during the debate, usually for 2–3 minutes each.

After the proposer, opposer, seconders and the movers of any amendments have spoken, the Chair will open up the debate to anyone present.

Giving way:	When a person is speaking, somebody else may ask them to give way – in other words, let someone else speak. This can be to clarify a point or to ask a brief question.

At the end of the debate, the amendments are voted on. Then the motion, as amended, is voted on.

5.2 Grooming

<table>
<tr><td>

Strand:
- Relationships and sex education

</td><td>

Resources:
- Book Two: pp. 32–33

</td></tr>
<tr><td>

Learning objective:
- To understand what grooming is
- To develop strategies to stay safe from the dangers of grooming

</td><td>

Key words:
  grooming, to go private, flattery

</td></tr>
</table>

- See the pre-lesson notes for lesson 5.1, which also apply here.

STARTER

- Elicit from students what grooming means and note their suggestions on the board before reading the introduction on page 32 of *Your Choice Book Two*. Ask students if they have heard of any cases of grooming in the media (e.g. Rotherham, Rochdale, Oxford). Only touch on these superficially and do not go into detail about them (see 'Guidlines on teaching sensitive material' below).

ACTIVITIES

- Ask students to read the 'Fact check', 'The tricks that are used to groom you' and Mared's Story. Then organise them into small groups to discuss what they think can be done to avoid each of the six online tricks that are mentioned.

- Still in their groups, ask students to read the 'Scenario' on page 33 and then do part **1** of the discussion activity. Bring the class back together and ask groups to share their suggestions. Ask what advice they would give to the young person in the scenario. Then continue the class discussion for questions **2** and **3**. *Answers: 2. You can't, and therefore you should always treat someone you meet online with caution. Don't meet people in person by yourself. If you do meet (not recommended), do so in a busy public place in the daytime, with a parent, carer or trusted adult. Don't reveal where you live or go to school. 3. Stop the conversation and report it – to parents, to school and if necessary, to the police.*

- Read the paragraph under the 'Discuss' box and make sure that students understand that the victims of grooming are never to blame.

PLENARY

- As a class, read the 'Case study – Rotherham', and then discuss what they can do to keep themselves safe from face-to-face grooming. This includes the answers to question **2** above, as well as never taking drinks, alcohol or drugs from a person you hardly know (and ideally not doing the latter two at all, even from people you do know).

EXTENSION

- Organise students into small mixed-ability groups to do the research and writing tasks.

Further information and support for teachers:

You may want to watch the series *Three Girls* from the BBC as background, but this is too hard-hitting for students of this age: www.bbc.co.uk/programmes/b08rgd5n

PHSE Association, Guidelines on teaching sensitive material: www.pshe-association.org.uk/news/warning-against-using-breck%E2%80%99s-last-game

BBC News, 'Instagram biggest for child grooming, NSPCC finds': www.bbc.co.uk/news/uk-47410520

NSPCC, 'Grooming': www.nspcc.org.uk/preventing-abuse/child-abuse-and-neglect/grooming/

Children's Society, 'Old enough to know better?': www.childrenssociety.org.uk/old-enough-to-know-better

Connect Safely, 'How to recognize grooming': www.connectsafely.org/how-to-recognize-grooming/

Further information and support for students:

Child Exploitation and Online Protection (CEOP): www.ceop.police.uk/safety-centre/

Thinkuknow: www.thinkuknow.co.uk/

Childline: www.childline.org.uk

Strand:	**Resources:**
• Relationships and sex education	• Book Two: pp. 34–35 • Worksheet 5.3

Learning objective:	**Key words:**
• To examine the dangers of sexting and identify ways of protecting yourself	sexting, social media, cyber-safety

STARTER

• Ask the class to suggest what they think sexting is and the dangers attached to it. Note their suggestions on the board.

ACTIVITIES

• With the class read the 'Fact check' and 'Think before you click' on page 34 of *Your Choice Book Two*, and then discuss the list of questions. Ask students if they were aware of the law and, if not, whether they were surprised about it. Ask whether the questions convince them that a young person should always refuse to send such pictures, and that no one should ever ask for them. Encourage the students to give reasons for their views.

• Ask students to read 'Amy's story' on their own and then to work in pairs on 'Your choice'. Invite pairs to share their responses with the class and ensure that they have distinguished correctly between fact and opinions. *Answers: 1. Opinion; 2. Fact; 3. Fact; 4. Opinion but wrong; 5. Opinion; 6. Opinion; 7. Fact.* Encourage the students to give reasons for their opinions in part **2**.

• Get students to read 'Ask Erica' on their own, or in pairs for students needing more support, and then to draft a reply to Harvey. Remind them to look back at the questions in 'Think before you click'.

• Ask students to read 'Sharing revealing photos and videos of yourself online' and the scenarios and advice that follow. In groups, encourage students to discuss each scenario in turn, thinking about what they would say to the people involved to try to convince them not to send the pictures. Then ask them to work in pairs to do the role play, bearing in mind what they've discussed.

PLENARY

• Hand out **Worksheet 5.3** and ask students to fill it in on their own, before working in groups to reflect on their responses. Encourage students to share what they have learned from the role plays and the rest of the lesson in a class discussion.

EXTENSION

• Ask students to research how the law on upskirting has recently changed as a result of a new Act of Parliament championed by MP Wera Hobhouse.

Further information and support for teachers:

UKCCIS advice for schools on preventative education and managing reports of sexting:
www.gov.uk/government/groups/uk-council-for-child-internet-safety-ukccis

NSPCC – Keeping children safe: support on sexting:
www.nspcc.org.uk/preventing-abuse/keeping-children-safe/sexting/

TES Online Safety Special Edition (2017):
www.tes.com/news/keeping-children-safe-online-tes-safeguarding-special-issue-free-download

Further information and support for students:

Childline, 'Sexting': www.childline.org.uk/info-advice/bullying-abuse-safety/online-mobile-safety/sexting/

Thinkuknow, Child Exploitation and Online Protection: www.ceop.police.uk/safety-centre/

Worksheet 5.3 Sexting role plays

Scenario 1: ....

What did it feel like playing this role?

....

What advice did you give?

....

What have you learned from this scenario?

....

....

Scenario 2: ....

What did it feel like playing this role?

....

What advice did you give?

....

What have you learned from this scenario?

....

....

Scenario 3: ....

What did it feel like playing this role?

....

What advice did you give?

....

What have you learned from this scenario?

....

....

Strand:	**Resources:**
• Social education	• Book Two: pp. 36–37 • Worksheet 6.1

Learning objective:	**Key words:**
• To understand what stereotyping is and the negative consequences it has • To be able to spot and challenge stereotyping	stereotyping, discrimination, racism, gender, sexism

STARTER

- Introduce the topic by eliciting the meaning of stereotyping from students, or providing them with the definition from the textbook. Ask students if they can think of any groups that are likely to be stereotyped (e.g. girls, boys, young people, older people) and note them on the board.

ACTIVITIES

- With the class, read the information on page 36 of *Your Choice Book Two*. Make sure that students realise that stereotyping can have serious negative consequences.

- Ask students to read the statements in the 'Discuss' box, either on their own or in pairs if they need more support, and decide which are based on stereotypes. Then organise them into groups to discuss their answers, giving their reasons. Monitor the discussions, providing feedback and answering questions.

- Explain to students that they are going to think about gender stereotyping. Get students, in pairs, to do parts **1** and **2** of 'Your choice'. When they have completed their tables, encourage students to discuss their choices with another pair and then with the rest of the class. Be sure to point out that any joking, sexist behaviour is inappropriate, and explain why.

- Get students to do part **3** of 'Your choice' in small groups and then, still in their groups, to do the discussion activity. If they can't think of any real-life examples, ask them to imagine what these experiences might have been like, in light of what they've learned.

- Ask students to read the information on page 37 and to answer the discussion questions in different groups. Bring the class back together to share responses and reasoning.

- Support students to do the research task, sourcing media images that reinforce stereotypes or misrepresent different groups, such as young men or women. With the students, choose the best examples and create a stereotyping wall chart for the classroom. Further material is available from the website links below.

PLENARY

- Hand out **Worksheet 6.1** and ask students to read the definition of positive discrimination and the six statements that follow it. Ask them to discuss which statements they agree with and whether they think that positive discrimination can ever be justified.

EXTENSION

- Based on their earlier research, get students to choose what they consider to be the worst example of stereotyping. Encourage them to write to the newspaper, magazine or media outlet that published it, challenging them on their stereotyping and requesting details of what policies the organisation has in place to combat stereotyping and discrimination.

Further information and support for teachers:

Anti-bullying support: www.ditchthelabel.org

BBC Bitesize, video clips on dealing with stereotyping: www.bbc.com/bitesize/topics/z3brd2p

Free TES resources on dealing with stereotyping:
www.tes.com/teaching-resource/challenging-stereotypes-and-discrimination-6298553

Worksheet 6.1 Positive discrimination

Positive discrimination means making sure that people such as women, members of minority ethnic groups and people with disabilities get a fair share of the opportunities available.
So, for example, you could positively discriminate for university applications by making it easier for students from a poorer social background to get into university, rather than requiring all applicants to have exactly the same A level grades.

The problem with positive discrimination is that somebody always loses in order for another person to gain. So, if we did allow a student from a poorer background to go to university, a student with higher grades from a richer background might miss out.

Although positive discrimination can be a blunt tool, in the case of UK universities, they use a student's background as only one of a number of factors to determine who goes to university. Others include the strength of an applicant's personal statement, references (including attendance and punctuality record), extra-curricular activities, including hobbies and interests, work experience, ethnic background, type of school attended and the most important factor – predicted exam grades.

Positive discrimination is used in a number of other areas in the UK. The Labour Party and the Liberal Democrats have used it to select more female and ethnic minority candidates to become MPs.

In groups, read the following statements. Which ones do you agree with? Give reasons for your views.

'It's right that a poorer student from a comprehensive should require lower entrance grades for university than a richer student from a private school. The latter has had a lot more support to get to uni – this levels out the playing field.'
Stephen, Cardiff

'Women should be elected to Parliament on their own merits, not simply because there are not enough of them.'
Jessica, Birmingham

'Positive discrimination can never be justified. There is always a loser, which is unfair.'
Charlie, Brighton

'Positive discrimination should only be used rarely, when every other option has been exhausted.'
Lisa, Edinburgh

'Positive discrimination should only be used occasionally – when candidates for a job are absolutely equal in terms of experience and qualifications. Then, the job should go to the ethnic minority candidate or the woman or the person with the disability.'
Sasha, Leeds

'We encourage positive action, not positive discrimination.'
Douglas, Bristol

Strand:
• Social education

Resources:
• Book Two: pp. 38–39
• Worksheet 6.2
• Photos of people from groups that may experience prejudice, such as homeless people, skinheads, travellers

Learning objective:
• To understand what prejudice is
• To understand why prejudice occurs, how to spot it and how to combat it

Key words:
prejudice, Roma, Gypsies, Travellers

STARTER

• Ask students to tell you something they learned about stereotyping in the last lesson and note their ideas on the board. Make sure that the definition of stereotyping is covered again. Elicit from students their understanding of 'prejudice' and then read the definition on page 38 of *Your Choice Book Two*.

ACTIVITIES

• Ask students to read the introduction and 'Are you prejudiced?' on page 38. You could show photos of homeless people sleeping rough, or skinheads walking down the street, to prompt discussion before getting students to do 'Your choice' on their own. Ask students what assumptions they make when they see these images. Is this stereotyping or prejudice, or both?

• Invite students to share their views and to compare them in a class discussion.

• Ask students to read the sections on 'Groups' and 'Belonging to groups' and then to do the writing task. Students who need more support can be paired up, while those requiring more challenge should be encouraged to think of all the different groups they belong to inside and outside school.

• Invite students to share their responses in a class discussion, encouraging them to find out what they have in common.

• Ask students to read the 'Fact check', 'Bailey's story' and 'Racism on Ryanair' and then, in pairs, to discuss the views in part **1** of the discussion activity.

PLENARY

• Organise students into groups to do part **2** of the discussion task. Then encourage them to share their answers and discuss them as a class.

RESEARCH

• Support students to research what hate crimes are most common in your town, area or region, and what is being done to combat such hate crimes.

EXTENSION

• Hand out **Worksheet 6.2** and ask students to work in groups to read the information and discuss the questions. Then discuss the answers as a class to agree a positive class approach to any new arrivals. In particular, ask students to describe how they would like to be treated when arriving at a new school.

Further information and support for teachers:
Free resources on racism and prejudice from the TES: www.tes.com/teaching-resource/racism-pshe-citizenship-lesson-11192377
Video resources on prejudice are available on this site: www.truetube.co.uk
Dealing with prejudice in schools: www.schooltools.info/prejudice-reduction/

'Gypsy, Roma and Traveller people have the worst outcomes of any ethnic group across a huge range of areas, including education, health, employment, criminal justice and hate crime. Too often local authorities and public services fail to differentiate between different groups who have different needs. Our inquiry has found that, while many inequalities have existed for a long time, there has been a persistent failure by both national and local policy-makers to tackle them in any sustained way. This failure has led to services that are ill-equipped to support Gypsy, Roma and Traveller people to use services that they need and are entitled to.

The term Gypsy, Roma and Traveller has been used by policy-makers and researchers to describe a range of ethnic groups or those with nomadic ways of life who are not from a specific ethnicity. In the UK, it is common to differentiate between Gypsies (including English Gypsies, Scottish Gypsy/Travellers, Welsh Gypsies and other Romany people), Irish Travellers, who have specific Irish roots, and Roma, understood to be more recent migrants from Central and Eastern Europe. In continental Europe, however, all groups with nomadic histories are categorised as "Roma", a much broader term that, while it includes Gypsies and Irish Travellers, is not the way in which most British communities would identify themselves.

Gypsies and some Traveller ethnicities have been recognised in law as being ethnic groups protected against discrimination by the Equality Act 2010.

The census recorded 58,000 people as Gypsy/Traveller in 2011 in England and Wales, with a further 4,000 recorded in Scotland. The Government acknowledges that this is likely to be an undercount, with estimates of between 100,000 to 300,000 Gypsy/Traveller people and up to 200,000 Roma people living in the UK.

Less than 5% of Gypsies, Roma and Travellers obtain 5 good GCSE passes at age 16.

A survey carried out by Traveller Movement, a national Gypsy, Roma and Traveller charity, found that, in 2017, 91 per cent of the 199 respondents had experienced discrimination and 77 per cent had experienced hate speech or a hate crime.'

Source: House of Commons Women and Equalities Committee, *Tackling inequalities faced by Gypsy, Roma and Traveller communities Seventh Report of Session 2017–19*

https://publications.parliament.uk/pa/cm201719/cmselect/cmwomeq/360/360.pdf

In groups, discuss the following scenario:

Imagine a Roma family have just moved into the area, and three children from this family are about to start at your school.

* What could you do to help them?
* How would you avoid being discriminatory or prejudiced towards them?
* What could you do to welcome them into the local area?

Recreational drugs

Strand:	Resources:
• Physical health and wellbeing	• Book Two: pp. 40–41
	• Worksheet 7.1

Learning objective:	Key words:
• To discuss the dangers of taking cannabis and MDMA	cannabis, weed, skunk, MDMA, addiction, overdose

STARTER

• Ask students what they already know about cannabis, including all the slang names for it, such as pot and grass. Note that skunk is a particularly strong strain of cannabis. Note these on the board, along with any myths about cannabis they mention. Cross out the myths as you go through the lesson.

ACTIVITIES

• Ask students to read the introduction on page 40 of *Your Choice Book Two* and all the information about cannabis. Then organise them into pairs to list all the arguments for and against decriminalisation and the legalisation of cannabis. Encourage students to compare their answers with another pair, giving reasons for their views. Bring the class back together to discuss what they've learned about cannabis and cross off any myths from the list on the board.

• Still in their pairs, ask students to do the research task about the legalisation of cannabis in Canada and then invite them to share their findings with the class.

• Organise students into groups of four to do the role-play activity at the top of page 41. Allow them time to prepare and then move around the class listening to the role plays and providing support where necessary. Invite two or three groups to perform their role play for the rest of the class.

• Ask students to read the information about MDMA and then do the 'Discuss' task in pairs. Invite pairs to share their lists in a class discussion. See if a consensus can be reached on a list of the top five things.

• Organise students into groups of three to do the role play and monitor these as before. Make sure that each person takes a turn in each role before they talk about what they have learned from the role play.

PLENARY

• Hold a class debate on the motion: 'Cannabis should be completely legalised in the UK'. Points student may wish to consider include decriminalisation (against the law with a fine) rather than full legalisation (no penalty).

RESEARCH

• Support students to find out about the medical uses of cannabis and then report back to the rest of the class. Find out the statistics about the number of hospital admissions for MDMA-related incidents. Are they on the increase and, if so, why?

EXTENSION

• Ask students to complete the wordsearch on **Worksheet 7.1**. *Answers: 1. cannabis, 2. MDMA, 3. legalise, 4. decriminalise, 5. addiction, 6. weed, 7. anxiety, 8. serotonin, 9. panic, 10. dealer, 11. synthetic, 12. overdose.*

Further information and support for teachers:

Mentor-ADEPIS briefing papers with ideas for lessons: mentor-adepis.org/planning-effective-education/

Cannabis, skunk and the teenage brain: parentinfo.org/article/cannabis-skunk-and-the-teenage-brain

'Signs and effects of teen ecstasy use':
www.verywellmind.com/ecstasy-and-teens-is-my-teen-using-ecstasy-2609546

Further information and support for students:

NHS, 'Cannabis: the facts': www.nhs.uk/live-well/healthy-body/cannabis-the-facts/

Teens Health, 'MDMA (Ecstasy)': kidshealth.org/en/teens/ecstasy.html

Brook, 'Drugs': www.brook.org.uk/your-life/drugs

Work out the answers to the following clues and then find the relevant words in the grid below.

1. The most popular illegal drug in the UK, which relaxes you and can make you feel hungry afterwards. (8)

2. An illegal party drug, used at raves and festivals, that heightens awareness. (4)

3. To make a drug fully legal for use. (8)

4. To make a drug less illegal by only having a fine for possessing it. (13)

5. What happens what you can't control wanting more of a drug. (9)

6. A slang word for ordinary forms of cannabis. (4)

7. A feeling of intense worry about what might happen. (7)

8. A chemical in the brain that affects mood. (9)

9. A strong feeling of fear that makes you act without thinking carefully. (5)

10. A person who sells illegal drugs. (6)

11. Describes a drug made from chemicals or artificial substances. (9)

12. When you take too much of a drug and there are serious negative side effects that can kill you. (8)

G	Y	L	Z	A	N	X	I	E	T	Y	U	F	T	G
S	O	E	T	J	D	Y	Q	E	U	G	W	I	C	Y
E	L	G	D	G	A	E	Z	P	I	X	E	F	A	L
R	R	A	P	S	P	N	A	E	R	K	E	F	N	S
O	C	L	A	F	G	X	L	L	Y	P	D	I	N	X
T	F	I	N	T	L	N	R	U	E	R	G	O	A	T
O	O	S	I	M	W	I	D	X	J	R	T	Q	B	J
N	I	E	C	A	D	D	I	C	T	I	O	N	I	A
I	N	D	E	C	R	I	M	I	N	A	L	I	S	E
N	N	A	M	E	Z	P	Q	D	Z	F	Y	H	R	T
A	Z	Z	K	O	V	E	R	D	O	S	E	D	V	Q
L	I	M	Q	U	H	Q	O	H	M	M	A	L	R	T
E	P	S	D	O	S	Y	N	T	H	E	T	I	C	B
R	G	A	B	M	T	V	N	O	J	L	O	Q	J	N
T	F	H	K	C	A	B	S	P	K	X	V	H	G	F

Strand:	Resources:
• Physical health and wellbeing	• Book Two: pp. 42–43 • Worksheet 7.2

Learning objective:	Key words:
• To understand what legal highs are and to examine their dangers	legal highs, LSD, acid

STARTER

● Elicit from students what is meant by 'legal highs', which 'legal highs' (now illegal) they have heard of, and any facts or myths they have heard about them (for example, the myth that they are safer than other drugs). Note these on the board, and cross out or correct the myths as you go through the lesson.

ACTIVITIES

● Ask students, in pairs, to read the information on page 42 of *Your Choice Book Two*, including the DEA article 'Spice' and the 'Fact check'. Refer back to the notes on the board from the starter and cross out or change anything as needed.

● Organise students into pairs to do the 'Research' task on page 43 and then ask them to share their findings with the rest of the class. Make sure that they have found accurate information and understand it (see the link below).

● Ask students, on their own, to read 'LSD' and 'Ask Erica' and then do the writing task. Invite a few students to share their replies with the class.

● Still on their own, ask students to read 'Amphetamines', including 'Freddie's story'. Then organise them into groups to do the discussion task.

● Read through the role-play task with the students and then organise them into groups to do the preparatory research on the effects, risks and statistics related to each drug.

PLENARY

● As a class, decide who is going to give a speech about which drug in the role play, and then encourage students to work in groups to help the speakers prepare their speeches. Use the websites below if required. The structure of the speeches should include a brief introduction, three main points and then a summing-up statement. Hand out **Worksheet 7.2** to help students with their preparation.

EXTENSION

● Chair the forum students have prepared for in the plenary and encourage comment and questions from the 'audience'.

Further information and support for teachers:

Talk to Frank, 'New psychoactive substances': www.talktofrank.com/drug/new-psychoactive-substances

BBC News, 'What exactly are legal highs?': www.bbc.co.uk/news/uk-32857256

The Week, 'What are legal highs and has the Government ban worked?': www.theweek.co.uk/legal-highs/59802/legal-highs-what-are-they-and-has-the-government-ban-worked

Further information and support for students:

Gov.UK, 'Drugs penalties': www.gov.uk/penalties-drug-possession-dealing

Childline, 'Drugs, alcohol and smoking': www.childline.org.uk/info-advice/you-your-body/drugs-alcohol-smoking/

Worksheet 7.2 Preparing a speech

Use the frame below to help you prepare the speech you are going to give in the forum.

Drug: ....

Effects:

....

....

Risks:

....

....

Statistics:

....

....

What will you include in your introduction?

....

....

....

What three main points will you include?

....

....

....

....

....

....

What will you include in your summing up?

....

....

....

Strand:	**Resources:**
• Physical health and wellbeing	• Book Two: pp. 44–45
	• Worksheet 7.3

Learning objective:	**Key words:**
• To discuss whether drugs can ever be safe	contaminated, dehydrated, overheat, drowsy, unconscious
• To debate whether some drugs should be legalised, or whether alcohol and tobacco should be made illegal	

STARTER

- Ask students if they think taking drugs, including smoking and drinking, can ever be completely safe. Make sure that the discussion leads to the conclusion that it cannot. Also explain that the risks can be higher with illegal drugs as you do not know where the drugs came from or what they contain.

ACTIVITIES

- With the class, read the information on page 44 of *Your Choice Book Two* (excluding the article) and then discuss the points that are raised. Ask whether they think allowing testing centres such as 'The Loop' is a good idea and whether they are surprised by anything they have read. Explain that it is possible to become addicted to some prescription drugs, particularly certain types of painkiller (opioids).

- Organise students into pairs and ask them to read 'Is legalisation the answer' and then to make a list of the pros and cons of legislation. Invite pairs to share their lists with the class and give their reasons.

- Ask students to read 'What to do in an emergency' on their own, and then divide the class into groups to do the discussion task that follows. For each of the emergencies listed, ask one group to share their response with the rest of the class and check that everyone agrees on the procedures to follow. Then ask them to work in pairs to produce the leaflet in the writing task.

- Hand out **Worksheet 7.3** and ask students to complete it individually or in pairs. *Answers: **1.** Because it's easy, cheap and convenient. **2.** Xanax (alprazolam) and Valium (diazepam); Ritalin (methylphenidate, a stimulant used to treat ADHD); pregabalin (used to treat epilepsy and anxiety); gabapentin (also used to treat epilepsy and nerve pain). **3.** Class C, 14 years. **4.** Greater internet regulation, educational awareness and greater action by the police to disrupt criminal gangs involved in the drugs trade.*

PLENARY

- Hold a class debate on the motion: 'Alcohol and tobacco should be made illegal and categorised as Class C drugs.' You may like to refer back to **Worksheet 5.1b** for guidelines on holding a debate and share some of the information from the Vox article listed below with students to help them prepare.

EXTENSION

- Ask students to think of how they could improve their leaflets from the writing task – for example, what images to use or how they could use headings and bullet points to make the information clearer.

Further information and support for teachers:

Vox, 'How scientists rank drugs': www.vox.com/2015/2/24/8094759/alcohol-marijuana

Talk to Frank, 'Drugs A–Z': www.talktofrank.com/drugs-a-z

Drug classifications: www.aleretoxicology.co.uk/en/home/support/drug-classifications.html

Opioid addiction: www.ukat.co.uk/prescription-drug-addiction/opioids-and-chronic-pain-in-the-uk/

Addiction to prescription drugs:
www.newscientist.com/article/2110089-addiction-to-prescription-drugs-is-uk-public-health-disaster/

Further information and support for students:

Childline, 'Drugs, alcohol and smoking': www.childline.org.uk/info-advice/you-your-body/drugs-alcohol-smoking/

Brook, 'Drugs': www.brook.org.uk/your-life/drugs

Worksheet 7.3 Q&A: Buying drugs online

Q: What is the problem and how widespread is it?

A: People are increasingly buying medications as well as illicit drugs online, amid reports of dependency, hospitalisations and even deaths around the UK. Experts are hearing more first-hand accounts of online drug purchases over the last year. The internet is a feature of daily life, and so cutting it out is almost impossible for those in recovery.

Q: Why are people buying drugs online?

A: Buying drugs on the web is relatively straightforward. Often it is seen as easier than finding and meeting a dealer, and some people mistakenly think buying online is safer. There are also reports of teenagers clubbing together to buy drugs such as Xanax in bulk.

Q: What kind of medications are people buying online?

A: The most common ones include anti-anxiety benzodiazepines such as Xanax (alprazolam) and Valium (diazepam); Ritalin (methylphenidate, a stimulant used to treat ADHD); pregabalin (used to treat epilepsy and anxiety); and gabapentin (also used to treat epilepsy and nerve pain).

Q: Why are people buying these drugs?

A: The drugs are, quite simply, 'in fashion' at the moment. The rise of Xanax use in the UK is thought to be influenced by trends in America, where it is widely prescribed and features in music, social media and online culture. Pregabalin was prescribed 5.5 million times in the UK in 2016 and is thought to be an effective alternative painkiller for people with opioid-use disorders.

Q: What is the law?

A: Buying online is no different to buying in person: the law relates to the substance being bought, not the method of purchase. Xanax is listed as a Class C controlled drug and the maximum sentence for possessing, supplying or importing a Class C drug is 14 years' imprisonment.

Q: What needs to be done?

A: Campaigners are calling for more information about the risks of taking unprescribed medications. Alongside better awareness for users, it wants healthcare professionals to educate people about the dangers. Speaking in parliament, Labour MP Bambos Charalambous called for the government to research the prevalence of Xanax use and respond to the growing mental health crisis among teenagers.

Source: : www.theguardian.com/society/2018/jan/27/addiction-clinic-teenagers-hooked-illegal-medicines

1. Why do people buy drugs off the internet? ....

   ....

2. What are the most common drugs bought off the internet? ....

   ....

3. What class drug is Xanax, what is the penalty for supplying it?

   ....

   ....

4. What do you think can be done about the problem?

   ....

   ....

   ....

7.4 Are you addicted to your mobile phone?

Strand:
- Physical health and wellbeing

Resources:
- Book Two: pp. 46–47
- Worksheet 7.4

Learning objective:
- To understand what smartphone addiction is and to explore ways of overcoming it

Key words:
smartphone addiction

STARTER
- Ask the class how long they spend on their mobile phone each day. What are they doing? How much time are they spending on each way they use their mobile phone? Is too much? What could they be doing with their time that is more productive instead?

ACTIVITIES
- Ask students, on their own, to read the introduction and the list of questions on page 46 of *Your Choice Book Two*, noting down yes or no answers to the questions. Then organise them into pairs to discuss their responses and whether either of them qualifies as being addicted to their phone.

- On their own again, ask students to read 'What is Smartphone addiction?' and 'Am I addicted to my smartphone?'. Then organise them into groups to discuss the question: 'What you would say to a person who spends too long on their mobile phone?' Invite them to share and compare their responses with the class and encourage them to give reasons for their views.

- On their own, or in pairs if they need more support, ask them to read 'Ask Erica' and write Erica's reply.

- With the class, read 'When the fun stuff stops being fun'. Ask student to do the 'Discuss' activity below the article in groups. Then bring the class back together to share responses and discuss suggestions for how to spend less time on smartphones and social media.

- Hand out copies of **Worksheet 7.4** for students to complete on their own. Then get them to compare and discuss their results with a partner, giving reasons for their views. Invite individuals to share some of their responses with the rest of the class.

PLENARY
- 'The benefits of smartphones outweigh the problems.' Hold a debate on this motion.

RESEARCH
- Keep a diary of when and where you use your mobile phone for at least a week. At the end, look at when you are using your mobile phone and for how long? Do the results surprise you? Do you think you need to cut down on your usage? Discuss the results with a partner, and give reasons for your views.

EXTENSION
- Encourage students to draw up a contract in which they and their parents/carers agree boundaries for their use of their mobile phones, including: time limits for sessions (e.g. taking a break at least once every hour); switch-off times at night (e.g. not using the phone while in bed); designated screen-free times (e.g. mealtimes, when there are visitors and one hour before you go to bed); guidelines about who they accept as friends on social media and about posting pictures; websites that are out of bounds.

Further information and support for teachers:

Relate, 'My teenage is always on the phone': www.relate.org.uk/relationship-help/help-family-life-and-parenting/parenting-teenagers/communicating-teens/my-teenager-always-their-phone

Child Mind Institute, 'When should you come between a teenager and her phone?' childmind.org/article/when-should-you-come-between-a-teenager-and-her-phone/

The Guardian, 'Mobile phone addiction': www.theguardian.com/technology/2018/jan/27/mobile-phone-addiction-apps-break-the-habit-take-back-control

Further information and support for students:

Rehab recovery from mobile phones: www.rehab-recovery.co.uk/articles/smartphone-addiction-infographic/

Worksheet 7.4 Smartphone use and addiction

Read the following statements about using a smartphone. Tick the appropriate box to say whether you agree or disagree with each statement.

Then compare your answers with a partner and share your views in a group or class discussion giving the reasons why you agree or disagree.

Statement	Agree	Disagree
Parents should not try to control how much you use your phone.		
You should switch your phone off whenever you are having a meal with family or friends.		
You can be friends with people all over the world thanks to your phone.		
Adults worry too much about the amount of time we spend on our phones.		
If phones had been around when they were teenagers, adults would understand why we use them so much.		
Smartphone addiction needs treatment like any other addiction.		
Everyone in the family should leave their phones switched off when they go to bed.		
The warning signs that a person is addicted to their phone are easy to spot.		
Smartphones are dangerous. You can never be sure of the true identity of the people you chat to.		
The benefits of smartphones outweigh the drawbacks.		
You should never spend more than an hour on your phone without taking a break.		
Parents should think about how much time they spend on their phones before criticising us.		

Strand:	**Resources:**
• Physical health and wellbeing	• Book Two: pp. 48–49 • Worksheet 8.1

Learning objective:	**Key words:**
• To examine the facts and myths around alcohol • To develop strategies to deal with the peer pressure around drinking alcohol	alcohol, peer pressure

STARTER

- Elicit from students what they already know about alcohol. Note any facts or myths on the board. (For example: myth – alcohol is less harmful than illegal drugs; fact – some religions forbid alcohol consumption.) Cross out and correct the myths as you go through the lesson.

ACTIVITIES

- Ask students to read the whole of page 48 of *Your Choice Book Two*. Then look with them at their initial ideas on the board and ask them to compare these with what they know now. Do they want to add, remove or change anything?

- Ask students to read the 'Fact check' on page 49 and then, in groups, to do the 'Discuss' task beneath it. Invite groups to share their views with the class, giving their reasons.

- Ask students to read 'Why do teenagers drink?' and then, in groups, to do the 'Discuss' task that follows. Remind them of the term 'peer pressure' and encourage them to consider this in their discussion.

- Organise students into pairs to do the research task. Make sure that both of the questions are researched by different groups. Then bring the class back together and ask some pairs to share their findings with the class, again making sure that both questions are covered (see the links below for '18 alcohol' and NHS). *Answers: 1. Ads must not be directed at people under 18 or contain anything likely to appeal to them by reflecting youth culture. 2. It is dangerous to spike another person's drink as you can't predict the effect it will have on them, for example how alcohol would interact with any medication they are taking. It may leave them vulnerable to rape or assault. Drink spiking is illegal and can result in 10 years in jail.*

- Hand out **Worksheet 8.1** for students to complete on their own. Once they have done this, organise them into groups to compare their answers and to agree a list of pros and cons of drinking alcohol. Invite some pairs to share their lists with the class. *Pros: feel relaxed, temporarily more energy, fewer inhibitions. Cons: hangover, dehydration, fewer inhibitions, cost, sickness.*

PLENARY

- Divide the class into four groups and get each group to stand in a different corner of the room. Explain that they are going to prepare for a class discussion about the drinking age: corner 1 will argue to cut the drinking age to 16, corner 2 to keep the drinking age at 18, corner 3 to raise the drinking age to 21, and corner 4 to ban drinking completely. Ask groups to discuss their viewpoint and come up with three reasons to support it. Then bring the class back to together to share and discuss their responses.

EXTENSION

- Ask students, in mixed-ability pairs, to research the effect of peer pressure in relation to drinking, using the links below. Then, based on their findings, ask them to create a short role play, with one person trying to encourage the other to drink and the other resisting. Invite some pairs to act out their role play in front of the class. Then encourage discussion of what students have learned from the role play.

Further information and support for teachers:

Mentor-ADEPIS research and briefing papers with ideas for lessons:
http://mentor-adepis.org/planning-effective-education/

Drinkaware, 'Teenage drinking': www.drinkaware.co.uk/advice/underage-drinking/teenage-drinking/

ASA/CAP, '18 alcohol', the law on advertising: www.asa.org.uk/type/non_broadcast/code_section/18.html

NHS, 'Drink spiking': www.nhs.uk/live-well/healthy-body/drink-spiking-and-date-rape-drugs/

1. Read each of the statements below. Put a tick in one of the columns to show whether you agree with the statement, disagree with it or are not sure.

Statement	Agree	Disagree	Not sure
'The world would be a better place if no one drank alcohol.'			
'People exaggerate the dangers of alcohol.'			
'I don't see what's wrong with drinking a lot and getting drunk.'			
'Alcohol is OK – provided you don't drink too much.'			
'People who get ill from drinking should have to pay for their medical treatment.'			
'Alcohol causes a lot of unhappiness.'			
'Alcohol gives a lot of people harmless pleasure.'			
'Anyone who drinks too much is taking a risk.'			
'People who drink alcohol lead more exciting lives than people who don't.'			
'People who get drunk should be locked up and have to pay a fine before they are let out.'			
'Teenagers who get drunk several times should have to observe a curfew.'			

2. In groups, discuss your views on the statements above, giving reasons for your views. Then list the top three reasons you can think of for drinking alcohol and the top three reasons against drinking alcohol.

Top three reasons **for** drinking alcohol:

....

....

....

Top three reasons **against** drinking alcohol:

....

....

....

Strand:	Resources:
• Physical health and wellbeing	• Book Two: pp. 50–51 • Worksheet 8.2

Learning objective:	Key words:
• To examine the dangers of alcohol poisoning • To discuss how strong different types of alcohol are and how long it takes to sober up	unit of alcohol, alcohol poisoning, sober, binge drinking

STARTER

* Ask students what they think is a safe amount to drink per week. Note the answers on the board and leave them up there as you will revisit them at the end of the lesson, asking students the same question.

ACTIVITIES

* Ask the students to read the information on page 50 of *Your Choice Book Two*, up to the end of 'Problems at school and with mental health'. In a class discussion, ask students what they think the most important piece of information is that they have read, giving reasons for their views.

* Ask students to read 'Sobering up – four dangerous myths'. Ask if they are surprised by what they have learned. Organise students into pairs or small groups to design a poster for underage teenagers describing the dangers of drinking and dispelling the myths about sobering up.

* With students, read 'Diary of a teenage alcoholic'; then organise them into small groups to do the writing task. Encourage them to think about everything they have learned so far and to refer back to their posters when deciding what to include in their PowerPoint presentation (see Extension activity below).

* Ask students, on their own, to do the 'Your choice' quiz. Check comprehension (e.g. binge drinking = drinking a large amount of alcohol in a very short period of time). Then invite students to share their answers in a class discussion. *Answers: false = 1, 4, 5, 6; true = 2, 3, 7, 8, 9, 10.*

* Hand out **Worksheet 8.2** for students to complete in pairs. This can be checked with the alcohol calculator in the links below. *Answers from weakest to strongest: 10 pints of the low alcohol beer = 1 unit (1 hour to leave body); 1 snakebite = 2 units (2 hours) although you are likely to feel worse for mixing the alcohol; 1.5 pints of lager, 3 shots of vodka or 3 small glasses of wine = 3 units (3 hours); 4 Jäger bombs = 4 units (4 hours); 5 shots of tequila = 5 units (5 hours); 3 pints of cider = 6 units (6 hours); a bottle of wine can have up to 9 or even 10 units in it, depending on its strength (9/10 hours); a 2-litre bottle of Diamond White (extra strong cider) is likely to have over 10 units of alcohol in it (10 hours+ for the alcohol to leave your body).*

PLENARY

* Ask students to read 'Drink wisely', but remind them that they are underage, referring them back to the 'Fact check' in the previous lesson. As a class, do the discussion activity and encourage students to suggest other advice. Then revisit the issue of safe drinking and the notes on the board from the beginning of the lesson.

RESEARCH

* Ask students, in pairs, to research the exact limits of alcohol consumption the doctors recommend and to compile these into an information leaflet.

EXTENSION

* Invite students to present to the class the PowerPoints they prepared during the lesson.

Further information and support for teachers:

NHS, 'Alcohol poisoning': www.nhs.uk/conditions/alcohol-poisoning/

Further information and support for students:

Drinkaware, 'Low risk drinking guidelines': www.drinkaware.co.uk/alcohol-facts/alcoholic-drinks-units/alcohol-limits-unit-guidelines/

UK Underage alcohol consumption: www.drinkaware.co.uk/research/data/uk-underage-consumption/

Worksheet 8.2 Units of alcohol

In pairs, look at the following table. Work out how many units of alcohol are contained in the drinks consumed. Decide who has consumed the most units and order them from the fewest to the most.

The following 'Drinkaware alcohol calculator' will help you work it out:
www.drinkaware.co.uk/understand-your-drinking/unit-calculator

Then estimate how long you think it would take for the alcohol to leave your body having drunk this amount. Compare your answers in groups and then ask your teacher for the correct results.

What a person has drunk	How many units of alcohol does this contain?	How long it takes for the alcohol to leave their body
4 Jäger bombs		
3 pints of cider		
3 small glasses of wine with 1 unit of alcohol in each		
1.5 pints of lager		
3 shots of vodka		
1 bottle of wine		
5 shots of tequila		
1 pint of snakebite – half lager, half cider		
10 pints of low alcohol 0.5% beer, with only 0.1 unit in per bottle.		
A 2-litre bottle of Diamond White cider from the supermarket		

Strand:	Resources:
• Physical health and wellbeing	• Book Two: pp. 52–53 • Worksheet 8.3

Learning objective:	Key words:
• To understand what alcoholism is, and • To recognise the main signs and dangers of alcoholism	alcoholism

• Alcoholism is a sensitive subject, which some students may have been exposed to or have direct experience of. Consider this before you teach this lesson and speak privately to any students you think may have been affected by the issue, outlining what the lesson will cover. Monitor them during the lesson and adapt it if necessary.

STARTER

• Ask students what is meant by the term 'alcoholism'. Elicit any facts they know and myths they believe about alcoholism and note them on the board. Correct the myths as you go through the lesson.

ACTIVITIES

• Ask students to read the introduction and 'Signs that a person may have a problem with alcohol' on page 52 of *Your Choice Book Two*. Then, as a class, discuss which are the easiest and which are the most difficult signs to spot, as well as what the most important signs are (e.g. being unable to start the day without a drink, having a hangover every day).

• Organise students into pairs to read 'Ask Erica' and then to do the discussion task. Invite pairs to share their ideas with the rest of the class. Then encourage students, working on their own, to write Erica's reply to Annie.

• Ask students to read all the text on page 53, and then organise them into small groups to do the discussion task.

• Support students to do the research task in pairs (see the Al-Anon link below) and then invite some of them to share their findings with the rest of the class. Please note that COAP, mentioned on page 53, has now been merged with Action on Addiction. You might like to look at the link below with the students.

PLENARY

• Ask students to discuss whether there should be a legal limit on what you can drink on a night out, and how this limit could or should be enforced. Also, should there be different age limits for different types of drinks for young people, with the drinking age for spirits being raised to 21, and for beer and lager being lowered to 16?

EXTENSION

• Hand out **Worksheet 8.3**. Ask students to read the statements on their own and then discuss in groups what they have learned from each of the statements.

Further information and support for teachers:

National Association for Children of Alcoholic Parents: www.nacoa.org.uk

'Worried about someone else's drinking': www.drinkaware.co.uk/advice/worried-about-someone-elses-drinking/

Children Harmed by Alcohol Toolkit (CHAT) and ADAM: www.chatresource.org.uk and www.chatresource.org.uk/adam/

Action on Addiction: www.actiononaddiction.org.uk/family-support

Alcoholics Anonymous: www.alcoholics-anonymous.org.uk/

Further information and support for students:

Al-Anon Family Groups, support for people affected by someone else's drinking: www.al-anonuk.org.uk/

Dennis — 'Alcohol ruined my sister's life. She was knocked down by a driver who was more than twice the amount over the legal limit. Now she's in a wheelchair.'

Nasreen — 'It is against our religion, so no one in my family drinks any alcohol. It doesn't stop us from enjoying ourselves.'

Theresa — 'People get a shock when I tell them my dad is an alcoholic. They think that alcoholics are down-and-outs. I couldn't accept it at first. Now I realise that he's sick and alcoholism is a disease. It affects the whole family. I just keep on hoping that one day he'll stop drinking.'

Aston — 'My grandfather died last year. He was only 56. There was something wrong with his liver, caused by drinking too much.'

Sam — 'Our lives have changed completely since mum and dad stopped drinking. It used to be totally chaotic. They seemed to be drunk all the time. It got so bad that I dreaded what I'd find when I got home from school. There was never any food in the house and we were always short of money. Now they both go to Alcoholics Anonymous. This year we may even have a holiday.'

Jason — 'My older sister's an athlete. She says alcohol is a poison and she doesn't want it messing up her body. She says she's never going to touch it.'

Abigail — 'My sister got so drunk she had to go to A&E and have her stomach pumped. She could have died from alcohol poisoning.'

Darren — 'I was with my friends and we'd all had too much to drink. We got into a fight and I ended up at the police station. My dad had to come and fetch me. It was embarrassing and humiliating. I was lucky that I just got a warning. I could have ended up with a criminal record.'

Discuss what you learn from these statements about the ways alcohol can affect people's lives.

Strand:	Resources:
• Physical health and wellbeing	• Book Two: pp. 54–55 • Worksheet 9.1

Learning objective:	Key words:
• To understand what a vaccine is and why it is important that everyone is vaccinated against common diseases	immunisation, vaccine, herd immunity

STARTER

• Elicit from students what a vaccine is. Ask what vaccines they know of and note them on the board.

ACTIVITIES

• Ask students to read the introduction and 'Immunisation' on pages 54–55 of *Your Choice Book Two*. Draw their attention back to the list on the board and ask if they would like to make any changes to the points listed, or to add or delete anything.

• Organise students into small groups to do the discussion activity, then invite them to share and compare their answers as a class.

• Ask students to read the text about breast cancer and testicular cancer. Clarify with students how often they should check themselves – the answer is once a month, from aged 20 onwards.

• Ask students to read the information about 'Thrush' and then on their own, or in pairs if students need more support, to read 'Ask Erica' and write her reply to Shannon. Then hold a class discussion to check that everyone has understood the information in the passage, and for everyone to share their replies.

PLENARY

• With students, discuss whether all vaccines should be legally enforced on children or whether it should still be up to the parents to decide. Note the case of measles in New York in Spring 2019, where the religious exemption against vaccination has been removed (see the link below).

RESEARCH

• Ask students to research what is meant by the term 'herd immunity', and why vaccines are so important to people with compromised immune systems, using the links below. *Answers to include: vaccines are necessary to protect those in the general population with compromised immune systems; herd immunity means preventing the spread of diseases across the general population by most people being immune.*

EXTENSION

• Hand out **Worksheet 9.1**. Ask students to read the information about the MMR vaccine on their own and then to work in small groups to produce a poster explaining why everyone should have the MMR vaccine. They could include their findings about herd immunity.

Further information and support for teachers:

NHS, 'How vaccines work': www.nhs.uk/conditions/vaccinations/how-vaccines-work/

NHS, 'When do teens need vaccines?': www.vaccineinformation.org/teens/schedules.asp

NHS, 'Childhood Vaccines Timeline': www.nhs.uk/conditions/vaccinations/childhood-vaccines-timeline/

BMJ Opinion – Should we consider compulsory vaccinations? blogs.bmj.com/bmj/2019/05/17/eleanor-draeger-we-have-reached-the-point-where-we-should-consider-compulsory-vaccination/

The Guardian – New York ends religious exemption for vaccinations:
www.theguardian.com/us-news/2019/jun/13/new-york-vaccines-measles-religion

Further information and support for students:

NHS, 'Childhood Vaccines Timeline': www.nhs.uk/conditions/vaccinations/childhood-vaccines-timeline/

NI Direct, 'Immunisation for teenagers between 14 and 18 years old':
www.nidirect.gov.uk/articles/immunisation-teenagers-between-14-and-18-years-old

The MMR vaccine is a vaccine that protects you against catching measles, mumps and rubella, which are three highly infectious diseases.

Measles

Before vaccination was introduced, measles outbreaks were common. Measles is spread by coughs and sneezes. The symptoms of measles can include fever, a runny nose, sore red eyes and a rash covering the whole body. Measles is still common in many parts of the world and can be very serious. One in 5000 people who catch measles is likely to die as a result.

Mumps

Mumps was also common among children before the introduction of vaccinations. Symptoms can include fever and headache. The most common symptom is a swelling of the glands under the ears. Around one in twenty people may have temporary hearing loss. Most cases of mumps now occur in young adults who have not received two doses of the MMR vaccine.

Rubella

Rubella, also called German measles, is now rare in the UK, as a result of vaccination. It is a mild illness with symptoms similar to a cold, aching joints and a rash. However, if a pregnant woman gets rubella, it can seriously affect the development of the unborn baby.

How does the vaccine work?

The vaccine makes your immune system produce cells that can recognise each of the three viruses that cause the diseases. So if you come into contact with any of these viruses, your immune system produces antibodies that protect you against it.

Who should get vaccinated?

The MMR vaccine is offered to all children in the UK in two doses – one just after their first birthday and the second at about the age of 3 years and 4 months.

If you weren't vaccinated as a child, or only received one dose, teenagers can arrange to be vaccinated by contacting your doctor.

How long does the MMR vaccine last?

The vaccinations for measles and rubella are 99% effective for over 20 years, while for mumps the figure is 88%.

Is the vaccine safe?

Research suggests that the vaccine is safe and that scares in the past about how it could cause autism were unfounded.

Use the information on this page to produce a poster designed to encourage parents to have their children vaccinated with the MMR vaccine.

Strand:	Resources:
• Physical health and wellbeing	• Book Two: pp. 56–57 • Worksheet 9.2 • School policy on allergies and medication

Learning objective:	Key words:
• To examine what the most common allergies are • To understand what anaphylactic shock is, and how epi-pens can be used to treat it • To understand what hay fever, asthma and eczema are, and how each can be treated	allergies, asthma, eczema, anaphylactic shock, epi-pen

STARTER

• Ask students what an allergy is, and what common allergies they know of. Note these on the board. If appropriate, ask the class if they or anyone they know has an allergy and to share their experiences.

ACTIVITIES

• Ask students to read the introduction and 'What causes an allergic reaction?' on page 56 of *Your Choice Book Two*. Discuss this with the class and include bee and wasp stings, hay fever and food allergies.

• With the class, read 'Anaphylactic shock'. Ask if anyone in the class carries an adrenaline auto-injector. If not, show them the one in the book (an Epi-Pen®) and explain how it is used (see the link below). (Note that the date for Natasha Ednan-Laperouse should be 2016.)

• Support students to do the research task about whether there should be changes to food labelling. Note that this may be affected by Brexit, as the EU currently sets food labelling rules.

• Ask students to read the rest of the text from 'Skin allergies – eczema' through to the end of 'Managing allergies'. Organise students into pairs to do the 'Discuss' activity, and then ask pairs to compare their responses in small groups. Points to listen out for and clarify: eczema is an allergic reaction, not a disease; it is not contagious; it can be treated with creams.

• Hand out **Worksheet 9.2** and ask students to do the 'True or false' activity in pairs, then invite some to share their responses with the rest of the class. Statements 1, 3, 5 and 6 are false – the rest are true.

• Organise students into pairs and support them to do the research task on page 57 about the school's policy on allergies. Then encourage pairs to write a leaflet offering advice and information to other students in the school about what to do if someone has a severe allergic reaction. Invite some pairs to share their leaflets and agree the most important information to include on it.

PLENARY

• Ask students to discuss what can be done to protect people with allergies, using the table in part **2** of **Worksheet 9.2**. Suggestions might include: making administering auto-injectors part of the secondary school curriculum; all packaged foods having to label ALL ingredients on the label; first aid training for all secondary school pupils; first aid awareness on allergies for primary school children.

EXTENSION

• Get students to find out online when hay fever sufferers are most at risk from pollen, and what the pollen forecast is today.

Further information and support for teachers:

NHS, 'Anaphylaxis': www.nhs.uk/conditions/anaphylaxis/prevention/
EpiPen® user guide: www.epipen.co.uk/patients/epipenr-user-guide

Further information and support for students:

Pollen forecast: www.metoffice.gov.uk/weather/warnings-and-advice/seasonal-advice/pollen-forecast
Asthma UK, 'Asthma and young people': www.asthma.org.uk/advice/manage-your-asthma/young-people
TeensHealth, 'Eczema': kidshealth.org/en/teens/eczema.html

Worksheet 9.2 Allergies

1. Read the statements below and decide which are true and which are false.

Statement	True	False
1. You can catch asthma off other people.		
2. Playing with dirt can be good for children as it activates their immune system and they get fewer allergies later in life.		
3. Doctors have a vaccination that can cure you of nut allergies.		
4. A wasp sting is less likely to cause anaphylactic shock to a person than a bee sting.		
5. Eczema is contagious, so you should always wash your hands if you have it.		
6. Allergies are always hereditary – if one of your parents has an allergy, you will have it as well.		
7. Hay fever is worse in the summer.		
8. Asthma is worse in big cities that have air pollution.		
9. You should never use another person's inhaler – you don't know what is in it.		
10. Hay fever can be treated with medicine from a pharmacy to reduce its effects.		

2. What are the top three things that can be done to help people with allergies? Why are these important?

Action	Why it is important
1.	
2.	
3.	

Strand:	Resources:
• Physical health and wellbeing	• Book Two: pp. 58–59 • Worksheet 10.1

Learning objective:	Key words:
• To understand how to look after your skin	acne, pores, follicles, ultraviolet rays, SPF

STARTER

• Elicit what problems can occur with your skin and why it is important to look after it. Note the best points on the board, to refer to later. Be sensitive to children who may suffer with complaints such as acne.

ACTIVITIES

• Ask students to read the introduction, 'Keeping your skin clean' on page 58 of *Your Choice Book Two*, followed by 'Acne: the facts' including 'How to deal with acne'. Ask the class if any of the advice surprises them and what advice they think is the most important.

• Organise students into groups to read 'Rose's story' and then to do the discussion activity that follows it.

• Now split students into pairs to do the role play, bearing in mind what they talked about in their discussion of Rose's story. Invite some students to share with the rest of the class how they would feel if they were the person being bullied.

• Still in their pairs, ask students to read 'Your choice' and decide which statements are facts and which are myths. Then get them to compare their answers with another pair before inviting some students to share their responses with the rest of the class. Make sure the students understand which are true and which are not. *Answers: 1. True; 2. False; 3. True; 4. True; 5. False; 6. True; 7. True; 8. True.*

• Ask students to read 'Tanning' and the 'Fact check' on skin cancer, before working in pairs on the role play on page 59. Then ask students to discuss what they have learned.

• Hand out **Worksheet 10.1**. There is no correct order, but note the following points: **a)** if you don't wear any protection you can still get sunburnt; **c)** you can still get sunburnt in the water, but are less likely to feel it; **d)** water-resistant sun creams are no stronger than those that aren't; **g)** you can still get burnt on a cloudy day; **h)** aloe vera may help after you get burnt, but it's better not to get burnt in the first place; **j)** cool sunglasses only provide protection against harmful UVA/UVB rays if they are labelled as such.

• Consolidate what students have learned from the worksheet by getting them to read 'Stay safe in the sun' on page 59. If appropriate, ask students to create a poster for other teenagers about staying safe in the sun.

PLENARY

• Organise students into small groups to do the 'Discuss' task on page 59. Then bring the class back together to share their opinions and reasoning.

RESEARCH

• Ask students to research why it may be a good idea to spend a short period in the sun, without sunscreen, when it is not too hot. They can use the NHS link below. *Answer: it boosts Vitamin D.*

EXTENSION

• Encourage students to do more research on sun creams, finding out what the difference is between UVA and UVB, and what the different SPFs (sun protection factors) actually mean. Ask them to write two or three paragraphs on what they find out.

Further information and support for students:

TeensHealth, 'Tanning for teens': kidshealth.org/en/teens/tanning.html

Sun protection advice: yourteenmag.com/health/physical-health/sun-protection-for-teenagers

Sunburn: www.skinsight.com/skin-conditions/teen/sunburn

NHS guidance on Vitamin D: www.nhs.uk/live-well/healthy-body/how-to-get-vitamin-d-from-sunlight/

Worksheet 10.1 Sun protection

Complete the table, ranking the ideas from 1–10, with 1 being the one you think best protects you from the sun and 10 being the one that protects you least, giving reasons for your views.

Idea	Ranking	Reason
a) Staying out of the sun between the hours of 11 a.m. and 3 p.m.		
b) Tanning for an hour, then spending an hour indoors		
c) Hiding in the swimming pool to protect yourself from the sun's rays		
d) Using a water-resistant SPF 15 sun cream – it's stronger, even if you don't go in the water		
e) Wearing a pair of UVA/UVB resistant sunglasses		
f) Using a SPF 30 sun cream if the sun is strong		
g) Only going out on a cloudy day, because you can't get sunburnt then		
h) Using aloe vera oil after being in the sun to reduce skin damage		
i) Wearing a hat		
j) Wearing a pair of cool shades		
k) Wearing a long-sleeved shirt and long trousers, to keep your skin out of the sun		

Strand:	Resources:
• Physical health and wellbeing	• Book Two: pp. 60–61 • Worksheet 10.2

Learning objective:	Key words:
• To understand how to care for your teeth, ears and eyes	bacteria, plaque, calculus, abscess, fluoride, gingivitis, tinnitus, decibels, ultraviolet rays

STARTER

• Explain the objective of the lesson, reading the introduction on page 60 with the class. Then focus on looking after your teeth. Ask students to write down what they think are the main causes of tooth decay. Compare their ideas. Stress that the two main causes are poor dental hygiene and poor diet.

ACTIVITIES

• Ask students to read 'Tooth decay and gum disease'. Show some images of tooth decay which can be found at photo libraries such as Shutterstock (www.shutterstock.com). Make sure students understand how plaque is formed and why it leads to tooth decay and gum disease.

• Go through the advice given in 'Top tips for healthy teeth' point by point. Ask: 'Why is it recommended that you see a dentist regularly?' Explain how a cavity can be filled before the tooth decays so much that it has to be extracted. Explain that it is a good idea to use a toothpaste with fluoride in as this helps to prevent tooth decay. Explain that they can find a local dentist, if they are not registered with one, by searching online through the NHS, and that dental treatment is free if they are under 16, or under 18 and in full-time education.

• Organise students into pairs to do the role-play activity. Invite pairs to perform their scenario for the rest of the class and agree the most persuasive arguments for going to the dentist.

• Still in pairs, ask students to do the writing task, thinking back on what they have learned and making sure they include all the most important points. Invite a few pairs to share their factsheet with the class.

• Ask students to read 'Caring for your ears' and then to do the 'Discuss' task in pairs. In a class discussion, ask how you can protect your ears when listening to music on your own. Ask what tinnitus is. Information on tinnitus can be downloaded from the Action on Hearing Loss website (see below).

• With students, read 'Caring for your eyes' and discuss why it is important to wear sunglasses with UV protection (they block out the sun's harmful rays). Go through the advice given in 'First aid for eyes' and discuss the reasons for each piece of advice.

• Ask students to work in pairs on the research task. Invite some students to share their posters and compare their recommendations for which sunglasses to buy and why.

PLENARY

• In a class discussion, ask students, without looking at their books, what they think is the best advice about how to care for their teeth, ears and eyes. List on the board each piece of advice they remember and ask them to give the reason for that advice. Then check with them in the book to see if they have missed anything important.

EXTENSION

• Ask students to complete **Worksheet 10.2**. *Answers: 1, 4, 6, 8 and 10 are false (6 is about teeth and 10 depends on the type of glasses); the rest are true.*

Further information and support for students:

Preventing tooth loss: www.humana.com/prevention-and-care/healthy-living-and-prevention/dental-health/tooth-loss

NHS, 'Tooth decay': www.nhs.uk/conditions/tooth-decay/

Hearing loss – Action on Hearing Loss: www.actiononhearingloss.org.uk/

The National Deaf Children's Society: www.ndcs.org.uk/

Sight loss – Royal National Institute for the Blind: www.rnib.org.uk/

The ABCs of sunglasses protection: www.eyesite.co.uk/news/abcs-sunglasses-protection/

Worksheet 10.2 Teeth, ears and eyes: true or false?

Read the statements below and decide which are true and which are false. Then write a sentence in the space provided giving the reason for your answer.

Statement	True	False
1. You have to pay for dental treatment from the age of 14. Reason:		
2. Bleeding from your gums is a sign of gum disease. Reason:		
3. You should buy a new toothbrush every six months. Reason:		
4. Tooth decay is caused by a virus that enters your mouth when you breathe. Reason:		
5. Exposure to loud noise can cause tinnitus. Reason:		
6. Gingivitis is an infection of the ear. Reason:		
7. Cotton wool will protect your ears from the loud music at festivals and concerts. Reason:		
8. You can always tell if you have an eye disease, because your eyes will hurt. Reason:		
9. If someone has a splinter in their eye, do not try to remove it. Reason:		
10. Wearing sunglasses protects your eyes from damage from the sun's rays. Reason:		

Caring for your feet and your back

Strand:	**Resources:**
• Physical health and wellbeing	• Book Two: pp. 62–63 • Worksheet 10.3

Learning objective:	**Key words:**
• To learn how to look after your feet and back	corns, calluses, verrucas, bunions, athlete's foot, in-growing toenails, backache

STARTER

• Read the introduction on page 62 of *Your Choice Book Two* with the class. Then focus on looking after your feet. Ask pairs: 'Why is it important to wear shoes that fit properly? What problems can result from ill-fitting shoes? How many of you have had a problem with your feet?' Encourage those who are willing to share their experiences to do so in a class discussion.

ACTIVITIES

• Ask students to read the 'Fact check' and 'Common foot problems' before getting into small groups to do the discussion task. Invite groups to share their views and reasoning with the rest of the class.

• Bring the class back together and discuss the 'Top tips for healthy feet', encouraging students to give reasons for each piece of advice.

• As a class, revisit the discussion about whether children should be allowed to wear whatever shoes they like to school and then taking a vote on the issue.

• As a class, do the first part of the research task and list the most common foot injuries. These could include broken ankle, broken toe, torn ankle ligaments, torn tendons, broken foot bones, puncture wound from stepping on something, torn nail. Put students in pairs and give each pair a different foot injury to research the answers to questions **2** and **3**. Invite pairs to share their findings in a class discussion.

• Ask students, on their own, to read 'Ask Erica' on page 63 and write a reply to Kelly. Invite a few students to share their responses with the rest of the class.

• Explain that you are now going to focus on looking after your back. Ask if any of the students ever get an achy back and what they think might be the cause (e.g. carrying heavy bags). Ask students to read 'Looking after your back' and the 'Fact check'. Then go through the 'Lighten the load' advice with them.

• Ask the class how they would lift a heavy object. Note their answers on the board. Then read the advice on 'How to lift heavy objects', highlighting any advice the students missed or got wrong.

• Organise students into pairs to read the advice on sitting properly and then do the discussion task that follows. Invite pairs to share their responses with the class and discuss the way students sit during lessons and at computers at school and at home. How many of them are conscious of their posture? What could they do to protect their backs when they are sitting?

PLENARY

• Hand out **Worksheet 10.3** for students to read and answer the questions. Then discuss their answers. *Answers: 1. Going through a growth spurt; 2. E.g. cricketers (stress fractures) and gymnasts (torn/strained muscles/ligaments); 3. Stiff back from sitting in one position; 4. Overweight – puts extra pressure on your back; 5. Too heavy bags can strain your back; 6. Lifting heavy objects incorrectly can strain your back; 7. Regular movement, massages, visit to a chiropractor (a back specialist).*

EXTENSION

• Ask students to research the RICE (or PRICE) strategy for dealing with injuries (see the weblink below).

Further information and support for teachers:

Children's feet and shoes: www.betterhealth.vic.gov.au/health/healthyliving/childrens-feet-and-shoes

Further information and support for students:

Safe lifting tips: www.nhs.uk/live-well/healthy-body/safe-lifting-tips/

How to sit correctly: www.nhs.uk/live-well/healthy-body/how-to-sit-correctly/

PRICE treatment for sports injuries: www.nhs.uk/conditions/sports-injuries/treatment/

Read the information about back pain and then answer the questions.

What causes back pain?

Emily Johnson explores the causes of back problems among teenagers.

There are a number of causes of back pain among teenagers. One of the reasons that teenagers suffer from back pain is that during puberty you go through a growth spurt. This can cause you to feel pain in your spine. This is more common in girls than it is in boys.

Another cause of back problems is injuries caused by sporting activities, such as playing football, tennis or cricket or doing gymnastics and weightlifting. A gymnast puts considerable stress on their back as does a fast bowler in cricket. Young fast bowlers can suffer stress fractures and gymnasts can injure themselves by falling or twisting awkwardly.

Teenagers who lead inactive lives can cause problems for themselves by spending too much time sitting in front of their computers. Unless the chair they use is the right height and offers plenty of support, they can develop poor posture, leading to back problems.

Inactive teenagers may be overweight. This too is a cause of back problems by putting stress on the lower back.

Another major cause of back problems is the weight of their schoolbags. A survey of 1126 students aged 12–18 published in the journal *Spine* found the weight of schoolbags a factor in many cases of back problems. A further survey found that carrying the bag on one shoulder also contributed to back problems. Schoolbags that are carried incorrectly or are too heavy may injure muscles and joints and can lead to severe pain in the neck, shoulders and back.

Teenagers can also injure their backs by not keeping their back straight when lifting heavy objects or by lifting objects that are very heavy and put too much strain on the spine.

1. Why can you get back pain in puberty?

   ....

2. Give two examples of people playing sport who can injure themselves.

   ....

   ....

3. Why is playing on a computer bad for your back?

   ....

4. What is the problem with being inactive?

   ....

5. How can schoolbags contribute to the problem?

   ....

6. Why is lifting objects sometimes a problem?

   ....

7. What other precautions or actions can you think of that would help your back?

   ....

   ....

Strand:	Resources:
• Physical health and wellbeing	• Book Two: pp. 64–65 • Worksheet 10.4 • pictures of people with tattoos, including pictures of neck, face and finger tattoos

Learning objective:	Key words:
• To explore why people get tattoos and piercings and the issues surrounding them	rite of passage, hepatitis, Maori

STARTER

* Read the introduction on page 64 of *Your Choice Book Two* with the class. Explain that the art of tattooing goes back thousands of years and that attitudes to tattooing depend on the society in which you live. Show pictures of people with tattoos, including pictures of neck, face and finger tattoos. Ask: 'Would you consider getting your neck, face or fingers tattooed? Is there a danger if your tattoos are visible of you being the victim of discrimination, for example from an employer?' Talk about how people from different generations may have different attitudes to tattoos and piercings.

ACTIVITIES

* Ask students to read 'Tattoos' and the 'Fact check' and then, in small groups, to do the 'Discuss' task that follows it. Invite students to share and compare their responses in a class discussion.

* Organise students into pairs to read 'If you are thinking of getting a tattoo' and then to discuss the questions. Invite pairs to role play a scene in which one person explains why they are thinking of getting a tattoo and the other explains why they would never get a tattoo. Allow some time to prepare for this.

* Ask students to read the information about 'Body piercing' on page 65, including the 'Fact check' and 'Tongue piercing'. With the class, discuss the questions in 'Your choice' and then take a vote on each one. If they think there should be laws about the ages at which you can have certain piercings, ask them what age they think this should be for each piercing, and why.

* Organise students into pairs to do the 'Role play', taking it in turns to be the dentist. Encourage some pairs to perform their scenario for the rest of the class.

* Still in their pairs, encourage students to do the 'Research' activity and then invite them to share their findings with the class. You could extend the activity by asking some pairs to find and research cultures other than the Maoris where tattooing and piercing has cultural importance.

* On their own, ask students to read 'Ask Erica' and then write her reply to Maria.

PLENARY

* Ask students, in pairs, to do the second part of the 'Write' task, thinking about everything they have learned in the lesson and including at least three pieces of advice each about tattooing and piercing. Encourage pairs to share and compare their articles with the rest of the class.

EXTENSION

* Read **Worksheet 10.4** with students to explore the difficulty of removing a tattoo. Ask the class: 'Would knowing the facts make you think more carefully about getting a tattoo?' Ask students to use the information to create a short information leaflet entitled, 'Tattoos: changing your mind'.

Further information and support for teachers

'7 things your teen needs to know about getting a tattoo' (includes images which students might find distressing): www.aftertheplayground.com/7-things-teen-needs-know-getting-tattoo/

'When are children old enough to have piercings': www.familylives.org.uk/advice/secondary/health-and-development/when-are-children-old-enough-to-have-piercings/

British Council, 'Tattoos and piercings' – video (4 mins): http://learnenglishteens.britishcouncil.org/study-break/youtubers/tattoos-piercings

Tattoos are no longer permanent, but removal can be a long and costly process.

Rebecca's story

Rebecca, a 24-year-old public relations executive from London, was just 16 when she decided to have an ankle tattoo – a weird symbol in black, green and purple, which she chose from a book on tattooing.

At first, she was pleased. 'It cost about £50 from a tattooist in Exeter,' she says,' and took about 50 minutes to complete. But over the past 5 years, I've come to find it embarrassing. I'm fed up with people asking what it means – because I don't know.'

She opted to have it removed by laser, which is a lengthy and costly procedure. 'I will have spent about £1000 in the end. I just want it gone.'

Your questions answered

Q: *How can I have a tattoo removed?*

A: A tattoo can be removed by a laser.

Q: *How long does it take to remove a tattoo?*

A: The tattoo is removed gradually and it can take ten or more sessions over a period of weeks or months.

Q: *Can I have a tattoo removed on the NHS?*

A: Most removals have to be paid for privately. Tattoo removal is not available on the NHS.

Q: *How much will it cost?*

A: The cost varies according to the size of the tattoo and can range from £50 to several hundred pounds per session.

Q: *Will the tattoo be removed completely?*

A: Some colours don't fade as well as others, and many tattoos aren't completely removed.

Q: *What is the chance of being left with a scar?*

A: There is about a 3 per cent chance of being left with a scar.

Strand:	Resources:
• Personal wellbeing and mental health	• Book Two: pp. 66–67 • Worksheet 11.1

Learning objective:	Key words:
• To understand what anger is and learn what makes you angry • To examine strategies for dealing with anger and for dealing with what happens after an argument	anger, anger reservoir, arguments, sorry

STARTER

- Divide the class into groups. Ask students to think of three things that they find easy to deal with but that might make others feel angry, and one thing that makes them really angry. Ask them to talk about these.

ACTIVITIES

- Ask students to read the introduction and 'What makes you angry?' on page 66 of *Your Choice Book Two*. Then ask them to do the 'Write' task that follows it using questions **1** to **3** of **Worksheet 11.1**.

- Organise students into small groups to do the 'Discuss' task. Encourage students who need more challenge to develop their self-awareness by thinking about what has made them angry in the past and whether they have any particular triggers. Invite students who are comfortable with this to share their experience with the class.

- With the class, read 'Anger reservoir'. Ask students the following questions: 'What's Nadia's problem with anger?' *(she stores anger in her body)*; 'What is a name for doing this?' *(an anger reservoir)*; 'What is Lisa's problem with anger?' *(she has a short fuse)*; 'Is everyone the same when it comes to anger?' *(no)*; 'What's the thing that you need to be aware of?' *(when your anger reservoir is full)*

- In groups of three, ask students to read 'What to do when you get angry' on page 67 and to talk about any other techniques they have to deal with anger. Encourage them to share their suggestions with the rest of the class before doing the 'Role play' and then discussing what they have learned from it. Invite a few students to share with the class the most important thing they've learned.

- In new groups, ask students to read 'After an argument' and then do the discussion activity that follows it. Again, invite students to share their views and reasoning with the rest of the class. Ask if anyone has any suggestions of their own to add to the list.

PLENARY

- As a class, read the poem 'Anger' and then do the 'Discuss' task. Ask students if they agree with the idea in the poem. Encourage them to bring into the discussion the things they have learned in the lesson about how to manage anger. Then ask them to write their own cinquain about anger (a cinquain is a five-line poem with a syllable pattern of 2, 4, 6, 8, 2). Students requiring more challenge can do this on their own; those needing more support can do it in pairs or in mixed-ability pairs.

RESEARCH

- Ask students to use the internet to find out about other strategies for dealing with anger (e.g. meditation, deep breathing, CBT).

EXTENSION

- Ask students to complete the rest of **Worksheet 11.1** (questions **4** and **5**).

Further information and support for teachers:

'8 ways to teach teenagers anger management skills':
www.verywellfamily.com/teach-teens-anger-management-skills-2609114

NHS, 'Teenage aggression and arguments':
www.nhs.uk/conditions/stress-anxiety-depression/teen-aggression-and-arguments/

Further information and support for students:

Childline, 'Anger': www.childline.org.uk/info-advice/your-feelings/feelings-emotions/anger/

Young Minds, 'Anger': https://youngminds.org.uk/find-help/feelings-and-symptoms/anger/

1. What makes you angry? List three things.

   a) ....

   b) ....

   c) ....

2. Are there any particular times of day that you often get angry?

   ☐ Morning   ☐ Evening

   ☐ Lunchtime   ☐ Late at night

   ☐ Afternoon

   Why do you think you are more likely to get angry at this time of day?

   ....

3. Which of the following states make you more angry or more likely to lose your temper?

   ☐ Feeling tired

   ☐ Feeling ill

   ☐ Feeling hungry

   Other ....

   Why do you think you are more likely to lose your temper when in this state?

   ....

4. What are the best ways to stop you getting angry?

   a) ....

   b) ....

   c) ....

5. What are the best ways for you to calm down?

   a) ....

   b) ....

   c) ....

Strand:	Resources:
• Personal wellbeing and mental health	• Book Two: pp. 68–69 • Worksheet 11.2

Learning objective:	Key words:
• To understand what jealousy is and to learn strategies for protecting yourself against jealousy • To identify when friends are jealous and learn strategies for dealing with this	jealous

STARTER

• Elicit from students the meaning of the word 'jealousy'. Ask a volunteer to describe a time or situation when they have felt jealous or have witnessed somebody else being jealous.

ACTIVITIES

• Ask students to read the introduction and 'Dealing with jealousy' on page 68 of *Your Choice Book Two*. Then put them into groups to do the discussion task.

• Now ask students read 'Protecting yourself against jealousy' and 'When you're feeling jealous' and then, still in their groups, to do the second 'Discuss' activity. Bring the class back together to share their views and give their reasons.

• Get students to read 'Dealing with jealous friends', and then organise them into pairs or groups of three to do the 'Role play'. If they work in threes, they should do the role play three times, with each person having the opportunity to observe the other two playing the two friends. Ask the students to compare what they have learned from watching and taking part in the role plays. Invite a few students to share what they've learned with the rest of the class – for example, there is always somebody or something you can be jealous of because you can't have or be everything; jealousy is a negative and pointless emotion – look for ways of turning it into something positive.

PLENARY

• Hand out copies of **Worksheet 11.2** and read it with the class. Explain that these are questions students could ask themselves if they think they are feeling jealous. In a class discussion, encourage students to say what they think the best questions are for helping a person to deal with jealousy.

RESEARCH

• Ask students to research the best ways of dealing with jealousy and to compare their findings with the techniques they have learned about in class. Has anyone found any new techniques or different approaches to managing jealousy? Ask them to share these with the rest of the class.

EXTENSION

• Ask students to write a blog post of two or three paragraphs for the school website on how to deal with jealousy, either in yourself or in someone else.

Further information and support for teachers:

'How to stop feelings of jealousy in teenagers': https://howtoadult.com/stop-feelings-jealousy-teenagers-7055.html

Further information and support for students:

Teen issues UK, 'Coping with a jealous friend': http://www.teenissues.co.uk/coping-jealous-friend.html

Childline, 'Jealousy': www.childline.org.uk/info-advice/your-feelings/feelings-emotions/jealousy/

Kids' Health, 'Jealousy – when it's all about you': www.cyh.com/HealthTopics/HealthTopicDetailsKids.aspx?p=335&np=287&id=2599

Worksheet 11.2 Dealing with jealousy

Questions to ask yourself about jealousy:

1. What exactly are you jealous of?

2. Is there anything you can do about the situation?

3. When you start feeling jealous, what helps you stop having these feelings and think about something else?

4. What is good that is going on in your life at the moment?

5. When you are in the midst of feeling jealous, what helps you break the pattern and think about something else?

6. In three years' time, will you still feel jealous about – or even remember – what you are currently jealous of? (If the answer is no, it is definitely not worth your time or feelings.)

7. What can you do to reduce your exposure to the thing that is making you jealous?

8. Have you discussed the issue with the person, if a person in particular is making you jealous?

9. Have you discussed the issue with somebody independent, so you can get some advice outside of the situation?

10. What are you going to do for yourself, taking time out for you, to make yourself feel better?

11.3 Dealing with fear

Strand:	Resources:
• Personal wellbeing and mental health	• Book Two: pp. 70–71 • Worksheet 11.2

Learning objective:	Key words:
• To learn strategies for dealing with fears, including fear of exams • To distinguish between a fear and a phobia	fear, phobia, panic attack

STARTER

• Read the introduction on page 70 of *Your Choice Book Two*, explaining what fear is. Ask students to suggest common fears that people have and note these on the board, but be sensitive to any fears students might express in the classroom (e.g. fear of public speaking, fear of getting an answer wrong in front of people).

ACTIVITIES

• Ask students to read 'Fear about exams' and then to do the discussion activity in groups. Bring the class back together to compare and discuss their answers.

• Organise students into pairs to read 'Your choice' and decide which things in the list are fears and which are phobias. Then encourage pairs to share their results with the class and compare them with other groups' suggestions. Note that this is a normative activity, where there are no right/wrong answers – almost all of the points listed could be phobias.

• As a stretch activity, ask students to think of any other phobias.

• Ask students to read 'Dealing with phobias' and 'Steve's story', and then to do the 'Discuss' activity that follows in groups.

• Hand out **Worksheet 11.3** and read through it with students before asking them to complete it. Then, in a class discussion, ask who found it helpful and why.

• Ask students to read 'Panic attacks' and 'After a panic attack or feeling frightened'. As a class, discuss what students think is the best way of dealing with a panic attack. Did they find the advice helpful?

• Organise students into pairs or groups to read 'Fear as fun' and then do the final 'Discuss' activity.

PLENARY

• Ask students to work in pairs to do the 'Research' task. You could ask half of the class to do the research and make the poster about advice on dealing with panic attacks, and the other half to do theirs on dealing with fears and phobias, explaining what the difference is between the two.

EXTENSION

• Look at the websites given below for students. In small groups, get students to discuss which ones give the best advice, giving reasons for their views.

Further information and support for teachers:

Psychology Today, 'Appreciating fear in adolescence': www.psychologytoday.com/us/blog/surviving-your-childs-adolescence/201311/appreciating-fear-in-adolescence

Very Well Family, 'How to help your teen conquer the fear of failure': www.verywellfamily.com/ways-to-help-your-teen-conquer-the-fear-of-failure-2609555

Further information and support for students:

NHS Moodzone, '10 ways to fight your fears': www.nhs.uk/conditions/stress-anxiety-depression/overcoming-fears/

NHS, 'Phobias': www.nhs.uk/conditions/phobias/

NHS Moodzone, 'How to deal with panic attacks': www.nhs.uk/conditions/stress-anxiety-depression/coping-with-panic-attacks/

Worksheet 11.3 Dealing with your fears

1. On a scale of 1 to 10, with 1 being not at all afraid, and 10 being very afraid, what are you afraid of? Write a score in the boxes for each of these common fears.

☐ Spiders	☐ Insects	☐ Heights
☐ Confined spaces (claustrophobia)	☐ Wide open spaces (agoraphobia)	☐ Dogs and other large animals
☐ The dark	☐ Snakes	☐ Deep water
☐ Crowds	☐ Public speaking	

Other (please specify) ....

2. What are you most afraid of?..

3. Do you have a big picture in your head of what you are afraid of?

   ....

4. What happens when you make a small picture in your head of this thing or the situation you are in?

   ....

5. What happens now when you imagine a picture of yourself with the thing or situation you are thinking of?

   ....

6. Now change this picture to black and white.
   How does this make you now feel about the thing or situation you are thinking of?

   ....

7. Now imagine a bubble around yourself whilst you are thinking about this thing or situation.
   How does that make you feel?

   ....

8. Imagine you had put yourself with this thing or situation 100 times, and every time everything had been OK. How does that now make you feel?

   ....

9. Image the one thing that would make you feel completely relaxed with this thing or this situation.
   How does that now make you feel?

   ....

10. Putting this all together, on a scale of 1 to 10, how afraid are you now of this thing or situation?

   ....

12.1 Signs of stress

Strand:	Resources:
• Personal wellbeing and mental health	• Book Two: pp. 72–73 • Worksheet 12.1

Learning objective:	Key words:
• To understand what stress is and identify the three main types of stress • To discuss successful strategies for dealing with different types of stress	stress, physical stress, mental stress

STARTER

• Ask students what they think stress is and how it can affect people. Draw out from their responses that there are three types of stress: mental, physical and emotional. Then read the introduction on page 72 of *Your Choice Book Two*. Ask students to suggest the signs of mental stress and make a list on the board.

ACTIVITIES

• Before reading any more of the text, ask students to do part **1** of the 'Discuss' activity on page 72, drawing a picture of a stressed person and then, in groups, comparing it with other people's.

• Still in their groups, ask students to read 'The mental signs of stress'. How does the list compare with the one on the board? Did the students suggest other signs not included in the book? Then ask students to do the rest of the discussion activity (parts **2–4**). Do they still think their pictures are a good representation of someone who is stressed? What, if any, changes would they like to make?

• Get students to read 'Physical signs of stress' and then to do the 'Your choice' matching activity on page 73 (they will read 'Johnny's story' later). Work through the answers in a class discussion and ask if anyone can think of any other solutions for the physical symptoms of stress. *Suggested matches: 1G, 2E, 3A, 4H, 5I, 6C, 7B, 8D, 9J, 10F, 11K.*

• Organise students into small groups to read 'Johnny's story' and then, through discussion, to do the first part of the research activity. *Answers: Johnny is suffering from stress caused by exams. He needs to find a strategy to deal with this. Karen has PTSD and needs to see a counsellor for therapy to deal with this.*

• In pairs, ask students to read 'The emotional signs of stress' and then to do part **1** of the 'Your choice' activity that follows it. Encourage pairs to compare their answers in groups and then do part **2** of the activity together.

PLENARY

• Hand out copies of **Worksheet 12.1** for students to complete on their own and then discuss in pairs if they feel comfortable doing so. Hold a class discussion to find out if students now feel better equipped to recognise and deal with stress.

EXTENSION

• Ask students to design their own stress management plan – see the links below.

Further information and support:

APA, 'How to keep stress in check': www.apa.org/helpcenter/stress-teens.aspx

TeensHealth, 'Stress': kidshealth.org/en/teens/stress.html

'For teens: creating your personal stress management plan': www.healthychildren.org/English/healthy-living/emotional-wellness/Building-Resilience/Pages/For-Teens-Creating-Your-Personal-Stress-Management-Plan.aspx

Worksheet 12.1 Knowing yourself and what stresses you

In order, from the most to the least stressful, write down what people or situations stress you and what difference being stressed by each one makes to you (for example, how do you feel, think and act when stressed?). Then in the final column, note down what you can do to avoid or remove this stress.

Compare your answers with a partner.

What stresses you – people/situation	What is the difference when they/it stress/stresses you?	What you can do to avoid or remove this stress
1.		
2.		
3.		
4.		
5.		
6.		
7.		
8.		
9.		
10.		

Strand:	Resources:
• Personal wellbeing and mental health	• Book Two: pp. 74–75 • Worksheet 12.2

Learning objective:	Key words:
• To examine the pros and cons of stress • To consider strategies on avoiding stress in the first place	stress, stress reservoir, FOMO

STARTER

• Ask students if they think stress can ever be a good thing. Try to draw out examples like going into survival mode in an emergency or encouraging revision at exam time. Then read the introduction on page 74 of *Your Choice Book Two*.

ACTIVITIES

• With students, read 'Pros and cons of stress'. Looking at the Yerkes-Dodson curve, discuss what it means and how it can help with managing stress.

• Organise students into pairs to do the 'Your choice' activity. Tell them to do the initial rankings (tasks **1** and **3**) on their own before comparing their answers with their partner (tasks **2** and **4**). In a class discussion, draw out where there were similarities and where there were differences. This should help students to see that there are some common causes of stress as well as other areas where stressors are more individual.

• Ask students to read 'Our stress reservoir'. Remind them of the anger reservoir that they found out about in lesson 11.1 and explain that this is a similar idea. Then get them to do 'Your choice' on page 75 in pairs. (Please note that in some editions of *Your Choice Book Two*, one of the ten ways to avoid stress it missing, namely: 'Never go to bed on an argument – always sort it out before going to sleep.' If it is missing from students' books, ask them to add it in to the list when they do 'Your choice'.)

• Get students to read 'Becca's story' and then do the discussion activity in groups.

• Organise students into pairs to do part **1** of the 'Write' activity, and then share and compare their posts in groups (part **2**). As a class, decide which are the best posts and why.

PLENARY

• Hand out **Worksheet 12.2** for students to complete on their own and then discuss their results in pairs or small groups.

RESEARCH

• Ask students to keep a diary of their stress levels over one or two weeks. Find time in a later lesson to encourage those who feel comfortable to compare their results in groups, and work out how they can best avoid the stress highlighted in their stress diaries.

EXTENSION

• Ask students to design their own questionnaire based on **Worksheet 12.2** and then pilot it on their classmates.

Further information and support for teachers:
Psycom, '6 common triggers of stress': www.psycom.net/common-triggers-teen-stress

Further information and support for students:
Childline, 'Anxiety, stress and panic': www.childline.org.uk/info-advice/your-feelings/anxiety-stress-panic
NHS, 'How to deal with stress': www.nhs.uk/conditions/stress-anxiety-depression/understanding-stress

Worksheet 12.2 How stressed are you? Quiz

Are you stressed? Look at the following statements. Ask your partner to answer each statement with the answer that best suits them. Then count up the number of A, B and C answers that they give. Then look at the feedback at the bottom of the sheet.

1. I always get the right amount of sleep. (A)
   I often wake up in the middle of the night. (B)
   I often oversleep and have trouble getting up in the morning. (C)

2. I find myself very short tempered when I disagree with someone. (B)
   I really don't care what other people are saying – I can't be bothered. (C)
   I pay attention to what others say and can be assertive when I disagree with them. (A)

3. I have a good strategy for revising for any exams or tests that are coming up. (A)
   I don't worry at all about exams or tests – there's no point – you're going to pass or fail them anyway. (C)
   I get really wound up by exams – and get a dry feeling in my mouth. (B)

4. Food doesn't really interest me. I only eat when I have to, and it doesn't matter what I eat. (C)
   I stuff myself with as much food as possible when I eat, and often don't really taste it. (B)
   I eat the right amount of food – slowly and carefully – and stop when I am full. (A)

5. I can be very sensitive. When something upsets me, I really know when it's happened – I can even have a physical reaction. (B)
   I react to upsetting situations, but can deal with them, put them in perspective, and get over them. (A)
   Nothing ever really upsets me. (C)

6. Sometimes everything gets too much for me – if it's too loud or there are too many people. (B)
   I find it best when I'm on my own and it's quiet and there's nothing to bother me. (C)
   I'm OK either on my own or with people, and I don't mind whether it's loud or quiet. (A)

7. I calm down quickly after an argument. (A)
   I get really involved in an argument and will think about it for days afterwards. (B)
   I don't get emotionally involved in arguments, I just say my piece and that's it. (C)

8. When playing video games, I find I can't stop – I have to get the top score, even if I often get a sore neck and headache afterwards or the next day. (B)
   I enjoy the competitive nature of video games, but only play occasionally. (A)
   I don't play games – what's the point? (C)

9. I feel tired all of the time. (C)
   I have just the right amount of energy. (A)
   I feel tired sometimes, and I always feel like I never get a break. (B)

10. I let things get to me sometimes, and then I make silly mistakes. (B)
    Things can get to me, but I'll get over them quickly. (A)
    Things never get to me. (C)

How did you score?

Mostly A – It sounds as if you are in control of yourself and are in balance.	**Mostly B** – It sounds as if you could be under some stress and should look at ways of dealing with stress in the next lesson.	**Mostly C** – It sounds as if you could be feeling a bit depressed and would benefit from looking at materials on depression.

12.3   Coping with stress

Strand:	Resources:
• Personal wellbeing and mental health	• Book Two: pp. 76–77 • Worksheet 12.3

Learning objective:	Key words:
• To understand how to deal with stress	emotional resilience, emotional stress

STARTER

• Elicit from students what they think the long-term effects of stress are and note these on the board. *Suggestions could include: lack of sleep, nervous exhaustion, irritability, unhappiness, depression, bad temper and shorter life expectancy.*

ACTIVITIES

• With students, read 'The long-term effects of stress' and the 'Research' task on page 76 of *Your Choice Book Two*. Ask what they think 'emotional resilience' might be and then get them to research it in pairs. Invite students to share their findings with the rest of the class.

• Still in their pairs, ask students do parts **1** and **2** of 'Your choice' before comparing their answers in groups (part **3**). Ask them to do part **4** in their groups, and then share and compare their responses in a class discussion.

• Organise students into pairs to read 'Caitlin's coping strategies' and then do the 'Discuss' task that follows it on page 77. Get students to compare their answers in groups.

• Ask students to do part **1** of the writing task on their own and then to get into pairs to compare their answers and do part **2** of the activity. *Suggested answers: 1. Talk to them, get them to see all sides of the situation, clarify whether it is the person or their behaviour that is causing the problem. Talk about resolving or avoiding the problem. 2. Break the pattern – get them a tea/coffee, have a chat, change the subject, do something different. 3. Change the topic of conversation or get the conversation to end. 4./5. Talk things through with them, make sure they exercise, have a cup of tea/coffee, give them time and space to relax.*

• Divide the class into groups to do the second 'Discuss' activity on page 77. Allow students enough time to think through the features and list the information before getting them to share their app ideas with the rest of the class. *Ideas of features include: music, regular breaks, study groups, rewards.*

PLENARY

• Ask students to read 'Study skills' and then to do the final 'Discuss' activity in groups. In a class discussion, encourage students to think about whether they feel better equipped to deal with stress in general as they reflect back on what they have learned in this lesson.

EXTENSION

• Organise students into pairs and hand out **Worksheet 12.3** for them to complete together. Encourage them to compare their answers and discuss what they have learned about themselves. Suggest that the also compare their answers with those to **Worksheet 11.1** to see if there are any similarities or patterns.

Further information and support for teachers:

Psychology Today, 'Top 10 stress busters for teens': www.psychologytoday.com/gb/blog/teen-angst/201411/top-10-stress-busters-teens

The Samaritans, 'Managing stress, making choices': www.samaritans.org/education/deal/coping-strategies/managing-stress

Further information and support for students:

Childline, 'Coping with stress': www.childline.org.uk/info-advice/your-feelings/anxiety-stress-panic/coping-with-stress/

NHS, 'How to deal with stress': www.nhs.uk/conditions/stress-anxiety-depression/understanding-stress/

Worksheet 12.3 Coping with stress

1. What makes you stressed? List three things.

   a) ....

   b) ....

   c) ....

2. Are there any particular times of day that you get stressed?

   ☐ Morning   ☐ Evening

   ☐ Lunchtime   ☐ Late at night

   ☐ Afternoon

   Why do you think you are more likely to get stressed at this time of day?

   ....

3. Which of the following states make you more stressed?

   ☐ Feeling tired

   ☐ Feeling ill

   ☐ Feeling hungry

   Other ....

   Why do you think more likely to feel stressed when in this state?

   ....

4. What are the best ways to stop you getting stressed?

   a) ....

   b) ....

   c) ....

5. What are the best ways for you to relax?

   a) ....

   b) ....

   c) ....

Strand:	Resources:
• Personal wellbeing and mental health	• Book Two: pp. 78–79 • Worksheet 13.1

Learning objective:	Key words:
• To understand the different types of bank account that exist • To clarify which sort of bank accounts are suitable for particular situations	bank account, current account, rate of interest, APR, savings account, online banking, bank card, cash machine, PIN code

STARTER

• Ask students for ideas about where they can store their money. Note different ideas on the board. Ask if any student has a bank account and, if so, what type. Then read the introduction on page 78 of *Your Choice Book Two* with the class.

ACTIVITIES

• Ask students to read 'Bank accounts: your questions answered' on page 78 and then test the class on the key vocabulary. This can be done in the form of a quiz with questions such as: 'What is a bank account? What is a bank card? How does online banking work', etc.

• Organise students into pairs to do the 'Research' task on page 79, summarising their results in a table. Note: they should find that savings accounts offer a higher rate of interest than current accounts, especially savings account where you can't get your money out immediately. (This will be a useful fact for the next lesson, 13.2, on saving and borrowing.) Also, the more you save, the higher the rate of interest will be.

• Hand out copies of **Worksheet 13.1**. Ask the students to complete part **1** either on their own or in pairs for students needing more support. Encourage students to compare their answers in groups and then do part **2** of the worksheet together. *Answers might include: To give you financial advice; to offer you different products that help you save money and earn interest on your savings; to offer you different products that help you borrow money; to help you manage your finances.*

• As a class, read and then discuss 'Keeping your bank account safe'. Which do they think are the most important pieces of advice? Why? Encourage students as a class to give different reasons for the points of view.

• Organise students into pairs to do the 'Write' task. Encourage them to do some research to see if they can find any additional advice about keeping their bank account safe. Other advice they might find is how to protect themselves against phishing (people trying to get their account details through fraudulent emails), fraudulent phones calls (another form of phishing), and making sure that old bank and credit cards are cut up and destroyed.

PLENARY

• Invite students to share the findings of the research they did for the writing task. Encourage some pairs to show their poster to the rest of the class and talk through their reasons for including what they have.

EXTENSION

• Ask students to research prepaid cards for under-18s (see the link below) and summarise their findings in an information leaflet for teenagers.

Further information and support for students:

Money.co.uk, 'Compare bank accounts for teenagers': www.money.co.uk/current-accounts/bank-accounts-for-teenagers.htm

'Top cards for under-18s': www.moneysavingexpert.com/banking/cards-for-under-18s/

Which?, Best bank accounts for children and teens: www.which.co.uk/money/banking/bank-accounts/best-childrens-bank-accounts-arspc9p7mk0y

Worksheet 13.1 What are banks for?

1. Look at the following table. Which of the functions of a bank do you think are the most important? Rank them from 1 (most important) to 10 (least important). Give reasons for your views when you fill in the table. Then compare your results with other people in your group.

Function	Ranking	Reasons
A place to store money safely		
A place to withdraw cash easily		
A place to pay other people easily		
A place for your employer to pay you easily		
A place to catch financial criminals and fraudsters		
A place to buy foreign currency when travelling abroad		

2. What other functions can you think of for banks? Give reasons for your views.

Function	Reasons

Strand:	Resources:
• Personal wellbeing and mental health	• Book Two: pp. 80–81 • Worksheet 13.2

Learning objective:	Key words:
• To identify the different ways of savings • To identify different ways of borrowing money, including highlighting the dangers of loan sharks	saving, premium bonds, loan sharks, rate of interest

STARTER

• Elicit from students whether they have ever saved up money for something. If so, what was it for and how did they save? Then read the introduction on page 80 of *Your Choice Book Two* with the class.

ACTIVITIES

• Ask students to read about the different ways of saving money on page 80. Then check comprehension with the class by asking the students to give an example of a formal way of saving (money in a bank account) and an example of an informal way of saving (spare change in a jar at home).

• Hand out copies of **Worksheet 13.2** for students to complete on their own or in pairs. Encourage them to compare their answers in groups. Then come together as a class to talk through the advantages and disadvantages and share some of the reasons for students' rankings. *Formal saving: you get a rate of interest; the money is safe (advantage); it's harder to get your money (disadvantage). Informal saving: no rate of interest, not as safe as a bank (disadvantage); easy access (advantage).* For question **2** students may suggest: *saving together as a group to gain a higher rate of interest; a credit union – where local people who have money lend it to others at a low rate of interest to help the local community; investing it in a local business – risky, you may get a higher rate of interest, or you may lose all your money.*

• Read through the 'Role play' with students. They can do this in pairs or in groups of three. If doing it in threes, the third person will observe the two who are acting out the scenario. Get students to take it in turns playing the different roles and being the observer and then to discuss what they think would be the best option for saving the money. Invite pairs or groups to share their opinions with the rest of the class.

• With the students, read through the five scenarios, **a)–e)**, in the 'Discuss' box. Then ask the students to work in small groups to discuss and answer the two questions about the scenarios.

• Ask students to read 'Why would you borrow money?', Joshua's story and 'Loan sharks' on their own, and then discuss these in groups or as a class.

PLENARY

• Ask students to do the writing task in mixed-ability pairs. Then bring the class back together and invite students to share their plan with the rest of the class. Note the best ideas as a list on the board.

EXTENSION

• Ask students to use the internet to find out more about premium bonds. They should use their findings to write a report of two to three paragraphs saying whether they would prefer to save money in premium bonds or with a savings account at a bank, giving reasons for their views.

Further information and support for teachers:

BBC, 'The dangers of loan sharks to be taught in schools': www.bbc.co.uk/news/business-26376737

'Two thirds of young people borrow money from invisible sources': www.moneyadvicetrust.org/media/news/Pages/Two-thirds-of-young-people-borrow-from-invisible-safety-net-of-family-and-friends.aspx

Further information and support for students:

Money Advice Service, 'Teenagers talking money': www.moneyadviceservice.org.uk/en/corporate/teenagers-talking-money-yphub

National Savings & Investments, Premium bonds: www.nsandi.com/premium-bonds

'Premium bonds: Are they worth it?': www.moneysavingexpert.com/savings/premium-bonds/

1. Look at the following ways of saving money. Which do you think are best? Which are the worst? Write the advantages and disadvantages of each and then rank each way of saving in order of preference. Compare your answers in groups and give reasons for why you ranked each way of saving.

Way of saving money	Advantages	Disadvantages	Ranking	Reason for ranking
Keeping spare change in a jar at home				
Putting money in a low-interest current account				
Putting money in a high-interest savings account				
Lending money to a friend, asking them to pay you back with interest				
Letting your mum and dad keep your savings				
Hiding a little bit of money under the bed every week				
Putting money aside at the end of every month with your brother, sister or a friend				

2. What other ways can you think of for saving money?

Way of saving money	Advantages	Disadvantages	Ranking	Reason for ranking

Strand:	Resources:
• Social education	• Student Book: pp. 82–83 • Worksheet 14.1

Learning objective:	Key words:
• To identify where laws come from and what laws apply to children at different ages • To discuss whether the current laws relating to smacking are appropriate	law, common law, case law, smacking, permission

STARTER

• Elicit from students the definition of a law (the rules that apply to everyone in the country), with examples. Ask where they think laws come from. Note their suggestions on the board.

ACTIVITIES

• Ask students, in pairs, to read 'Types of law' on page 82 of *Your Choice Book Two*, including 'A gap in the law' and then to ask each other questions to check their understanding. Suggestions: What are the most important types of law? *(statute laws passed by Parliament)*; What is a gap in the law called when a judge makes a ruling on it? *(common law)*; What are laws based on judges' rulings in the past called? *(case law)*. Then organise students into groups and support them to do the 'Your choice' activity.

• Get students to read 'Children in care', including Tina's and Joe's stories, and then do the discussion activity in groups. Share some responses in a class discussion.

• Ask students to read 'Discipline and smacking' on their own and then to discuss in groups whether they agree with smacking. Help students to do the research task on the latest changes to the law on smacking in Scotland and Wales, using news websites.

• Ask students to do the writing task, thinking about what they have learned about the proposed changes to the law in Scotland and Wales.

• Organise students into groups to read 'You and the law in school'. Then do the 'Discuss' task that follows.

PLENARY

• Bring the students back together to share and compare groups' responses to the discussion task as a class. Then look back at the points you noted on the board at the start of the lesson. Would students answer the questions differently now?

RESEARCH

• Hand out **Worksheet 14.1** and ask students to complete the first column in pairs or groups, researching online to find the answers. Invite some students to share their answers: *1. 18 except for local elections in Scotland and for the Scottish Parliament, where it is 16; **2.** 14; **3.** 10 (8 in Scotland); **4.** 15; **5.** Any age; **6.** 18; **7.** 16 (for a moped; older for more powerful motorbikes); **8.** 17; **9.** 18; **10.** 5; **11.** 16; **12.** 16.*

EXTENSION

• Organise students into mixed-ability pairs to fill out the second and third columns of **Worksheet 14.1**. Then compare these views as a class.

Further information and support for teachers:

'The law on smacking children': childlawadvice.org.uk/information-pages/the-law-on-smacking-children

Taking children on holiday in term time: www.moneysavingexpert.com/family/school-holiday-fines

Further information and support for students:

NSPCC, 'A child's legal rights': www.nspcc.org.uk/preventing-abuse/child-protection-system/legal-definition-child-rights-law

'What age can I?': www.themix.org.uk/crime-and-safety/your-rights/what-age-can-i-9102.html

Worksheet 14.1 At what age can you...?

Look the following laws that exist for young people. Fill out the table with what you think is correct, and then check your answer with a teacher. Then decide what laws you would change, and what age you would have instead. Give reasons for your views.

The Law	Current age	What you would change the age to?	Why?
1. Age you can vote			
2. Age an adult can open a bank account for you that you can access			
3. Age at which you are responsible for a crime			
4. Age at which the police can take your fingerprints with your parents' consent			
5. Age your parents can get a passport for you			
6. Age you are legally an adult			
7. Age you can get a licence to drive a motorbike			
8. Age you can get a licence to drive a car			
9. Age you can leave school or training			
10. Age you must start school			
11. Age you can join the army			
12. Age you can consent to sex			

14.2   You and the police

Strand:	**Resources:**
• Social education	• Book Two: pp. 84–85 • Worksheet 14.2

Learning objective:	**Key words:**
• To understand the job of the police and to know what rights you have with regard the police • To discuss whether or not there should be ID cards in the UK	police, arrest, ID cards

STARTER

- Elicit from students what they think the job of the police is. Note their suggestions on the board and refer back to the list at appropriate points in the lesson.

ACTIVITIES

- Ask students to read the introduction and 'Attitudes towards the police' on page 84 of *Your Choice Book Two* and then, in groups, do the discussion task. Invite groups to share their responses with the rest of the class.

- Hand out **Worksheet 14.2** for students to complete in pairs and then compare their answers in groups. Go through the questions with the class and make sure they all know the correct answers: *False are **2** and **3** – you can remain silent, but if you do remain silent and then reveal something later on in court, it may count against you. For **5** and **9** you have to be 15 or over for fingerprints and DNA samples to be taken with your parents' permission, or 17 without their permission.*

- With students, read the 'Fact check' and then discuss the information as a class. Ask if the students were surprised by any of the statistics.

- Ask students to read 'ID cards' on their own and then do the writing task. Invite individuals to share some of their for and against arguments with the rest of the class.

- Organise students into pairs to read the section on 'Terrorism' and then do the 'Research' task. You could direct students to the weblinks on counterterrorism below. Allow some time for them to find the information and answer the questions. Then bring the class together to share and compare their responses and reasons.

PLENARY

- Ask students to read 'Arrests' and then do the 'Your choice' activity on their own, before getting into pairs to compare their answers. Invite individuals to share their responses with the rest of the class and make sure they all know the correct answers. *Answers: **1.** Offences you can be arrested for: all of them, although refusing to give name and address is unlikely. **2.** Court summons: all of them, although again unlikely for refusing to give name and address or minor acts of vandalism as a first offence.*

EXTENSION

- Ask students to research the Validate UK ID card (see the link below) and summarise what they think the advantages might be and why someone would or wouldn't want to get one.

Further information and support for teachers:

The Independent – terrorist attacks foiled in 2019: www.independent.co.uk/news/uk/crime/terror-attacks-plots-uk-police-tips-concerns-appeal-foiled-brexit-basu-a8741411.html

The latest counterterrorism statistics can be found by searching on GOV.UK: https://www.gov.uk/

Further information and support for students:

Lawstuff, 'If you are arrested': lawstuff.org.uk/police-and-law/if-you-are-arrested

ID cards for teenagers: www.validateuk.co.uk

Crime and policing in England, Wales and Northern Ireland: www.police.uk

Read the statements below and decide which are true and which are false.

Statement	True	False
1. Anybody can be arrested by the police.		
2. Anyone can make a citizen's arrest by shouting 'I arrest you in the name of the law' and calling the police.		
3. You have the right to remain silent.		
4. If you are under 16, the police must inform your parents that you have been arrested.		
5. The police can take your fingerprints, whatever your age.		
6. You are entitled to free legal advice if you are arrested.		
7. At the police station, the police don't have to keep you arrested – they can let you go if it was a minor matter.		
8. The police can choose to give you a formal written warning rather than charge you. This doesn't mean that you have been found guilty. It does mean the police keep a record of what happened, and this can be taken into account if you are arrested for the same offence again		
9. The police can take a sample of your DNA. Even if you are released without charge, they can keep this on file for a certain period.		
10. The police can apply to a judge to search your home if they suspect evidence is there of you committing a crime.		

Strand:	Resources:
• Social education	• Book Two: pp. 86–87 • Worksheet 15.1

Learning objective:	Key words:
• To understand the two different types of democracy: direct and indirect	democracy, direct democracy, representative democracy, referendum, initiative

STARTER

• Elicit from students what they think the meaning of the word 'democracy' is. With them, read the introduction on page 86 of *Book Two* and see how the information compares with their suggestions.

ACTIVITIES

• Ask students to read 'Representative democracy' and then support them to do part **1** of the 'Research' task in pairs. Strictly speaking, the UK is a constitutional monarchy because we still have a royal family. However, laws are made and put into effect by the legislature.

• Divide the class into four groups to do part **2** of the research task. Ask each group to research one of the devolved assemblies, using the BBC Bitesize links below, and then to write two to three paragraphs about their institution. Invite groups to report their findings in a class discussion.

• Organise students into groups and support them to do 'Your choice' at the top of page 87.

• Ask students, on their own or in pairs for students who need more support, to read 'Votes at 16' and the statements in 'Your choice'. Get them to discuss, in groups, which statements they agree or disagree with, giving reasons for their views.

• Ask students to read 'Direct democracy' and then hand out **Worksheet 15.1** for them to do tasks **1** and **2** in pairs. Then explain that at the end of the lesson they are going to participate in a debate. Tell them to read task **3** on the worksheet and then divide them into two groups, one for and one against the motion. Allow them some time to discuss their allocated point of view, using the information on the worksheet. You might also like to refer back to **Worksheet 5.1b** for guidance on holding debates.

• Support students to do the research task on direct democracy in Switzerland. There are some useful videos on YouTube about this if they search 'Switzerland's direct democracy'.

PLENARY

• Chair the debate that students prepared for earlier in the lesson and take a final vote to decide whether the majority of the class agrees or disagrees with the motion.

EXTENSION

• Hold an election to elect a class representative, to represent students' views to the school authorities. This can be done in stages: asking for candidates (any student nominated by two others); holding a quick hustings, where each candidate says why they want to be the class representative; allowing the class to ask questions; then voting. If more than two candidates are nominated, you can either use a simple first-past-the-post system or you can use the alternative vote system, whereby students vote for their candidates in order of preference. If no candidates get 50%+1 of votes in the first round, then the candidate with the least votes is eliminated. Their second preferences are counted and reallocated, until either a candidate achieves 50%+1 of the votes or there is only one candidate left, who is the winner.

Further information and support for teachers:

House of Commons and House of Lords: www.parliament.uk/commons and www.parliament.uk/lords

Further information and support for students:

The Scottish Parliament: https://www.bbc.com/bitesize/clips/zdmkq6f

The Welsh Assembly: https://www.bbc.com/bitesize/clips/z6fmpv4

The Northern Ireland Assembly: https://www.bbc.com/bitesize/clips/zwhjxnb

You Gov, 'For and against: Lowering voting age':
yougov.co.uk/topics/politics/articles-reports/2012/02/15/and-against-lowering-voting-age

The case of Austria – what happened when voting at 16 was introduced:
www.euronews.com/2018/09/11/what-does-voting-at-16-change-the-case-of-austria

Worksheet 15.1 Direct versus indirect democracy

1. Look at the arguments for and against direct and indirect democracy. Rank each set of arguments in order of strength, with 1 as the strongest and 4 as the weakest.

   1. ....   2. ....

   3. ....   4. ....

2. Decide which system you prefer. Give reasons for your views.

....

....

....

....

....

For direct democracy:	Against direct democracy:
• It is the most democratic form of government, because everyone gets a say. • It is the most transparent form of government. • It forces people to listen to all minority voices, because everyone has a vote. • It is very responsive, allowing decisions to be challenged and changed quickly. • It is now a lot faster, thanks to the development of the internet.	• It is very expensive. • It is very time consuming. • In a close decision, it can lead to the majority forcing their wishes on a minority. • The general public may not have the expertise to make decisions. • It can lead to contradictory decisions, such as when the public wants a lot of things for free and to cut taxes.
For indirect (representative) democracy:	**Against indirect (representative) democracy:**
• It is less expensive. • It is less time consuming. • It is practical. • It has a good track record of working. • It allows experts to develop, who have a better understanding of policy. • Decisions can be made with an overview, such as balancing spending commitments with taxation. • It can allow freedom from politics, allowing people to switch off and live their lives.	• It is less transparent. • It can be unrepresentative, with minority voices being drowned out by the majority. • It can be unresponsive, particularly between elections. • It encourages apathy, by allowing people to switch off, thus not taking a real interest in what is going on. This means that politicians can get away with bad decisions.

3. You are now going to take part in a class debate on the motion:

   'This house believes that direct democracy is better than indirect democracy.'

   Your teacher will tell you whether you are going to argue for or against the motion.

Strand:	Resources:
• Social education	• Book Two: pp. 88–89 • Worksheet 15.2 • The Declaration of Human Rights (downloadable from the link below)

Learning objective:	Key words:
• To understand what is meant by 'human rights' and to identify the most common human rights	human rights, European Convention on Human Rights, freedom of expression, Universal Declaration on Human rights

STARTER

• Elicit from students what a human right is and what they think their human rights are. List the answers on the board.

ACTIVITIES

• Ask students to read the introduction on page 88 of *Your Choice Book Two* and 'The European Convention on Human Rights. Organise them into groups to do the 'Research' and 'Discuss' activities. Then invite groups to share their choice of the most important rights, giving their reasons.

• With the class, read 'The Universal Declaration of Human Rights'. Then do the 'Discuss' activity on page 89. A pdf file of the document can be downloaded from the link below or students can look at it online.

• Hand out **Worksheet 15.2** for students to do in pairs or small groups. Ask them to share and compare their answers in a class discussion. *Answers: Any age – freedom of movement, freedom from slavery, the right to have a family, freedom from torture, freedom of speech. Age 14 – A job excluding paper rounds (11). Age 16 – to own a pet, to vote in local elections in Scotland and for the Scottish Parliament (18 for all other elections/parts of the UK), to get married (with parental consent, 18 without), to leave home with parental permission, to be tried as an adult with a fair trial. Age 18 – to stand for election, for the minimum wage, for guns under strict licensing, to own a home.*

• Ask students to read 'The European Charter of Fundamental Rights'. Then organise them into groups of three to do the 'Research' task. Do this by asking a student from each group to read out a point from their document and see if the students in the other two groups have something comparable. Ask more confident students to deal with the European Charter of Fundamental Rights, which is more complicated than the other two documents. Make sure that each student has access to one of the three documents, all of which can be accessed online or downloaded from the links below.

PLENARY

• Get students to read and 'The UN Convention on the Rights of the Child' on page 89 and then, in pairs, to do the 'Your choice' activity. Then hold a class discussion on which rights are the most important. Answers may be necessities – right to food, water, shelter, clothing and security.

EXTENSION

• Organise students into groups and ask them to imagine they are designing their own country. What rights should they include in their new country? Why? Then as a class, debate the different rights and decide what you would do as a class.

Further information and support for teachers:

'How human rights protect young people': rightsinfo.org/human-rights-protect-young-people/

The European Convention on Human Rights: www.echr.coe.int/Documents/Convention_ENG.pdf and rightsinfo.org/the-rights-in-the-european-convention/

'Rights of the Child': fra.europa.eu/en/theme/rights-child

The Universal Declaration of Human Rights: www.un.org/en/universal-declaration-human-rights/

The European Charter of Fundamental Rights: ec.europa.eu/info/aid-development-cooperation-fundamental-rights/your-rights-eu/eu-charter-fundamental-rights_en

Worksheet 15.2 What rights when?

Look at the following list of rights. At what age do you think you have each of these rights in the UK?

Right	Age in the UK
The right to own a pet	
The right to vote	
The right to get married	
Freedom of movement	
Freedom from torture	
The right to have a family	
The right to leave home	
Freedom of speech	
The right to stand to be elected as a politician	
The right to a minimum wage	
Freedom from slavery	
The right to a fair trial	
The right to a job	
The right to a home	
The right to own a gun	

Strand:	**Resources:**
• Social education	• Book Two: pp. 90–91
	• Worksheet 15.3

Learning objective:	**Key words:**
• To understand the different types of pressure groups and examine the range of campaign methods pressure groups use	pressure groups, single-issue groups, sectional groups, lobbying, petitions, civil disobedience, direct action

STARTER

* Elicit from students what they think a pressure group is, with examples. Note their suggestions on the board.

ACTIVITIES

* Ask students to read the introduction and 'Single-issue groups' on page 90 of *Your Choice Book Two* and then to do the research task on their own. Invite some students to share their findings with the class.

* Ask students to read 'Sectional groups' and then organise them into groups to discuss which sort of pressure group they think is most important, and why. Encourage groups to share and compare their views with the rest of the class. Refer students back to the suggestions on the board and decide which of their groups were single-issue and which sectional.

* Read the first paragraph of 'Campaign methods' with the students and then tell them that you would like them to do some jigsaw reading. Organise them into groups of up to eight and explain that each person in the group will read about a different campaign method and then explain it to the other members of the group or, in pairs, to the class as a whole.

* Do the 'Discuss' activity as a class. Ask students if they can think of examples of other campaigning methods they may have come across on social media or through publicity stunts. Encourage them to draw on what they have learned in this lesson about campaigning methods and about democracy in earlier lessons to help them decide which methods they think are most effective.

* Support students to do the 'Research' activity. The answer to question **2** is that a party seeks power, putting candidates forward for election, and will have policies across a wider area, while a pressure group only seeks influence and usually in a very specific area.

* Ask students to use **Worksheet 15.3** to prepare for a debate on pressure groups. Split the class into three groups: one to argue that pressure groups are bad for democracy, one to argue that they are good and one to represent those who are not sure. Ask group 1 to list arguments why pressure groups are bad for democracy and group 2 to list arguments why pressure groups are good for democracy.

PLENARY

* Chair the debate. Arguments for them helping democracy include: more participation, opportunity for tension release (participation between elections), providing education, providing expertise. Arguments for them hindering democracy: elitism, not transparent/opaque, small minority can hijack the will of the majority, illegal activities.

EXTENSION

* Organise students into mixed-ability pairs and ask them to research one of the campaign methods in more detail. They should then summarise their findings in two to three paragraphs, including a recent example they have found.

Further information and support for teachers:

Insider pressure groups – Video (3.5 minutes): www.bbc.com/bitesize/clips/zhrkq6f

Outsider pressure groups – Video (1.5 minutes): www.bbc.com/bitesize/clips/zws34wx

Further information and support for students:

BritPolitics, 'What are pressure groups?': www.britpolitics.co.uk/what-are-pressure-groups

Pressure groups in Scotland: www.bbc.com/bitesize/guides/zj37hyc/revision/9

Hold a debate on the following motion:

> **'This house believes that pressure groups hinder democracy overall.'**

Group 1   Spend 10 minutes thinking about all the reasons why pressure groups hinder democracy.
Choose one person who will open the debate for you – known as the proposer – to speak for
5 minutes. They need to be a good public speaker. Choose a different person to sum up at the
end. They should be good at summarising and responding.

Group 2   Spend 10 minutes thinking about all the reasons why pressure groups help democracy.
Choose one person who will open the debate for you – known as the opposer – who will speak
for 5 minutes. They need to be good at responding and thinking on their feet. Choose a different
person to sum up at the end. They should be good at summarising and responding.

Group 3   Think of all the questions you would like to ask.

List here arguments why pressure groups hinder or help democracy, or questions you would like to ask:

1. ....

....

2. ....

....

3. ....

....

4. ....

....

5. ....

....

The debate will run in the following order:

* The proposer will speak.
* Then the opposer will speak.
* Then there will be questions and anyone can speak.
* Then the person summing up against the motion will speak.
* Finally, the person summing up for the motion will speak.
* Then everyone will vote.

Strand:	**Resources:**
• Social education	• Book Two: pp. 92–93
	• Worksheet 15.4

Learning objective:	**Key words:**
• To understand what organ transplant and assumed consent are	organ transplant, genetics, stem cell research
• To find out about stem cell research and identify its pros and cons	

STARTER

• Revisit what the word 'consent' means. Discuss the idea of informed consent, when someone can give medical consent on your behalf if you are in a situation where you cannot.

ACTIVITIES

• Ask students to read the introduction, 'Blood donation' and 'Organ donation and assumed consent' on page 92 of *Your Choice Book Two*.

• Organise students into pairs to do the 'Research' task on page 93 (answers to the questions in part **1** can be found on the 'Give blood' website, via the link below). Invite some students to share with the class whether or not they will give blood when they're older, explaining their reasons.

• Again in pairs, ask students to do 'Your choice'. Give them copies of **Worksheet 15.4** to help them with this. They can do part **1** to get them thinking about how they feel themselves about organ donation and then they can write their 'Your choice' responses in parts **2** and **3**. Invite some pairs to share their responses to **2** and **3** with the rest of the class.

• Ask students to read 'Stem cell research', including 'Research controversy' on page 93. Read the questions in the discussion task with the class and then give them time to think about their answers before discussing them in groups.

PLENARY

• Invite students to contribute to a class discussion on stem cell research, sharing and comparing their opinions from the group discussion.

RESEARCH

• Max and Kiera's law is a law that was passed recently to encourage organ donation. Organise students into mixed-ability pairs to research this law and write two or three paragraphs about what they have learned, using the weblink below.

EXTENSION

• Ask students to design a poster promoting the importance of organ donation and informed consent. The poster should also advise people about how to make sure they are on the donor register and that their family knows what their wishes are.

Further information and support for teachers:

Give blood: www.blood.co.uk/

Organ donation: www.organdonation.nhs.uk/

NHS, Blood and transplants: www.nhsbt.nhs.uk/who-we-are/a-history-of-donation-transfusion-and-transplantation/

'Types of stem cells and their uses': www.eurostemcell.org/types-stem-cells-and-their-uses

Further information and support for students:

Max's and Kiera's law: www.bbc.co.uk/newsround/47374529

Worksheet 15.4 Organ donation

1. Look at the following form. These options have been used by the NHS in the past for people who wish to donate organs after their death.

   What would you be willing to donate? Tick the relevant boxes.

In the event of my death, I give my consent for the following organs to be used for the purpose of organ transplant:

☐ Heart ☐ Corneas

☐ Lungs ☐ Pancreas

☐ Kidneys ☐ Tissue

☐ Liver ☐ Small bowel

☐ I am happy for any part of my body to be used for organ transplant after my death.

☐ I am happy for any part of my body to be used to medical research after my death.

☐ In the event of my death, I want NHS staff to contact my family to discuss how my wishes for my organs to be used can be carried out, in line with my religious and personal beliefs.

☐ I do not give my consent for any of my organs to be used in organ transplants and/or medical research after my death.

---

2. Give three reasons in favour of having an 'opt out' system of organ donation.

   ....

   ....

   ....

3. Give three reasons why people might object to this.

   ....

   ....

   ....

Strand:	**Resources:**
• Social education	• Book Two: pp. 94–95
	• Worksheet 16.1

Learning objective:	**Key words:**
• To understand the different types of disability	disability, physical disability, learning differences, dyslexic, autism
• To examine the different strategies that can be used to help people with disabilities, autism and learning difficulties	

STARTER

* Elicit from students what a disability is, what sort of disabilities there are and how people with a disability may be discriminated against.

ACTIVITIES

* Ask students to read the introduction and the paragraph on physical disabilities on page 94 (not including Jamal's story) and the first paragraph about learning differences on page 95 of *Your Choice Book Two* to prepare them for the 'Research' task (which they will do later in the lesson).

* Organise students into groups to read Jamal's story and then do the discussion activity that follows. Make sure they all understand what indirect discrimination is: when a person is discriminated against by accident. For example, a Jewish boy brings his lunch to school and asks for it to be heated, because he only eats certain food that has been specially prepared (Kosher). The school says no, students can't use the microwave. The Jewish student has been indirectly discriminated against because of his religion.

* Organise students into mixed-ability groups to do the writing activity, using **Worksheet 16.1** for parts **2** and **3**. Compare their design suggestions in a class discussion and then agree on the best design, incorporating features from other designs that they may have missed. As a stretch activity, these suggestions can be sent to the local council's education department, to influence future school design.

* Tell the students they are going to do 'jigsaw reading', with half of the students reading Anna's story and the others reading Toby's story on page 95. They should then do the relevant 'Discuss' activity for their story. Then bring the class together to discuss the two stories and share their ideas. Encourage each half of the class to contribute about both stories.

* Organise students into mixed-ability pairs to complete the 'Write' activity, imagining they were planning a day out in London, with Jamal, Anna and Toby coming along.

* Now ask students to do the 'Research' task on page 94 in pairs, teaming more-confident students with those needing more support. Ask them to choose either physical disabilities or learning difficulties and to find out what is being done to fight discrimination and prejudice against this particular type of disability.

PLENARY

* Bring the whole class together to discuss the results of the 'Research' task.

EXTENSION

* Encourage them to write two or three paragraphs summarising their findings from the plenary.

Further information and support for teachers:

National Autistic Society: www.autism.org.uk/about.aspx

British Dyslexia Association: www.bdadyslexia.org.uk/educator/hints-and-tips-secondary

Scope – support for families with physically disabled children: www.scope.org.uk/advice-and-support/families-with-disabled-children/education/

Mencap – support for families of children with learning disabilities: www.mencap.org.uk/advice-and-support

Worksheet 16.1 Designing your own school

1. How many floors will your school have? ....

2. How many main entrances will your school have? ....

3. What access arrangements will your school for students with physical disabilities have?

   ....

   ....

4. Will your school have hearing loops, to help students who are hard of hearing?

   ....

5. How many steps will there be in your school? ....

6. If your school has more than one floor, will there be a lift? ....

   ....

7. Will your school have coloured lines on the floor to help visually impaired students and students with learning difficulties easily find their way around?

   ....

   ....

8. How will your school use technology to make lessons accessible for everyone?

   ....

   ....

9. How will your school make its environment as positive and welcoming to everyone as possible?

   ....

   ....

   ....

10. Is there anything else you can think that should go in your school's design?

   ....

   ....

   ....

   ....

Strand:	**Resources:**
• Social education	• Book Two: pp. 96–97
	• Worksheet 16.2

Learning objective:	**Key words:**
• To understand ageism and identify what discrimination occurs against younger and older people in society	dementia, Alzheimer's disease, living wills, advocate
• To examine strategies to help discrimination against young people, and against older people, particularly those with dementia and/or Alzheimer's disease	

STARTER

* Ask students to imagine being old and to suggest the sort of problems they might face. Note these on the board.

ACTIVITIES

* Ask students to read the introduction on page 96 and then to do the first 'Discuss' activity in pairs. Invite students to share and compare their answers with the rest of the class. Strategies for challenging these statements include asking: How do you know? Is that always the case? Is this unfair? (And if so, why?)

* Ask students to read 'Ageism against children and young people' and then, in groups, to do the second 'Discuss' activity. Encourage students to share their experiences of ageism with the rest of the class and compare groups' responses to parts **2** and **3** in a class discussion.

* Ask students to read 'Ageism towards older people' and 'Busting the myths'. As a class, go through the achievements listed in 'Busting the myths' again and do the 'Discuss' task on page 97 together. Do students find different things surprising, or do they all have similar opinions? Refer back to the problems noted on the board at the beginning of the lesson and ask students to consider whether they might have given some ageist responses that they'd now like to rethink.

* In pairs, ask students to read 'Dealing with dementia and Alzheimer's', including 'Living wills' and 'Advocate', and then to do the final discussion task in groups. Ask students to share with the class their suggestions for other things that could be done to prevent discrimination against people with dementia and Alzheimer's disease.

PLENARY

* Hand out **Worksheet 16.2** for students to work on in groups. Then share responses in a class discussion.

EXTENSION

* Ask students to discuss what they think the challenges are for older and young people in their area, and to draw up a strategy to help deal with these. They could use the list of questions on **Worksheet 16.1** as a starting point to discuss what needs to improve in their local area.

* Encourage students to send their strategies to the local council and invite a speaker to come in to say what is being done to help young people in their local area.

Further information and support for teachers:

Equality and Human Rights Commission, 'Age discrimination': www.equalityhumanrights.com/en/advice-and-guidance/age-discrimination

Dementia UK, 'Getting support': www.dementiauk.org/get-support

Alzheimer's Society, 'Get support': www.alzheimers.org.uk/get-support

Personnel Today, 'Age equality: five examples of discrimination against young workers': www.personneltoday.com/hr/age-equality-five-examples-discrimination-young-workers

Worksheet 16.2 Challenging ageism

Challenging ageism is important. Even if you are not directly involved, it is important to challenge ageism, otherwise, the person being discriminatory gets away with their behaviour.

Look at the following situations. What is wrong in each situation? What would you do to challenge each sort of behaviour:

1. A young person pushes in front of an elderly woman in the bus queue. 'You were being too slow', they say to her.

2. A frail elderly woman gets on a train and wants to sit on a seat, but it's blocked by a mother with a pram. The mother refuses to move the pram.

3. An elderly man is waiting to cross the road. A middle-aged woman grabs him by the arm and helps him across, although he didn't want any help and was happy to take his time.

4. A pensioner couple are waiting at the bar. The barman keeps ignoring them and serving younger people.

5. A volunteer who has helped at her local after-school club is told that she can no longer come and help because she has just turned 70.

6 A male pensioner is waiting to see the latest *Star Wars* film at the cinema. Two young girls shout: 'What are YOU doing here? You're far too old to get this!'

7. A group of teenagers are hanging out at the park, playing football and having fun together. Two older women tell them to stop messing around and ask if they would like a place of their own to go to as the park is for children.

8. A young person finds it very difficult to find a part-time job because there are always candidates with more experience than her. At a job interview she is told, 'You look much too young for this position'.

 © HarperCollins*Publishers* Ltd 2019

Strand: • Personal wellbeing and mental health	**Resources:** • Book Two: pp. 98–99 • Worksheet 17.1
Learning objective: • To assist students in choosing their GCSE options	**Key words:** choice, GCSEs

STARTER

• With the class, read the introduction and 'Making the right decision' on page 98 of *Your Choice Book Two*. Then ask students to do the 'Your choice' activity which will encourage them to think about how and why they make the decisions they do.

ACTIVITIES

• Ask students to read 'Choosing the right subjects' and then, in mixed-ability pairs, to do the discussion activity. Invite some students to share their responses with the rest of the class.

• Ask students, on their own, to read 'Changing subjects' on page 99 and then to do the 'Write' task. Ask them to do the discussion activity in pairs, thinking about the answers they gave in the writing task and what they've learned so far in the lesson.

• Support students to do the 'Research' task. They should do this individually before getting back into their earlier pairs to discuss their findings and work out whether the GCSE choices they discussed in the previous task match up with the sort of qualifications they need for the career they researched. Monitor this closely.

• Ask students to read 'Breaking targets into chunks' and then do the writing task that follows. As a way of structuring this task, hand out **Worksheet 17.1**, which consists of a 'goals pyramid', with the near future at the bottom and the far future at the top. Ask students to complete each level of the pyramid with their ultimate goal at the top and, below that, what they need to do in each time period in order to progress towards their ultimate goal. Students can then compare their pyramids with one another, checking how realistic each other's plans are.

PLENARY

• Ask students to discuss their pyramids and assess whether their targets for each stage are realistic enough, taking positive and constructive feedback from other students.

EXTENSION

• Ask students to list their potential GCSE subject choices and then discuss these with their parents or carers.

Further information and support for students:

Youth Employment UK, 'Choosing GCSE options – 19 questions to ask yourself': www.youthemployment.org.uk/choosing-gcse-options-19-questions-ask/

Success at School, 'Careers advice for teenagers': successatschool.org/blog/515/Careers-Advice-for-Teenagers

'Smart goal-setting for teens': 7mindsets.com/smart-goal-setting-for-teens/

Making informed A level choices: www.informedchoices.ac.uk/

Complete each level of the 'goals pyramid' below.

* Write in your ultimate goal at the top.
* In each layer below that, write what you need to do in that time period in order to progress towards your ultimate goal.

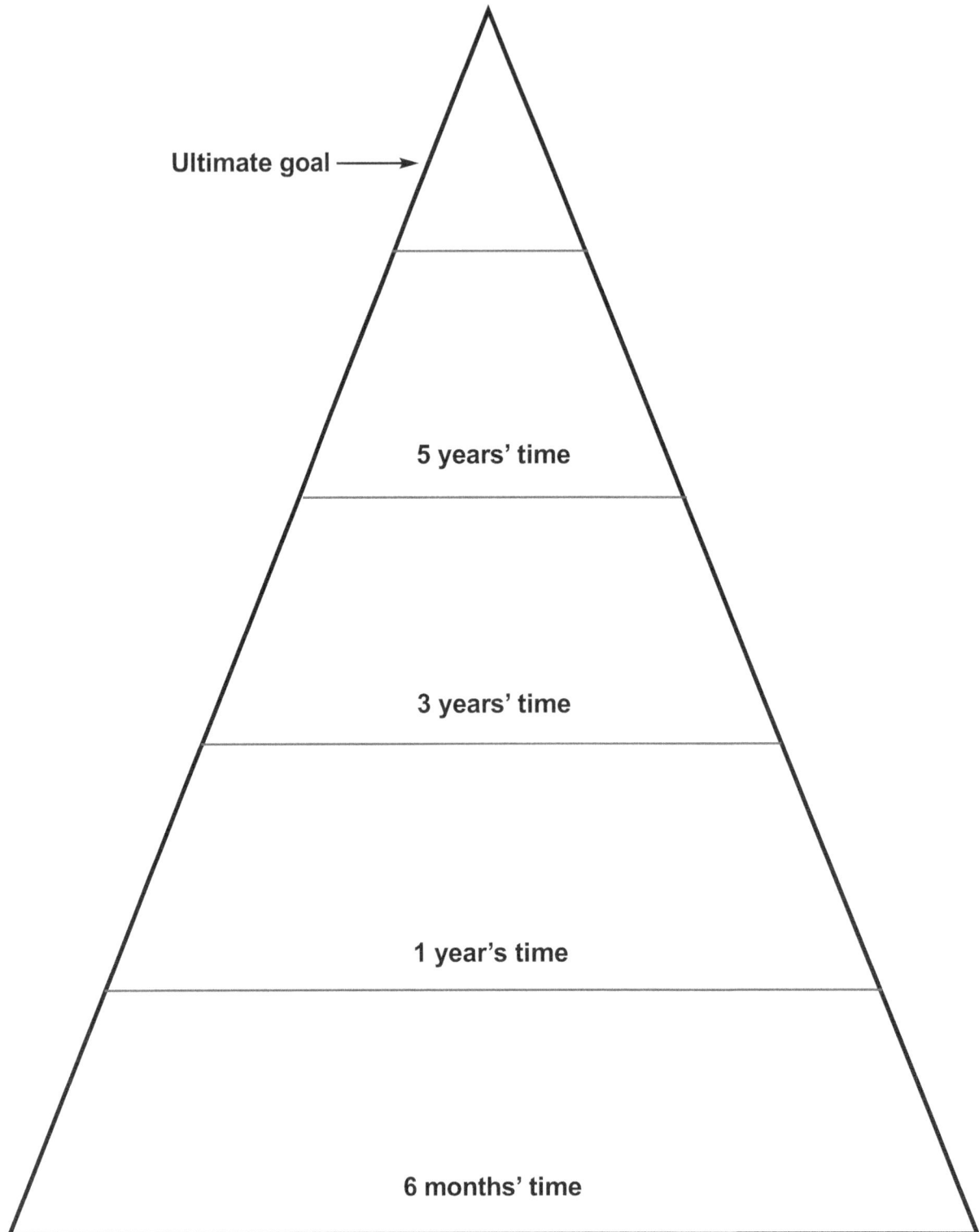

Ultimate goal ⟶

5 years' time

3 years' time

1 year's time

6 months' time

Strand:	**Resources:**
• Personal wellbeing and mental health	• Book Three: pp. 6–7 • Worksheet 1.1

Learning objective:	**Key words:**
• To understand why confidence is important and how to build up confidence in difficult situations	confidence, thoughts, feelings and behaviours

STARTER

* Write 'confidence' on the board. Ask the class what difference being confident can make to a person. Get them to specify particular situations to put it in context, e.g. 'being able to ask a stranger for directions', 'jumping off a high diving board'. Write the responses around the word 'confidence' to build up a picture of what a person with confidence looks like in action.

ACTIVITIES

* Pick one of the situations provided in the starter activity. Draw an outline figure on the board and invite students to suggest what thoughts, feelings, physical sensations and behaviours that person would be having/showing in that situation if they were confident. Draw a second figure and use a different colour to write the equivalent thoughts, etc. of someone with low confidence in the same situation. Elicit that it is our thoughts and behaviours that we are most in charge of, and that practising these can help build our confidence.

* Ask students to read the confidence diagram on page 6 of *Your Choice Book Three* and do the writing activity, using **Worksheet 1.1**. They could do this on their own on in pairs, depending on how much support they need. Then ask them to work in pairs to do the discussion activity that follows.

* Read the 'Research' task with students and encourage them to do it outside classroom time.

* Ask students to read 'Boosting your confidence' and 'Tara's story' on page 7 and then discuss the questions in the 'Discuss' box in small groups. Ask for volunteers to feed back their responses to the rest of the class.

* Read the 'Your choice' activity with the class. Then organise the students into pairs either to discuss the statements or to pick one of them to role play. Choose volunteers to share their ideas or to do their role play for the class.

PLENARY

* Ask students to write a short statement about what they have learned about confidence in the lesson. Encourage them to relate it to a specific situation where they lack confidence, with suggestions as to how to build confidence instead.

RESEARCH

* Ask students to use the internet to discover how a hero of theirs, such as a singer or sportsperson, developed their own confidence.

EXTENSION

* Ask students to choose one area of their life where they want to build their confidence. (Working in pairs to pinpoint this area is helpful.) Encourage them to use one of the ideas from this lesson to help them move forward in that area in the next week, and write a short statement outlining what happened.

Further information and support for students:

Childline, 'Building confidence and self-esteem': www.childline.org.uk/info-advice/your-feelings/feelings-emotions/building-confidence-self-esteem/

Prince's Trust, 'Building confidence': www.princes-trust.org.uk/help-for-young-people/tools-resources/building-confidence

---

Area where you have LOW confidence:

....

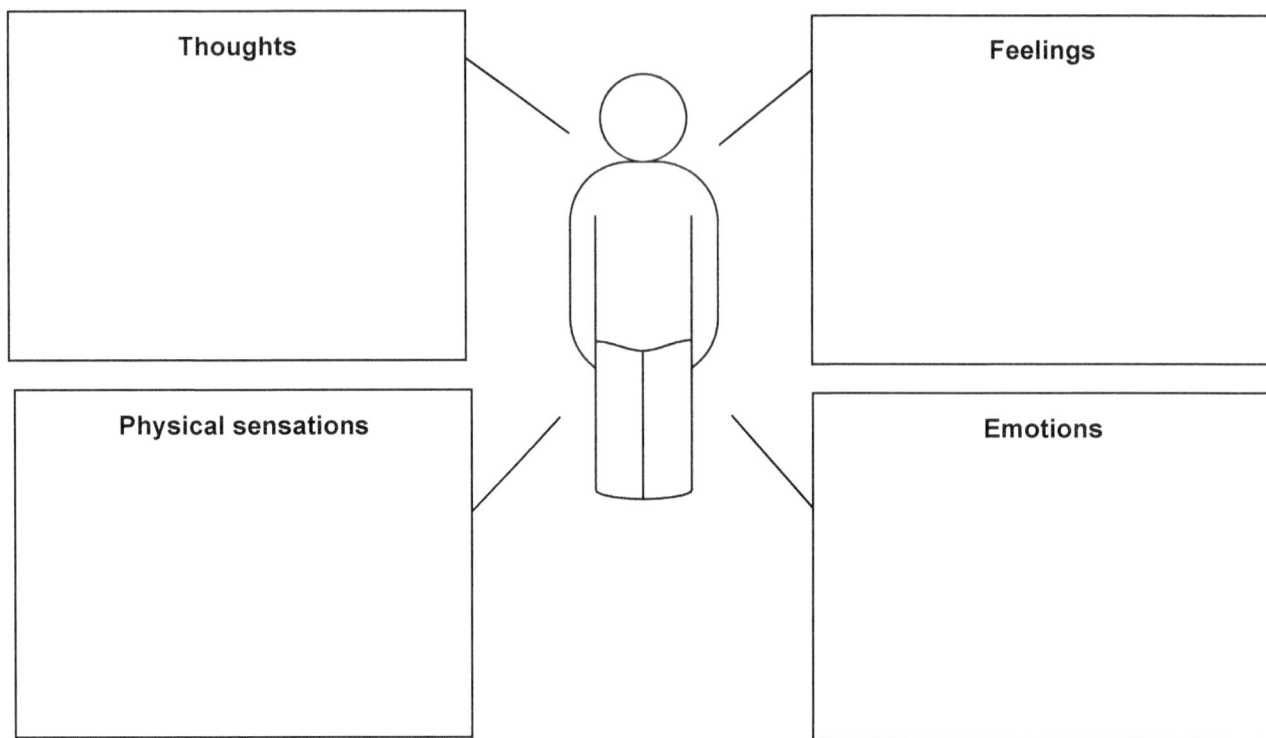

| Thoughts | Feelings |
| Physical sensations | Emotions |

Area where you have HIGH confidence:

....

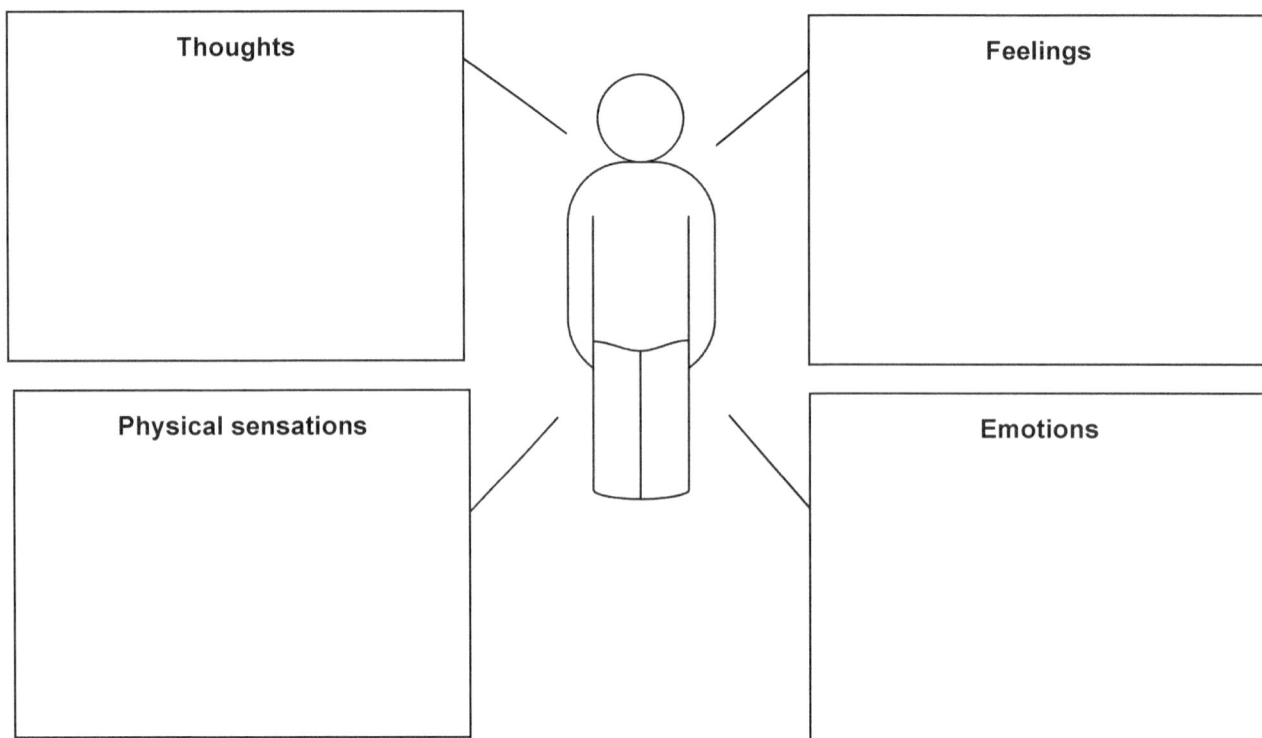

| Thoughts | Feelings |
| Physical sensations | Emotions |

Strand:	Resources:
• Personal wellbeing and mental health	• Book Three: pp. 8–9 • Worksheet 1.2

Learning objective:	Key words:
• To understand what self-esteem is and why it is important • To learn ways of developing self-esteem	self-esteem, self-acceptance, perfectionism

STARTER

• Recap lesson 1.1 and ask the class what the difference is between confidence and self-esteem. Work towards a definition of self-esteem (e.g. 'Self-esteem is about valuing and accepting yourself, whatever your achievements', as on page 8 of *Book Three*). Then read and discuss 'Why self-esteem is important'.

ACTIVITIES

• Ask students to read 'Myths that lower our self-esteem' and 'How to build self-esteem – the four keys' and then, in small groups or pairs, to do the first part of the 'Discuss' task. Give students **Worksheet 1.2** in order to help them identify their positive qualities. Emphasise that this activity is a crucial step in freeing up their thinking in order to acknowledge and accept good things about themselves. This may be difficult at first, because they may not be used to acknowledging these things, so working with a supportive partner may help. Alternatively, the exercise can be given to students to take away and complete on their own, over a period of time, and/or with the help of a supportive family member.

• Organise students into pairs to work on parts **2** and **3** of the discussion task. You may need to go through a class example first to gather the sorts of critical judgements and predictions that our minds come up with, and identify ways of challenging these thoughts.

• Ask students to read the statements in 'Your choice' and discuss their views with a partner. Select some volunteers to feed back to the class.

PLENARY

• Read out the posts from Riley and Jess and then ask students to do the 'Write' task, using the skills they have practised in the lesson. Ask for volunteers to share their responses with the class.

EXTENSION

• 'You yourself, as much as anyone in the entire universe, deserves your love and affection' (the Buddha). Ask students if they agree with this statement. Ask them to discuss it in pairs or small groups and then, on their own, to write a paragraph giving reasons for their view.

Further information and support for teachers:

Good Therapy, 'How to help teens manage their emotions and accept their feelings', another aspect of developing self-esteem: www.goodtherapy.org/blog/how-to-help-teens-manage-their-emotions-and-accept-their-feelings-0705175

Mind Moose, 'The importance of developing healthy self-esteem in children and young people': www.mindmoose.co.uk/2016/10/04/the-importance-of-developing-healthy-self-esteem-in-children-and-young-people/

The Guardian: 'Why Dutch teenagers are among the happiest in the world': www.theguardian.com/world/2018/jun/17/why-dutch-bring-up-worlds-happiest-teenagers

Further information and support for students:

Childline, 'Building confidence and self-esteem': www.childline.org.uk/info-advice/your-feelings/feelings-emotions/building-confidence-self-esteem/

The Children's Society, 'Self-esteem': www.childrenssociety.org.uk/mental-health-advice-for-children-and-young-people/self-esteem

One way of building your self-esteem is to make a list of your qualities, skills, talents and strengths. This will help to develop your positive sense of yourself, and bring to mind things that you may not generally notice about yourself.

Under the heading 'My positive qualities' (below), list as many good things about yourself as you can think of. Give yourself time to do this, and make sure you are relaxed and alone when you do it. Add things to the list as the days pass. Enjoy seeing it build up and read it frequently.

Here are some questions you can ask yourself if you have difficulty identifying your good points:

* **What do you like about yourself**, however small and fleeting?
* **What positive qualities do you possess?** You don't have to possess these for the whole time, or to a great degree!
* **What have you achieved in your life, however small?** Think small – have you learned to swim?
* **What challenges have you faced?** What anxieties and problems have you faced, and what skills did you use to manage these?
* **What gifts or talents do you have, however modest?** What things can you do well (NB not perfectly)?
* **What skills have you acquired?** Academic, domestic, people, technical, sporting, leisure and work skills.
* **What do other people like or value in you?** What do they ask you to do or compliment you on?
* **What qualities and actions that you value in others do you share?** Sometimes it's easier to see the strong points in other people than in yourself.
* **What aspects of yourself would you appreciate if they were aspects of another person?** Write down something that would count as a positive if it applied to someone else.
* **What small positives are you discounting?** You don't discount small negatives, so don't discount small positives either!
* **What are the bad things that you are *not*?** If it's hard to say that you are kind, at least start by saying that you are not cruel!
* **How might another person who cared about you describe you?** People who know you often have a kinder, more balanced perspective on you.

My positive qualities

....

....

....

....

....

....

....

....

....

....

Strand:	Resources:
• Personal wellbeing and mental health	• Book Three: pp. 10–11 • Worksheet 1.3

Learning objective:	Key words:
• To explore what challenges teenagers face and • To learn how to build resilience when faced with those challenges, with a focus on coping with friendship issues	challenge, change, resilience, friendship

STARTER

• Ask the class what challenges they face as a teenager. Write these on the board. Include emotional and developmental challenges as well as challenges that family life and the outside world may throw at them. Read the introduction on page 10 of *Your Choice Book Three* with the students, followed by 'Teenage pressures'. This will help them to recognise that being a teenager is difficult and challenging, and that they need to be kind to themselves and build up skills to meet these challenges.

ACTIVITIES

• Ask students to read 'Building resilience' and then to do the first 'Discuss' activity. You may need to prompt the class with suggestions for difficult situations – at school, at home, in relationships, etc. What is difficult for one person may not be difficult for another. In the feedback, collect all the strategies, including ones that are additional to those listed in the article. Students could write them on sticky notes and display them on the wall.

• Give students **Worksheet 1.3** and tell them to work with a partner to identify a present or future problem where they need to dig deep and build resilience. They use the same checklist as in the previous exercise and write down what strategies they could use.

• Ask students to read 'Coping with friendship issues' and then do the second 'Discuss' activity in small groups. Invite groups to feed back their findings to the rest of the class.

• Organise students into pairs to do the role play giving advice to Olivia. Rather than advising Olivia to ditch her friends, encourage the role play to move in the direction of practical steps Olivia can take to build her resilience in this situation – for example, by communicating assertively, taking control, taking care of herself and getting the situation in perspective.

PLENARY

• Ask students to do the 'Write' task to complete the statement: 'When times are hard, remember these three key things...'. Ask for volunteers to share what they have written. Re-emphasise the term 'resilience' to encompass these strategies.

EXTENSION

• Ask students to watch the Prince's Trust podcast by the model Iskra Lawrence on how to deal with setbacks (you can find this on YouTube using the search terms 'Iskra Lawrence Princes Trust setbacks'). Ask them to identify which of the points she makes speaks most to them.

Further information and support for teachers:

Public Health England, 'Dealing with change': campaignresources.phe.gov.uk/schools/topics/rise-above/overview?WT.mc_id=RiseAboveforSchools_PSHEA_EdComs_Resource_listing_Sep17

Building resilience in young people: www.worthit.org.uk/blog/building-resilience-young-people/ and schools.au.reachout.com/articles/building-resilience-in-young-people-resource

Further information and support for students:

NHS video explaining resilience and ways to build it: www.healthforteens.co.uk/feelings/resilience/video-5-ways-to-build-resilience/

Worksheet 1.3 Resilience

Resilience is the ability to adapt well in the face of hard times. First describe the problem that is affecting you. Then think about each of the ways in which you could build your resilience to cope with that problem.

Problem: ....

1. **Communicate.** Who could you talk about your problems with? How can you keep connected? Who can you spend good quality time with? How can you channel your emotions?

   ....

   ....

   ....

   ....

2. **Take care of yourself.** How can you be kind to yourself? What treats can you give yourself? Are you getting enough sleep? Are you demanding perfect standards of thought or behaviour?

   ....

   ....

   ....

   ....

3. **Stick to a routine.** Identify some fixed points to anchor you. What could be a good routine (at school/home)? How can you help yourself stick to this? Identify a place free from stress and anxieties that can act as a haven (at school/home or with friends).

   ....

   ....

   ....

   ....

4. **Take control.** How can you take back control? Do you need to take decisive action? What smaller steps can you take? Remember: any steps are an achievement.

   ....

   ....

   ....

   ....

5. **Keep the problem in perspective.** Don't assume that the worst will happen – or has already happened. Ask yourself, 'Will this matter in a year from now?' Think of a time when you faced up to a different challenge. Identify the good times as well – in the past and the future.

   ....

   ....

   ....

   ....

1.4   Problem-solving

Strand:	Resources:
• Personal wellbeing and mental health	• Book Three: pp. 12–13 • Worksheet 1.4

Learning objective:	Key words:
• To explore a technique of problem-solving	problem-solving

STARTER

- Brainstorm different problems that come up in life – however trivial. Write these on the board. Despite the wide range of problems students are likely to have suggested, ask if each one would require a completely separate range of strategies to solve it. If not, what sorts of skills can we use to tackle *any* problem? Get students to discuss this briefly in pairs and then begin to gather some of their ideas in a separate brainstorm.

ACTIVITIES

- Read the introduction on page 12 of *Your Choice Book Three* with the class. Explain that there are many problem-solving approaches, so it helps to explore one and see if it is beneficial. Ask students to read about the Sx4 method of problem-solving on pages 12 and 13. Then ask them to discuss this in pairs before working on one of the problems in the 'Discuss' exercise, using the template in **Worksheet 1.4**. Ask for volunteers to do a short presentation and share their problem-solving approach.

- Organise students into pairs to do the 'Role play' activity. The friend supporting the one with the problem may want to refer to their notes on the Sx4 method, or even get their partner to fill in a blank copy of **Worksheet 1.4** as they discuss it together. Emphasise to students that writing things down can help embed things in the memory as well as reinforce commitment to a course of action.

PLENARY

- Ask students to write down the single most helpful aspect of problem-solving they have learned. Invite feedback from volunteers and ask them how they are going to remember that tip, and elicit ways of doing this.

- Get students to think of a problem of their own using **Worksheet 1.4** and to complete the exercise in 'Your choice' on page 13. If they cannot identify a problem for themselves, then they could either think of a problem that a friend or family member has at the moment or imagine a problem that could come up for them in the future.

EXTENSION

- Ask students to think about how learning from their mistakes or from situations which have not gone well can help them to solve them solve problems in the future. Ask them to write one paragraph about a past situation that did not go well and one paragraph about what they have learned from this.

Further information and support for teachers:

i News, 'Teens fail to see value in "vital" problem-solving skills' – an article on the importance of teenagers developing their problem-solving skills, and yet the low importance given to problem-solving: inews.co.uk/news/education/teens-fail-see-value-vital-problem-solving-skills/

ReachOut.com, 'Problem-solving and teenagers': parents.au.reachout.com/skills-to-build/connecting-and-communicating/problem-solving-and-teenagers

---

Worksheet 1.4 The S×4 method of problem-solving

1. State the problem

State the problem as clearly as possible. Make sure it is something that is in your control.

....

....

2. List possible solutions

Think of as many solutions as possible to your problem and write them down.

....

....

....

....

....

3. Select the best solution

Now choose the best solution. You may need to list the advantages and disadvantages of your proposed solutions first.

....

....

....

....

4. See how it works

Draw up a plan of action. Identify the separate steps.

....

....

....

....

....

If it's successful, keep doing it. If it's not, work out what went wrong and adjust the solution or try another solution from your list.

Note: If your problem is causing huge stress or trouble for you, you may need more help. If, for example, you are too depressed or anxious to solve your problems effectively on your own, you should talk to a trusted adult or seek help from a GP.

Strand:	**Resources:**
• Relationships and sex education	• Book Three: pp. 14–15 • Worksheet 2.1 (cut into cards) • Screen shots of celebrities

Learning objective:	**Key words:**
• To build understanding and acceptance of the many and various ways in which young people develop sexually at puberty • To explore the issues around coming out as gay or trans	sexuality, sex, sexual development, coming out, gender

STARTER

• Display screen shots of celebrities who have come out as gay or trans, such as Tom Daley and Caitlyn Jenner. If possible, include those whose developing sexual awareness has been very difficult (e.g. through repression or bullying) and those for whom it has been less problematic. Ask what the connection is between them, and then what their different experiences have been. Get some quick suggestions from students as to what factors may make coming out more or less difficult.

ACTIVITIES

• Ask students to read page 14 of *Your Choice Book Three*, about the young people's experiences of their developing sexuality. Then organise them into small groups to do the 'Discuss' activity. Give each group a set of the cards on **Worksheet 2.1**. Tell them that these are descriptions of sexual behaviours and attitudes. Explain that you want them to put these into three piles – healthy, unhealthy and not sure. Emphasise that 'healthy' relates to emotional wellbeing as well as physical health, e.g. issues of respect, equality and consent. Unhealthy sexual behaviours and attitudes are ones that impact adversely on the person's or partner's physical health as well as undermining respect, equality and consent. Then ask groups to share what they put in the 'not sure' pile and say briefly what the different opinions were in the group about it. (At this stage, do not try to make distinctions between sex and gender, as this is complex and will be the focus of a later lesson.)

• Ask students to read the article 'Coming out' on page 15 on their own and then, in small groups, to do the discussion activity. Ask the groups to draw up a list of the three things that could be most beneficial for someone in deciding to come out, and the three things that may be most difficult for them. Collate the group feedback on the board under two headings: 'Benefits' *(draw out things such as: being yourself, unloading the burden, living as you want to live, meeting other gay people)* and 'Considerations' *(draw out aspects such as: homophobia/transphobia, safety, being rejected/judged).*

• Ask students to read 'Ask Erica' and discuss the issues in pairs before doing the 'Write' task on their own.

PLENARY

• Ask students to write down the most important thing they have learned in this lesson. Invite volunteers to share what they have written.

EXTENSION

• Ask students to adapt the writing activity into role plays. These will only be effective with groups of students who are at ease with role playing and openly exploring issues of sexuality. Make sure the students understand that they are **not** expected to play themselves and their experiences.

Further information and support for teachers:
LGBT inclusivity, Stonewall: www.stonewall.org.uk/best-practice-toolkits-and-resources-0

Further information and support for students:
LGBT Youth Scotland have useful coming out guides for LGB and trans young people:
www.lgbtyouth.org.uk/resources/?topic=Coming&type=All
Childline, 'Sexuality': www.childline.org.uk/info-advice/your-feelings/sexual-identity/sexual-orientation

Having sexual fantasies	Having a crush on someone older
Pressuring someone into having sex	Having sex at age 14
Using pornography	Not being that interested in sex
Thinking about sex all the time	Going out with someone just because all your friends are
Being attracted to both boys and girls	Not using contraception
Practising safer sex	Using contraception

Strand:	**Resources:**
• Relationships and sex education	• Book Three: pp. 16–17 • Worksheet 2.2 • A current advert with strong gender roles

Learning objective:	**Key words:**
• To explore what influences our views about sex and gender	sexuality, gender, men, women, manhood, pornography

STARTER

• Display a current advert to the class, one with strong gender roles, such as an advert for perfume. Ask for quick responses to these questions: 'What does it say about men? About women? About sex and relationships? Specifically, what characteristics of men/women are shown as being positive/rewarded? What characteristics are absent or portrayed negatively? How influential is such a diet of stereotypes on our attitudes to sex and gender?'

ACTIVITIES

• Ask students to read the introduction and 'Thinking about our influences' on page 16 of *Your Choice Book Three*. Ask them to rate, in order of importance, the influences listed on their own views and behaviour. Explain that 'culture' means the general attitudes of the society they are living in. You may also want to unpack 'media' into smaller categories, as music, videos and social media. Ask students to discuss their ratings in small groups and invite groups to share their findings.

• With students, read 'The man box'. Ideally also watch the TED talk (see weblink below) and then discuss it with the class. Organise students into small groups to do the 'Discuss' activity at the top of page 17 and then invite them to share their responses. Regroup students into pairs to construct a similar 'woman box' of the culturally acceptable ways in which women are socialised.

• Get students to read Jez Franks' article on pornography and the 'Fact check' that follows it. Then organise students into small groups to do the second 'Discuss' task and invite feedback. *(For question 2, elicit answers such as parents, good friends, trusted adults, RSE lessons, advice columns.)*

PLENARY

• As a class, read 'Your choice' on page 16 and then construct an ideal word picture of man or woman on the whiteboard. What would a man/woman look like if we weren't in these boxes? Would the picture for a man look any different from that of the woman? Raise these questions rather than trying to answer them.

RESEARCH

• Ask students to research what the law is relating to porn and under-18s and write down three key facts. Remind them that it is illegal to watch pornography under age 18 and it is a crime for someone, especially an adult, to send you pornography, or to encourage or pressure you to watch it. If they have experienced this or seen something they find upsetting, they should talk to a trusted adult. Students can write their own safety plan using **Worksheet 2.2**.

EXTENSION

• Ask students to write a statement about what they would say to their own children about what it means to be a man or a woman.

Further information and support for teachers:

'PSHE & RSE: The impact of porn on the young': www.sec-ed.co.uk/best-practice/pshe-rse-the-impact-of-porn-on-the-young/

Further information and support for students:

Brook advice on porn: www.brook.org.uk/your-life/porn

Tony Porter's gripping and moving TED talk on the 'man box' (NB it includes a description of rape): www.ted.com/talks/tony_porter_a_call_to_men

NSPCC article, 'Online porn': www.nspcc.org.uk/preventing-abuse/keeping-children-safe/online-porn

---

Use the box below to develop a safety plan.

How I will keep myself safe

If someone is sending me pornography or sexual images, or encouraging me to watch pornography, I will:

1. Talk to one of these trusted people:

....

....

....

2. Take this action:

....

....

....

....

....

....

3. Remind myself of this law:

....

....

....

....

....

....

Strand:	Resources:
• Relationships and sex education	• Book Three: pp. 18–19 • Pictures of gender-ambiguous people • School's inclusion policy

Learning objective:	Key words:
• To understand the complexities and nuances of gender identity with a particular focus on transgender	sex, sexuality, gender (identity), LGBT+, transgender

STARTER

• Understanding the difference between sex and gender is an essential starting place for gender-aware RSE. Write 'sex', 'sexuality' and 'gender' on the board and ask students for definitions. Write their suggestions under each headword. This should display a lot of confusion – be sympathetic and understanding, but use the material to come to a clearer definition of each term. (See the definitions provided at the start of the 'Fact check' box on page 18 of *Your Choice Book Three*.)

ACTIVITIES

• Ask students to read the introduction and the 'Fact check' definitions on their own and then to do the 'Discuss' task. Next, ask them to produce a 'true/false' quiz about gender terminology for their partner. Ask which, if any, terms caused confusion or controversy, and try to clarify these terms as a class.

• Get students to read 'Myths about being trans' and 'How to support a trans friend'. Then organise them into small groups to do the 'Discuss' task that follows.

• In the same groups, ask students to discuss how schools can make LGBT+ students feel welcome and safe. You may want them to consider any or all of the following: changing rooms, toilets, uniform, bullying, use of language, safe areas, liaison with teachers/governors, written policies. (See also the extension activity below.) Get feedback from groups as to the key phrases/policies they have agreed on.

PLENARY

• Display a series of pictures of gender ambiguous people. Ask for class responses to each in turn as to whether they are male or female. Ask: 'Does it matter if there is confusion, or if you can't decide? How useful are the categories anyway?' End by asking students to write a short statement about anything new they have learned about gender. Students could look at the gender unicorn on the Trans Student website (www.transstudent.org/gender) if they want to explore further their own thoughts feelings about their gender identity and/or sexuality. The 'gender unicorn' is a useful way to think about gender, as it breaks down gender identity vs. gender expression vs. biological sex, and separates sexual orientation from gender.

• Encourage students to do the 'Research' task to find out what kinds of support are available on the internet for young people questioning their gender identity.

RESEARCH

• Now ask students to research the school's inclusion policy to discover what policies are in place to make LGBT+ students feel safe and welcome. What would they change, if anything?

EXTENSION

• Encourage students to use the phrases/policies they have developed in the activity on making LGBT+ students safe (see above) to design a poster for the school noticeboard advertising these policies.

Further information and support for teachers:

PSHE Association: www.pshe-association.org.uk/content/government-equalities-office-anti-homophobic

Further information and support for students:

Mermaids UK, support for young people questioning their gender: www.mermaidsuk.org.uk

Trans Student Educational Resources, a youth-led organisation dedicated to transforming the educational environment for trans and gender-nonconforming students: www.transstudent.org

Gendered Intelligence – works with the trans community: genderedintelligence.co.uk/professionals/cpd

Transfigurations – support organisation: transfigurations.org.uk/helpline-support/

3.1   Women's rights

Strand:
- Relationships and sex education

Resources:
- Book Three: pp. 20–21
- Worksheets: 3.1a, 3.1b
- School's equal opportunities policy

Learning objective:
- To learn about the fight for women's rights and identify the inequalities that remain, in the UK and rest of the world

Key words:
women's rights, equal rights, education

STARTER

- Hold a class discussion on equal opportunities at school. Ask: 'Does your school treat girls and boys equally?' Display the school's equal opportunities policy. How effective is it in stopping discrimination? For example, do the school uniform rules discriminate against girls? Are the lessons 'gender inclusive', i.e. do teachers stress women's achievements as much as men's? Invite groups to rate how girl-friendly the school is on a scale of 1–10 (1 = very low, 10 = very high). Invite them to share their views. Does anyone think boys are discriminated against?

ACTIVITIES

- Read the introduction on page 20 of *Your Choice Book Three*, followed by 'Women's rights in the UK – the successes' and 'The challenges that remain'. Then read the questions in the 'Discuss' box and ask pairs to discuss one of them. Next, hold a class discussion tackling each question in turn. This activity can be supplemented by asking students to complete the multiple-choice quiz on **Worksheet 3.1a**. *Answers: 1(a), 2(a), 3(a), 4(c), 5(c), 6(b), 7(b), 8(a), 9(c), 10(c)*

- Ask students to complete the 'Research' task on page 21. They may find the Fawcett Society link below helpful here.

- Read the article 'Malala's story' with the class and then allocate groups to discuss the questions. Ask groups discussing the same question to compare their responses and then share similarities and differences with the rest of the class.

- Ask students to read 'Women in sport' and then to do the 'Research' activity that follows it. They may be interested to read the information about the history of women's football in the UK on **Worksheet 3.1b** as context for this task.

PLENARY

- Get students to write down the most important thing that they have learned about women's rights in this lesson. Ask volunteers to share what they have written.

RESEARCH

- Ask students to research how Plan International UK are campaigning for the rights of girls (see weblink below). Which do they think is the most inspiring campaign and why?

EXTENSION

- Ask groups to draft either an email to the Minister for Women and Equalities saying what they think their priorities should be, or a proposal to the school council saying what they think needs to be done to improve equal opportunities at the school.

Further information and support for students

Fawcett Society, 'Equality. It's about Time' – a timeline of women's rights: www.fawcettsociety.org.uk/equality-its-about-time-timeline-of-womens-rights-1866-2016

Read more about the history of women's football and the game today: *Here Come the Girls* by Helena Pielichaty. See collins.co.uk/products/9780007464913

Women in Sport, 'Campaigning': www.womeninsport.org/about-us/campaigning/

Plan International UK, a charity promoting equality for girls all over the world: plan-uk.org/act-for-girls

Circle the correct answer.

1. What percentage of MPs in the House of Commons are women? (2019)

    (a) 32%   (b) 51%   (c) 63%

2. What percentage of chief executives of the top 100 UK companies are women? (2018)

    (a) 6%   (b) 34%   (c) 42%

3. What percentage of high court judges are women? (2018)

    (a) 22%   (b) 32%   (c) 47%

4. When was rape in marriage made a crime?

    (a) 1884   (b) 1919   (c) 1994

5. When did Major General Susan Ridge become the first female senior officer in the British Army?

    (a) 1939   (b) 1978   (c) 2015

6. How many pregnant women and working mothers are estimated to be made redundant or pressured to leave their jobs each year?

    (a) 3000   (b) 54 000   (c) 87 000

7. What proportion of women have experienced sexual harassment in the workplace?

    (a) 34%   (b) 52%   (c) 67%

8. What proportion of these women reported the harassment to their employer?

    (a) 20%   (b) 52%   (c) 80%

9. What is the maximum punishment that women in Northern Ireland seeking an abortion can face?

    (a) no punishment – abortion is legal in Northern Ireland

    (b) community sentence

    (c) life imprisonment

10. What proportion of UK companies pay men on average more than women?

    (a) a quarter   (b) half   (c) over three-quarters

- Wall paintings showing women playing football have been found in China.
  They date from around AD 25–220. That's nearly 2000 years ago.
- There are reports of ladies' matches between England and Scotland in 1881.
- The first known club team, the British Ladies Football Club, was formed in 1895.

[…] So what happened? How come most women's teams today only date back to the 1970s and 80s?

Men, that's what happened. They just wouldn't take women seriously. I'm not saying all men. Some were supportive. The British Ladies were trained by a Tottenham Hotspur player, J W Julian, for example. But, by and large, men didn't take kindly to women playing football. In Scotland, some of the 1881 matches didn't finish because the crowd got angry. The police had to step in and stop the women from being hit. The papers thought these early matches were the 'beginning and end for the ladies' game'.

[…] The end – no chance! Not with women like **Nettie Honeyball** around. Nettie was the one who formed the British Ladies Football Club (BLFC). She was all for equal rights. She thought that if women wanted to play football, they should. She said they weren't just 'useless ornaments'. […]

Nettie split the squad into two sides. Although they were all from the London area, one was called 'North' and wore red. The other was called 'South' and wore light blue. The first time they played, at a ground in Crouch End, London, 10 000 people came to watch. It was a huge event. North won 7–1.

[…] Between March 1895 and June 1896, the BLFC played 75 matches throughout Britain and Ireland, mainly against each other. Nothing was heard of them after 1896, but Nettie had proved her point.

The next time female footballers got noticed was during the First World War (1914–1918). When the men went to fight, the women went to work. A lot of them went to work in munitions factories, making ammunition and weapons. All workers were encouraged to play sport and most factories had a women's football team. The matches raised a lot of money for charity.

One team, from Preston in Lancashire, became famous. They were the Dick, Kerr Ladies, named after their factory, Dick, Kerr & Co Ltd. They were the first women's team to wear shorts. They were the first to play overseas (in France). They once played in front of a record crowd of 53 000 (Boxing Day at Everton FC's ground, Goodison Park, in 1920).

The Dick, Kerr left-winger, Lily Parr, was the first woman in the National Football Museum Hall of Fame. In her career she scored over 1000 goals. Probably only Pelé has scored more. What a legend.

When the war ended, women's football was as popular as ever. In fact it was too popular. Guess what the English FA did?

In 1921 they banned women from playing on their grounds. They gave rubbish reasons. They said the money raised for charity wasn't being checked properly. Then they said: 'We feel that the game of football is quite unsuitable for females and ought not to be encouraged.'

The ban meant teams couldn't play at decent grounds or have proper referees. None of the matches and leagues was seen as 'official'. In other words, they didn't count.

The FA didn't lift the ban until 1971. That's 50 years later.

from Helena Pielichaty, *Here Come the Girls*

Violence against women

Strand:
- Relationships and sex education

Resources:
- Book Three: pp. 22–23
- Worksheet 3.2 cut into cards

Learning objective:
- To learn about violence against women, focusing on sexism, harassment, domestic abuse and FGM

Key words:
violence against women, sexism, harassment, domestic abuse

STARTER

- Write 'sexism' on the board and elicit a definition from the students. Write out a dictionary definition: 'Prejudice or discrimination, usually against women, on the basis of sex'. Then add the word 'casual' in front of 'sexism' and ask what this means. Elicit that, even though the law in the UK forbids gross discrimination, casual sexism is a huge problem in society. Ask what sorts of things may count as casual sexism and write them on the board; examples include sexist jokes, street calling, patronising comments, offensive language, double standards (e.g. around behaviour in relationships), unwanted touching, assumptions about women's roles/abilities. If you feel it's appropriate, invite students to share examples that they have experienced or witnessed, but be sure to handle this sensitively. What do they feel about being the victims of casual sexism?

ACTIVITIES

- Ask students to read the introduction and 'Sexism and hate crimes' on page 22 of *Your Choice Book Three*. Then ask students to do the 'Research' activity in pairs (see the link to the Everyday Sexism Project below). Invite pairs to share their responses with the class.

- Organise students into groups to discuss the opinions in the 'Your choice' activity, then to read 'What is sexual harassment' and do the 'Discuss' activity that follows. Invite a spokesperson for each group to report back to the class. Ask what action they think should be taken against anyone who sexually harasses someone either at work, in public or at school.

- Now ask students to read the section on 'Domestic abuse' on their own and then get back into their groups to do the second 'Discuss' activity. Be aware that there may be students who have experienced abusive behaviour in their homes.

PLENARY

- Ask students to draft a letter to their local MP focusing on the one issue that has most affected them in the lesson and asking for more action to be taken, giving reasons. Ask volunteers to read out their letters.

RESEARCH

- Get students to research what help is available for those suffering domestic abuse. They could begin with the Women's Aid website listed below

EXTENSION

- Distribute the cards on **Worksheet 3.2**. These list many of the manifestations of violence against women. The cards can be used in different ways, e.g. ranking (which are the worst and why?), selection for further research or discussion, or even personal responses at seeing the vast number of forms that violence against women can take, leading to such questions as 'Why are women treated in this way?'. Explain any of the forms of violence that may be unfamiliar, such as FGM and breast ironing.

Further information and support for students:

Everyday Sexism Project – cataloguing instances of everyday sexism: everydaysexism.com

Women's Aid – national charity working to end domestic abuse: www.womensaid.org.uk

Contacting your local MP: www.parliament.uk/get-involved/contact-your-mp

Rape	Marital rape
Domestic violence	Honour killings
Forced marriage	Coercive control
Stalking	Sexual harassment
Forced prostitution	Forced sterilisation
Stoning for adultery	Female genital mutilation (FGM)
Breast ironing	Cyberbullying

Strand:	Resources:
• Relationships and sex education	• Book Three: pp. 24–25

Learning objective:	Key words:
• To learn about forced marriage and other aspects of honour-based abuse, and FGM	forced marriage, violence against women, FGM, honour-based abuse

STARTER

• Show the government's Forced Marriage Unit video (see the link below) and ask for students' responses. The video is hard-hitting and aims to highlight the impact of forced marriages on victims and their families. Please view before sharing it with the class (it features intimations of rape/abuse).

ACTIVITIES

• Ask students to read the section on 'Forced marriages', including the 'Fact check' and 'Nazanine's story' (page 24 of *Your Choice Book Three*). Make sure that you emphasise the difference between arranged marriages and forced marriages, as they are often confused (arranged marriages are discussed on page 49). Ask students to use the internet to research what advice and support is available to those at risk of forced marriage, and to list three key pieces of advice.

• Ask students to read 'Honour-based abuse' and to do the 'Discuss' activity in small groups. The discussion of the use of the term 'honour' turns on the positive connotations that the word can have. Some people argue that this puts the victims of honour-based abuse at a disadvantage. Others say that it is a useful term because it specifies why the violence is being perpetrated and therefore makes strategies to restrict it more focused. The term is understood in the communities where the violence occurs, and it is 'owned' by survivors. The discussion can be broadened into one about how much a society allows communities to follow their own cultural practices – bearing in mind the law of the land.

• Ask students to read the section on FGM, including the 'Fact check'. Then ask them to do the 'Research' activity using the WHO website and to discuss the questions in groups. *Answers to part 1 may include: (a) regarded as a traditional, cultural practice; (b) difficulties in menstruation, urinating and giving birth, and in having and enjoying sex; (c) through education, supporting care professionals who are opposed to FGM; (d) emotional support, group support, specialist clinics.*

PLENARY

• Ask students to identify the one issue that has most affected them in the lesson. How has it affected them and what action can they take?

EXTENSION

• Ask students to discuss why there have been so few convictions for practising FGM in the UK (the first prosecution was in 2019; it has been a criminal offence since 1985). Elicit that the offence is often committed on very young children, supported by close family members, and that taboos surrounding the practice prevent many victims from speaking out.

Further information and support for teachers:

Amnesty International's teaching resources on forced marriages: www.amnesty.org.uk/blogs/classroom-community/education-resources-forced-marriage

Further information and support for students:

Government Forced Marriage Unit video (2 minutes): www.gov.uk/government/news/new-video-shows-the-devastating-impact-of-forced-marriage

World Health Organization on FGM: www.who.int/reproductivehealth/topics/fgm/en/

Karma Nirvana – supporting victims of honour-based abuse and forced marriage: karmanirvana.org.uk

The government information on forced marriage: www.gov.uk/stop-forced-marriage

Useful fact-based brochure on responding to FGM prepared by the CHANGE project: forwarduk.org.uk/wp-content/uploads/2014/12/CHANGE-Responding-to-FGM-A-Guide-for-Key-Professionals.pdf

Strand:	Resources:
• Relationships and sex education	• Book Three: pp. 26–27 • School inclusion policy

Learning objective:	Key words:
• To learn about the fight for LGBT+ rights and the inequalities that remain, in the UK and the wider world	LGBT+ rights, gay rights, equal rights

STARTER

• Show a video about what it means to be a young gay or trans person and the difficulties they face, such as the one from the Stonewall YouTube channel (see links below). Discuss the issues raised by the film.

ACTIVITIES

• Ask students to read the introduction, 'Fact check' and 'LGBT+ rights under the law in the UK' on page 26 of *Your Choice Book Three*. Then ask them to do the 'Research' activity; they could either choose one of the events in the 'Fact check' timeline or you could allocate different events to different students/groups. In the feedback, ask students/groups exactly what effect the event has had on the lives of LGBT+ people and society in general.

• Ask students to read 'Homophobic, biphobic and transphobic bullying' (pp. 26–7) and 'How to deal with bullying' (p. 27) and discuss their reactions to the facts and views expressed as well as the questions in the 'Discuss' activity. Be aware that there may be students in the class who have suffered or are the victims of such bullying.

• Ask students to read 'LGBT+ rights abroad' and to do the 'Research' activity, investigating either one of the countries listed or any other country where persecution of LGBT+ people still persists. Sex between people of the same sex is no longer as widely criminalised as it used to be, but over 70 nations still have laws against it. The number of nations with anti-gay laws dropped from 92 in 2006 to 72 in 2019.

PLENARY

• Ask the students to work in pairs to discuss the statements in 'Your choice' on page 27 before feeding back to the class. Then ask students to write a statement about the one thing that they themselves could do to be more LGBT+ inclusive. Ask for volunteers to share their statements.

RESEARCH

• Ask students to research what your school's inclusion policy says about LGBT+ students and then write a statement about the one thing that would make the school more LGBT+ inclusive.

EXTENSION

• In pairs, ask students to role-play a scene involving two friends, one of whom sensitively but firmly points out to the other that they are out of order because they've made a homophobic, biphobic or transphobic comment. Ask for feedback: what approach is most likely to be effective? humorous? serious? angry? Why is it important for peers to call out discriminatory behaviour?

Further information and support for teachers:

A range of responses to homophobic and transphobic language and gender stereotyping can be found in the Trans Inclusion Schools Toolkit (2018) produced by Brighton and Hove City Council and Allsorts Youth project, uploads-ssl.webflow.com/5888a640d61795123f8192db/5bb6216a5253bf4eea4ebeb9_Trans_Inclusion_Schools_Toolkit_Version_3.2_2018.pdf

Countries where homosexuality is illegal: 76crimes.com/76-countries-where-homosexuality-is-illegal

PSHE Association: www.pshe-association.org.uk/content/government-equalities-office-anti-homophobic

Further information and support for students:

Stonewall and Young Stonewall websites (click on the YouTube icon at the top right of each website to access their short videos): www.stonewall.org.uk or www.youngstonewall.org.uk

Strand:	**Resources:**
• Social education	• Book Three: pp. 28–29
	• Worksheet 4.1

Learning objective:	**Key words:**
• To explore the problem of racism in education and at work, and identify what can be done to combat it	racism, educational racism

STARTER

• Ask students to define what they think racism is. Note a good definition on the board *(treating someone as inferior because of their race, with race defined in the Equality Act as including a person's colour, ethnicity, nationality, or ethnic or national origins)*. Then read the definition in the introduction on page 28 of *Your Choice Book Three*.

ACTIVITIES

• Ask students to read 'Educational racism' in groups and then look at the situations in the first 'Discuss' activity. Ask: 'Do you think teachers have different expectations for different groups of students? Why?' All are discriminatory. Point out direct or overt discrimination in **a)**, **b)**, **c)** and **e)**. Point out how **d)** may be indirect or covert discrimination – the school may not microwave food for anyone. However, this is still discrimination because the school hasn't considered this student's needs.

• Organise students into groups to read 'Banning religious symbols' and then do the 'Discuss' task below it.

• In France, it is illegal to wear any sign of faith in school. Ask the students to read the 'Research' task in pairs (or on their own for students requiring more challenge). Then support them to research the subject before writing their report. *Advantages: there is a secular environment where everyone is treated equally; it means there is a public/private divide. Disadvantages: restricts freedom of expression; discriminates against minority groups who may be uncertain of their identity in majority white French society.*

• Get students to read 'Employment racism' and the 'Fact check' as a class. Concept-check the class with question: 'How can somebody be discriminated against at work?' *Answers: hiring or not hiring someone, refusing a pay rise or promotion, firing or keeping someone – all on the grounds solely of ethnicity.*

• Ask students to do the 'Discuss' task on page 29 in groups and then invite them to share their views and reasoning with the rest of the class. *Suggested responses: **1.** Equal opportunities (use the school's policy if you have it in advance as an example). **2.** Verbal warning, written warning, compulsory equal opportunities training, ruling out promotion, final written warning, termination of contract. **3.** Regard it as a factor helping towards promotion and pay rises, employee of the month. **4.** Equal opportunities training, sessions to find out about other cultures on specific days (e.g. Muslims – Ramadan; Hindus – Diwali; Americans or any nationality – their Independence Day).*

• Ask students to read 'Racism in sport: Kick It Out', and then to work in groups to do the 'Write' task based on what they have learned from the article.

PLENARY

• Lead a class discussion about the extent to which racism is a problem in your local area, and what part students can play in combating it. Make sure students back up their opinions with facts. You may wish to research this area in advance, using the internet to see what racism has been reported in your local media over the last 12 months. Alternatively, you can give this to students as a research task.

EXTENSION

• Hand out copies of **Worksheet 4.1** and ask students to discuss, in pairs, what they would do in each situation. Invite pairs to compare their solutions as a class and discuss any differences.

Further information and support for teachers:

The Guardian, 'Record number of UK children excluded for racist bullying':
www.theguardian.com/education/2018/nov/30/record-number-of-uk-children-excluded-for-racist-bullying

'Six classroom activities to spark discussion on racism and privilege' (an Australian perspective):
http://inservice.ascd.org/six-classroom-activities-to-spark-discussion-of-racism-and-privilege/

Worksheet 4.1 Combating educational racism

Look at the following table. What do you think can be done to combat each instance of educational racism? Give reasons for your views.

Problem	Solution and reasons
A teacher always asks every student in a class a question, except for the Asian students.	
A university is in an area where 10% of all school students are black, but only 5% of its students are black.	
A local school refuses to let a student study Mandarin A level in the school timetable with the lessons paid for privately, even though the student has Chinese heritage.	
A school gives Muslim students time off to celebrate Eid, but doesn't give Sikh and Hindu students the time off to celebrate Diwali.	
In your class, the white students always sit in one group, and the black students in another group. The two groups never mix.	
In the English course, most of the books studied are by white authors, with a few black authors, but never any black female authors.	
A teacher keeps using examples from the UK, Canada, Australia and New Zealand when talking about the British Empire in history lessons. They ignore India, South Africa and other Commonwealth countries that were part of the British Empire.	
In school assemblies, only Christian holidays are mentioned and celebrated. There is no discussion of Muslim festivals such as Eid, or Sikh and Hindu festivals such as Diwali.	
A teacher won't give a student who has recently arrived from Poland extra time to complete tasks. The student is clever but is still learning English and thus struggles in class.	

Strand:	Resources:
• Social education	• Book Three: pp. 30–31 • Worksheet 4.2 • Copies of the school's equal opportunities policy • An article about UKIP or the Brexit Party

Learning objective:	Key words:
• To distinguish between racism and xenophobia • To examine what equal opportunities are	racism, xenophobia, prejudice, discrimination

STARTER

* Ask students to state what they think discrimination is. Note a good example on the board and then read the introduction on page 30 of *Your Choice Book Three*. Allow some discussion of what is and is not discrimination.

ACTIVITIES

* Hand out copies of the school's equal opportunities policy and read through it with students. Ask students to do the 'Research' task on page 30 in pairs and then feed back to the class as a whole.

* Get students to read 'Racism and xenophobia', and then share with them your chosen article about UKIP (or the Brexit Party, Nigel Farage's next party). Read part **1** of the 'Discuss' activity with students and ask pairs to talk about it and decide what they think. Invite pairs to compare their answers with another pair, and then ask the groups of four to do part **2** of the 'Discuss' activity. Finally, bring the class back together to share their views on both parts of the activity.

* Still in their groups, ask students to read 'No platform versus freedom of speech' and then to do the discussion task that follows it. Invite groups to share their views with the class.

* Then ask students to read 'Institutional racism and the police', including the article from *The Guardian*, and do the next 'Discuss' task in small groups. *Answers: **1.** Racial disparity refers to a different proportion of people being stopped and searched from one ethnic group compared to another. **2.** Yes, this should help, as officers from BAME backgrounds may spot issues affecting BAME people that other officers might miss (e.g. a Muslim student legitimately out late at night, trying to get something to eat before sunrise – because its Ramadan). However, the best thing would be greater training for all officers.*

PLENARY

* Remind students about the discussion of the school's equal opportunities policy. Hand out copies of **Worksheet 4.2** for pairs to consider what they would include in their own equal opportunities policy for the school. Compare ideas as a class.

EXTENSION

* Support students to work in small groups do the 'Research' task about the murder of Stephen Lawrence and the Macpherson Report. Their report should include three paragraphs relating to three facts:
1. The initial police investigation was bungled. 2. The police were judged to be institutionally racist and many changes came about as a result. 3. Two of the murderers were eventually convicted years later.

Further information and support for teachers:

Stephen Lawrence Charitable Trust, Resources for schools:
www.stephenlawrence.org.uk/resources/secondary-ks3-ks4/

BBC Teach, 'Stephen Lawrence: The murder that changed a nation': www.bbc.com/teach/class-clips-video/citizenship-gcse-stephen-the-murder-that-changed-a-nation/zmncpg8

Further information and support for students:

Action for children, Equal opportunities policy: www.actionforchildren.org.uk/what-we-do/about-us/equality-and-diversity/

BBC News, Stephen Lawrence murder – timeline: www.bbc.co.uk/news/uk-26465916

Look at the characteristics listed in the table below. Which do you think should be included in your equal opportunities policy and why? What characteristics are essential to include to meet the school's requirements under the Equalities Act? Is there anything else you would want to include? Fill in the table, giving reasons for your views.

Characteristic	Should it be included and, if so, why?
Race	
Religion	
Geographical origin (e.g. North v South of England)	
Class or social-economic background	
Accent	
Nationality	
Sexuality	
Gender at birth and/or trans individuals	
Students with physical disabilities	
Students with mental disabilities	
IQ	
Lifestyle choice	
Age	

What other groups should be in your equal opportunities policy? Give reasons for your views.

....

....

....

....

....

5.1   Safety at parties

<table>
<tr><td>

Strand:
- Relationships and sex education

</td><td>

Resources:
- Book Three: pp. 32–33
- Worksheet 5.1

</td></tr>
<tr><td>

Learning objective:
- To examine the dangers of going to a party and to identify steps that can minimise them

</td><td>

Key words:
alcohol, partying, spiking, unconscious

</td></tr>
</table>

STARTER

- Ask students to imagine they have been invited to a party in the evening, some distance from where they live, and to make a list of the potential dangers. Invite individuals to share their ideas with the class and compile a list on the board.

ACTIVITIES

- Ask students to read all of the information on page 32 of *Your Choice Book Three* and then to discuss it in pairs. Tell them to do the 'Your choice' activity on their own and then to get back into their pairs to discuss their choices, before sharing their answers in groups.

- Next, ask students to do the 'Write' activity on their own and then compare their list with the concerns listed in the starter activity. Bring the class back together to discuss their lists and ask whether they want to add anything else to the list from the starter.

- Ask students to read the section on 'Spiking drinks', including the 'Fact check', 'Top tips on how to protect your drinks' and 'Lucy's story'. Organise the students into groups to answer the six questions in the 'Discuss' activity. Then invite groups to share their answers with the class. Are there differences in opinion between the groups?

- Ask students to read 'If things go wrong' and then support them to do the 'Research' task.

PLENARY

- Lead a class discussion on whether there should be a code of acceptable behaviour at parties. If so, what do they think it should include?

RESEARCH

- Ask students to summarise the advice given in the three weblinks for students below and then to produce a poster on the dangers of spiked drinks with information included from the NHS and the police.

EXTENSION

- Hand out copies of **Worksheet 5.1** and ask students to complete part **1** in pairs. As a stretch activity, students requiring more challenge can do part **2**, thinking up other scenarios either to discuss themselves or to put to other students.

Further information and support for teachers:

Drinkaware, 'Teenagers, parties and alcohol': www.drinkaware.co.uk/advice/underage-drinking/teenagers-parties-and-alcohol/

The Guardian, 'Teenage parties – a parents' guide': www.theguardian.com/lifeandstyle/2014/sep/05/teenage-parties-a-parents-guide

Further information and support for students:

NHS, 'Drink spiking and date rape drugs': www.nhs.uk/live-well/healthy-body/drink-spiking-and-date-rape-drugs/

Kids helpline, 'Partying safely': kidshelpline.com.au/teens/issues/partying-safely

Met Police, Crime prevention advice, 'Spiked drinks – what you need to know': www.met.police.uk/cp/crime-prevention/drugs/spiked-drinks/

Worksheet 5.1 Problems at parties

1. In pairs, read the statements below and rank them in order of seriousness (1 = most serious). Then complete the table, giving your reasons and suggesting solutions.

Statement	Ranking	Why?	Solution
a) You find a person searching through everyone else's coats.			
b) A group of friends trick a girl so that she misses the last bus home and will have to walk two miles on her own in the dark.			
c) A group of teenagers decide to try sniffing glue at the party, just for a laugh.			
d) Somebody offers you an unknown drink. After you've drunk it, they tell you it's snakebite – lager and cider mixed together.			
e) You see three guys pestering a girl and making sexual comments at her, and she's clearly uncomfortable.			
f) A teenager drinks so much alcohol they fall unconscious.			

2. Stretch activity: What other scenarios can you think of? How serious would you rank them? What would you do to sort out these other scenarios? Give reasons for your views.

Strand:
- Relationships and sex education

Resources:
- Book Three: pp. 34–35
- Worksheet 5.2

Learning objective:
- To understand the importance of protecting your online reputation and the steps you can take to do this

Key words:
social media, post, fake news

STARTER

- Ask students if they have ever regretted posting something on social media. Note examples under the following categories on the board: Posts that led to arguments, Fake news, Embarrassing photos, Inappropriate content, Opinions you no longer hold, Posts that make you look stupid.

ACTIVITIES

- Ask students to read the first three paragraphs on page 34 of *Your Choice Book Three*. Ask them to discuss, in small groups, what they think is the biggest problem from the four bullet points listed and why. Invite students to share their responses with the rest of the class.

- Ask students to read 'Online obsession' and 'Brian's story'. Then, as a class, discuss the questions in the 'Discuss' activity on page 35, just in relation to Brian's story. *Suggested answers: 1. Brian became obsessed with his body, started lying and stopped eating properly. 2. He could have stuck to a sensible diet and told his parents the truth. 3. Avoid glorifying such behaviour. Instead, challenge it and explain why over dieting can led to problems.*

- Organise the students into pairs. Ask half the pairs to read Stacey's story and half to read Gemma's story, and then to answer the 'Discuss' questions for each. *Suggested answers: Stacey – 1. Not reading what she was reposting. 2. Read what she reposts first; realise that likes on social media are no substitute for real-life relationships. 3. Challenge a person and point out what they are sharing online. Gemma – 1. Not checking Sam's real identity with him. 2. Find out early on who a person really is – check out their profile and try to find out whether their picture is real. (You could Google them to confirm their identity or you could ask them to send you a custom pic – a selfie where they hold a piece of paper with a message you have given them.) 3. Challenge a person as to their real identity.*

PLENARY

- Bring the class back together and discuss what Stacey and Gemma could have done differently, encouraging pairs to share their responses to the discussion questions. Then refer back to the list on the board from the starter activity and ask students what they have learned from this lesson. Would they add any other categories? Would they add any other examples now they have learned about digital consent?

RESEARCH

- Hand out **Worksheet 5.2** to pairs. Ask them to complete the questionnaire with a group of students at school. You can compare the results in your next lesson. Do the results suggest young people are careful about how they use social media?

EXTENSION

- Organise students into pairs. Ask them to complete the 'Your choice' activity on page 35, by ranking the different statements in order of importance. Students should then compare their answers with another pair, giving reasons for their views.

Further information and support for teachers:

Childnet: www.childnet.com

Further information and support for students:

Teens Health, 'Protecting your online identity and reputation': kidshealth.org/en/teens/online-id.html

Think u know, 'Keeping yourselves safe, keeping the internet fun': www.thinkuknow.co.uk/11_13/

Brook, 'Stay safe online': www.brook.org.uk/your-life/category/staying-safe-online

Worksheet 5.2 Social media and you

In pairs, read the statements below and answer each question with yes, no or don't know.

Are there any other questions about sensible use of social media that you would like to add? If there are, write them in the blank rows at the bottom of the table.

Question	Yes	No	Don't know
Do you always check what you repost or share on social media?			
Do you think you spend too long on social media?			
Are you too concerned with what other people say about you on social media?			
Do you think people pay too much attention to social media?			
Have you ever posted a photo of someone online without asking them first?			
Have you ever really regretted posting a photo on social media?			
Have you ever really regretted liking a post on social media?			
Have you ever really regretted writing something on social media?			

6.1 Heroin and cocaine

Strand:
- Physical health and wellbeing

Resources:
- Book Three: pp. 36–37
- Worksheet 6.1

Learning objective:
- To understand the dangers of cocaine and heroin, and the differences between them

Key words:
heroin, cocaine, addict

STARTER

- Ask students what they already know about heroin and cocaine. Note their ideas on the board. Correct any myths and highlight any facts as you go.

ACTIVITIES

- Ask students to read the information about heroin on page 36 of *Your Choice Book Three*. Then, with the students, look at the notes on the board from the starter activity and ask them if there's anything they'd like to change or add to the information about heroin. Do the same with the information about cocaine.

- Organise students into small groups to read the 'Fact check' on page 37 and then do the 'Discuss' task that follows it. Invite groups to share their answers and discuss any differences in opinion. Then ask them, still in groups, to do the 'Write' task. Encourage groups to share their petitions in a class discussion.

- Ask students, individually, to read the article and 'Ask Erica' on page 37 and then to draft Erica's reply to Maxine, working in pairs if they need more support. Erica's reply should include: *the health risks; the fact that he may be charged by the police and then prosecuted, which could affect his career; the addictive nature of drugs; the amount of money he is spending on them; how it will feel worse in the long run.*

- Ask students to do the 'Your choice' quiz on their own and then check their answers with a partner. Ask them to stay in their pairs to do the writing task. When pairs have swapped quizzes and answered the questions, ask them to work together in a group to check the answers. *Answers: 1. Can be true; 2. False; 3. False; 4. True – risk of catching infections such as hepatitis or HIV; 5. True.*

- Hand out copies of **Worksheet 6.1** and ask students to complete part **1** in pairs. *Answers: Both cocaine and heroin are class A drugs, and both are highly addictive. Cocaine can be snorted, while heroin is usually injected. Both drugs can cause serious health problems and have more dangerous side effects if combined with drugs or alcohol. Both carry the risk of overdose, which can lead to death. Addicts of both drugs do cost the country tens of thousands of pounds in crime.*

- The discussion in part **2** of **Worksheet 6.1** is subjective and is a good way to start the plenary. It is worth stressing again to students that both drugs are highly dangerous and addictive, which is why they have a class A classification. Students may think it is safe or fun to experiment, but experimentation can quickly lead to addiction.

PLENARY

- In a class discussion, ask students what the most surprising thing is that they have learned about cocaine and heroin today. Make sure they understand that they should refuse these drugs if they are ever offered them and inform the authorities, such as teachers and staff if at school, and the police if outside school.

EXTENSION

- Organise students into small groups to write their own quiz about cocaine and heroin, based on what they have learned in the lesson. Get groups to swap quizzes and do them, then check their answers.

Further information and support for teachers:

Mentor-ADEPIS research and briefing papers with ideas for lessons: http://mentor-adepis.org/planning-effective-education

NHS, 'Drug addiction: getting help': www.nhs.uk/live-well/healthy-body/drug-addiction-getting-help

Brook: www.brook.org.uk/your-life/drugs

Information about drugs: www.talktofrank.com

1. Add a tick to the relevant column in the table to show whether each statement applies to cocaine or heroin. Tick both boxes if it applies to both drugs.

Statements	Applies to cocaine	Applies to heroin
Restricted class A drug		
Is highly addictive		
Can be snorted up the nose		
Can be injected		
Can cause serious physical health problems		
Is very dangerous when taken with other drugs or alcohol		
Can cause serious side effects		
Carries the risk of overdose, which can lead to death		
An addict costs the country, on average, tens of thousands of pounds in crime		

2. What else do you know about these drugs that you can add to the table? Use the blank rows and the end and tick the relevant columns.

Strand:	Resources:
• Physical health and wellbeing	• Book Three: pp. 38–39 • Worksheet 6.2 • Book Two Worksheets 5.1b and 15.3 • School drugs policy

Learning objective:	Key words:
• To discuss how schools should deal with drugs • To discuss how students should deal with drugs and drug gangs they may encounter	drugs, gangs, county lines

STARTER

• With the class, read the two questions at the start of page 38 of *Your Choice Book Three* and ask students how they think the school should deal with drug incidents at their school.

ACTIVITIES

• Ask students to read 'A firm stand' on page 38 and then to do the 'Discuss' activity in small groups, comparing the school counsellor's view with their own ideas in the starter activity.

• Ask students if they know what the school policy is towards drug taking, or where to find it. If it is available on the school website, direct them to this. If not, hand out hard copies and then organise students into pairs to do the 'Research' activity.

• Next, ask students to read 'Drugs on the street' and the 'Fact check' before doing the 'Discuss' task on page 39 in small groups. Invite groups to share their views in a class discussion.

• Ask students to read 'Portugal takes a different approach' and then to get into groups to do 'Your choice'. Explain that they will use their notes for a class debate at the end of the lesson.

PLENARY

• Organise a class debate on whether any drugs should be decriminalised in the UK, using the links given in the websites below. Useful guidance on holding a debate is given on **Worksheets 5.1b** and **15.3** in *Your Choice Book Two*.

EXTENSION

• Hand out copies of **Worksheet 6.2** for students to complete. They will need to use the internet to search for the answers. *Answers: 1. False – it depends on the school's drugs policy and the police; 2. True; 3. True; 4. False – the police can search you, if they have reasonable suspicion; 5. True; 6. True; 7. True; 8. False – the same drugs are illegal in all parts of the UK; 9. False; 10. False – any student expelled from school for any reason has a right of appeal if the school is run by a local authority.*

• As a stretch activity, ask students to design their own drugs quiz in pairs. The quiz should be based on information they have learned from this spread and their internet research.

Further information and support for teachers:

Daily Mail, 'Britain tops teen drugs league': www.dailymail.co.uk/news/article-24749/Britain-tops-teen-drugs-league.htm

Time, Portugal and decriminalisation: http://time.com/longform/portugal-drug-use-decriminalization

'Mixed results for Portugal's great drug experiment': www.npr.org/2011/01/20/133086356/Mixed-Results-For-Portugals-Great-Drug-Experiment

Further information and support for students:

Mentor, 'Get the facts about young people and drugs': mentoruk.org.uk/get-the-facts/

What happens when a child gets caught with drugs in school? www.inbrief.co.uk/child-law/children-with-drugs-in-school/

Worksheet 6.2 Quiz: drugs and teenagers

Write T or F in the second column below to say whether each statement is true or false. For those that are false, explain why in the third column.

Statement	True or false?	If it's false, why?
1. You will always be arrested if you are found to have illegal drugs in school.		
2. Nearly 40% of teenagers have tried some sort of illegal drug.		
3. The most popular illegal drug among teenagers is cannabis.		
4. The police do not have a right to search you for drugs.		
5. Teenagers who are addicted to drugs often steal to support their habit.		
6. There is a range of help available to teenagers who are addicted to illegal drugs.		
7. A number of US states and Canada have now decriminalised cannabis.		
8. Different drugs are illegal in Scotland from in England, Wales and Northern Ireland.		
9. Your school can suspend and expel you for carrying drugs.		
10. If you are expelled from school for dealing in drugs, you have no right of appeal.		

<table>
<tr><td>

Strand:
- Relationships and sex education

</td><td>

Resources:
- Book Three: pp. 40–41
- Worksheet 7.1 cut into cards

</td></tr>
<tr><td>

Learning objective:
- To understand how pregnancy occurs, what to do if you are pregnant, and about miscarriage and fertility

</td><td>

Key words:
  pregnancy, miscarriage, fertility

</td></tr>
</table>

STARTER

- Ask students to read 'How does pregnancy happen?' on page 40 of *Your Choice Book Three*. Follow up with a quick quiz to test their understanding, e.g. 'Does the penis have to be in the vagina for conception to occur?' *(No, just the sperm)*; 'Can you get pregnant at any time in the menstrual cycle?' *(Yes, but most likely at ovulation; remember, sperm can live in the vagina for up to 7 days, and if you have a short cycle, ovulation may be earlier than you think.)*

ACTIVITIES

- Organise students into small groups to read 'How can you tell if you are pregnant' and 'Taking the test'. Then give each group a set of cards cut out from **Worksheet 7.1** and ask them to construct a timeline using the cards. Ask them: 'When would you do/feel these things after unprotected sex?' and tell them to place the cards at the relevant points on the timeline. This physical approach helps address students' need to know what to do when they think they may be pregnant. Circulate around the groups and address any questions or ask for clarifications (e.g. 'What different things could bleeding mean?'). Bring together groups' knowledge by constructing a similar timeline on the board.

- Ask students to work in pairs to do the 'Discuss' activity at the top of page 41. Invite pairs to share their responses. Ask: 'How might girls' reactions differ from those of boys?'

- Get students to read the article 'Miscarriage' and then to discuss it in small groups. To test/reinforce their understanding, ask students what signs they would look out for, what they would do and where they would go for help.

- Read the information about 'Fertility' with students and then ask them to do the second 'Discuss' task in small groups. Invite groups to share their responses.

- Ask students to do the 'Research' task, investigating what options are open to same-sex couples who want to start a family.

PLENARY

- Ask students to write down the most important thing they have learned this lesson. Ask for volunteers to share what they have written.

RESEARCH

- Ask students to research what happens when a couple who want to have a baby attend a fertility clinic.

EXTENSION

- Get students to research teenage pregnancy rates in the UK in the last 10–15 years and identify the factors that have helped to reduce the rate.

Further information and support for teachers:

ScienceSplained, Celebrity Pregnancy (scroll to 'Sex education video for Society of Endocrinology'), a fun but explicit video which explains how conception happens: www.sciencesplained.com

Further information and support for students:

Detailed guide to pregnancy from the charity Tommy's: www.tommys.org/pregnancy

Brook, a video of a teenager's experience of miscarriage: www.brook.org.uk/your-life/miscarriage-at-7-weeks-holly-maes-story

For teenage pregnancy rates see:
www.local.gov.uk/sites/default/files/documents/15.7%20Teenage%20pregnancy_09.pdf
www.bbc.co.uk/news/health-43506784 and www.bbc.co.uk/news/health-42655079

Worksheet 7.1 Pregnancy timeline

1	2	3	4	5	6	7
			DAY			

8	9	10	11	12	13	14
			DAY			

15	16	17	18	19	20	21
			DAY			

22	23	24	25	26	27	28
			DAY			

unprotected sex	emergency contraception (EHC)	missed period/ lighter period	feeling bloated
sore breasts	bleeding	talk with partner	talk with parents/carers
go to GP	take a pregnancy test	take a second test	

Strand:	**Resources:**
• Relationships and sex education	• Book Three: pp. 42–43 • Worksheet 7.2

Learning objective:	**Key words:**
• Understanding the different options young people have if pregnancy occurs, with a focus on the facts about abortion	pregnancy, abortion, adoption, parenthood

STARTER

• Write the word 'Abortion' on the board and brainstorm students' thoughts and ideas. Put each idea as a single word or phrase around the central word, e.g. choice, rights, shame, time limits, life, loss. Ask students which of the words/phrases may have a factual basis and which are more open to personal (subjective) views.

• Introduce the lesson as an exploration of the different options available to young people at pregnancy. One of these is abortion. Ask what the others are. Read the introductory paragraphs on page 42 of *Your Choice Book Three* to the class.

ACTIVITIES

• With the students, read 'Abortion – the facts', including 'Polly's story' and the 'Fact check', followed by 'The law on abortion'. Then ask them, in pairs, to draw up a 'true/false' quiz of six questions to ask their partner to test their knowledge.

• Organise students into small groups to discuss the statements about abortion on **Worksheet 7.2**. Invite groups to feed back their views in a class discussion. Which statements were easy to agree with and which generated more discussion?

• Ask students to read the information on 'Adoption' and then do the 'Discuss' activity as a class. Be sensitive to the feelings and views of students who may themselves be adopted.
Possible answers: 1. Advantages = not terminating the pregnancy; allowing a childless couple to bring up a child in better circumstances. Disadvantages = letting go of a child after bonding for 9 months; the physical and emotional demands of pregnancy and childbirth. 2. Anxiety, contentment, guilt, joy, shame, regret – the whole gamut of feelings.

• Ask students to read 'Keeping the baby' and then to do 'Your choice' in small groups. You could tell them that teenage fathers can find themselves paying for a child's upkeep for two decades, until the child is 18, and often beyond. The cost of raising a child in 2019 was estimated at £230 000.

PLENARY

• Ask students, on their own, to do the 'Write' activity. Invite individuals to share their writing and discuss their responses with the class.

EXTENSION

• Set up a role play for students to do in pairs: 'Imagine that you or your partner has become pregnant. Role-play discussing your options with a friend or parent. Take it in turns to be (a) a 15-year-old; (b) a 17-year-old. Will your discussion be different in each case?'

Further information and support for teachers:

Brook's 90-page resource on the subjective issues around abortion (NB produced before the abortion law in the Republic of Ireland was changed in 2018):
www.brook.org.uk/attachments/Abortion_decisions_and_dilemmas.pdf

Further information and support for students:

'Pregnant and don't know what to do?' an FPA information leaflet is available at:
https://sexwise.fpa.org.uk/unplanned-pregnancy/pregnant-and-dont-know-what-do

Brook's abortion factsheets: www.brook.org.uk/shop/category/resources/P10

Worksheet 7.2 Abortion: what do you think?

Read the following statements and tick the relevant column to say whether you agree or disagree with each one. Write any additional comments you have in the final column.

Statement	Agree	Disagree	Comments
1. If everyone used contraception, there would be no need for women to have abortions.			
2. Abortions should only be available for medical reasons.			
3. It's too easy for women to have an abortion in the UK.			
4. A man should take responsibility for his child even if it was the woman's choice to continue with the pregnancy.			
5. It is too hard for women to have abortions in the UK.			
6. It is a woman's right to decide what to do with her own body.			
7. If you are old enough to have sex, you're old enough to live with the consequences and to have a baby.			
8. Making women feel guilty about abortions won't stop abortions happening.			
9. Teenagers can be good parents.			
10. Abortions should be harder to access in order to encourage women to continue with pregnancy.			
11. If a man wants to be an active father, he should be able to stop his partner having an abortion.			
12. Young people need to know about abortion in case they or their partner ever need one.			

Source: Brook, *Education for Choice – Abortion: decisions and dilemmas*

<table>
<tr><td>**7.3**</td><td colspan="2">**Teenage parents**</td></tr>
</table>

Strand:	**Resources:**
• Relationships and sex education	• Book Three: pp. 44–45
	• Worksheet 7.3
	• Book Two Worksheets 5.1b and 15.3

Learning objective:	**Key words:**
• To explore the reality of being a teenage parent	teenage parents, baby

STARTER

• Show the short documentary 'Teenage parents' (see the link below) produced by eleven teenage parents in 2011. They talk about the challenges and rewards of being young mums and dads. Draw out the different views and experiences, focusing on the key issues of support, sacrifice/challenge and love.

ACTIVITIES

• Ask students to read the article 'So much to do as a teenage parent' on page 44 of *Your Choice Book Three*, followed by 'Fathers' rights' and the 'Fact check' on page 45. The statistics in the Fact check are from the pdf 'Teenage pregnancy and young parents' (see the weblink below).

• Organise students into pairs to discuss what they have learned, using the 'Discuss' questions on page 45 as a starting point.

• Give each pair a copy of **Worksheet 7.3** and ask them to write three key things in each of the categories around the figure of the dad and then to do the same with the figure of the mum. Then bring the class together to share the things they listed. Bring out any overlap or differences in the views about the needs and rights of mum and dad. Take care to listen out for and challenge any stereotyping.

• Alternatively, you could allocate half the class to complete the notes about dad and the other half to complete the notes about mum, and/or you could divide the exercise according to students' gender. Whichever option you choose, follow it up with the whole-class discussion outlined above.

• Ask students to do the 'Write' activity on page 45. Encourage them to think about their thoughts and feelings as they considered in this lesson what it is like to be a teenage parent. The lesson on pregnancy (7.2) should be relatively fresh in their minds; if not, you may need to recap with the whole class the sorts of thoughts and feelings that may occur if a teenager or their partner gets pregnant.

• Ask students to do the 'Research' task, in pairs. Invite students to share their findings with the class and encourage them to add to their lists any sources other pairs found that they did not.

PLENARY

• Ask students to write down three positive aspects of starting a family as a teenager and three negative aspects. Invite volunteers to read out their lists.

EXTENSION

• Conduct a class debate on the motion 'Teenagers make just as good parents as adults do'. You can refer back to **Worksheets 5.1b** and **15.3** in Book 2 for guidance on holding a debate.

Further information and support for teachers:

'Teenage pregnancy and young parents':
www.local.gov.uk/sites/default/files/documents/15.7%20Teenage%20pregnancy_09.pdf

Further information and support for students:

Into Film Shorts, Teenage parents (video): search on YouTube for 'Teenage parents babes first light'.

Gov.UK – information on parental rights and responsibilities: www.gov.uk/parental-rights-responsibilities/who-has-parental-responsibility (The law is slightly different for births registered in Scotland and Northern Ireland.)

Gingerbread – providing information on benefits, money, housing and childcare to single parents or young women who are pregnant and living with a parent: www.gingerbread.org.uk

Worksheet 7.3 Being a teenage parent

Teenage dad

What he needs to do for his child:

1.

2.

3.

What he needs to do for himself:

1.

2.

3.

What he needs to do for his partner:

1.

2.

3.

His rights:

1.

2.

3.

Teenage mum

What she needs to do for her child:

1.

2.

3.

What she needs to do for herself:

1.

2.

3.

What she needs to do for her partner:

1.

2.

3.

Her rights:

1.

2.

3.

Strand:	Resources:
• Relationships and sex education	• Book Three: pp. 46–47 • Worksheet 7.4 • Pictures of children at different ages (for the starter activity)

Learning objective:	Key words:
• To understand the needs of children at different ages • To explore the roles and responsibilities of parents	parenting, children, mother, father

STARTER

* Display pictures of children at different stages of development – baby, toddler, primary school age, teenage – and brainstorm with the class what the students think their needs are. Say that you will be exploring this in more detail in the lesson.

ACTIVITIES

* Ask students to read 'What do children need?' on pages 46–47 of *Your Choice Book Three*. Divide the class into groups, allocating each group one of the four stages of development for part **1a** of the 'Discuss' activity (the child's key needs).

* In the same groups, give students a different age group for part **1b** of the discussion activity (the parents' key skills). Invite groups to present their findings to the rest of the class so they have a spread of information across the four stages. Bring out what skills may be needed across all stages, and how these may change according to context. For example, attending to a child's health and safety may mean making sure a toddler learns not to run across the road, but also that a teenager knows about STIs. Hand out copies of **Worksheet 8.3** to help groups collate their ideas, and/or to record notes taken while watching other groups' presentations so that they have a comprehensive record.

* Organise students into pairs to do part **2** of the first 'Discuss' activity, thinking about the differences in how they were parented when they were at primary school compared with how they are parented now. Ask pairs to compare and discuss their responses.

* Ask students if the lesson has made them see parenting in a different light. Then ask them to work in small groups to do the second 'Discuss' activity. Ask them what they think is the key skill/quality they need to work on to be a good enough parent. Invite groups to share their opinions.

PLENARY

* Ask students to read the poem 'What is a mother?' and discuss the questions that follow. Be sensitive to any student whose relationship with their mother is difficult, or whose mother is very ill or has died, or who is not present in their lives for any other reason. Then ask them, individually, to do the writing task.

EXTENSION

* As a development of the plenary, ask students to write their version of the poem or song 'What is a father?' Again be sensitive to any students who may have a difficult relationship with their father or whose father is not present in their lives for whatever reason.

Further information and support for students:

Useful materials can be found on the website on Family Lives: www.familylives.org.uk

BBC, 'Parenting': www.bbc.co.uk/parenting

NSPCC, 'Positive parenting': https://learning.nspcc.org.uk/research-resources/leaflets/positive-parenting

Worksheet 7.4 What do children need?

Fill in this grid to remind yourself of what good parenting is for children of different ages.

Child's age	Child's key needs	Key skills that parents must have
Baby		
Toddler		
Primary school child		
Adolescent		

Strand:	**Resources:**
• Relationships and sex education	• Book Three: pp. 48–49 • Worksheet 8.1 cut up into cards

Learning objective:	**Key words:**
• To explore the legal, emotional and practical characteristics of different types of committed, long-term partnerships	marriage, civil partnership, cohabiting, arranged marriage, forced marriage

STARTER

• Display photos of couples getting married and point out the ones on page 48 and 49 of *Your Choice Book Three*. Brainstorm students' views on marriage and write key words on the board. Highlight the diversity of opinions. Explain that you will be exploring the issue of committed relationships further in this lesson and that marriage is only one of several different forms.

ACTIVITIES

• Ask students to read the information on 'Marriage', 'Civil partnerships' and 'Living together (cohabiting)', including the 'Fact check', on their own. To test their knowledge, give small groups a set of cards from **Worksheet 8.1** and ask them to allocate each card to one or more of the forms of partnership. (The card 'Available only to same-sex couples' may soon not apply to any of the forms of partnership as the law around civil partnerships changes.)

• Ask students to discuss part **1** of 'Your choice' in small groups. Invite groups to feed back their opinions to the rest of the class.

• Organise students into different small groups to do the whole of the 'Discuss' task. Again, invite groups to share their views with the rest of the class.

• With the students, read the section on 'Arranged marriages' and make sure that they understand the difference between arranged marriages and forced marriages as the two can be confused. Then ask the students to work in pairs to do part **2** of the 'Your choice' activity.

PLENARY

• Ask students to do the 'Write' activity, for which they consider the pros and cons of different kinds of partnership. Ask for volunteers to read out what they have written.

EXTENSION

• Ask students to research the views on marriage, civil partnerships and cohabiting of different members of their wider family. Is there a difference in views depending on the generation? Have older relatives changed their views as society's attitudes have changed?

Further information and support for teachers:

Citizens Advice, 'Living together, marriage and civil partnership': www.citizensadvice.org.uk/family/living-together-marriage-and-civil-partnership

BBC News, article on civil partnerships, article: www.bbc.co.uk/news/uk-politics-45714032

'What is the difference between arranged marriage and forced marriage?': https://www.highspeedtraining.co.uk/hub/arranged-marriage-forced-marriage/

Further information and support for students:

The Guardian, Video about the first same-sex marriages in Britain featuring the couple shown on page 48: www.theguardian.com/society/2014/mar/29/gay-couples-wed-same-sex-marriage

MARRIAGE	CIVIL PARTNERSHIP
COHABITING	Can take place in a church, register office or 'approved premise'
Can be civil or religious	Can take place in a register office or 'approved premise'
The partners exchange vows	Available only to same-sex couples
Gives tax benefits to a partner when they pass on their property to the other on death	Does not give partners automatic rights to each other's property
Does not entitle you to inherit anything from your partner	You have certain responsibilities for your partner under the law

Strand:	Resources:
• Relationships and sex education	• Book Three: pp. 50–51 • Worksheet 8.2 • Pictures of celebrity couples (for starter activity)

Learning objective:	Key words:
• Explore what skills are needed to make a long-term relationship with a partner work	relationship, commitment, communication, consideration, compromise, cooperation

STARTER

• Show pictures of celebrity couples, some in a loving relationship, some who have split up, and some who have public differences. Ask what students think has caused these situations. To start them thinking about the issues, broaden the question out to 'What makes relationships work?' and 'What makes relationships fail?'.

ACTIVITIES

• Get students to read the article 'Committed relationships are good for your health' on page 50 of *Your Choice Book Three* and to do the 'Discuss' task that follow it in small groups. Invite groups to share their views and discuss any differences with the class.

• Then ask them to read 'What's the best thing about a committed relationship?' and, still in their groups, to do the 'Your choice' activity on page 50. The cards on **Worksheet 8.2** can be used to help them to rank the different benefits in order. Ask for feedback from the groups and discuss the differences in opinion between students.

• Organise students into different small groups to read the article 'Oiling the wheels of a relationship' and discuss the four Cs. Encourage them to come up with other factors to help keep a relationship together. Then ask them individually to do the 'Your choice' activity on page 51, writing the paragraph giving their reasons.

• With the students, read the two scenarios in the final 'Discuss' activity and then ask them to discuss the situations in groups. Ask them to think about what the effect is on the relationship and which of the 'four Cs' they could use to keep the relationship running smoothly.

PLENARY

• Ask students: 'If you were in a committed relationship, what do you think would be the most important thing you would work at or pay attention to in order to make the relationship successful?'. Ask the students to write down their ideas. Then invite a selection of responses and ask for reasons.

EXTENSION

• Working in pairs, ask students to adapt one of the scenarios in the 'Discuss' task into a role play. Make sure at least one pair does each scenario and then invite them to perform their role play for the class.

Further information and support for students

Psychology Today, 'Relationships': www.psychologytoday.com/gb/basics/relationships

Psychology Today, '8 ways to make your relationship work better': www.psychologytoday.com/gb/blog/emotional-fitness/201309/8-ways-make-your-relationship-work-better

Brook, 'Relationships': www.brook.org.uk/your-life/category/relationships

Time article, 17 strategies for keeping relationships together: http://time.com/4927173/relationships-strategies-studies/

Companionship

Sharing ordinary things with someone you love and building that sharing up over the years.

Security

I feel supported in the things I do. I can rely on my partner to back me up, and to be there for me. That makes me feel stronger as a person.

Teamwork

We work together and pool our resources. So financially it makes sense, but we also bring different skills to the complex task of making life work.

Children

To me, bringing children up in a relationship that is strong and reliable is the most important thing. They need that stable structure in which to grow.

Love

If you truly love someone then you'll want to spend your life with them. It's a deeper feeling than the love you can have with friends or casual partners.

Developing as a human being

A committed relationship makes demands on the couple, but precisely because of that it allows you to grow emotionally and not get stuck in a rut.

Strand:	Resources:
• Physical health and wellbeing	• Book Three: pp. 52–53

Learning objective:	Key words:
• To understand how our body image of ourselves is created, the role social media has in this, and how important it is to have realistic role models in the media	social media, body image, photoshopped, role model

STARTER

* Ask students when the last time was that they looked at a photo of a friend online. Ask why they think it is important to put photos of themselves on social media. Note their answers on the board. *Suggestions may include: to feel good about themselves; to show people what they are doing; to show off a hairstyle, clothes or a fashion trend; to connect with friends.*

ACTIVITIES

* Ask students, in groups, to read the introductory paragraph and 'Social media' on page 52 of *Your Choice Book Three*. Then ask them to do the 'Discuss' task that follows. Students may quickly agree with statements 1 or 2. Statement 3 (Amy) is subjective, whereas statement 4 (Tomas) will require research to prove whether it is true or not *(it is true – the question is to what extent they are altered).*

* In the same groups, ask students to read 'Body image' and 'The unrealistic model' before discussing the 'Your choice' questions on page 52. Bring the class back together and invite students to share their answers in a class discussion. *Suggested answers: the media (magazines, the internet, TV), friends, people at school, siblings, parents.*

* Organise students into pairs to discuss question **1** in 'Your choice' on page 53 (the answers are subjective). Then ask them to compare their answers with another pair before moving on to discuss question **2**. Bring the class back together to share and discuss their answers.

* With the class, discuss the idea of a disclaimer on digital photos. Students could research the example of France, where photos in adverts must carry a disclaimer telling the viewer or reader if images have been digitally enhanced.

PLENARY

* Read 'Does it matter who we see in the media?' and 'Real Beauty – getting it right and wrong' with the class, and then answer the 'Discuss' questions on page 53. *Suggested answers: **1.** Yes; **2.** Yes; **3.** Yes; **4.** No, men are not judged as much. Reasons why for **1.** to **3.** – Role models are important as they teach us what is normal and we identify with them.*

EXTENSION

* Ask students to write a letter, either to themselves as they are now about their own body image now or from themselves in their 20s or 30s to their younger teenage self. They could look at the Telegraph article below as an example.

Further information and support for teachers:

Article to discuss with students, 'How to prevent the media from damaging your teen's body image': www.verywellfamily.com/media-and-teens-body-image-2611245

Further information and support for students:

#thisboytalks – site supporting teenage boys on male body image: http://boysbiggestconversation.com/

Daily Telegraph (Australia), 'Dear teenage me, stop worrying about your body': www.dailytelegraph.com.au/rendezview/dear-teenage-me-stop-worrying-about-your-body/news-story/7bce2a9770bf7e0004cdacb984e0c7cb

Strand:	Resources:
• Physical health and wellbeing	• Book Three: pp. 54–55 • Worksheets 10.1a, 10.1b

Learning objective:	Key words:
• To understand what an eating disorder is • To examine the common causes of eating disorders	eating disorder, anorexia, bulimia, binge eating

• Please note, the curriculum gives the following advice for this subject: 'Eating disorders and extreme weight loss are a specialised area and schools should use qualified support or advice as needed. Schools may consider accessing support from the NHS or local specialist services who may be able to provide advice and CPD for teachers.'

STARTER

• Ask students what they think an eating disorder is and if they know the names of any disorders. Write these on the board.

ACTIVITIES

• Ask students to read the introduction on page 54 of *Your Choice Book Three* and then ask them if they would like to add anything to the notes on the board or change anything.

• Ask students to read the section on 'Anorexia' on page 54 and then, in small groups, to do the 'Discuss' task on page 55. Ask them, still in their groups, to read the extract from Emma Woolf's book on page 54 and to talk about this in their groups. Then bring the class back together and invite groups to share their responses with the rest of the class. Ask: 'What you think Emma means by "I feel most trapped by my illness" or "I feel distinctly not part of the family"?'

• Organise students into pairs to do the first 'Research' task – about the charity Beat. Encourage them to share their report with another pair and see if either of them would like to add anything to their report.

• Organise the class into three groups, A, B and C and hand out copies of Worksheet 10.1a. Read the instructions with the students and make sure everyone understands what they have to do. After the initial groups have answered the questions allocated to them, reorganise them into new groups of three, comprising one student from each of the initial groups, to share their answers.

PLENARY

• Compare answers in a class discussion: *1. No; 2. Yes; 3. Yes; 4. Tooth decay, gum disease, throat infections and mouth ulcers; 5. Your body doesn't absorb all the nutrients it should do; 6. As a mental health problem; 7. Yes; 8. No; 9. Getting people to think differently; 10. Yes; 11. Yes; 12. Yes; 13. Yes; 14. Discuss the problem with a responsible adult; 15. The UK's eating disorder charity.*

• Support students to do the 'Research' task using the NHS website. Invite students to share their findings with the rest of the class.

EXTENSION

• Distribute copies of **Worksheet 10.1b** for students to work on in pairs. *Suggested answers:* **Brian** *is binge eating. This started when his parents split up. He needs to plan his meals with healthy snacks and the occasional treat – with advice from a doctor or dietician. He could also see a counsellor and look at strategies to avoid binge eating.* **Kate** *may have anorexia. This seemed to start when she hit puberty. She should see a doctor immediately to discuss her weight loss, as anorexia is an extremely serious medical condition.* **Joe** *is suffering from bulimia. This started after his dad's death. He should see a doctor immediately, as bulimia is also a serious medical condition needing professional help. He should also see a counsellor, to help him deal with the grief from his dad's death.*

Further information and support for teachers:

'Helping someone with an eating disorder': www.helpguide.org/articles/eating-disorders/helping-someone-with-an-eating-disorder.htm

Anorexia and bulimia care: www.anorexiabulimiacare.org.uk/help-for-you

Further information and support for students:

Beat Eating Disorders, UK eating disorder charity: www.beateatingdisorders.org.uk

Young Minds, advice and support on eating disorders: youngminds.org.uk/find-help/conditions

---

Worksheet 10.1a Eating disorders

Group A   Read the section on 'Bulimia' on page 55 and answer questions 1–5.

Group B   Read the section on 'Treating anorexia, bulimia or an eating disorder' on page 55 and answer questions 6–10.

Group C   Read the section on 'Signs and symptoms that you may have an eating disorder' on page 55 and answer questions 11–15.

Then, in groups of three, with one person from each group, discuss your answers, giving reasons for your group's choices.

Group A – questions on bulimia:

1. Is bulimia an easy problem to spot? ....

2. Do people with bulimia binge eat? ....

3. Can bulimia be dangerous? ....

4. What other problems has bulimia been linked to? ....

5. What is another problem of bulimia? ....

Group B – questions on treating anorexia, bulimia or an eating disorder:

6. How should we treat anorexia and bulimia? ....

7. Can anorexia and bulimia be addictive? ....

8. Is a diet a long-term solution for these conditions? ....

9. What is the key to dealing with anorexia and bulimia? ....

10. Will people suffering from bulimia and anorexia need professional support? ....

Group C – questions on signs and symptoms of that you may have an eating disorder:

11. Do symptoms vary from person to person? ....

12. Can a person eat too little and suffer from one of these conditions? ....

13. Can a person eat too much and suffer from one of these conditions? ....

14. What should the first step be? ....

15. What is Beat? ....

Worksheet 10.1b Eating disorders: case studies

In pairs, read the case studies below and think about the following questions:

- What eating disorder might the person be suffering from in each case?
- When did each eating disorder start?
- What help should each person seek and from whom?

Give reasons for your views.

Brian's story

I've always loved food. When I was at primary school, I used to love eating cakes, sweets and chocolate. I'd eat as much as I could. However, things changed when my parents split up when I was 9. It really shook me up. I began to feel negative about things. When I felt bad, I'd comfort myself by having another piece of cake or something sweet. I began to always make sure mum had bought me some cake and there was always some at home when I needed it.

Now I'm older at secondary school. We've got exams, and I've got a problem. At the slightest stressful thing, I'm eating cake, sweets or chocolate. On a bad day, I will have between 4 to 8 junk food snacks in one day. I've begun to put on a lot of weight. Some friends have noticed and are concerned, and some horrible kids at school have begun teasing me and calling me names. Which of course makes me want to go and eat more. I really don't know what to do.

Kate's story

When I was 11, I started going through puberty. I didn't like it. Suddenly all these curves started appearing. I put on a bit of weight over the summer holidays. As a result, I decided I wanted to be thinner.

At first, I was only watching what I ate. Then I discovered calories and became obsessed with counting them. As a result, I began to eat less and less, and made excuses to eat on my own, so other people didn't see how little I ate.

At 13, my mum became concerned, as I had lost so much weight. I told her it was only a phase, and that it is much better to be thin rather than fat.

My mum wants to take me to the doctor, but I think I'm fine. I mean, I'm not that thin so not eating must be fine, right?

Joe's story

When my dad died, I put on a lot of weight. All of us were shocked in the family, so we just ate to survive. I had a really bad diet then.

I managed to lose the weight at the gym, but I swore I'd never go back there. Then on the first anniversary of my dad's death, I began to worry what would happen if I put the weight on again. That's when I first made myself sick after a meal.

I thought, this is great, I've found a way of keeping my weight down. However, being sick can really burn your throat and it hurts my gums. I've done this three or four times now, but I'm wondering if I'm really doing the right thing?

Youth crime

Strand:	Resources:
• Social education	• Book Three: pp. 56–57 • Worksheet 11.1

Learning objective:	Key words:
• To understand why young people commit crime, and what sort of sentences apply to different crimes	crime, offence, sentence, youth court

STARTER

* Give students two minutes to list the most common crimes they can think of. Invite students to share their lists and note all the crimes on the board to refer to during the lesson.

ACTIVITIES

* Ask students to read the introduction and 'Reasons for committing crimes' on page 56 of *Your Choice Book Three* and then, in groups, to do the first 'Discuss' activity. Invite groups to share their responses in a class discussion, and to think about other reasons for committing crime (e.g. boredom, revenge).

* Read through the 'Role play' activity with students and then organise them into groups of three to act it out. Make sure that they take turns to be the person who is reluctant to take part in the illegal activity. The illegal activity might be trespassing on private property, creating graffiti, shoplifting, or similar. Encourage the best groups to perform their role play for the rest of the class and then discuss any issues they raise.

* Ask students to read 'Natalia's story' on page 57 and then to do the next 'Discuss' task in small groups. Invite groups to share their responses with the class.

* Now ask students to read 'Youth courts' on page 56, including 'What sentences can youth courts give?' (page 57), and then to work in pairs on the 'Your choice' activity. Encourage pairs to share their responses with another pair and then with the rest of the class. Discuss differences of opinion – point out that some sentences will have to be custodial (see **Worksheet 11.1** below).

* Support students, in pairs, to do the 'Research' activity, investigating exactly what happens in a youth court and finding answers to the questions they would have if they were summoned to attend a youth court. Check students' understanding of the different sentences and then invite them to share their questions and answers with the rest of the class.

* Hand out copies of **Worksheet 11.1** for students to complete in pairs and then invite some to share their suggested sentences with the rest of the class. Work through the sheet with the class, telling them the maximum sentence for each crime: *1. 4 years in jail; 2. 10 years in jail; 3. 10 years in jail; 4. 10 years in jail; 5. a life sentence; 6. 14 years in jail; 7. £10 000 fine; 8. 6 months in jail and a £5000 fine; 9. 10 years in jail; 10. 14 years in jail.*

PLENARY

* Lead a class discussion on what students think the age of criminal responsibility should be for different crimes, including shoplifting, vandalism, knife crime and murder, asking them to give reasons for their views. Note that the age of criminal responsibility in the UK is 10 (apart from Scotland, where it is 8), but children aged 10–17 are tried differently from adults aged 18 and over. Shoplifting and vandalism may result in a caution for a first offence. Knife crime will result in a custodial sentence on the second or third offence. Murder is always going to result in a custodial sentence of some kind.

EXTENSION

* Ask students, in pairs, to research what a 'youth caution' is, using the Youth Justice Legal Centre link below.

Further information and support for students:

UK Government, 'Youth courts': www.gov.uk/courts/youth-courts

Sentencing Council, 'Types of sentences for young people': www.sentencingcouncil.org.uk/about-sentencing/young-people-and-sentencing/types-of-sentences-for-young-people/

Youth Justice Legal Centre, 'Youth caution': yjlc.uk/youth-caution/

Worksheet 11.1 Crime and sentencing

Look at the crimes listed in the table. Write down what you think the sentence ought to be for each of the crimes. Then check your answers with your teacher. Do any of the answers surprise you? Give reasons for your views.

Crime	Your sentence	Actual sentence
1. Carrying a knife		
2. Rioting		
3. Cruelty to a person under 16		
4. Making threats to kill		
5. Murder		
6. Committing FGM (see Unit 3.3)		
7. Employing illegal immigrants		
8. Failing to stop at a road accident you were involved in		
9. Fraud		
10. Burglary		

Strand:	Resources:
• Social education	• Book Three: pp. 58–59 • Worksheet 11.2

Learning objective:	Key words:
• To examine the dangers of carrying a knife and knife crime	gang, knife crime

STARTER

* Ask students when the last knife crime incident they heard about was in the media, and what occurred. (The chances are there will have been a knife crime death in the news in the two weeks before your lesson. Research this in advance and have the details with you to discuss if required.)

ACTIVITIES

* Ask students to read the section on 'Gangs' on page 58 of *Your Choice Book Three* and then to do the 'Your choice' activity in groups. Invite groups to share their lists with those of other groups and compare them in a class discussion. Are the lists very different, or are there lots of similarities?

* Either on their own, or in pairs if students need more support, ask students to read 'Ask Erica' and then to do the 'Write' task that follows it. Invite a few students to share their replies and discuss any differences in their advice.

* Organise students into groups to read 'Knife crime' on page 59 and the 'Fact check', before doing the 'Discuss' task considering suggestions for how to reduce knife crime. Invite some groups to share their answers with the rest of the class, giving reasons for their views.

* Now working in pairs, ask students to read 'Teenagers talking about knife crime' and then to do the 'Discuss' activity that follows. Invite some pairs to share their answers with the rest of the class, giving reasons for their views. As a stretch activity, ask students to come up with additional statements.

* Ask students to read 'What is joint enterprise?' and make sure they all understand it.

* Organise students into groups of three to do the 'Role play'. Explain that one of them should play the parent and one the teenager, with the third observing what is going on to feed back to the others afterwards. Make sure that everyone has a go in each role before they compare notes about what they have learned.

* Hand out copies of **Worksheet 11.2** for students to read the information and answer the questions. *Answers: 1. 215; 2. Number of men and boys killed in stabbings; 3. Men and boys; 4. 61; 5. More people died as a result of knife crime (215 as opposed to 32).*

PLENARY

* Hold a debate of the motion 'This house believes that there should be zero tolerance for knives and knife crime'. You can refer back to **Worksheets 5.1b** and **15.3** in *Book Two* for guidance on holding debates.

EXTENSION

* Ask students, in pairs, to design a poster to be displayed in school warning about the dangers of knife crime and/or joining a gang. Include the following: *Joining a gang – increased risk of violence, bullying, being encouraged to do something illegal, aggression, interference with school and family life, danger that this affects not just you but also your family and friends. Dangers of carrying a knife – feeling safe when you may not be, increased level of aggression and violence, being in trouble with school and parents, being caught by the police and prosecuted, danger of serious injury or death to you and others.*

Further information and support for teachers:

The Guardian, 'Knife crime: how teenagers cope with daily life on the front line': www.theguardian.com/uk-news/2018/nov/10/london-knife-crime-lives-transformed-by-mentoring

No knives, better lives – the facts from a Scottish perspective: noknivesbetterlives.com/young-people/the-facts/

NSPCC, 'Gangs and young people': www.nspcc.org.uk/preventing-abuse/keeping-children-safe/staying-safe-away-from-home/gangs-young-people/

Worksheet 11.2 Knife crime and young people

Read the article and then answer the questions below.

Stabbing deaths among young people hit eight-year high

Police recorded 61 deaths in 16–24 group and a total of 215 fatal stabbings in England and Wales

By Alan Travis

The number of teenagers and young adults stabbed to death in England and Wales reached the highest level for eight years, official figures show.

Police recorded a total of 215 fatal stabbings in the 12 months to March 2017. This was a similar number to the 212 recorded for the previous 12 months, but a 16% increase over the 186 in the year to March 2015.

The number of women and girls who died as a result of knife crime last year was 51, the lowest number in a decade. The number of men and boys killed was 164, the highest since 2009, the Office for National Statistics said.

'Male victims aged 16 to 24 years and 35 to 44 years have seen the biggest increases over the last year, with both groups having 10 more homicides than in the year ending March 2016,' the ONS said.

The detailed figures show that 10 teenagers aged 16 to 17 and 51 young adults aged 18 to 24 died as a result of knife crime in 2016–17. The combined figure of 61 is the highest since 2008–09, when 67 young people were killed in stabbings.

Six under-16s died as a result of knife crime in 2016–17. The number has fluctuated since the last peak of 14 in 2010–11.

Thirty-two people died in shootings last year, seven more than in the previous year and 11 more than in the year to March 2015. However, gun offences are still 45% below the level seen a decade ago.

The Guardian, Thursday 8 February 2018

1. How many knife crimes resulted in someone dying between April 2016 and March 2017?

   ....

2. What in the statistics was the highest figure since 2009?

   ....

3. Who are usually the victims of knife crime, according to the statistics?

   ....

4. How many young people (aged 16–24) died as a result of knife crime in the year to March 2017?

   ....

5. Did more people die as a result of gun crime or knife crime in the year to March 2017?

   ....

12.1 Fake news

<table>
<tr><td>

Strand:
- Social education

</td><td>

Resources:
- Book Three: pp. 60–61
- Worksheet 12.1
- Articles from different sources on a topical controversial issue (see Research below)

</td></tr>
<tr><td>

Learning objective:
- To understand what fake news is
- To examine the different ways of spotting a fake news story

</td><td>

Key words:
fake news

</td></tr>
</table>

STARTER

- Ask students if they think they can believe everything they read on the internet. Elicit examples of false stories (e.g. when it was claimed that there were only very small numbers of protesters during US President Donald Trump's visit to the UK in June 2019) and then define 'fake news'.

ACTIVITIES

- Ask students to read the introduction and the 'Case study' on page 60 of *Your Choice Book Three* and then to do the 'Discuss' task in groups. Invite some groups to share their responses with the rest of the class, giving reasons for their views.

- Now ask students to read 'Fake news on social media', 'Responsibility for fake news' and the 'Case study' on page 61. (Please note that there is some text missing from the top of page 61; it should read: 'For example, during the 2016 US election, it was discovered that dozens of United States political news websites had been launched from the small Macedonian town of Veles. Almost all these sites supported Donald Trump, mostly with fake news stories which were then shared via Facebook.')

PLENARY

- With the class, read through the advice in the 'Discuss' box on page 61. Then organise students into groups to consider the questions. Bring the class back together to discuss groups' opinions on the advice and to make sure students understand how they can implement these suggestions.

RESEARCH

- Organise the students into groups and hand out copies of **Worksheet 12.1**. Find a controversial news story that has occurred recently (this will require you to search the internet and prepare these in advance) and give each group a different version to check; for example, give one a tabloid newspaper (e.g. *The Sun*) version, one a broadsheet version (e.g. *The Times*), one a social media version, one a left-wing newspaper (e.g. *The Guardian* or the *Mirror*) and one a right-wing newspaper (e.g. the *Mail* or *The Telegraph*). Then draw the class together to discuss the following questions: 'Which version of the story seems most reliable or accurate? How can we tell?'

EXTENSION

- Ask students to research what the UK Parliament has done to prevent fake news and what social media companies said to Parliament the last time they appeared there. Ask them to write two to three paragraphs summarising their findings.

Further information and support for teachers:

BBC, 'Fake news: Can teenagers spot it?': www.bbc.co.uk/news/technology-46206675

The anti-vaccination movement – video for teachers to use clips from:
www.futurelearn.com/courses/social-media-in-healthcare/0/steps/9757

Further information and support for students:

Teen Vogue, 'The best tips for spotting fake news in the age of Trump': www.teenvogue.com/story/the-best-tips-for-spotting-fake-news-in-the-age-of-trump

BBC Newsbeat, 'YouTube to offer fake news workshops to teenagers':
http://www.bbc.co.uk/newsbeat/article/39653429/youtube-to-offer-fake-news-workshops-to-teenagers

1. **Does it come from a reliable news organisation?**

   Does the story come from a reliable news organisation, such as the BBC, Sky News or a major newspaper? Or is the story the opinion of one person on the internet? What information can you find on the website about the people who have produced it?

2. **How professional is the story or photo?**

   Is the story well written? Or it is badly written, with spelling mistakes? If it's a photo, does it look real, or does it look like a fake? The more mistakes a story contains, the more likely it is to be unreliable.

3. **Does the story contradict itself?**

   A story that contradicts itself is much more likely to be unreliable. A story that presents the same set of facts and is coherent is more likely to be genuine.

4. **Does the story just present one point of view?**

   Is there other evidence that backs up the story or photo from another source? If the story says 'Donald Trump is against this', do other newspapers, online articles or news organisations say the same thing?

5. **Are you seeing the full picture?**

   Are there other facts, information or pictures that add to or detract from the story?

6. **Does the headline match the picture or story?**

   How accurate is the headline? Is it a fair representation of the story? Or does it exaggerate or emphasise one part of the story for effect?

7. **What is the past record of the news organisation where you got the photo or story from?**

   Do they have a track record for producing good reliable stories or photos? Or do they have a history of political bias and exaggeration?

8. **What does your gut feeling tell you?**

   Do you think you are being lied to? If so, check the story more closely and look for other sources to check what you are reading.

12.2 Radicalisation

<table>
<tr><td>

Strand:
- Social education

</td><td>

Resources:
- Book Three: pp. 62–63
- Worksheet 12.2

</td></tr>
<tr><td>

Learning objective:
- To understand what radicalisation is
- To identify ways of preventing and reporting it

</td><td>

Key words:
radicalisation, Prevent

</td></tr>
</table>

STARTER

* Ask students what they understand by the term 'radicalisation'; then read with them the definition at the beginning of page 62 of *Your Choice Book Three*.

ACTIVITIES

* Ask students to read all the information on page 62 and then to do the 'Discuss' activity in groups. Invite groups to share their responses with the class, giving reasons for their views.

* Then ask students to read Kamran's story on page 63 and, still in groups, to do the next 'Discuss' task. *Answers:* **1.** *Factors that made Kamran vulnerable: he was the only Muslim student at the school; he had communication difficulties; his mother was very ill which may have affected him emotionally; he had unsupervised access to the internet.* **2.** *To help him get a different view, he got a mentor, Daud, who engaged Kamran with his passion for football and helped him explore Islam at the local mosque.*

* With the class, read 'What you can do'. Organise students into pairs and ask them to rank the advice in order from the most to the least effective, in their opinion, before doing the final 'Discuss' activity. Other ways of protecting themselves might include speaking to a wide range of people with different views, and making sure that nobody isolates them to teach them just one extreme point of view. Explain that if they are uncomfortable with what is being said or being shown to them, they should tell a teacher, parent or responsible adult.

* Bring the class back together and ask pairs to share their views and their reasons in a class discussion.

* Hand out **Worksheet 12.2** for students to do in pairs or small groups.

PLENARY

* Ask pairs to do the 'Write' task and encourage them to use the vocabulary from **Worksheet 12.2** where appropriate. Support them to find out more on the Educate Against Hate website (link below) and then to discuss their findings. Invite some pairs to share their emails with the rest of the class.

* You could also discuss with students what they think are the main dangers of being radicalised in your local area, and what can be done to combat this. *Answers may include: material on social media from radical or terrorist groups; interacting with people who know radicals who have returned from fighting in Syria or other countries; being drawn into far-right groups.*

EXTENSION

* Explain to students the school's duty under the Prevent strategy, and what policies and procedures the school has in place to stop and deal with radicalisation. Use the BBC story below, and discuss with students whether the number of students being referred to Prevent is appropriate, and why.

Further information and support for teachers:

BBC, 'Prevent scheme: Anti-terror referrals for 2,000 children': www.bbc.co.uk/news/uk-41927937

Child Law Advice, 'Radicalisation in schools and The Prevent Duty': childlawadvice.org.uk/information-pages/radicalisation-in-schools-and-the-prevent-duty/

Gov UK, article on the Prevent strategy: www.gov.uk/government/speeches/safeguarding-our-young-people-from-becoming-radicalised-is-difficult-but-vital-work-article-by-amber-rudd

Educate Against Hate – practical advice and information on protecting children from extremism and radicalisation: educateagainsthate.com

Worksheet 12.2 Radicalisation wordsearch

Find the following words or phrases in the wordsearch below. Look up each one in a dictionary (e.g. at Collinsdictionary.com). As you find each word, talk with a partner about how it relates to the topic of radicalisation.

Radicalisation	Extremist	Isolation
Prevent	Fundamentalist	Grooming
Terrorist	Moderate	Brainwashed
Far right	Reasonable	Internet

A	A	O	R	B	R	N	R	H	H	J	X	Z	T	G	X
P	Q	K	F	R	R	E	Q	F	A	R	R	I	G	H	T
N	C	M	U	A	J	N	A	I	K	F	H	M	N	Z	K
D	B	O	N	I	S	V	A	S	C	Z	L	R	W	R	U
A	S	D	D	N	T	E	R	R	O	R	I	S	T	R	M
H	U	E	A	W	W	H	M	F	M	N	K	P	B	G	U
X	S	R	M	A	F	G	I	S	O	L	A	T	I	O	N
Y	W	A	E	S	X	J	W	F	F	C	A	B	Y	K	L
C	M	T	N	H	P	M	N	K	V	K	X	B	L	P	A
R	G	E	T	E	N	Y	A	T	R	I	E	Y	L	E	N
C	L	R	A	D	I	C	A	L	I	S	A	T	I	O	N
Y	C	Z	L	F	Q	M	G	R	O	O	M	I	N	G	F
Z	C	I	I	J	E	X	T	R	E	M	I	S	T	I	H
R	X	Z	S	X	S	F	I	F	O	B	T	A	G	Z	Q
V	X	K	T	Z	Y	W	I	I	N	T	E	R	N	E	T
C	T	P	R	E	V	E	N	T	H	Q	K	X	C	P	P

Strand:	Resources:
• Social education	• Book Three: pp. 64–65 • Worksheet 12.3

Learning objective:	Key words:
• To understand our personal responsibility for what we post on social media, and the responsibilities of the media companies and others	duty of care

STARTER

* Ask students: 'What responsibilities do you think you have when posting something on social media?' Write their suggestions on the board and refer back to these, when appropriate, during the lesson.

ACTIVITIES

* Ask students to read the introduction on page 64 of *Your Choice Book Three* and then to do the 'Discuss' activity in pairs or groups. Invite students to share their responses and reasons in a class discussion.

* Ask students to read 'Social media and the law' and then organise them into pairs to do the 'Write' activity on page 65. Use the HireRabbit link below for examples and get general feedback from students as a class. Students can then use the internet to compare their codes of conduct with other codes of conduct, to see what they could add and what a company may have missed out.

* Hand out copies of **Worksheet 12.3** for students to complete in pairs. When they have done this, ask them to compare their answers with those of another pair before you share the answers with the class. *Answers: 1, 2, 4, 6, 7, 8, 10 are true; 5, 9 are false; 3 is false at the time of going to press but GCHQ have proposed a plan which would allow them to eavesdrop on encrypted chat.* (You may need to explain the term 'deep web' for question **7**: this refers to everything we are unable to see on the world wide web using regular search engines, including encrypted or password-protected sites, email, banking and messaging services.)

* As a stretch activity, students could research whether any legal cases or changes have occurred recently involving social media (for example, YouTube changing their policy in June 2019 and removing a large number of hate speech videos from its platform).

* Ask students, in groups, to read 'Social media and responsibility' and the two case studies on page 65, and then to discuss what they learn from each.

PLENARY

* Read 'Your choice' with the class and discuss the questions. Encourage students to give reasons for their views.

EXTENSION

* Ask students to research the right to be forgotten (see the link to *The Guardian* article below) and to write a report of two to three paragraphs explaining the concept and supporting or arguing against the proposal.

Further information and support for students:

The Guardian, 'Social media firms face crackdown over child protection': www.theguardian.com/society/2019/feb/05/social-media-firms-face-crackdown-over-child-protection

HireRabbit, '5 terrific examples of company social media policies': http://blog.hirerabbit.com/5-terrific-examples-of-company-social-media-policies/

The Guardian – the right to be forgotten, 'Ministers back campaign to give under-18s right to delete social media posts': www.theguardian.com/media/2015/jul/28/ministers-back-campaign-under-18s-right-delete-social-media-posts

Worksheet 12.3 Online literacy and responsibility

Read the following statements in the table below and decide which ones you think are true and which are false.

Statement	True or false?
1. You can be taken to court for writing something that is untrue about a celebrity on twitter.	
2. Extremist groups will try and trick you into sharing their content, which helps them to build support for their views.	
3. The government has the power to spy on every private WhatsApp message you have ever written.	
4. You can be banned from Facebook or Twitter for sharing inappropriate material, such as hate speech.	
5. The government has the power to automatically monitor all of your emails and read them, even though it may not know what it is looking for.	
6. Many social media companies have material on self-harm that they should have taken down, but haven't.	
7. Most of the material on the internet we can't see, because it is part of the deep web, which is more difficult to access, but there is no control over what is put up there.	
8. The police can track your location through your mobile phone signal.	
9. The government is constantly spying on you by turning on the camera on your computer and mobile phone.	
10. You should never send a naked photo of yourself online or through social media, even if the picture disappears quickly (as on Snapchat), because it is possible for the recipient to screenshot it and share it.	

Attending to your wellbeing

Strand:
- Personal wellbeing and mental health

Resources:
- Book Three: pp. 66–67
- Worksheet 13.1

Learning objective:
- Exploring wellbeing and how we can attend to it and enhance it

Key words:
wellbeing, happiness

STARTER

- Write 'wellbeing' on the whiteboard and ask students to call out whatever comes to mind, including definitions, thoughts and feelings. Note students' suggestions on the board around the central word. Try to draw out that the term 'wellbeing' refers to a whole range of feelings, both physical and mental, and that these are related. Ask: 'What things can we do to enhance our wellbeing?' and say that you will be exploring some of those things in the lesson.

ACTIVITIES

- Ask students to read the introduction and 'Children less happy with their lives' on page 66 of *Your Choice Book Three*, and then to do the 'Discuss' task in small groups. Ask each group to feed back their findings to the rest of the class. You could get the groups to rank the factors listed in order of importance and compare their rankings in the feedback, discussing any differences of opinion.

- As a class, look through 'Your choice' on page 66 and the quiz questions on page 67. Then hand out **Worksheet 13.1** for students to work through the quiz on this. Encourage them to count up the number of **a)**, **b)** and **c)**s, and then to read 'What's your score?'. They should then discuss with a partner what they have learned about themselves and what they may need to do to enhance their wellbeing.

PLENARY

- Organise students into pairs to do the 'Your choice' activity on page 67. Ask volunteers to share what they have written.

RESEARCH

- Ask students to research the connection between physical activity and wellbeing and/or diet and wellbeing, and to present their findings to the class. They could use the Mind website as a starting point (see links below).

EXTENSION

- Ask students to research the levels of wellbeing among one or more members of their wider family and/or friends. They can do this using copies of the quiz on **Worksheet 13.1.** Encourage the students to discuss with those family members the areas where they might be able to improve their wellbeing and how they could do this.

Further information and support for teachers:

Children's Society, Good Childhood Report 2018: www.childrenssociety.org.uk/good-childhood-report

Further information and support for students:

Mind, 'Food and mood' – on the relationship between diet and well-being: www.mind.org.uk/information-support/tips-for-everyday-living/food-and-mood/#.XOfniI97mUk

Mind, 'Physical activity and your mental health': www.mind.org.uk/information-support/tips-for-everyday-living/physical-activity-and-your-mental-health/about-physical-activity/?o=28048#.XOfoHY97mUk

Answer this quiz to see how good you are at maintaining your mental wellbeing. Keep a record of your answers. Then check your score and discuss with a friend what you have learned about yourself, and what you could do to help yourself.

1. **Having fun**. Doing things that cheer you up is an obvious way of feeling better. How often do you let yourself feel happy, e.g. by being with friends who make you laugh, or treating yourself with something you like?

    a) often   **b)** sometimes   **c)** hardly ever

2. **Self-esteem**. Accepting yourself as a person builds your resilience. How good are you at feeling OK about yourself even when you don't achieve, or when you get criticised?

    a) pretty good   **b)** sometimes good, sometimes not   **c)** not very good

3. **Eating well**. Your diet is more important for mental health than you may think. Do you:
    a) have a balanced diet
    b) have good days and bad days
    c) have a lot of junk food and sugary drinks?

4. **Sleep**. Not enough sleep, or poor-quality sleep, affects our energy and mood. How is your sleep?

    a) good (7+ hours per night)   **b)** average   **c)** poor (5 or fewer hours)

5. **Getting active**. Physical exercise is a mood-booster. Regular walking is just as good as aerobic exercise. How often do you exercise each week?

    a) most days   **b)** some days   **c)** rarely

6. **Sharing your feelings**. Talking about how you are to someone you trust makes problems more manageable and builds emotional intelligence. How good are you at sharing your feelings?

    a) I often do this   **b)** I sometimes talk about how I feel   **c)** I keep my feelings to myself

7. **Connecting with others.** We are social beings, so developing good relationships with family, friends and community is vital to our wellbeing. How much effort do you put into your relationships?

    a) a lot of time and effort   **b)** they are quite important   **c)** they aren't important to me

8. **Hobbies and interests**. Learning new skills keeps you mentally alert and interested, and connects us with others. What time do you give to learning new skills or to your existing hobbies?

    a) a lot   **b)** some   **c)** hardly any

9. **Giving to others**. Kindness and helping others gives us a sense of purpose and strengthens our relationships. Volunteering, helping someone, or even just a kind word – every little helps. How much do you give to others?

    a) a lot   **b)** some   **c)** hardly at all

10. **Being aware of yourself and the world**. Practising mindfulness can help us enjoy the world and manage stress. How much do you really notice what's going on in the present moment – in yourself and in the world around you?

    a) I regularly take time to notice things
    b) sometimes I stop and notice how I am feeling
    c) I always dash from one activity to another

What's your score?

Mostly a) – You are doing lots of valuable things to help your mental wellbeing.	**Mostly b)** – You are doing some things to help your mental wellbeing, but there is more you could do if you wanted to.	**Mostly c)** – There are plenty of things you could do to improve your wellbeing.

13.2   Mindfulness

Strand:	**Resources:**
• Personal wellbeing and mental health	• Book Three: pp. 68–69 • Worksheet 13.2 • Raisins and a printed version of mindful eating practice with a raisin

Learning objective:	**Key words:**
• To learn about and practise mindfulness to enhance wellbeing	mindfulness, mental health, wellbeing

STARTER

* Write the word 'mindfulness' and ask students what they think it means. Ask them to call out any words and phrases they associate with it and note these on the board around the word without judgment. Underline the ones that relate directly to your own definition – a good definition is 'Paying attention (or being aware) (a) on purpose, (b) in the present moment, (c) without judgement'.

ACTIVITIES

* Give each student a raisin (checking for possible allergies first) and take the class through a mindful eating practice. There are many versions of this, such as the one at the link below. Then organise students into small groups to discuss what they got from the exercise. Invite groups to feed back and ask any questions that they couldn't resolve. Hand out **Worksheet 13.2**, which uses a similar technique to bring mindful awareness to any eating experience. Encourage students to use it when eating one meal or snack per day for a week.

* Ask why practising mindfulness – either formally (i.e. with a regular formal practice) or informally (i.e. bringing an openness and present-moment awareness to our day-to-day existence) – may help us. Encourage students to relate their responses to their experience of the mindful eating exercise. Elicit that instead of being trapped inside our minds, worrying or distracted by the world, we can learn to really be where we actually are. This helps to bring us greater calm and fulfilment. Then ask them to read 'Why practise mindfulness?' on page 68 and to think about part **1** of 'Your choice'. Invite them to share ideas.

* With the class, read 'Watching the thought train' and then ask students to do part **1** of the 'Discuss' task. Read out the steps of the thought train, allowing students the time to relax and close their eyes. When the exercise is over, organise students into small groups to do the rest of the 'Discuss' activity. Encourage students to practise 'watching the thought train' over a period of a week or two. It can be hard at first, but even noticing the difficulty is an achievement.

* Read through the 'Write' task with students and encourage them to do the two activities over the next week. Tell them that you will be asking for their feedback on the exercises in a future lesson. Stress that the walking exercise isn't just a memory game – students could write a few words as they use their senses to identify things on their walk. These could be very small things, such as paint peeling off a window pane. The intention is to wake up to the sights, sounds and smells of the present moment.

* Allow time for students to do the 'Research' activity, finding out about the apps in the lesson and then trying them out in their own time.

PLENARY

* Ask students to choose one mindful practice to explore and to write themselves a note of what it is, when they will do it and for how long, and the benefits they hope for. Invite volunteers to share their responses.

EXTENSION

* Ask students to develop part **2** of the 'Write' activity so that they pay close attention to their emotions through a single day, charting their levels (1–10) of stress, sadness, happiness and calmness on the hour every hour. What do they notice?

Further information and support for teachers:

Mindful eating practise with a raisin: www.mynutritionclinic.com.au/wp-content/uploads/2016/12/Mindful-eating-with-a-raisin.pdf

Mind, 'Mindfulness': www.mind.org.uk/information-support/drugs-and-treatments/mindfulness/#.XRS_Hnt7kWo

Worksheet 13.2 Mindful eating practice

Use your experience of eating to bring present-moment awareness to your day-to-day existence. For a week, eat one meal, or one snack, mindfully in this way and see what effect it has. Does it enhance your appreciation of simple but vital things, such as the flavours, tastes and texture of food? Does it allow you to slow down and focus on the present moment instead of following your mind as it jumps from thought to thought? Note down your experience in the table below.

1. Sit attentively with your next meal in front of you. Close your eyes and notice your body posture. Slowly breathe in and out and let any tension move out of your shoulders, arms, chest and legs as you gently scan your body. Continue slowly to move the air in and out of your nose and mouth for a few breaths. Then open your eyes again.

2. Take time to look at exactly what is on your plate. Look carefully at the shapes and sizes, colours and textures. Do you notice smells? Do you notice any urge to start eating, or to think about something else?

3. Feel the weight of your knife, fork or spoon as you lift it. Slowly raise the first forkful to your mouth. Notice the smells of the food and the body's digestive system preparing itself to receive the first mouthful.

4. Slowly open your mouth and place the food on your tongue for a moment without biting into it. Feel what you mouth wants to do with this food. Take a few moments before you bite into it. Feel its texture on your tongue and in your mouth. What do you taste? Observe yourself carefully while you chew and swallow mindfully.

5. Repeat till the plate is empty. Whenever your mind wanders, bring your attention gently back to the food and to your sensations.

Date	Food/meal	Comments/observations

Strand:	Resources:
• Personal wellbeing and mental health	• Book Three: pp. 70–71 • Worksheet 13.3

Learning objective:	Key words:
• To explain what mental ill-health and mental illness are, attitudes to mental health, and how to check one's own mental health	mental health, mental ill-health, mental illness, mood

STARTER

• Draw the mental health spectrum diagram on the board (see page 70 of *Your Choice Book Three*). Ask students for words and phrases associated with each stage of the spectrum (e.g. happy, calm, balanced under 'healthy') and write them around the relevant slot on the spectrum. Then get students to read the introduction and 'A spectrum of mental health'. Explain or elicit the difference between mental ill-health and mental illness (and, if it comes up, mental disability, which is a permanent condition). Emphasise that anyone can develop mental health problems depending on circumstances.

ACTIVITIES

• Ask students to read 'Different names for different problems' and 'Myths about mental illness' and then to do the 'Discuss' task in small groups. Ask each group to come up with two questions that they would like to ask a mental health professional and write these down. Invite groups to share their responses and answer any questions they have. Assess if there are any trends in students' concerns. The statistics about young people in 'Myths about mental illness' come from the NHS Digital survey 'Mental Health of Children and Young People in England'.

• Still in their groups, ask students to do the 'Research' task and then invite them to share their findings and thoughts with the rest of the class.

• Hand out **Worksheet 13.3** and go through the questionnaire 'What's your mood?'. Ask the students to do the second 'Discuss' task on page 71 in small groups and then share responses in a class discussion. Explain that when a distressed mood seems to last for a long time (here, two weeks), it may be helpful to think in terms of mental health problems and try to make changes or seek help. (This is why students are asked to repeat the questionnaire in a fortnight's time.) Also tell them that thoughts of self-harm or death (Q9) are quite common; it is only when they become obsessive or turn into actual plans that action needs to be taken. You can ask students to complete the questionnaire in class or to take it away to complete it at home.

PLENARY

• Invite the students, in pairs, to list the points they would make to try to reassure a friend who confides in them that she is feeling ashamed, upset and worried because her mum has developed a mental illness. Encourage them to share their ideas in a class discussion.

EXTENSION

• The NHS survey 'Mental Health of Children and Young People in England', published in 2018, suggests that young women aged 17–19 were twice as likely as their male peers to experience poor mental health. Ask students to discuss why this might be (e.g. additional pressures on girls to conform to standards of looks and behaviour).

Further information and support for teachers:

NHS survey of children's mental health (2017): digital.nhs.uk/data-and-information/publications/statistical/mental-health-of-children-and-young-people-in-england/2017/2017

The Guardian – a good article analysing the NHS survey:
www.theguardian.com/society/2018/nov/22/mental-health-disorders-on-rise-among-children-nhs-figures

MindEd – educational resources on children and young people's mental health www.minded.org.uk

Further information and support for students:

For information about mental health problems, visit the website of Mind, www.mind.org.uk, and the Moodzone section of the NHS website, www.nhs.uk/conditions/stress-anxiety-depression

Think about your mood over the past two weeks. How much do you agree with the following statements about your mood? Give a rating between 1 and 10 for each one, where 1 = completely disagree and 10 = completely agree. Write your ratings in the boxes in the **Date 1** column.

		Date 1:	Date 2: ....
1.	Over the last two weeks you've had little interest in doing the stuff you usually enjoy doing.	☐	☐
2.	Over the last two weeks you'd describe your mood as down, low or hopeless.	☐	☐
3.	Over the last two weeks you've had trouble falling asleep or have had trouble getting out of bed (even on a non-school day!).	☐	☐
4.	Over the last two weeks you've lacked energy and felt tired all the time.	☐	☐
5.	Over the last two weeks you've had little appetite or found yourself comfort-eating.	☐	☐
6.	Over the last two weeks you have felt like a bit of a failure at work, home or school.	☐	☐
7.	Over the last two weeks you've found it hard to concentrate on work or even things like watching TV.	☐	☐
8.	Over the last two weeks you've noticed a change in your mannerisms – you feel either slow and sluggish or buzzing and hyper.	☐	☐
9.	Over the last two weeks you've thought about harming yourself or thought about your own death.	☐	☐
10.	Over the last two weeks your mood has made it difficult for you to do your normal day-to-day activities.	☐	☐

Add up your score. If your score is higher than 50, can you say why? Are you having a bad time of it at the moment? (For example, if you're having a relationship break-up, you may well score over 50.) If you CAN'T identify a life event or a reason why you might be feeling so blue, perhaps it's time to think about your mental wellbeing.

Do the questionnaire in another two weeks, writing your ratings in the **Date 2** column. Has anything changed? It could be that a couple of days off, or being kind to yourself, is all you need right now, but MAYBE it's time to seek some support. There's plenty of it out there (see Unit 13.4).

Adapted from Juno Dawson, *Mind Your Head*

Getting help and giving help

Strand:	**Resources:**
• Personal wellbeing and mental health	• Book Three: pp. 72–73
	• Worksheet 13.4

Learning objective:	**Key words:**
• To explore how to seek help for mental health issues and how to support someone with mental health problems	support, help, mental health

STARTER

• Ask the class: 'How can you tell if a friend is in a period of low mood or suffering from bad mental health?' With the students' help, draw up a checklist of signs that a friend is struggling with mental health issues. What signs may indicate that you need to encourage them to seek professional help?
(For example: when it's hard to do normal things; when the symptoms last for at least a fortnight)

ACTIVITIES

• Ask students to read 'Getting help' on pages 72–73 of *Book Three*. Divide the class into groups and allocate a different section to each group, asking the groups to feed back the key points to the class.

• Ask students to do the 'Research' task on Kooth and The Mix, assessing the websites' usefulness and accessibility for teenagers looking for help.

• Ask students to read out Faisal's and Maya's experiences ('Discuss' activity). Ask them to discuss these experiences – and their own – in small groups. Ask each group to come up with a list of advantages and disadvantages of using social media to help with mental health issues and collate these on the board.

• Ask students to read 'Giving help'. Divide them into small groups to discuss the advice and do the second 'Discuss' task, deciding which are the three best tips. Share groups responses in a class discussion. Have they listed different tips? What are their reasons for choosing the tips they have?

• 'If your mate's acting differently, ask twice.' This is the slogan of a campaign by Time to Change, a charity that works to end mental health discrimination. Ask students: 'Is this a good slogan? What does it mean? Why would we need to ask people twice if they are OK?'

• Organise students into pairs to do the 'Role play'. Before they reverse their roles, invite students to share with the class anything they learned or any difficulties they encountered.

PLENARY

• Hand out **Worksheet 13.4** and ask students to use the information and ideas from this lesson to complete their own checklist of how to seek help. They can take the worksheet home and adapt it into a more readily accessible form, e.g. put it on their phones.

EXTENSION

• Ask students to write a blog called 'Look out for your friend – spotting the signs of mental illness' to be posted on an internet forum. This could then be used as a springboard for recording a short podcast, either individually or in small groups.

Further information and support for students:

The Epic Friends website is a lively resource aimed at helping teens understand mental health issues and support their friends through problems: epicfriends.co.uk

Kooth, an online counselling and emotional wellbeing platform for young people: www.kooth.com

The Mix, providing free, confidential support for young people: www.themix.org.uk/mental-health

'When I talked to my friends and family', a video of young people's experiences in asking for help: www.mind.org.uk/information-support/mental-health-in-our-own-words/

Worksheet 13.4 Getting help for mental health problems

If your mood has made it difficult for you to do your normal day-to-day activities, then you need to seek help. Fill in this checklist *when you are thinking clearly* – don't wait until you are in a low mood! Get a friend or a trusted adult to help you, if you like. Then refer to it when you are struggling with your mental health.

I can talk about my mood, or the things that are troubling me, to these people:

1. ....

2. ....

3. ....

I can look at these websites and/or post on the forums here:

1. ....

2. ....

3. ....

I can phone these professional organisations:

1. The Samaritans: 116 123

2. ....

3. ....

These techniques or activities usually help me improve my sleep, diet and physical wellbeing:

1. ....

2. ....

3. ....

These activities help me to improve my mood (e.g. walking, fun activities, a favourite mindfulness practice):

1. ....

2. ....

3. ....

If you think you need urgent help and may be at risk of harming yourself or others, you should contact your GP or visit your local NHS walk-in centre or the closest A&E department straight away.

Strand:	Resources:
• Personal wellbeing and mental health	• Book Three: pp. 74–75
	• Worksheet 13.5

Learning objective:	Key words:
• To understand what anxiety is and the common forms in which it presents as a disorder	anxiety, fear, mindfulness
• To learn mindful methods of managing anxiety	

STARTER

• Put the word 'anxiety' on the board and ask for students' immediate reactions. Write these words/phrases around the central word. Discuss their reactions, which will probably be negative. Read the introductory text on page 74 of *Your Choice Book Three*, but don't look in detail at the diagram yet. Explore the positive reasons why we feel anxious *(we are hard-wired to think and feel in this way, to escape what we perceive as 'danger')*, and ask students to think of any times when feeling anxious has helped. In this way, the discussion can move to a more nuanced understanding that anxiety itself isn't bad, but too much anxiety can lead to problems, and that we are partly in control of how much we increase that natural level of anxiety.

• Please note that this lesson takes a mindful approach to managing anxiety, in line with lesson 13.2. There are many other approaches, including those that challenge negative thoughts and actively calm physical sensations.

ACTIVITIES

• Ask students to remember a time when they were very anxious. Suggest some scenarios (e.g. about to ask someone out, before an exam). It helps if they spend a few moments with their eyes closed visualising the occasion. Ask what thoughts, physical sensations and actions/urges came to mind. Gather their responses on the whiteboard in a diagram like the one on page 73. Emphasise that these are natural responses and not harmful in themselves. The trick is not to let them overwhelm us, or to act on them too much, or they could develop into an anxiety disorder – a mental health problem. Now, with the class, look at the diagram in the book and see how closely it matches with the one on the board.

• Ask students to read 'Anxiety conditions' and 'Managing anxiety', including Noah's story. (A more comprehensive list of anxiety conditions is provided in **Worksheet 13.5**.) Then ask them to do the 'Discuss' task in pairs.

• Then ask students to do the 'Research' activity. Hand out **Worksheet 13.5** to help them with this and encourage them to visit the websites below.

PLENARY

• Ask students to adapt their answer to part **3** of the 'Discuss' activity into a self-help checklist. Encourage them to visualise the situation of great anxiety that they thought of earlier, and explore what it feels like to respond to their anxious feelings with techniques of mindfulness, acceptance and non-avoidance.

EXTENSION

• Ask students to research apps for managing anxiety, such as Fear Tools – Anxiety Kit (note: this uses cognitive behavioural approaches) and SAM: Self-help for Anxiety Management. Which would they recommend and why?

Further information and support for students:

Anxiety UK, a charity supporting people living with anxiety: www.anxietyuk.org.uk

Epic Friends, a website to help young people help friends they think may have mental health problems: epicfriends.co.uk

There are several TED talks on anxiety, including:
www.ted.com/talks/olivia_remes_how_to_cope_with_anxiety?language=en

Worksheet 13.5 Common anxiety disorders

Anxiety disorder	What you may experience and how you may behave, if you have the disorder
Social anxiety (or social phobia)	If you suffer from social phobia, you are very fearful of social situations, especially where you think you may be judged by others. You are very anxious when you're with other people, and very self-conscious – your thoughts focus on how badly you are coping or coming across. As this causes a lot of distress, you will typically try to avoid or escape from social situations as much as you can, or keep yourself 'safe' by various means (avoiding conversation, looking for escape routes, etc).
Generalised anxiety disorder (GAD)	You are suffering from GAD if you worry excessively about a number of events and activities, and the worry causes you great distress or negative effects such as muscle tension, lack of concentration, poor sleep, irritability, restlessness and fatigue. You are overly concerned about events that you cannot control or predict, and you may avoid such events. You may even worry about the effects of worrying, but you still seem to be unable to stop.
Panic disorder and agoraphobia	If you have recurrent panic attacks, or have had panic attacks in the past, you may have a persistent fear or worry about having attacks in the future. Basically, you are fearful of experiencing fear, and the slightest indication from your body (or mind) that you are fearful can be enough to trigger a 'fight or flight' reaction. Agoraphobia means avoiding places where you think you may have a panic attack, and where escape may be difficult.
Phobias	If you have an excessive or unreasonable fear of a particular situation or object, then you are suffering from a phobia. The most common phobias are fear of animals (e.g. spiders, dogs), heights, closed spaces, blood and injuries, storms and lightning, and flying. When you are exposed to the feared object, you are immediately and intensely frightened, and you have an urge to escape and avoid the object.
Obsessive compulsive disorder (OCD)	You have OCD if you feel compelled to carry out certain acts in order to feel at ease. You worry a lot about your own or others' physical safety, or about contamination. Common actions are washing hands or checking; sometimes the acts are purely in the mind, e.g. counting or ritual repetition or dwelling on a mental image. Either way, the compulsions gradually become more dominating and increase your anxiety overall.
Stress and burn-out	Stress is a very general term that is best defined by the thought: 'I can't cope with the demands that are made on me at the moment.' This may be partly because you underrate your abilities, and/or you fear failure. The stress response involves high levels of adrenalin and an over-alert, tense mood as part of the 'fight or flight' reaction. If constant stress is ignored, it can lead to burn-out – complete physical and mental exhaustion.
Physical problems and health anxiety	Anxiety and stress are felt in the body, so high levels of anxiety may lead to physical problems, such as stomach and digestive troubles, headaches, raised blood pressure, worsening asthma, difficulty sleeping, nausea or diarrhoea. These can cause you additional worry, and so worsen the physical symptoms. If you become obsessed with physical sensations and preoccupied with thoughts of being seriously ill, this is called health anxiety.
Post-traumatic stress disorder (PTSD)	If you have suffered or witnessed a traumatic event or series of events, such as a car crash or an attack, it is natural to experience extreme stress reactions. These may include vivid memories or 'flashbacks' of the event(s), being physically very wound up, and the urge to avoid certain people or situations associated with the event(s). Usually these symptoms fade, but if they persist over months and years, you may be suffering from PTSD.

13.6 Managing depression

Strand:
- Personal wellbeing and mental health

Resources:
- Book Three: pp. 76–77
- Worksheet 13.6

Learning objective:
- To understand what depression is and to learn mindful methods of managing it
- To understand self-harm

Key words:
depression, self-harm

STARTER

- Show the first half of the video (see below) 'I had a black dog: his name was depression' (up to 2:20) and invite students to recall what features the black dog of depression is given.

ACTIVITIES

- Ask students to read the sections on 'Symptoms', 'Causes' and 'Treatment' of depression on page 76 of *Your Choice Book Three*. Then ask them to do the 'Write' activity. They could use **Worksheet 13.6** as a template for their diagram. *(Typical depressive thoughts are 'What's the point?', 'I can't face ...'; typical sensations are very low energy or irritability; typical urges are to stay in bed, or eat too much/too little.)* Ask for volunteers to share their diagrams and draw up a class version on the board.

- Organise students into small groups to read the article 'Managing negative thoughts' and 'Ask Erica' on page 77, and then to discuss which they think is the best strategy in the article before moving on to the 'Write' tasks. Do any of the students have a strategy of their own they could add?

- Play the second half of the video 'I had a black dog: his name was depression' and write on the board all the suggested approaches for managing and treating depression.

- With the class, read the article on 'Self-harm' and then discuss it. Discussion of this topic should be tightly managed, given that it is likely to be a live issue for some class members.

PLENARY

- Do the discussion part of 'Your choice' as a class and then ask students, individually, to do the second part of 'Your choice', designing a self-help card for things that they can do if they feel depressed.

EXTENSION

- Ask students to research two or three of the stories about depression in the 'Your stories' section of the Mind website (see below). What helped these people to manage their depression?

Further information and support for students:

Mind, the mental health charity, 'Your stories': www.mind.org.uk/information-support/your-stories/

'I had a black dog: his name was depression' video: www.who.int/mental_health/advocacy/videos/en/

Some ideas that can help someone who is self-harming can be found at http://epicfriends.co.uk/self-harm

Young Minds, 'Depression': youngminds.org.uk/find-help/conditions/depression

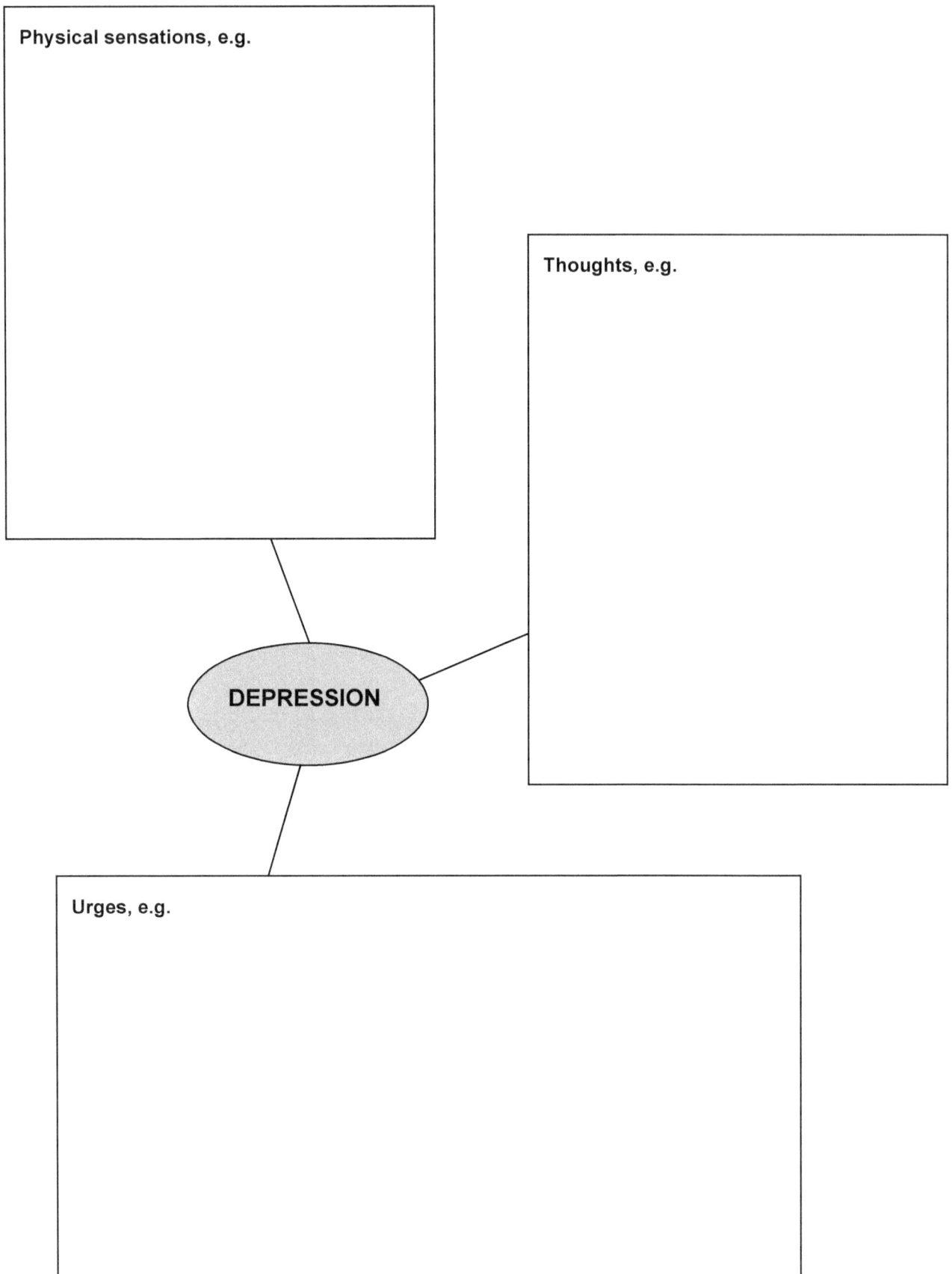

Physical sensations, e.g.

Thoughts, e.g.

DEPRESSION

Urges, e.g.

Strand:	Resources:
• Personal wellbeing and mental health	• Book Three: pp. 78–79 • Worksheet 14.1

Learning objective:	Key words:
• To define gambling, explore why people gamble, how much it affects young people and the different views that people hold about it	gambling, money, debt, gaming, betting, National Lottery

STARTER

* Ask the class for a definition of gambling, before providing the definition in the Gambling Act 2005: 'betting, gaming or participating in a lottery'. Ask for the legal age for: **1.** gambling in a casino (18); **2.** gambling online (18); **3.** taking part in the National Lottery (16).

* Ask why young people gamble. Note students' suggestions on the board and then ask them to rank these in order of importance.

ACTIVITIES

* Following on from the second starter activity, ask: 'So why are we exploring gambling when most forms of gambling are banned for children?' Elicit that rates of gambling among young people are growing.

* Ask students to read the introduction, the 'Fact check' and 'The National Lottery' on page 78 of *Your Choice Book Three* and discuss the arguments for and against participating in the lottery. Then do the first 'Discuss' activity as a class. (Note that the figures in the National Lottery pie chart only add up to 99p because they have been rounded up/down to the nearest whole number.)

* Ask students to read the 'Teenage boys' article on page 79, and then organise them into small groups to do the 'Discuss' task that follows it. The article does not mention that 14% is two percentage points lower than in 2016, and represents a continuation of the longer-term decline seen since 2011, when 23% of 11–15 year olds in England and Wales had gambled in the past week. Distribute **Worksheet 14.1** to the groups and ask them to discuss the statistics and to write down the statistic that most concerns them. Compare different groups' responses. Where was there a difference of opinion and why?

* With the class, read the quotes in 'Why do young people gamble?' on page 79. Then ask students to use this and the material from the starter activity to help them to do the 'Write' activity.

* Ask the class to read the views in 'Your choice' and then ask individuals to share their views in a class discussion. Elicit that most people will have a less black-or-white view. You could get students to form a spectrum line in the classroom, one end being 'Gambling is totally fun and harmless', the other being 'Gambling is wrong and dangerous'. The students then take their place on the spectrum depending on the view they have formed during the lesson. Ask specific questions of individuals about the dangers/morality, etc. of gambling to refine where they are on the spectrum.

PLENARY

* Following on from the last activity, ask students to write a personal statement of their views about gambling, giving reasons to back up their view.

EXTENSION

* As a class, make a list of all the moral and religious arguments against gambling. Discuss each argument and ask students to say why they agree/disagree with it. The list could include: *It's a sin because you should trust in God, not luck, to provide your needs; It's wrong because you win money by luck rather than earning it; It causes misery because it can lead people into debt; People spend money on gambling that could be spent in better ways; It can be addictive and therefore encourage people to steal to fund their habit; It can make people lie and cheat.*

Further information and support for teachers:

Most of the statistics are from the Gambling Commission, especially their report 'Young People and Gambling': www.gamblingcommission.gov.uk

Further information and support for students:

The National Lottery website: www.national-lottery.co.uk

Young People and Gambling 2018

GAMBLING COMMISSION

Data source: Ipsos MORI Young People Omnibus
Sample: 2,865 11-16 year olds drawn from 86 academies and maintained secondary and middle schools in Great Britain
Method: Self-completion online and pen and paper surveys conducted with whole classes under supervision
Fieldwork dates: 5 February - 2 July 2018

Gambling participation

14% have spent their own money on gambling in the past week

c.450,000 11-16 year olds

Compared to:

- **13%** who've drunk alcohol
- **4%** who've smoked cigarettes
- **2%** who've taken illegal drugs

18% of boys **9%** of girls

Online behaviour

- **6%** have used a parent's account to gamble online
- **13%** have played online gambling-style games
- **12%** follow gambling companies on social media

Seen gambling advertising

66% on TV
59% on social media
53% on other websites

Past week gambling participation: trend

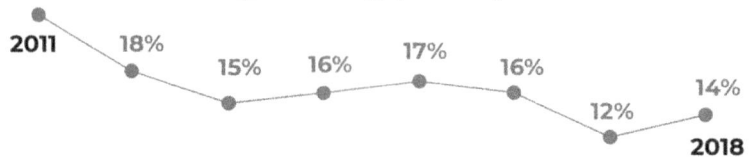

23% 2011
18%
15%
16%
17%
16%
12%
14% 2018

Most common past week gambling activities

Private bets **6%**
Scratchcards **4%**
Fruit/slot machines in pubs, clubs or arcades **3%**
Playing cards **3%**

Parents

- **26%** have seen their parents gamble
- **60%** think that their parents would prefer them not to gamble

only **19%** of parents set out strict rules on gambling

In-game items (in computer games/apps)

31% have paid or used in-game items to open a loot box

3% have ever bet with in-game items

Problem gambling

1.7% are problem gamblers

c.55,000 problem gamblers

- **2.2%** are at-risk gamblers
- **32.5%** are non-problem gamblers
- **63.6%** don't gamble at all

Strand:	Resources:
• Personal wellbeing and mental health	• Book Three: pp. 80–81 • Worksheet 14.2

Learning objective:	Key words:
• To explore problem gambling, especially as it affects young people	gambling and gaming, problem gambling, addiction, skins and loot boxes

STARTER

• Ask the class: 'When does gambling become a problem?' and note students' responses on the board. Problem gambling is defined as gambling that disrupts or damages personal, family or recreational pursuits. Explain that gambling can be as addictive as drugs and alcohol.

ACTIVITIES

• Ask students to read 'What is problem gambling?' on page 80 of *Your Choice Book Three*, followed by 'What turns gambling into problem gambling?' and the 'Fact check' box. Then ask them to discuss the views and facts in small groups. Ask the groups to come up with the top three factors that they think may lead someone to develop a gambling problem. Gather these in a whole-class discussion.

• Give each group a copy of **Worksheet 14.2** and ask them to discuss how problem gambling could affect people's lives (in both the short and long term), writing their ideas on the outline of the body. Suggest that they think about the effects of gambling on these areas: emotions, relationships, physical health, mental health, schoolwork, employment, police records, financial situation. Invite a spokesperson from each group to share their worksheets in a whole-class discussion.

• Ask students to read 'Gambling and gaming' and 'Beware of loot boxes' on page 81. Then ask them to do the 'Your choice' activity in small groups, discussing whether they think loot boxes and similar features should count as gambling and be restricted.

• Organise students into small groups to do the 'Write' activity, designing a flow chart to be displayed in a youth club or on a school noticeboard. Ask pairs of groups to share their charts and compare them.

PLENARY

• Set up a class debate on the issue of loot boxes. Highlight the point made in Marcus' blog that skins and loot boxes in online games should count as gambling because the player is risking something of value in the hope of winning something else. They encourage risk-taking and gambling-style behaviour, which could potentially be harmful to gamers later in life.

EXTENSION

• Organise a class debate: 'This class believes that skins gambling should be illegal for under-18s.' You can refer to **Worksheets 5.1b** and **15.3** from *Book Two* for guidance on holding a formal debate.

Further information and support for teachers:

BeGambleAware gives advice about problem gambling and materials for teachers: www.begambleaware.org

Further information and support for students:

BBC Newsround, videos and other material on children and gambling (July 2018): www.bbc.co.uk/newsround/44736452

Write on and around this person the ways in which problem gambling could affect his or her life.

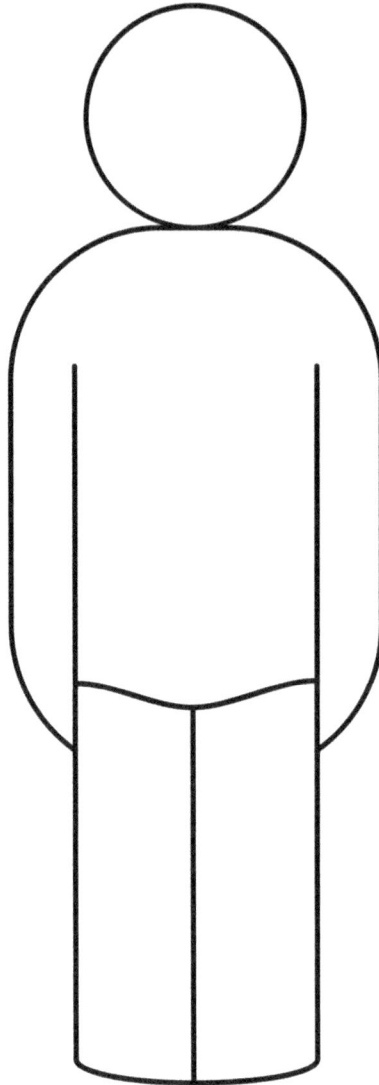

14.3	How to manage gambling

Strand:	**Resources:**
• Personal wellbeing and mental health	• Book Three: pp. 82–83 • Worksheet 14.3 • A video of the famous Marshmallow test

Learning objective:	**Key words:**
• To spot signs of problem gambling and explore what we can do to manage gambling	problem gambling, advertising, temptation, impulsive behaviour, delayed gratification

STARTER

• Ask students: 'A young child is put in a room with a marshmallow and told that if they don't eat it, they can have two marshmallows in 15 minutes. What would the child do?' Show a video of the famous Marshmallow test (you can find this on YouTube). Ask what this may tell us about gambling and how to resist it (issues of temptation, impulsive behaviour, delayed gratification). Make sure that students are aware of any advice and support they can access if they are concerned about any of the issues explored in the lesson. Reassure students that this is confidential, and they can be anonymous. This should include the school's own arrangements as well as external provision (see Further information below).

ACTIVITIES

• Ask students to read the introduction, the article 'We should be protecting our children' and the 'Fact check' on page 82 of *Your Choice Book Three*. Then organise them into small groups to do the 'Discuss' task about the guidelines for advertising gambling.

• Still working in small groups, ask the students to read 'Spot the signs of a gambling problem', 'Now get to grips with the problem' and 'Stay in control'. Ask them to discuss which they think are the best strategies, depending on the context (e.g. gambling alone/online/with friends). Ask the class if they can come up with any other suggestions for self-management. Refer back to the idea of delayed gratification from the starter activity. How could students reward themselves for resisting gambling? (A fuller list of the criteria for a gambling problem is provided on **Worksheet 14.3**, which consists of a series of questions used internationally by academics and researchers to screen problem gambling among 11–16-year-olds, using the DSM-IV-MR-J problem gambling screen.)

• Ask students to read 'How to help someone with a gambling problem' and then to do the 'Write' activity on their own. Invite students to share their tips with the rest of the class and discuss any differences. Then ask students to do the 'Discuss' task in pairs before bringing the class back together to share their answers.

• Support students to research GambleAware and GamCare (see the links below) to discover what advice they offer about gambling problems and assess, as a class, how accessible it is for young people.

PLENARY

• Organise students into groups of three to do the 'Role play' activity. Invite groups to perform their role play in front of the class. Ask students to note any different or additional things the friend under pressure could say. Alternatively, the Chloe/Nadia scenario in the 'Discuss' task could be adapted as a role play.

EXTENSION

• Organise a class debate on whether gambling companies should be allowed to advertise during football games, on players' shirts and in stadiums (9 out of the top 20 football teams in the UK were sponsored by gambling companies in 2018).

Further information and support for students:

Childline – 0800 1111 or www.childline.org.uk – offers a range of ways to talk to a trained counsellor, including via email and an online chat service. Calls are free from a landline or mobile.

The National Gambling HelpLine number is 0808 8020 133.

GambleAware offers advice about responsible gambling and gambling problems: http://www.gambleaware.co.uk

GamCare offers advice about gambling problems including a helpline and online chat service: http://www.gamcare.org.uk

Worksheet 14.3 Signs of problem gambling

Use this checklist of questions to assess whether gambling is a problem for you. Circle the answer that relates to you in each case. Then read the box at the bottom of the page.

The list of questions can also be used as a helpful reminder of the sorts of behaviours that you may spot in a friend or other teenager who you suspect is developing a gambling problem.

1. Have you found yourself thinking about gambling or planning to gamble?

      a) often   **b)** sometimes   **c)** never

2. Have you needed to gamble with more and more money to get the amount of excitement you want?

      a) sometimes or often   **b)** rarely   **c)** never

3. Have you felt bad or fed up when trying to cut down on gambling?

      a) sometimes or often   **b)** rarely   **c)** never

4. Have you ever spent much more than you planned to on gambling?

      a) often   **b)** sometimes   **c)** never

5. Have you gambled to escape from problems or when you are feeling bad?

      a) sometimes or often   **b)** rarely   **c)** never

6. After losing money on gambling, have you returned another day to try to win back the money you lost?

      a) more than half the time   **b)** less than half the time   **c)** never

7. Has your gambling ever led to your telling lies to family, friends or others?

      a) sometimes   **b)** hardly ever   **c)** never

8. Have you ever taken money without permission from your family, your dinner money, your fare money, money from things you have sold, or from somewhere else, to spend on gambling?

      a) yes   **b)** no

9. Has your gambling ever led to arguments with family, friends or others, or you missing school?

      a) yes   **b)** no

Each **a)** response = 1 point. If the total score is 4 or more, this indicates a problem gambler. A score of 2 or 3 indicates as at-risk gambler. A score of 0 or 1 indicates a non-problem gambler.

If you are concerned about the results of this survey:

- Childline – 0800 1111 or www.childline.org.uk – offers a range of ways to talk to a trained counsellor, including via email and an online chat service. Calls are free from a landline or mobile.
- The National Gambling HelpLine number is 0808 8020 133.
- GambleAware offers advice about responsible gambling and gambling problems: www.gambleaware.co.uk
- GamCare offers advice about gambling problems including a helpline and online chat service: www.gamcare.org.uk

Strand:	Resources:
• Personal wellbeing and mental health	• Book Three: pp. 84–85 • Worksheet 15.1

Learning objective:	Key words:
• To explore your rights and responsibilities as a consumer and how to seek redress if the goods/services are inadequate	consumer, rights, Consumer Rights Act 2015, services, refund

STARTER

* Write the word 'consumer' on the board and ask the class what it means. Repeat with 'goods' and 'services'. Read the introduction on page 84 of *Your Choice Book Three* with the class and then invite students to share examples of when they or their families have had to complain about goods or services. What happened? Can the class work out what their rights were from these examples? For example, if someone took a damaged garment back to a clothes shop, did the shop have to replace or refund it, even if it was in a sale? *(Yes)*

ACTIVITIES

* Ask students to read 'Your rights when shopping' (including the 'Fact check') to find out about the rights introduced in the starter activity. For the 'True or false?' section, you can either ask students to read this on their own, or read out the proposed facts and get students to jot down whether they think they are true or false, then elicit replies from the class. They can then read the section themselves to consolidate their knowledge. (The Consumer Rights Act 2015 became law on 1 October 2015. It replaces and simplifies three consumer laws: the Sale of Goods Act, Unfair Terms in Consumer Contracts Regulations, and the Supply of Goods and Services Act.)

* Hand out **Worksheet 15.1** to small groups. Instruct them to discuss the situations and then answer the questions. Invite groups to feed back what they have written to the whole class and discuss where there are confusions. *Answers: 1. Demand a refund. Sale goods are not exempt from the Consumer Rights Act. 2. The delay and increased charge are reasonable, so he cannot make a valid complaint under the Consumer Rights Act. 3. Although it's not Lola's legal right to ask for a refund after 30 days of buying the bag, she can still ask for a repair or replacement. 4. He should complain citing the Consumer Rights Act.*

* With the class read 'How to make a complaint' on page 85 and go through the steps outlined in the diagram. Then organise the students into pairs, first to do the 'Write' activity and then to do the 'Role play'. You might like to get pairs to share their lists and decide as a class whether or not they are right.

* For the role play, you may need to supply some helpful phrases to the 'customer', such as 'Under the Consumer Rights Act ...'. You could suggest ways in which the shop assistant could prevaricate, e.g. 'But you bought it in the sale', or 'Do you have a receipt?' or 'You must have damaged the trainers yourself'. In all cases, emphasise the importance of speaking assertively rather than aggressively.

PLENARY

* Ask students to close their books and write down one important feature of the Consumer Rights Act. Invite some students to share their responses with the class.

EXTENSION

* Ask students to design a poster outlining consumers' rights when shopping.

Further information and support for teachers:

Consumer Rights Act 2015: www.which.co.uk/consumer-rights/regulation/consumer-rights-act

Further information and support for students:

Resolver provides free guidance with shopping problems and ensures your complaint is heard and addressed: www.resolver.co.uk

Citizens Advice provides step-by-step guides and template letters for making formal complaints: www.citizensadvice.org.uk

Money Saving Expert has step-by-step help for making complaints, with template letters: www.moneysavingexpert.com/shopping/how-to-complain

1. Cameron bought a pair of trainers that were reduced in a sale from £89 to £49. When he got home, he noticed that the stitching was coming away down the side of one of them. He assumed that the price was reduced because the trainers were damaged so it wasn't worth complaining.

   What are Cameron's rights? ....

   ....

   What do you advise Cameron to do now? ....

   ....

   ....

2. Kelvin's amplifier needed repairing before a gig he was putting on the following week, so he took it to the local music shop. They gave him an estimate of £50 for the repair and said it would be ready in time for the gig. It wasn't ready, as it took an extra two days, and the repair turned out to be £55.

   What are Kelvin's rights? ....

   ....

   What do you advise Kelvin to do now? ....

   ....

   ....

3. In October, Lola bought an expensive sports bag as a Christmas gift for her sister. When her sister opened it on Christmas day, she found that the zip was faulty. Lola had kept the receipt but when she took it back to the shop, the manager refused to exchange it or refund the money. He said that Lola must have broken the zip herself and she should have brought it back within 30 days of the purchase.

   What are Lola's rights? ....

   ....

   What do you advise Lola to do now? ....

   ....

   ....

4. Theo hired an angle grinder and paid a £50 deposit. When he got it home, he couldn't get it to work. The manager of the tool hire firm claimed that Theo had broken it and refused to return the deposit.

   What are Theo's rights? ....

   ....

   What do you advise Theo to do now? ....

   ....

   ....

Strand:	Resources:
• Personal wellbeing and mental health	• Book Three: pp. 86–87 • Worksheet 15.2 cut into cards

Learning objective:	Key words:
• Exploring what it means to be responsible consumers in order to encourage sustainable financial management	money, borrowing, designer clothes, consumer responsibility, ethical consumer, Fairtrade

STARTER

• Ask if any students refuse to buy particular products on principle. If so, ask what those principles are. Gather lots of examples on the board, but do not allow discussion or judgement – the aim is to introduce the idea that we have choices and as consumers we can put our principles into action. Examples might include: not buying certain products (sweatshop clothes), buying ethical products (toilet rolls made from recycled paper), boycotting the products of a company (e.g. Nestlé) or even of a country.

ACTIVITIES

• Ask students to read the introduction and 'Your choice' on page 86 of *Your Choice Book Three*. Then put them into groups and give each group one of the cards from **Worksheet 15.2** – these are the seven statements listed in 'Your choice', describing attitudes to spending and borrowing. Say that each member of the group must give their view of the statement on their card; then together they should explore what lies behind the different ideas and opinions. There is also one blank card – ask each group to come up with a similar saying or attitude about spending and borrowing. Ask for a spokesperson from each group to feed back the views and any key difference of opinion to the rest of the class.

• Ask students to read the magazine article 'Designer clothes – for and against'. They then could discuss the issue in small groups before doing the 'Write' task. (Regarding Mark's opinion about the high standards that designer brands have to follow, because of their exposure to publicity, it's worth noting, that Nike and other brands have been involved in scandals around exploitative labour practices.) As a follow-up, ask the groups to do the 'Discuss' task and then collect their ideas on the board or display them on cards around the room.

• Ask students to read 'Your responsibilities as a consumer', 'Why buy ethically?' and 'What is Fairtrade?' on their own. Then organise them into small groups to do the 'Discuss' task on page 87. Ask for feedback from the groups.

• Ask students to do the 'Research' task in pairs and then share their findings with the rest of the class. Discuss the idea of being or becoming a Fairtrade school and draw out students' opinions on this.

• Read out the dilemmas in 'Your choice' and quickly collect some ideas from the whole class before asking students, individually, to write a statement of where they stand on each issue.

PLENARY

• Ask students if they will think differently in any way about how they spend their money as a result of the lesson, and if so, how.

EXTENSION

• Ask students, in groups, to discuss how we can change our habits as consumers to combat climate change. Get each group to list five key actions and share them in a whole-class discussion.

Further information and support for teachers:

A useful guide for teachers and students that aims to help students become savvy buyers and borrowers: http://images2.moneysavingexpert.com/attachment/teen_cash_guide.pdf

Further information and support for students:

Ethical Consumer is an organisation that highlights the ethics of products and companies: www.ethicalconsumer.org

Fairtrade website: www.fairtrade.org.uk

How to become a Fairtrade school: schools.fairtrade.org.uk

'Never borrow money under any circumstances.'

'If you look after the pennies, the pounds will look after themselves.'

'Never buy on impulse. Research before you buy.'

'Paying more for big brands is a waste of money.'

'It's a shop's job to make money out of you, so you have to watch out.'

'If you lend money to your friends, you will lose your friends.'

'You can always rely on your parents to help you out.'

Strand:	**Resources:**
• Social education	• Book Three: pp. 88–89
	• Worksheet 16.1

Learning objective:	**Key words:**
• To define climate change, and to understand what can be done to reduce climate change	climate change, species extinction, global warming

STARTER

• Give students, working in pairs, two minutes to list all the things they think the phrase 'climate change' refers to. Note their ideas on the board to refer back to during the lesson.

ACTIVITIES

• Ask students to read the introduction on page 88 of *Your Choice Book Three* and then support them to do the 'Research' task in pairs, using the BBC link on Greenpeace and Trump below. Draw the class together by discussing what they think about the article. Link this to previous material on fake news (see lesson 12.1).

• Ask students to read 'Global warming' and 'Case study – the Maldives' before doing the first 'Your choice' on page 89 in pairs. Fact check the article by asking the following questions: How many islands are there in the Maldives? *(over 1000)*; How high are the Maldives? *(There is no point in the Maldives over 5 metres high, making it very vulnerable to flooding.)*; How many people live in the Maldives? *(over 430 000)*; When might the entire country be underwater? *(during the next 30–40 years)*

• Discuss the 'Your choice' questions as a class. *Suggested answers might include: we have a moral responsibility to save the Maldives, and that our behaviour is part of the problem.*

• Next, ask students to read 'Air pollution' and 'Case study – Southampton's polluted air' before working in groups on the second 'Your choice' activity. Monitor groups and discuss the suggested answers. Students will have to make a trade-off between improving the city's air and economic growth and jobs in Southampton. Invite groups to share their ideas with the class. Clarify that there is no one correct answer to this.

• Hand out **Worksheet 16.1** for students to do in pairs. When everyone has finished, give them the answers: *1, 11 and 12 are false; the rest are true*. Then organise students into groups to discuss which facts surprise them the most, giving reasons for their views.

• Ask students to read 'Species extinction' and then do the 'Research' task in pairs. Students could look at the other areas of the UK, such as England, Scotland or Northern Ireland, or a less industrialised country such as Indonesia or Brazil. Invite pairs to share their findings with the rest of the class.

PLENARY

• Lead a class discussion on what students as individuals, in their families and as a class can do to take action to help avoid climate change and reduce species extinction. You might like to use some of the links below to give them some ideas.

EXTENSION

• Ask students to research Greta Thunberg, the students' strike and the extinction rebellion. As students feed back their findings, ask whether civil disobedience such as blocking traffic can ever be justified when it comes to climate protest.

Further information and support for teachers:

The *Telegraph*, 'The Greta Thunberg generation: how children are pushing their parents to go greener': www.telegraph.co.uk/family/life/greta-thunberg-generation-children-pushing-parents-go-greener/

BBC News, Extinction rebellion blocks roads: www.bbc.co.uk/news/uk-england-london-47935416

Further information and support for students:

'6 ways to help fight climate change': www.teenvogue.com/story/6-ways-to-help-fight-climate-change

Worksheet 16.1 Climate change: true or false?

Read the following statements. Which ones do you think are true and which false? Make your predictions with a partner. Then check your answers with your teacher.

Statement	True or false?
1. There is no way of stopping climate change. We might as well just get used to the idea.	
2. In the next 50 years, the Arctic will become ice-free during the summer.	
3. Central London should already be underwater due to our changing climate. The only reason it isn't is due to the Thames barrier.	
4. Whatever happens, global temperature will rise by 1°C over the next 50 years – even if we stopped all CO_2 emissions right now.	
5. Climate change will benefit some people. For example, people will be able to produce more wine in the south of England as the country gets hotter.	
6. Some people and some countries will suffer more due to climate change.	
7. The biggest polluting fuel that we burn is coal when it comes to greenhouse gases.	
8. Nuclear energy can be a way of producing a lot more energy, without polluting greenhouse gases.	
9. We could generate enough energy for the entire planet just by covering Western Australia in solar panels – if we could find a way of transmitting the energy around the planet.	
10. The biggest problem is if the permafrost – semi frozen ground – melts in places like Greenland and Russia. This will release more methane, a gas that will accelerate climate change even further.	
11. If we all drove electric cars, it would eliminate all the CO_2 produced by personal transport.	
12. China produces the most pollution of any country in the world.	

Strand:	Resources:
• Social education	• Book Three: pp. 90–91 • Worksheet 16.2

Learning objective:	Key words:
• To understand climate change and to examine what can be done to combat it	climate change, plastic pollution, deforestation

STARTER

• Ask students to name everything plastic they use in an average week. Explain that you will come back to plastic during the lesson.

ACTIVITIES

• Ask students to read the introduction, 'Sustainable development' and the case study on plastic. Then ask them, in pairs, to do the 'Discuss' activity, naming everything they can see in the classroom that is plastic. Ask them to talk about what substitutes could be used and invite pairs to share their suggestions.

• Still in their pairs, support students to do the 'Research' activity and then invite pairs to share their findings with the rest of the class.

• Ask students to read 'Sustainable solutions' and 'Energy consumption', before doing the 'Your choice' activity in pairs. Encourage pairs to compare their answers in groups.

• Hand out **Worksheet 16.2** for students to work on in pairs. When they have finished, ask them to compare their rankings with another pair and explain their reasoning.

• Ask students to read 'Food and water consumption' and then to do the 'Discuss' activity in groups. You could also ask if they think we should we use more chemicals or GM crops when producing food. Then invite groups to share their responses in a class discussion, giving reasons for their views.

• Next, ask students to read 'Protecting natural resources' and do the 'Research' task that follows it, using the link below.

PLENARY

• Ask students what they think their parents might be willing to do in order to live a greener lifestyle. Include suggestions like family holidays in the UK, eating less meat and dairy, buying more locally produced goods, recycling, switching to an electric car, cycling, walking or using public transport. Make a list of the most popular suggestions and place them on the board.

EXTENSION

• Ask students to research what is being done to reduce plastic in their local area. Examples might include whether any supermarkets have got rid of plastic bags or plastic packaging altogether, beach cleaning, park litter picking, and plastic recycling schemes from the local council.

Further information and support for teachers:

BBC Future, 'How should we manage nuclear energy?': www.bbc.com/future/story/20170622-how-will-we-manage-nuclear-energy-in-the-21st-century

BBC News, 'Laser drones protect Scottish forests': www.bbc.co.uk/news/uk-scotland-48380213

Further information and support for students:

The Vegan Society: www.vegansociety.com

Teen Ink, 'Stop deforestation': http://www.teenink.com/hot_topics/environment/article/170409/Stop-Deforestation

Greenpeace: www.greenpeace.org.uk

Worksheet 16.2 Dealing with environmental issues

In pairs, look at the following statements. Rank them in the order you think would be most effective in dealing with climate change. Then discuss your answers in groups. Give reasons for your views.

Statement	Ranking
A) We should build lots more nuclear power stations to reduce our CO_2 emissions.	
B) We should persuade China to adopt a greener strategy. It doesn't matter if we prevent the third runway from being built at Heathrow, if China is building 50 new runways each year.	
C) We need the USA to come back into the Paris Climate Change Agreement, as it uses 40% of the world's energy each year.	
D) We should all become vegetarian, if not vegan, to reduce our meat consumption. Cows are a major produce of methane – a greenhouse gas.	
E) The Government is wrong to cut subsidies for wave, wind and solar power in the UK. We should subside these industries so we can continue to be a world leader in this technology. It's good for the environment and good for jobs.	
F) Genetically modified foods are safe – we should eat a lot more of them.	
G) The main problem is in the less industrialised world – the industrialised countries should persuade less industrialised countries to become green right now, rather than encouraging them to move into un-environmental economic growth.	
H) Plastic is the biggest danger to our health – we should ban all non-recyclable plastic right now.	
I) All major cities in the UK should have a congestion charge, to combat air pollution.	
J) Bolivia has a Government department – a ministry for mother earth – which is there to protect the natural environment and biodiversity of the country. We should do the same.	
K) We all need to work from home more – so that we're not travelling all over the place using energy – or switch to a four-day week, which would also help unemployment.	
L) We need to recycle more: this is the one thing that would make a real difference.	

Strand:	Resources:
• Social education	• Book Three: pp. 92–93 • Worksheet 16.3

Learning objective:	Key words:
• To examine the difference between absolute poverty and relative poverty, in more industrialised and less industrialised countries	poverty, absolute poverty, relative poverty, more industrialised country, less industrialised country

• Note – Before teaching this topic, consider whether you need to make any adjustments to be sensitive to your students' situation, e.g. if you have students whose families are in poverty.

STARTER

• Elicit what the word poverty means to students. Note the definition on page 92 of *Book Three* on the board. Ask them: 'Does poverty in the UK mean the same as poverty in a less industrialised country?'

ACTIVITIES

• Ask students to read 'Poverty and more industrialised countries' and check their comprehension by asking, for example: 'How many children live below the poverty line in the UK?' *(1 in 4)*; 'What is relative poverty?' *(Relative poverty is a measure of how one person's wealth relates to the average in that country.)*

• Next, ask students to read the 'Fact check' box. As a class, discuss which point students think is the most important, and why. There is no one correct answer to this, but one response might be that half of the people locked into poverty are disabled.

• Organise students into small groups and ask them to do the 'Discuss' task on page 92. Monitor closely, drawing out the problems people may have (e.g. no fresh food without a fridge, no clean clothes because there is no washing machine). Bring the class together and ask them to give reasons for their responses.

• Next, ask students to read 'Poverty and less economically developed countries' and 'Monique's story' before doing the next 'Discuss' task in new pairs. Then get pairs to compare their answers in groups, giving reasons for their views. *Answers may include: no regular showers or baths; having less free time or time to study; possible dangers of the walk to get water; the impact of walking five miles every day.*

• Ask students to read 'Relative poverty in less industrialised countries', and then support them to do the 'Research' task about Zimbabwe.

• Organise students into groups to do the final 'Discuss' task.

PLENARY

• Invite students to share and compare their responses to the discussion task. Then broaden the discussion out to talk about whether we have a moral responsibility to reduce poverty, both in the UK and in less industrialised countries, and if so, what steps or policies that might involved. Suggestions might include keeping the commitment of 0.7% of GDP (our wealth) for international aid each year; buying Fairtrade products where possible (so the producer in a developing country gets a fair deal); more charity work; more support for international organisations such as the UN (where richer countries pay more into UN budgets and poorer countries benefit from UN programmes).

EXTENSION

• Hand out **Worksheet 16.3** and read through it with the class, explaining that there are no correct answers. Check that students understand each action that is proposed. Divide the class into pairs and get them to rank each of suggestions, discussing their reasoning. Then compare the answers as a class. The stretch activities on **Worksheet 16.3** could be set as homework.

Further information and support for teachers:

The Guardian, 'Young people are angry': www.theguardian.com/society/2018/may/13/young-people-are-angry-meet-the-teenage-activists-shaping-our-future

The Borgen Project, '10 effective ways to fight poverty': borgenproject.org/10-ways-fight-poverty/

Worksheet 16.3 Priorities for reducing poverty

Look at the following list of actions that could reduce poverty. Which ones would you prioritise? Why? Rank each one in order. Give reasons for your views.

Statement	Ranking
A) Deal with climate change. Otherwise, the problem of poverty is only going to get worse, as water shortages will affect up to 3 billion people by the end of the century.	
B) Stop dealing with corrupt governments. The UK and other countries should break off ties with countries that abuse human rights.	
C) Introduce a tax on financial transactions to fund education around the world. Such a tax (known as a Tobin Tax after its creator James Tobin) would generate over £40 billion, ensure everyone got a good education and would, according to some economists, lead to a massive amount of economic growth.	
D) Make international trade fairer. Unfair trade rules, such as tariffs on importing food into the EU, suit more industrialised countries, who set the rules, and penalise less industrialised countries. There should be a level playing field.	
E) Combine making international trade fairer by cutting international aid at the same time, so that a real free market exists across the world.	
F) Improve health care across the industrialising world, by providing more healthcare workers with basic knowledge. This would result in less production being lost to people being ill and would make less developed countries richer.	
G) Increase aid to poorer countries and support less developed countries' own plans for development. Doing this would help less developed countries earn their way out of poverty in the long run, and would still respect locally democracy in these countries.	
H) Cut tax-dodging by multinational and transnational companies, which simply move production, on which they're taxed, to the country that has the lowest tax rate. If all countries acted together, the companies would have to pay the tax. It is estimated that poor countries lose over $160 billion each year in lost taxes. This would also help more developed countries as well.	

Stretch activities:

Research either:

1. Corruption in a less developed country and what effect it is having on that country.

2. The Tobin Tax: What is it and what difference could it make around the world?

Strand:	Resources:
• Social education	• Book Three: pp. 94–95 • Worksheet 16.4

Learning objective:	Key words:
• To define what genetically modified means • To examine the arguments for and against GM crops and genetically modified babies	gene, genetically modified, GM crops

STARTER

• Elicit from students what they think GM means. Write a definition on the board (e.g. plants and animals that have had one or more genes changed, for example so that they resist pests and disease better). Ask students if they would eat GM food, and why/why not.

ACTIVITIES

• Ask students to read 'Genetically modified (GM) crops' and the poem 'Modified progress' on page 94 of *Your Choice Book Three*. Organise students into groups to do the discussion task. Points to consider: **1.** Whether the ends justify the means, or whether it is never acceptable to break the law. **2.** They are probably not sure. You could look with them at the informative Food Standards Agency website, link included below. **3.** You may get some different responses, e.g. that there is a moral difference because a cow is a sentient being that is aware of its own surroundings, or that there isn't a difference because changing a plant's genetic make-up may produce negative effects for the ecosystem.

• Invite groups to share their responses with the class, giving reasons for their views.

• Next, ask students to work in pairs to read 'Cloning' and 'Case study – Genetically modified babies' and then do the 'Discuss' task that follows it. Again, invite pairs to share their responses with the class and give reasons for their views.

• Support students to work in pairs to do the 'Research' activity about genetically modified babies, using some of the links below.

PLENARY

• Encourage pairs to share their findings from the research with the rest of the class and then lead a class discussion about the ethics of genetically engineered babies. Point out that, on the one hand, serious genetic diseases and defects can be eliminated but, on the other hand, we are messing with nature and don't always know the full consequences.

EXTENSION

• Give students copies of **Worksheet 16.4** and ask them to complete the crossword on genetic engineering. *Answers: 1. Feed; 2. Environment; 3. Breeding; 4. Trial; 5. Direct action; 6. Genetic; 7. GM crops; 8. Cloning; 9. Herbicide; 10. Resistant; 11. Frankenstein; 12. Seed; 13. Dolly; 14. DNA; 15. Pesticide.*

Further information and support for teachers:

Food Standards Agency, GM foods: www.food.gov.uk/safety-hygiene/genetically-modified-foods

Teen Link , GM food: www.teenink.com/hot_topics/health/article/340987/Genetically-Modified-Foods

Guardian, 'Nobel winners slam Greenpeace for anti GM campaign': www.theguardian.com/environment/2016/jun/30/nobel-winners-slam-greenpeace-for-anti-gm-campaign

Independent, 'Medical dilemma of 'three-parent babies': www.independent.co.uk/news/science/medical-dilemma-of-three-parent-babies-fertility-clinic-investigates-health-of-teenagers-it-helped-9690058.html

'China says doctor who claimed using CRISPR to make gene-edited babies acted on his own': www.statnews.com/2019/01/21/china-doctor-gene-edited-babies/

Worksheet 16.4 Genetic engineering crossword

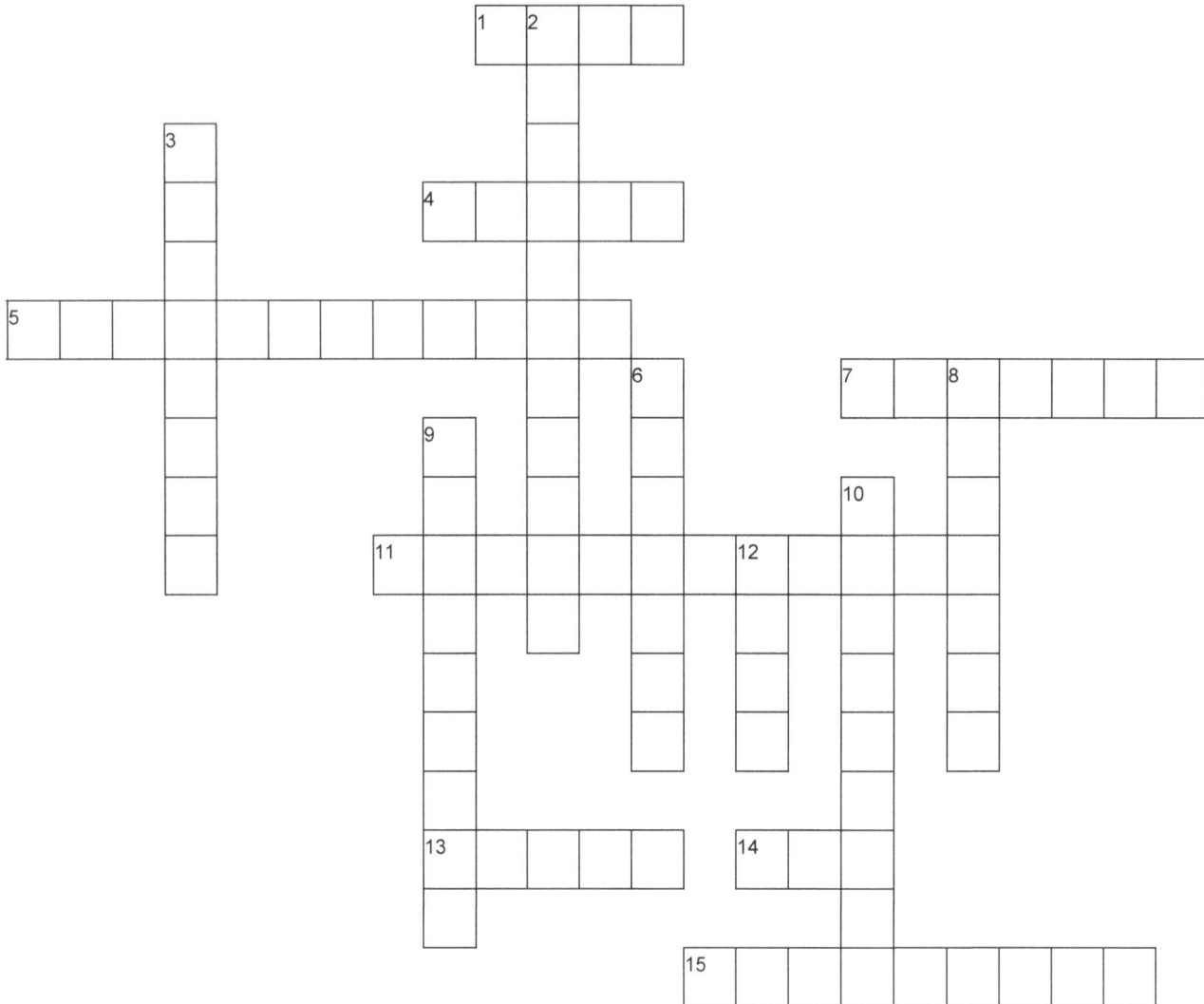

Clues

Across

1. Nourishment given to animals (4)
4. Testing out a crop in a small area to see if it works (5)
5. Form of political protest that immediately affects the issue being campaigned on (6,6)
7. Term for plants grown for food that have been changed using genetic engineering (2,5)
11. Name used to describe GM food connected with a fictional monster (12)
13. Name of the world's first cloned sheep (5)
14. The building blocks of our bodies (3)
15. Chemical used to reduce the number of insects that damage crops (9)

Down

2. The natural world that surrounds us (11)
3. Way of manipulating the offspring of animals or plants naturally (8)
6. Something that relates to our genes (7)
8. Taking a cell from one living thing and using it to make a copy (7)
9. Chemical used to stop weeds growing (9)
10. An animal or crop that is immune to a particular disease or pest (9)
12. What all plants grow from (4)